READING MEMORY IN EARLY MODERN LITERATURE

'He who remembers or recollects, thinks', declared Francis Bacon, drawing attention to the absolute centrality of the question of memory in early modern Britain's cultural life. The vigorous debate surrounding the faculty had dated back to Plato at least. However, responding to the powerful influences of an ever-expanding print culture, humanist scholarship, the veneration for the cultural achievements of antiquity and sweeping political upheaval and religious schism in Europe, succeeding generations of authors from the reign of Henry VIII to that of James I engaged energetically with the spiritual, political and erotic implications of remembering. Treating the works of a host of different writers, from the Earl of Surrey, Katherine Parr and John Foxe, to William Shakespeare, Mary Sidney, Ben Jonson and Francis Bacon, this study explores how the question of memory was intimately linked to the politics of faith, identity and intellectual renewal in Tudor and early Stuart Britain.

ANDREW HISCOCK is Professor of English at Bangor University, Wales. He teaches and publishes widely on early modern literature in British and European contexts. His earlier monographs include *Authority and Desire: Crises of Interpretation in Shakespeare and Racine* (1996) and *The Uses of this World: Thinking Space in Shakespeare, Marlowe, Cary and Jonson* (2004). He edited the 2008 *Yearbook of English Studies* devoted to Tudor literature, and his edited critical collection *Middleton: Women Beware Women* appeared in 2011. He is co-Editor of the academic journal *English*, and is about to take up his roles as Editor (English Literature) of the *Modern Language Review* and as Series Editor for the *Yearbook of English Studies*.

READING MEMORY IN EARLY MODERN LITERATURE

ANDREW HISCOCK

CAMBRIDGE UNIVERSITY PRESS
Cambridge, New York, Melbourne, Madrid, Cape Town,
Singapore, São Paulo, Delhi, Tokyo, Mexico City

Cambridge University Press
The Edinburgh Building, Cambridge CB2 8RU, UK

Published in the United States of America by Cambridge University Press, New York

www.cambridge.org
Information on this title: www.cambridge.org/9780521761215

© Andrew Hiscock 2011

This publication is in copyright. Subject to statutory exception
and to the provisions of relevant collective licensing agreements,
no reproduction of any part may take place without the written
permission of Cambridge University Press.

First published 2011

Printed in the United Kingdom at the University Press, Cambridge

A catalogue record for this publication is available from the British Library

Library of Congress Cataloguing in Publication data
Hiscock, Andrew, 1962–
Reading memory in early modern literature / Andrew Hiscock.
p. cm.
Includes bibliographical references and index.
ISBN 978-0-521-76121-5 (hardback)
1. English literature – Early modern, 1500–1700 – History and criticism.
2. Memory in literature. I. Title.
PR428.M44H57 2011
820.9′358–dc23 2011030491

ISBN 978-0-521-76121-5 Hardback

Cambridge University Press has no responsibility for the persistence or
accuracy of URLs for external or third-party internet websites referred to in
this publication, and does not guarantee that any content on such websites is,
or will remain, accurate or appropriate.

For Stephen

SOCRATES: But I've forgotten to mention your artful technique (as it seems) of memory
Plato, *Lesser Hippias*

Remembering is merely safeguarding something entrusted to the memory
Seneca, *Ad Lucilium Epistulae Morales*

We are naturally prone to applaud the times behind us and to villify the present
Sir Robert Naunton, *Fragmenta Regalia or Observations on Queen Elizabeth, her times and favourites* (1633?)

If anyone should feel inclined to over-estimate the state of our present knowledge of mental life, a reminder of the function of memory is all that would be needed to force him to be more modest.
Sigmund Freud, 'The Psychopathology of Everyday Life' (1901)

Scientists discover way to reverse loss of memory. Patient recalls forgotten events after accidental breakthrough in surgery.

Scientists performing experimental brain surgery on a man aged 50 have stumbled across a mechanism that could unlock how memory works. The accidental breakthrough came during an experiment originally intended to suppress the obese man's appetite, using the increasingly successful technique of deep-brain stimulation. Electrodes were pushed into the man's brain and stimulated with an electric current. Instead of losing appetite, the patient had an intense experience of *déjà vu*. He recalled, in intricate details, a scene from 30 years earlier. More tests showed his ability to learn was dramatically improved when the current was switched on and his brain stimulated ... The treatment for obesity was unsuccessful.
Independent, 30 January 2008

Contents

List of figures	*page* viii
Acknowledgements	ix
Introduction: 'the dark backward and abysm of time'	1
1 'To seke the place where I my self hadd lost': acts of memory in the poetry of Henry Howard, Earl of Surrey	37
2 'Remembre not (lorde) myne offences': Katherine Parr and the politics of recollection	65
3 'Better a few things well pondered, than to trouble the memory with too much': troubling memory and martyr in Foxe's *Acts and Monuments*	90
4 Text, recollection and Elizabethan fiction: Nashe, Deloney, Gascoigne	113
5 The Doleful Clorinda? Mary Sidney, Countess of Pembroke, and the vocation of memory	138
6 'Tell me where all past yeares are': John Donne and the obligations of memory	165
7 'Of all the powers of the mind … the most delicate and fraile': the poetry of Ben Jonson and the renewal of memory	192
8 'This art of memory': Francis Bacon, memory and the discourses of power	219
Notes	246
Select bibliography	286
Index	314

Figures

1 *An Allegory of Prudence*
  By Titian © The National Gallery, London. Oil on canvas, c.1550–65. This image is reproduced by kind permission of The National Gallery Picture Library, London. *page* 19
2 Henry Howard, Earl of Surrey
  By unknown artist © National Portrait Gallery, London. Oil on canvas, c.1546. This image is reproduced by kind permission of The National Portrait Gallery, London. 46
3 Mary Herbert, Countess of Pembroke
  Early seventeenth-century engraving by Simon de Passe © National Portrait Gallery, London. This image is reproduced by kind permission of The National Portrait Gallery, London. 141
4 Francis Bacon, *Historia Ventorum*
  From *Historia Natvralis et Experimentalis ad Condendam Philosphiam siue, Phænomena Vniversi: Quæ est Instaurationis Magnæ Pars Tertia* (1622), pp. 51–2. These items are reproduced by permission of The Huntington Library, San Marino, California. 235
5 Francis Bacon
  By Nicholas Hilliard © National Portrait Gallery, London. Watercolour and bodycolour on vellum laid on card, 1578. This image is reproduced by kind permission of The National Portrait Gallery, London. 244

Acknowledgements

This body of research has had a long gestation period and there are a great number of people to whom I owe a large debt of thanks. I would like to thank Bangor University and the Arts and Humanities Research Council for awarding me terms of research leave to complete this project, and Linda Jones, Research Administrator at Bangor University, who invested so much time and energy in overseeing the preparation of this manuscript in its final stages. Sarah Staunton and Becky Taylor at Cambridge University Press have never failed to offer thoughtful advice and patient assistance in response to my numerous queries, which I have appreciated enormously. I would also like to thank Rosina Di Marzo and Paul Smith at Cambridge University Press for overseeing the final preparation of this script for publication and the Press Readers for the attentive and detailed readings they devoted to my research. My thanks go to the staff of Bangor University Libraries, the British Library and the Bodleian Library for their swift assistance with my enquiries, and to the York Museums Trust (York Art Gallery), the National Gallery, London, the National Portrait Gallery, London and the Huntington Library, California for their very generous permission to reproduce the images contained in this volume. I wish to extend a very special mention of thanks to my good friend of longstanding, Liz Godbeer, Minoan archaeologist and Head of Collections Management at the York Museums Trust for all her assistance in facilitating the reproduction of the Parmigianino cover image.

I express my sincere thanks to my colleagues at the School of English, Bangor University, who have always been willing to offer me scholarly advice and leads for my research – in this context, I would especially mention my fellow early modernists, Tom Corns, Ceri Sullivan and Helen Wilcox. I have also benefited from the research of a host of other colleagues in the College of Arts and Humanities at Bangor University in memorial studies, most particularly Helena Miguélez-Carballeira,

Robert Pope, Laura Rorato, Anna Saunders and Catrin Williams, who have always been willing to discuss cultural contexts, ancient and modern, for memorial writing with me. I remain grateful for the friendship and support received from Richard Dutton, Mike Pincombe and Greg Walker; and would like to thank Anne Lake Prescott for kindly sharing her research on Anne Dowriche, to Lina Perkins Wilder for kindly sharing her research on Thomas Tomkis's playtext *Lingua*, and to Ruth Evans for kindly sharing her research with me relating to Chaucer and memory.

During the time in which this volume was being prepared, I had the privilege to present, explore and respond to questions about elements of this research at academic colloquia. I would like to thank the organisers of the many and varied conferences to which I was invited: Sarah Alyn-Stacey, Director of the Centre for Medieval and Renaissance Studies, Trinity College Dublin; Marco Formisano, Humboldt-Universität zu Berlin; José Gonzales de Sevilla, Department of English, University of Alicante; Jerome de Groot ('Renaissance Imprisonment' conference at the Tower of London); Dalia El-Shayal and her colleagues, Department of English, University of Cairo; Beatrice Groves, Tudor Reading Group, Faculty of English, University of Oxford; Giovanni Iamartino, Università degli Studi di Milano; Holger Klein, School of English, Salzburg University; Kristin Kuutma, University of Tartu, Estonia; Rob Maslen, School of English & Scottish Language & Literature, Glasgow University; Jean-Claude Mailhol, Université de Valenciennes; Efterpi Mitsi, Kapodistrian University of Athens; Kate Hodgkin at the University of East London; and Myriam-Isabelle Ducrocq and Sandrine Parageau at Paris X Nanterre. I would also like to thank Carla Dente, University of Pisa, for her kind invitation to the European Shakespeare Research Association Conference, which allowed me to further my interests in early modern/modern translation with reference to this project. Some early versions of the research pursued in this volume have appeared in print, though the materials have continued to undergo revision and development since that time. I would like to thank the editors for their kind permission to represent some of my research materials from the following: Mike Pincombe (ed.), *The Anatomy of Tudor Literature* (Aldershot: Ashgate, 2001), pp. 34–43; Claire Jowitt (issue editor), *Women's Writing* 9:2 (2002), 177–93; John Batchelor (series editor), *Yearbook of English Studies* 31:1–2 (2008), 68–85; Ken Newton (former editor of *English*), *English* 52:202 (Spring 2003), 1–19.

Once again, I would like to thank Siân, Bronwen and Huw for their love and support throughout the period in which this volume was being prepared – it would not have been possible without you.

Reading Memory in Early Modern Literature was dedicated to Stephen from its very earliest beginnings and he remains at the very heart of its memorialising and of my own everyday selves.

Introduction: 'the dark backward and abysm of time'

PROSPERO   Canst thou remember
   A time before we came unto this cell?
   I do not think thou canst, for then thou was not
   Out three years old.
MIRANDA Certainly, sir, I can.
PROSPERO By what? by any other house or person?
   Of any thing the image tell me, that
   Hath kept with thy remembrance.
   …
                  What seest thou else
   In the dark backward and abysm of time?
   …
ARIEL Is there more toil? Since thou dost give me pains,
   Let me remember thee what thou hast promis'd
   Which is not yet perform'd me.
   …
PROSPERO   Dost thou forget
   From what a torment I did free thee?
   …
CALIBAN This island's mine, by Sycorax my mother,
   Which thou tak'st from me. When thou cam'st first,
   Thou strok'st me, and made much of me …
                     Shakespeare, *The Tempest*,
         1.ii.38–44, 49–50, 242–4, 250–1, 333–5[1]

In many ways the entire unfolding of *The Tempest* is framed by coercive acts of memory prompted in the minds of the island inhabitants by keen experiences of absence and lack. Such retrospective endeavours excite many of these figures not only to recall their implication in the *doings* of the past but, equally importantly, to 'remember themselves' – to reflect urgently upon the ethical business of self-government. More generally, these carefully orchestrated performances compel audiences on- and off-stage to ponder, like Miranda, their own trajectories from a 'dark backward'. As may be witnessed in the extracts above from the second scene of Shakespeare's play, this symbolic practice of remembering is disciplinary in nature. Here, Prospero (and he has a number of imitators among the islanders) seeks to control those around him by carefully monitoring the relationships between memory and epiphany for his growing community, attempting to allow only restricted access to the changeful materials of the past.

The narrative drive in *The Tempest* to structure human experience in terms of recovery and retrieval is clearly in evidence from our very first encounters with those who find themselves on the magic island: in Act One we are swiftly presented with an all too persuasive human order in which the organising principles of society depend strategically upon the flexing of (selective) memory, the spectacle of violence and access to secret knowledge. In recent times Paul Ricoeur has invited his readers to consider that the revisiting of the past may not only disclose expectations relating to the ways in which our cultural identities are formulated but also open up 'forgotten possibilities, aborted potentialities, repressed endeavours in the supposedly closed past. One of the functions of history in this respect is to lead us back to those moments of the past where the future was not yet decided, where the past was itself a space of experience open to a horizon of expectation.'[2] Clearly, the subject positions of agency that Ricoeur describes here are eminently attractive to both Ariel and Caliban: instead of sharing Prospero's appetite for fixity (a bid for *emplotment* in Ricoeur's critical lexis[3]), these minions wish to interrogate the master's wisdom, and thus cumulatively offer competing angles of vision on a past that attend most particularly to questions of trauma, violation and obligation. Prospero is continually pained by the realisation that those around him are unwilling or unable to perform the labours of memory that define his very existence; yet in this final phase of his island residence he is condemned to maintain relationships with these unruly underlings in order to frame authoritative narratives of sovereignty and identity for the newly arrived Europeans.

An account of the (often desperate) competition for cultural narrativisation that lies at the heart of *The Tempest* also shapes this present study. Charting the burgeoning debate concerning memory through the strategic textual interventions of a series of early modern writers, I seek to uncover the ways in which sixteenth- and early seventeenth-century writers fully exploited the intellectual riches of the classical and medieval centuries on the subject made available by the increasingly vigorous industry of the printing presses. However, equally importantly, this study highlights how these philosophical and theological legacies were expressed in English textual cultures as a response to: the traumas of religious schism and widely articulated desires for social mobility; the pervasive European influences of *Petrarchismo*; the radically changing constructs of intellectual and cultural leadership; as well as the challenges posed by those who sought scientific and technological innovation. For a society that was enormously diversifying its understandings of epistemology and, indeed, ontological difference, it was inevitable that key concepts associated with acts of cognition, such as *memoria*, would undergo intense and sustained interrogation.

Each of the chapters that follow engages with some of the major perspectives upon memorial debate during the Tudor and Jacobean periods (Platonic, Aristotelian, Augustinian, rhetorical, historiographical, somatic, technological) and the various discussions relating to different decades, different authors, different reading communities, different textual genres are designed to be open – suggestive – rather than exhaustive. The very different narrative techniques and reading strategies that early modern writers employed to examine the status and functions of memory not only point to a consuming interest of critical speculation from the reign of Henry VIII to that of James VI/I but also to the Age's radically changing formulations of subjectivity that coexisted and spoke to each other across social, intellectual and religious divides.

THE ANXIETY OF MEMORY

Andreas Huyssen has proposed for contemporary audiences that 'It does not require much theoretical sophistication to see that all representation – whether in language, narrative, image, or recorded sound – is based on memory'.[4] And, as we have seen, nowhere does this become more evident than in a work such as *The Tempest* whose intrigue has its roots in the protagonist's failure to 'remember' his own ducal obligations of service. As the play opens, Miranda is beginning to negotiate the disorienting possibilities of adult experience, and is progressively exposed to the uneasy economy of control at work on the island. Nonetheless, if her father seeks to restrain those around him with a *grand narrative* of the past, Shakespeare's late romance (like his earlier tragedy *Hamlet*) urges us repeatedly to consider the desperate struggle that is being enacted to establish what *should be* remembered and to consider the very partial nature of any human act of memory. If, in the *Arcadia*, Sidney's 'good Kalander' submits (aptly in the Shakespearean context of this discussion) that 'too much thinking doth consume the spirits and oft it falles out, that while one thinkes too much of his doing, he leaues to doe the effect of his thinking', we directly learn that even this bountiful host did not stint in remembering 'how much *Arcadia* was chaunged since his youth ... according to the nature of the growing world, stil worse and worse'.[5] Indeed, the irrepressible, unmasterable, competitive, multifarious nature of memory is a subject that has preoccupied much cultural debate in recent years. Pierre Nora has argued for a memory that is 'par nature, multiple et démultipliée, collective, plurielle et individualisée', whereas Mary Warnock has drawn attention in an equally telling manner to the profoundly individuated nature of recollection: 'Insofar as each living creature persists through time as a separate distinguishable individual thing, it can be said to have its own history, to live its own life. Therefore each has its own memory and makes its own choices in the light of its own past.'[6]

That the past may be subject to revision clearly renders Prospero and all the other islanders progressively insecure. Indeed, this seemingly obsessive theme runs the length of the play and has a direct analogue in the anxieties repeatedly expressed in the anti-theatrical literature of the early modern period – anxieties that theatregoers (among other hedonists) would succumb to all kinds of amnesia and 'forget' themselves in the seductive environment of the *wooden O*. In a fairly representative specimen of this writing, *Spiritus est vicarius Christi in terra* (1577), John Northbrooke lamented that

> we kepe ioly cheare one with an other in banquetting, surfeting and dronkennesse, also we vse al the night long, in ranging from town to town and from house to house with Mummeries and Maskes, Diceplaying, Carding and Dauncing, hauing nothing lesse in our memories than the day of death: for Salomon, byddeth vs remember our end and last day, and then we shal neuer do amisse: but they remember it not, therfore they do amisse.[7]

Interestingly, the Oxford academic John Rainolds would take up this enquiry with renewed vigour in *Th'overthrow of stage-playes* (1599), attacking the temptations supposedly on offer in the theatre environment with remorseless moral outrage. However, Rainolds's wide-ranging account of sinful practices linked to the theatre would not have come as a surprise to his readers on this occasion: for his Oxford printer, John Lichfield, had helpfully taken the trouble in a prefatory discussion to set the reader's pulse racing by summoning up the whole panorama of a fallen populace that seemed to have severed all links with its spiritual and moral inheritance and given itself over to the forbidden fruits of forgetfulness.[8]

Inevitably, the early modern reader was also repeatedly encouraged to ponder the antithesis to the amnesiac horde and to greet with rejoicing those enviable individuals who unfailingly displayed the gifts of a well-tempered memory. The popular collection *A Helpe to memory and discourse with table-talke as musicke to a banquet of wine* (1619, attributed to William Basse) organised such meditations in dialogue form:

> Q. Who haue the best naturall Memories?
> A. They that exercise them most, and abuse them least: and therefore I haue knowne diuers vnlettered persons trusting onely to strength of Memory, could record and retaine much more then the Scholler or Penman that committeth all to Record.[9]

Discussions such as these clearly demonstrate the breadth of early modern memorial debate, and Shakespeare's *The Tempest* reflects upon and interrogates at length many of the contemporary expectations surrounding the faculty. This present study not only explores the very different cultural appetites and motivations that governed the cultural perception of memory in the early modern period, it also seeks to throw light upon the ways in which more modern fixations with remembering (in terms of formulating an index to selfhood, consolidating structures of cultural ownership and privilege, or restoring collapsed mythologies of belonging, for example) may find analogues or counter-evidence when we travel back to the documents of the sixteenth and seventeenth centuries. It has become a common practice in contemporary debates, most especially those spanning our very own millennial divide, to scrutinise the ways in which memory is constituted culturally and to promote its operations as the *raw material* for productions of the self, despite its seemingly weakening hold on our cultural life. In his collection *Twilight Memories* Huyssen draws attention to 'the deepening sense of crisis' in our experience of modernity, which, he insists, is triggered by 'the reproach that our culture is terminally ill with amnesia'.[10] Striking a similarly plangent note in *Les Lieux de mémoire*, Pierre Nora contends that 'On ne parle tant de mémoire que parce qu'il n'y a plus'.[11] It is sobering to remember that such lines of thinking were frequently also being attributed with a specifically moral character some four hundred years earlier, as may be witnessed in William Rankins's tract *A Mirrour of Monsters* (1587). In this particular case, an exhaustive review of the general malaise of human delinquency is linked specifically to the faulty operations of memory:

> *Pythagoras* might warne men to auoyde such folly. But the infection of this vice is so contagious, that as the Ryuer *Laethes* maketh hym that drynketh therof, presentlie to forget his own condition & former deedes, so this damnable vice of idlenes, so besotteth the sences, and bewitcheth the myndes of menne, as they remembred not the profitable fruites of vertuous labor.[12]

As we have seen, an analogous fear of memorial (and, thus, ethical) failure in his fellow creatures is clearly uppermost in the mind of Shakespeare's usurped ruler on the magic island. When Prospero performs his memorial labours at the beginning of the play in the desire to 'enlighten' his servants, his daughter and the new arrivals, he has also determined to renew power relationships in this society by stressing the burdens that his accounts of the past impose. In opposition to the unruly factions who seek to author their own destinies, Prospero reminds his various subjects of their own decaying knowledge and his own inevitable status as patriarch. As the historian J. H. Plumb underlined in *The Death of the Past*, in times of conflict 'the past has to be fought for as well as the present. Authority, once achieved, must have a secure and usable past'.[13] The deeply precarious nature of such an undertaking can only impress upon audiences on- and off-stage the very fragility of the social network that they inhabit – a network that requires constant renewal through acts of memory. Painfully aware of the terrifying provisionality of his own political order, Shakespeare's protagonist finds himself for most of the play attempting to shore up the collapsing limits of memory with spectacular acts of violence.

EARLY MODERN MEMORY AND ANTIQUITY

In her landmark study of medieval constructions of memory, Mary Carruthers observed that in our post-Romantic world 'when we think of our highest creative power, we think invariably of the imagination ... Ancient and medieval people reserved *their* awe for memory.'[14] Carruthers's study (like Frances Yates's *The Art of Memory*, Paolo Rossi's *Logic and the Art of Memory* and, more recently, Janet Coleman's *Ancient and Medieval Memories*, Lina Bolzoni's *Gallery of Memory* and Mary Warnock's *Memory*)[15] has highlighted in a highly illuminating manner the ways in which a discourse of *memoria* became institutionalised in medieval culture and played a strategic role in the cultural debates of antiquity.[16] Indeed, an abiding interest in the properties of this faculty is recorded in the earliest writings of the Western tradition. Memory was imagined as the goddess Mnemosyne by the earliest Greeks, and among her offspring sired by Zeus (or Apollo) were traditionally numbered the nine Muses. An account of such mythologies clearly lived on into the Roman period, for Plutarch argued in his *Moralia* for the faculty's importance, as may be witnessed in the 1532 edition translated by Sir Thomas Elyot: 'Aboue all thynges the memorie of chylderne is to be exercised and kepte in vsage: for that is as it were the store house of lernynge … Memorie is named the mother of Muses.'17 And, indeed, an appreciation of the exalted status accorded to Memory was common currency throughout the early modern period: in Book Three of *The Faerie Queene*, we discover Spenser hailing Clio, the Muse of history, as 'my dearest sacred Dame, | Daughter of *Phebus* and of *Memorye*' (III.iii.4); and in *The Castel of Memorie … Made by Gulielmus Gratarolus Bergomatis Doctor of Artes and Phisike. Englished by Willyam Fulwood* (1562) the reader is reminded that 'the poetes not without a cause haue feyned wisdome to be the daughter of Memory'.[18]

The imbrication of cultural expectations surrounding wisdom, history and memory had clearly been occupying thinkers since earliest times, and in his dialogue *Meno* Plato made one of his most influential contributions to this debate. Here, the mentor Socrates impresses upon the young Meno that, 'As the soul is immortal, has been born often and has seen all things here and in the underworld, there is nothing which it has not learned; so it is in no way surprising that it can recollect the things it knew before, both about virtue and other things'.[19] The later *Phaedo* affirms that memory (rather than instruction) is the vital resource for the recapturing of residual knowledges surviving from prenatal engagement with a higher realm of Being, or Forms: the mentor Socrates argues that 'if we acquired … knowledge before birth, then lost it at birth, and then later … we recovered the knowledge we had before, would not what we call learning be the recovery of our own knowledge, and we are right to call this recollection'.[20] Equally evocative for later generations was the assertion made in *Theaetetus* that the faculty of memory might be construed symbolically as 'a block of wax' lodged in our spiritual being ('larger in one person, smaller in another'):

> SOCRATES We may look upon it, then, as a gift of Memory, the mother of the Muses. We make impressions upon this of everything we wish to remember among the things we have seen or heard or thought of ourselves; we hold the wax under our perceptions and thoughts and take a stamp from them, in the way in which we take the imprints of signet rings. Whatever is impressed upon the wax we remember and know so long as the image remains in the wax; whatever is obliterated or cannot be impressed, we forget and do not know.[21]

Plato revealed in these constructions of memory not only a theory of human epistemology but a key perspective upon a transcendent realm whose mythic wisdom symbolises a desperately needed possibility of redemption for humanity from this sublunary world. Platonic dualist thinking (which maintained an emphasis upon an absolute ontological division and hierarchical distinction between the contrary motions of the physical and spiritual realms of experience) also became a recurring referent in many early modern considerations of memory. In *Phaedo*, for example, the mentor Socrates asks, 'When then ... does the soul grasp the truth? For whenever it attempts to examine anything with the body, it is clearly deceived by it ... And indeed the soul reasons best when ... taking leave of the body and as far as possible having no contact or association with it in its search for reality.'[22] Crucially, within these writings, Plato's reader is reminded repeatedly that true knowledge is stimulated by meditative enquiry and recollection, rather than engagement with the material environment in which the body is compelled to exist. If, on occasions, Plato does acknowledge that the disorienting experience of temporality (which itself serves to impair the soul's powers of understanding) may engender forms of recollection, such mental reflexes are governed by the senses, and thus of a lesser order. Genuine apprehension represents engagement with a higher reality, because this faculty of memory was formed in, and belongs to, the realm of Being, or Forms. The Platonic concentration upon learning as remembrance was clearly an avenue of enquiry with which Florio's Montaigne was acquainted, even if he expressed little affection for its premises:

it were necessarie they [our souls] should (being yet in the body) remember the said knowledge (as Plato said) that what we learn't, was but a new remembering of that which we had knowne before: A thing that any man may by experience maintaine to be false and erronious.[23]

In a culture that was obsessively concerned with the interpretation of the past, it comes as no surprise that early modern intellectuals frequently returned to the consideration of memory as a consuming source of vigorous, if ultimately irresolvable, debate. Prospero's attempts in *The Tempest* to refresh power relationships with the resources of memory has its counterparts in a host of other textual interventions from the period. Florio's Montaigne submits (rather disingenuously) that 'it is commonly seene by experience, that excellent memories do rather accompanie weake judgements',[24] whereas his younger contemporary Francis Bacon responded, on occasions, more flexibly to the veneration with which earlier generations had greeted this most perplexing of human faculties:

one of the moderns has ingeniously referred all the powers of the soul to motion, and remarked on the conceit and precipitancy of some of the ancients, who in too eagerly fixing their eyes and thoughts on the memory, imagination, and reason, have neglected the Thinking Faculty, which holds first place. For he who remembers or recollects, thinks; he who imagines, thinks; he who reasons, thinks; and in a word the spirit of man, whether prompted by sense or left to itself, whether in the functions of the intellect, or of the will and affections, dances to the tune of the thoughts.[25]

This concern with memory's role in the process of cognition would again be taken up later in the seventeenth century in an equally celebrated manner by the political theorist Thomas Hobbes with the contention that 'He that perceiues that he hath perceived, *remembers*'.[26] However, it is to the ever-changing mental landscapes of Montaigne's *Essais* (or rather John Florio's early seventeenth-century translation, *The Essayes or Morall, Politike and Millitarie Discourses of Lo: Michaell de Montaigne*) that we will return most often as a constant companion in the course of this study in order to contextualise the very multifarious nature of early modern debate upon memory. It is Montaigne's willingness to respond to a whole range of different discourses that had currency during the early modern period that inevitably marks him out as an invaluable guide. His quicksilver intelligence ran in a host of often contradictory directions as his prose meditations unfolded, and nowhere is this more evident than in his investigations into memory. Interestingly, despite his alignment of the faculty with 'weake judgements' in his essay 'Of Lyers', elsewhere, in 'Of Presumption', he is disarmingly eager to affirm that

Memorie is an instrument of great service, and without which, judgement will hardly discharge his duty, whereof I have great want ... if I must remember a discourse of any consequence, be it of any length, I am driven to this vile and miserable necessitie, to learne every word I must speake, by rote; otherwise I should never doe it well or assuredly ... Memorie is the receptacle and case of knowledge. Mine being so weake, I have no great cause to complaine if I know but little. I know the names of Artes in Generall and what they treate of, but nothing further. I turne and tosse over bookes, but do not studie them ... The Authours, the place, the words, and other circumstances, I sodainely forget: and am so excellent in forgetting, that as much as any thing else I forget mine owne writings and compositions.[27]

At the dawn of the modern period, Sigmund Freud's *The Psychopathology of Everyday Life* invited readers to consider such contentions in the light of his theories of paramnesia ('the mechanism of false recollection' and strategic forgetfulness) and psychic repression.[28] However, four centuries earlier, the very compendious nature of Montaigne's speculations meant that he not only engaged with a great variety of memorial speculations, he also unfailingly stressed for his own readers that an appreciation of the faculty was intimately bound up with an understanding of how their everyday selves were constructed.

MATERIAL MEMORY

In William Fulwood's *Englishing* of Gratarolo's treatise *The Castel of Memorie* (1562), the Elizabethan reader was treated to some strategic insights into the conflicted nature of memorial debate:

> Memorie is by the whiche the mynde repeateth things y^t are past. Or it is a stedfast perceiuyng in the mynde of the disposition of thinges and wordes. Or as (Aristotle supposeth) it is an imagination, that remaineth of such thinges as the sense had conceyued. Also by the sentence of Plato, Memorie is a sense of a safetie (or safe reteining of things): for the soule obtaineth by the office of the senses whatsoeuer thinges thaunce under the sense, and therefore it is the beginninge of an opinion.[29]

Here, readers were not only encouraged to acknowledge the legacy of Platonic thinking in this debate but asked to attend to the culturally pervasive traditions of Aristotelian thinking. The thorny problem that afflicts Shakespeare's Prospero, the parentage between memory and lack, was also of profound significance in Aristotle's thinking. Plato had promoted the analysis of memory as a focus for meditative, nay mystical, enquiry: as we have seen, in his writings memory often constitutes a precious route of retreat from the rigours of temporal existence. Nonetheless, it is clear that both Plato and Aristotle attributed to memory a pre-eminent status in their respective endeavours to define the nature of the human condition: Aristotle, for example, affirmed in *The History of Animals* that 'Many animals have memory, and are capable of instruction; but no other creature except man can recall the past at will'.[30] In *De Memoria et Reminiscentia* he stressed that memory is most commonly activated by mental visualisations of contiguous and/or antithetical images from the material world of that which is sought by the mind. Thus, the human memory, like a pictorial thesaurus, is often governed by associative laws; and, in opposition to Platonic thinking, Aristotle conceived of memory not as primarily concerned with transcendent intimations, but as structured by a psychic vocabulary of physical objects, situations and images derived from mortal experience:

> if asked, of which among the parts of the soul memory is a function, we reply: manifestly of that part to which imagination also appertains; and all objects of which there is imagination are in themselves objects of memory, which those which do not exist without imagination are objects of memory incidentally.

One might ask how it is possible that though the affection is present, and the fact absent, the latter – that which is not present – is remembered. It is clear that we must conceive that which is generated through sense-perception in the soul, and in the part of the body which is its seat, – viz. that affection the state whereof we call memory – to be some such thing as a picture. The process of movement stamps in, as it were, a sort of impression of the percept, just as persons do who make an impression with a seal.³¹

Characteristically, Aristotle's discussions of the faculty return repeatedly to the question of human sense impressions (notably, the pictorial), and it should be stressed this paradigm for discussion would persist for thousands of years: at the beginning of the modern period, for example, in his landmark study *Matière et mémoire* (1896) Henri Bergson acknowledged that, despite contemporary crises of interpretation surrounding the faculty, 'on both sides it is agreed that we can only grasp things in the form of images, we must state the problem in terms of images, and of images alone'.³²

Aristotle's enquiries in *De Memoria et Reminiscentia* are firmly rooted in the quotidian operations of memory and self-conscious acts of recollection and, once again, this is a distinction that has endured as an extraordinarily potent model, remaining valuable for generations of theorists. Jung, for example, was eager to have his reader differentiate between 'direct' and 'indirect' memory (the latter being 'an unconscious perception that enters the brain passively [that] can spontaneously activate a related association and in this way reach consciousness').³³ However, in Aristotle's *De Memoria et Reminiscentia*, a work that appears to have been conceived as a sister work to *De Anima*, recollection is often envisaged in terms of a physical search (*memoria rerum*): the human ability to remember is articulated with a lexis of sight, of visual identification – 'Without an image thinking is impossible'.³⁴ From this perspective, human narratives of memory are commonly organised around mental images (which are themselves diminished imprints of former experience or sensation). In opposition to Plato's projection of a unified fund of immutable truth that the human spirit may attempt to tap through contemplative investment (*theoria*), notably through the endeavours of memorial revelation, Aristotle attends to a theory of human epistemology (*phronesis*) rooted for the most part in the pragmatic interrogation of material experience. In many ways, Aristotle's often proves to be a more sobering theory of *memoria* because we are asked to testify repeatedly to the fact that our human powers to recollect are not only earth-bound but inevitably partial and subject to decay. Nonetheless, if he stresses (like Plato) that memory is inevitably a meditation upon absence, Aristotle appears most exercised in *De Memoria et Reminiscentia* by the proposition that the faculty might be shaped and developed by the visual replaying and revisiting of prior cycles of temporal experience. In addition, he repeatedly distinguished between the ways in which memory responded to the imprint of sense-perceptions and the conscious act of recollection, arguing that

> It has been already stated that those who have a good memory are not identical with those who are quick at recollecting. But the act of recollecting differs from that of remembering, not only in respect of time, but also in this, that many also of the other animals have memory, but, of all that we are acquainted with, none, we venture to say, except man, shares in the faculty of recollection. The cause of this is that recollection, is, as it were, a mode of inference. For he who endeavours to recollect infers that he formerly saw or heard, or had some such experience, and the process is, as it were, a sort of investigation.[35]

Equally importantly for the early modern period, Aristotle was interested in the question of mental retentiveness and the ways in which repetition or mnemonics might assist our mental labours. Indeed, in order to address this problem, he can be found at points to advocate beginning *in medias res* in narratives or sequences of associated ideas that we wish to retain or to summon up for particular occasions.[36]

Such thinking was to prove enormously influential and there developed a significant subgenre of instructional manuals that sought to advise readers upon the cultivation and refinement of 'artificial memory' (or the deliberate training of the faculty): these frequently involved exercises of mental imaging and often relied strategically upon laws of association. Indeed, at the close of the early modern period, John Aubrey related in his *Brief Lives* that the 'naturall memorie' of Thomas Fuller 'was very great, to which he added the Art of Memorie: he would repeat to you forwards and backwards all the signes from Ludgate to Charing-crosse'.[37] Such feats worthy of marvel had been recorded since earliest times. In *De Oratore*, Cicero celebrated for his readers the achievement of the poet Simonides of Ceos (c.556 BC – 468 BC), who was able to remember the seating positions (and thus identities) of the guests at a feast after the collapse of a building in which the gathering had taken place.[38] In the preface to Book One of his *Controversiae*, the Elder Seneca remembered an earlier time when his memory had been prodigious: 'When two thousand names had been reeled off I would repeat them in the same order; and when my assembled school-fellows each supplied a line of poetry, up to the number of more than two hundred, I would recite them in reverse.'[39] And, in his *Naturalis Historia*, the imagination of the Elder Pliny was also excited by the belief that the Persian king Cyrus could name all his soldiers and that Lucius Scipio could identify the whole Roman population by name.[40] Furthermore, it appears that the appetite for such spectacular performances was clearly alive and well in the early modern period, as we learn in the Induction to John Marston's drama *The Malcontent* (c.1603):

SINKLO My cousin hee hath an excellent memory indeed, sir.
SLY Who, I? I'll tell you a strange thing of myself, and I can tell you, for one that never studied the art of memory 'tis very strange, too.
CONDELL What's that, sir?
SLY Why, I'll lay a hundred pound, I'll walk but once down by the Goldsmith's Row in Cheap, take notice of the signs, and tell you them with a breath instantly.
LOWIN 'Tis very strange.[41]

More generally, within the context of early modern memorial debate, Leonard Cox's *The Art or Crafte of Rhetoryke* (1532) is not unrepresentative in linking questions of memorial performance specifically to another Aristotelian emphasis upon the importance of the moral probity (*ethos*) of those who would engage in public service to the *polis*: 'he that wyll for the confyrmyng of his purpose declare & proue y^t it is honest & commendable y^t he entendeth to persuade hym: behoueth to haue perfyte knowlege of ye natures of vertues'.[42] Such moralising of memorial discourse clearly continued on into the next century: in John Brinsley's *Ludus literarius* (1612), the reader is reminded that 'we must always looke to that diuine Caueat, that we neuer helpe the minde by any filthy obiect'.[43] Furthermore, John Willis's slightly later *Mnemonica, or The Art of Memory drained out of the pure Fountains of Art & Nature* (first published in Latin in 1618 with the first complete English translation published in 1661) repeatedly draws attention to the ethical discipline necessary, among a great number of other requirements, for the successful exercise of the faculty.[44] Indeed, the initial training of the memory with rudimentary exercises is repeatedly linked in his discussions to the exercise of virtue.

[Among those things that are most harmful to the memory are:] VI. *Venus*, i. if it be immoderate ... VII. Coldnesse of the hinder part of the head, of the neck, stomack, belly and feet. VIII ... In windy or moist places ... XI. Filthy desires, as avarice, envy, thirst of revenge, lust, love of harlots, and the ardent Passion, *Love*. XIII. Disorderly reading of Books, imitating Children in trivial Schools.[45]

Here, we witness an enduring cultural fascination with the ontological links that may exist between the performance of memorial prowess and the disciplined conduct of mind and body. Thus, in her study *Memory*,

Mary Warnock enquires in a timely manner, 'What is it about memory that inevitably brings in the physiological?'[46] Certainly, such a question looks back to the very heart of Aristotelian thinking in this field. In opposition to the assertions of his mentor Plato, Aristotle argued in *De Memoria et Reminiscentia* that the capacity to remember was shaped by the given constitution of a human body: he conceived of the possibility that certain individuals might enjoy a particular *hexis* or *pathos* that furnished them with a heightened ability to recollect. Given that he returned repeatedly to the symbiosis that existed between the motions of memory and body, it is unsurprising that recollection is often scrutinised explicitly in *De Memoria et Reminiscentia* in somatic terms:

> That the affection is corporeal, i.e. that recollection is a searching for an image in a corporeal substrate, is proved by the fact that some persons, when, despite the most strenuous application of thought, they have been unable to recollect, feel discomfort, which even though they abandon the effort at recollection, persists in them none the less; and especially persons of melancholic temperament. For these are most powerfully moved by images … Infants and very old persons have bad memories, owing to the amount of movement going on with them; for the latter are in process of rapid decay, the former in process of vigorous growth; and we may add that children, until considerably advanced in years, are dwarf-like.[47]

In the memorial literature that developed in succeeding ages, such concerns with anatomy and humoral predispositions were often yoked with an equally enthusiastic engagement with questions of environments and dietary regimes conducive to the nurturing of the body's ability to remember. These investigations, which clearly preoccupied Aristotle, had attained wide currency in memorial speculations by the sixteenth century. In Richard Edwards's drama *Damon and Pithias* (performed 1564–5, published 1571), Damon casually informs his companion, 'Ah Stephano, small diet maketh a fine memorie'.[48] Such commonplace conclusions were supported by an ever-growing corpus of writing circulating in Europe since medieval times. In his *Rhetorica novissima* (completed 1235) Boncompagno da Signa had stressed that 'whenever food and drink are consumed unnaturally, they cannot be digested owing to a lack of natural heat. For this reason, a harmful vapor rises up like a whirlwind, and heading for the brain overfills its membranes; consequently sense perception is impeded and the memory chamber is obscured'.[49] In a wide-ranging discussion of such publications, Paolo Rossi also draws particular attention to the *De omnibus ingeniis augendae memoriae* (1481) by the Italian scholar Giammichele Alberto da Carrara, which not only reflected in detail upon the benefits of disciplining the mind with assiduous training but also, following in the footsteps of Galen, Avicenna and Averroes, upon ailments detrimental to the memory and the therapies and remedies that might be employed to counteract their effects.[50] As far as English print culture is concerned, the abiding interest in the interrelations between humoral dispositions, diverse human habitats and dietary regimes may be witnessed at length in *The Castel of Memorie*. Here, the reader is warned sternly that

> this untemperatnes of the brayne commeth many tymes of ill nourishement, sometyme of the unwholesome ayres that is aboute us … If the hurting of the Memory come by vehement purgations and other unmesurable emptiness, or of dryness it must onely be remedied by good & nourishing meates … The braynes of a henne dothe helpe the witte and the Memorye, in such sorte that it hathe broughte some agayne to their wittes, that beganne to dote.[51]

By 1642, Thomas Fuller might be discovered throwing up his hands regarding such considerations: despite a belief that '*Moderate diet and good aire preserve Memory,*' he conceded, 'what aire is best I dare not define, when such great ones differ. Some say a pure and subtle aire is best, another commends a thick and foggy aire* [* *Plato, Aristotle, Tully.*].'[52]

MEMORY TRAINING

If we turn our attentions more specifically to the works of Latin writers, one of the most striking features of much of the memorial literature that survives is that, for the most part, the more metaphysical enquiries, relating to ontology or epistemology, which had frequently preoccupied their Greek predecessors, are marginalised or dispensed with altogether. The clearest statements of memorial training to be found in the period are developed in the anonymous collection *Rhetorica ad Herennium* (86–82 BC?), in Cicero's *De Oratore* (55 BC) and in Quintilian's *Institutio oratoria* (*c.*AD 95). Although these collections each in their own way bear witness to an Aristotelian emphasis upon the mental replaying of images/ objects/situations drawn from the material world (*memoria rerum*), there remains an abiding interest in the pragmatics of memorial training (the cultivation of 'artificial memory') and how this might relate to linguistic performance (*memoria verborum*). Thus, the *Rhetorica ad Herennium* underlines that, unlike 'natural memory', which is 'embedded in our minds … The artificial memory is that memory which is strengthened by a kind of training and system of discipline'.[53] More generally, Latin writers concerned themselves principally with *memoria* as a key procedure alongside *inventio* (generation of material), *dispositio* (marshalling of material), *elocutio* (linguistic embellishment) and *actio* (oratorical display) for public rhetorical performance in the *civitas*. In the *Rhetorica ad Herennium* the reader is invited to cherish 'the treasure-house of the ideas supplied by Invention … the guardian of all the parts of rhetoric, the Memory'; and, for centuries to come, memorial literature published in Europe would rehearse these premises as they had been set down for discussion in the Roman period.[54]

Cicero, Quintilian and the author of the *Rhetorica ad Herennium* all advocated an exercise of memory that relied upon the powerful resources of the visual imagination. Particular attention was devoted to the mental imaging of a complex architectural structure or landscape in which every chamber or building would contain a piece of relevant information:

> Some place is chosen of the largest possible extent and characterised by the utmost possible variety, such as a spacious house divided into a number of rooms … The first thought is placed, as it were, in the forecourt; the second, let us say, in the living room; the remainder are placed in due order … as soon as the memory of the facts requires to be revived, all these places are visited in turn and the various deposits are demanded from their custodians.[55]

In such discussions, we are left in no doubt that in the successful flexing of his expert memory, the orator would be confirmed in his elevated cultural position as a premier citizen and custodian of the collective past.

The systemisation of memory retrieval in rhetorical, philosophical and occult writing during the medieval centuries in Europe has been the focus of groundbreaking studies such as those already acknowledged by Frances A. Yates, Mary J. Carruthers and Janet Coleman. As far as English print culture was concerned, a conspicuous intervention in this area was made by one of the most widely read memorial tracts of the early modern period, Pietro da Ravenna's *Phoenix sive artificiosa memoria* (Venice, 1491).[56] This was translated by Peter Copland and published in *c.*1548 as *The Art of Memory, that otherwyse is called the Phenix*. The English readers of Ravenna's tract were called upon to prepare themselves for a vigorous training in the business of mental imaging, and from the prefatory discussion they are invited to nourish great expectations: 'easyly & in short tyme [you] may touch ye summite, & reach ye heyght of th[is] art.' Moreover, this induction into a new field of learning should be viewed, we are told, as an initiation into a mystical art that 'semeth more to be inuented by dyuyne inspyracion than by arte or scyence of mankynde'.[57] Nonetheless, a number of elements of this methodology and discourse had already established some currency in England by the mid-sixteenth century when Copland's translation was published. In some sixteenth-century editions of Stephen Hawes's *Pastime of Pleasure* (1st edn 1509), for example, Dame Rhetoric advises the orator in verse that he should select 'sundry ymages' and maintain 'inwarde, a recapitulation | Of eche ymage' that may be drawn upon 'In due order, maner, and reason', so that 'is enprynted, in his propre mynde | Euery tale'.[58] In the collection printed by Caxton and entitled *The myrrour [and] dyscrypcyon of the worlde* (1527; 1st edn 1481), there is similarly a consideration in the larger discussion of rhetoric of the 'Ars memoratiua Or memory'. Here, once again, the intimate relationship between the formulation of memoryscapes and the exercise of *memoria verborum* is established: 'in this arte of memory thou muste haue places which shal be to the lyke as it were perchment or paper to wryte vppon[.] Also insteade of thy lettres thou must ymagyn Images to set in the same places.'[59]

However, as will become evident in the course of this study, the *ars memorativa* was not assimilated effortlessly into English intellectual life. A number of humanist scholars, most notably Erasmus, proved to be resisting readers of this literature and questioned how receptive one should be to its precepts when considering the education of new generations of students. Once again, it was becoming increasingly apparent that the business of recollection might have profound repercussions upon the manner in which human epistemology was conceived. Strategically, Cicero had asked in his treatise *De Oratore*, 'Do you not see how great a responsibility the orator has in historical writing?', and this enquiry continued to prove highly relevant for early modern authors.[60] Fulwood's translation of *The Castel of Memorie* thundered, 'take Memorye away: What is a man? What can he doe? | or els what can he say?'; and ten years later John Foxe was heard to exclaim in the *Pandectae locorum communium* (1572), 'what can poets, what can historians, what can rhetoricians, and orators … provide by their art without memory, or by their memory without noting the places?'[61] Nonetheless, as Walter Ong and Paolo Rossi have demonstrated, the influential writings of Pierre de la Ramée (Ramus) in the second half of the sixteenth century proposed the replacing of rote-learning and imaginative memoryscapes (and thus the general intellectual undertaking of the *ars memorativa*) with an emphasis upon ordering and method: memorial prowess was now to be facilitated in all forms of argumentation (including oratory) by carefully sequenced taxonomies, logically descending from the general subject areas to particular classifications.[62] Thus, Ramist thinking sought to extricate memory from the imaginative clutches of rhetorical mnemnotechnology and to relocate it within a methodology of dialectic and logic. A leading international apologist for Ramist logic, William Temple, took up the role of secretary from 1594 to Robert Devereux, second Earl of Essex. The latter owned books by Ramus and was the dedicatee of Ramist publications such as Richard Harvey's *Ephemeron* (1583) and *Philadelphus* (1593). Earlier in the Elizabethan period, Gabriel Harvey had composed an elegy to his revered Ramus, *Ode Natalitia* (1575); and Abraham Fraunce clearly displayed his acquaintance with Ramist thinking in *The lawiers logike* (1588).[63]

Yet this is not to say that a knowledge of the *ars memorativa* completely lapsed from consciousness as the early modern period progressed. *An Apology for Poetry* indicates that Philip Sidney knew enough of the subject to argue that 'even they that have taught the art of memory have showed nothing so apt for it as a certain room divided into many places well and thoroughly known'.[64] Indeed, his lovelorn shepherds, Claius and Strephon, at the opening of the *Arcadia*, return nostalgically to a site of encounter with the departed Urania, recalling 'as this place serued vs to thinke of those thinges, so those thinges serue as places to call to memorie more excellent matters'.[65] Thomas Watson (who is mostly remembered now for his poetic collection *Hekatompathia* (1582)) published his own prose work *Compendium memoriae localis* in 1585. Repeatedly acknowledging Cicero as the authority for much of his discussion, Watson's study notably refrains from engaging with Ramist thinking, and instead distinguishes carefully between *memoria naturalis* and *memoria artifitiosa*, rehearsing familiar ideas inherited from classical writers on the training of memory. And John Willis is discovered in his later *Mnemonica* (1618 and 1661) at great pains to have his reader summon up mentally an imposing structure, and to 'suppose the Edifice to be of twelve yards in length within the walls, in breadth six yards, and in height seven yards'.[66]

MEMORY, VIRTUE AND PROVIDENCE

Building upon moral discourses in evidence from earlier Greek writing, in *De Inventione* Cicero defined virtue in terms of Wisdom (*Prudentia*), Justice (*Iustitia*), Courage (*Fortitudinis*) and Temperance (*Temperantia*). Like these other qualities, Wisdom or Prudence (which is the faculty governing moral knowledge) might be, according to Cicero, subdivided – subdivided in this case into *memoria*, *intelligentsia* and *providentia*. Within the terms of the discussion, these subdivisions are shown to relate closely to the three chronological planes of human experience – past, present and future:

Memory, virtue and providence

Figure 1. Titian, *An Allegory of Prudence* © The National Gallery, London. Oil on canvas, *c*.1550–65.

Wisdom is the knowledge of what is good, what is bad and what is neither good nor bad. Its parts are, memory, intelligence and foresight. Memory is the faculty by which the mind recalls what has happened. Intelligence is the faculty by which it ascertains what is. Foresight is the faculty by which it is seen that something is going to occur before it occurs.[67]

Fernando Bouza has justly underlined that in the early modern period 'writing was not considered the sole expression of humans' essential capacity to create memory. The same power was attributed to painted or sculpted images and to the spoken word.'[68] Indeed, the potency of Cicero's intellectual paradigms promoted in *De Inventione* may be demonstrated in the fact that they continued to be debated for centuries to come, and their legacies may be identified as one of shaping forces upon the symbolic architecture of Titian's *An Allegory of Prudence* (Figure 1), for example, executed 1550–65. Here, the Senex (thought to be Titian himself) is firmly aligned with *memoria*, lodged above the ravenous wolf's head of the tricephalous beast. The leonine strength of maturity or *intelligentsia* (thought to be Titian's son, Orazio) is also counterpointed by the meeker, canine version of youth or *providentia* (thought to be the family cousin, Marco Vecellio). The whole pictorial scene is bound together, unusually within Titian's *œuvre*, by a distinctly Ciceronian sentiment: 'EX PRATETERITO PRAESENS PRVDENTER AGIT NI FUTURA ACTIONE DETVRPET' ['from the past, the present acts prudently, lest it spoil future actions'].[69] The elderly Titian may be affirming the need for good government among his own kin in this instance, but in Cicero's writings the more general concern was that memory should be exercised in order to preserve evidence of human greatness and to restore (moral) direction to a society that has allowed knowledge (and the obligations) of its distinguished past to lapse.

With the advent of the Christian era, the discussions by Latin writers of the life-enhancing possibilities afforded by the resources of memory would often be re-addressed in terms of spiritual experience. Christian theologians, at least as far back as Saint Augustine, had recognised the significance of memory and of the skills of public performance in coming to understand some of the mysteries of spiritual interiority. The Church Father set forth in *De Trinitate* a key Christianised paradigm (adapted from Cicero's enquiries) whereby the rational soul was divided into *memoria*, *intelligentia* and *providentia*; in this way, Augustine envisaged an analogue to the Holy Trinity in memory, understanding and will – 'these three are one, one life, one mind, one essence'.[70] Moreover, elsewhere in the *Confessions*, we are presented with an exemplary spiritual history; and, most influentially, Augustine is often seen to conceive of memory in explicitly spatial terms: 'I come to the fields and vast palaces of memory, where are the treasuries of innumerable images of all kinds of objects brought in by sense-perception.'[71] Throughout his writings the faculty is presented as a spacious mental receptacle and/or landscape in which the past is preserved; and, as Mary Warnock has pointed out, in succeeding centuries there emerged 'a strong and natural tendency … to think of memory as a kind of storehouse. There is a spatial metaphor involved here, which we find it difficult to repress'.[72]

Clearly, in pondering the workings of the faculty and the human capacity for sense-perception, Augustine's *Confessions* acknowledges at least in part the authority of Aristotelian thinking (and diction). Indeed, in direct comparison with many of the enquiries in *De Memoria et Reminiscentia*, Augustine's narrative also meditates upon the relationships between memory and body ('just as food is brought from the stomach in the process of rumination, so also by recollection these things are brought up from the memory')[73] and the challenges posed by false and/or creative memory. More generally, in privileging a theory of human retrospection that engaged directly with a higher, redemptive realm of spirituality, Augustine's investigations into the nature of memory inevitably bear witness in part to the influence of Platonic idealism:

> the memory contains the innumerable principles and laws of numbers and dimensions. None of them has been impressed on memory through any bodily sense-perception … Yet we would not speak about them at all unless in our memory we could find not only the sounds of the names attaching to the images imprinted by the physical senses, but also the notion of the things themselves. These notions we do not receive through any bodily entrance.[74]

Augustine's narratives unveil a human condition in which memory retrieval emerges as a divinely ordered vocation, a source of orientation for the soul's cathartic spiritual journeying. As a consequence, the Church Father is found to ponder again and again the relationships between retrospection and the desperate need of the human spirit for self-scrutiny: Augustine's speaker is able to assert as an ontological given, 'It is I who remember, I who am mind', and thus he labours towards the piecing together of a greater spiritual unity.[75] This growing knowledge of spiritual identity is not thoroughly prenatal in origin, but clearly involves an epiphanic form of remembering and reappraisal. In this radical rescripting of human experience in the *Confessions*, Augustine's speaker appeals not only for a renewed sense of spiritual direction from the Godhead, but interrogates some of the fundamental axes through which we organise temporal existence: 'Thus my boyhood, which is no longer, lies in past time which is no longer … neither future nor past exists … The present considering the past is the memory, the present considering the present is immediate awareness, the present considering the future is expectation.'[76]

This crucial link that Augustine forges between the exercise of memory and the commitment to spiritual renewal would be taken up energetically in subsequent centuries. Cicero's moralising of *memoria* and Augustine's Christian theologising of this discourse proved enormously influential upon pre-eminent medieval thinkers such as Albertus Magnus and Thomas Aquinas, who both executed commentaries of Aristotle's *De Memoria et Reminiscentia*. In his tract *De Bono* Albertus promoted memory as a valuable ethical resource – a resource that may be seen to shape wise conduct and to reinvigorate the human commitment to virtue. Like

Aristotle, Albertus affirmed that memory was governed by visual stimuli ('Memory ... does not take place without a mental image'[77]) and by the humoral disposition of the individual. However, central to Albertus's intellectual undertaking in this area was his positioning of memory at the heart of the Christian's moral life: 'Prudence is the knowledge of the good and evil of actions; this knowledge, moreover, is greatly aided by events that have already happened, because by means of the past it will know in what way it should manage itself in the future; therefore memory should be part of prudence.'[78] Thus, while the mind of Albertus was clearly exercised by the mnemonic techniques that the Roman theorists of rhetoric held in such affection, he endowed the knowledge of the past with significance pre-eminently in that it should be seen as a principle for ethical and spiritual self-government:

> memory takes in an event that is past as though it stayed ever-present in the soul as an idea and as an emotional effect upon us, and so this event can be very effective for providing for the future. Moreover, I say 'to stay in the soul as an idea' meaning an idea of good and evil, and 'as an effect', meaning how much it affected positively or harmed those performing it.[79]

In his own writings, Aquinas would take up these very emphases in his mentor's thinking, asserting that 'it is in the nature of prudence that prudent people are directed through those courses of action which are at hand by a consideration not only of the present circumstances but also of past events'.[80] In his commentary of *De Memoria et Reminiscentia* Aquinas also acknowledged the Aristotelian contention that the memory may be exercised most successfully with the assistance of sequential procedures.[81] Most importantly, in the *Summa Theologiæ* he also invested much energy in inviting his reader to acknowledge the validity of Aristotle's materialist thinking, rather than that of Plato's dualism:

> if the soul does have a natural knowledge of everything, it would seem impossible for it to be so forgetful of this natural knowledge that it would not know that it had such knowledge. For no one forgets things that are naturally known ... We should therefore conclude that the soul does not know material things by means of naturally innate species.[82]

More generally, if the interest in memoryscapes and visual stimuli did not abate in these centuries, the medieval veneration for the faculty of memory also played a key role in the formulation of normative models of Christian observance. In this context, we might note the 'many goostly medytacyons & instruccions to all maner of people' of the late twelfth- and early thirteenth-century Archbishop of Canterbury,

Edmund of Abingdon, in *The myrrour of the chyrche*: 'Thinke dylygently inwardly & often what ye be[,] what ye haue ben & what ye shall be ... call to your remembraunce & thinke often how ye haue done grete euylles & many & how ye haue loste grete goodes & many.'[83] Emphasis in this period was being placed increasingly by the Church upon the interdependency of memory and worship (most notably, in the commemoration of the dead, the veneration of saints and in monastic practices and writings that focused precisely upon the enhancement of spiritual interiority). Furthermore, by the fourteenth and fifteenth centuries, monastic communities (like the communities of European courts and universities) were discovering increasing numbers of exceptionally talented scholars in their midst who were determined to revisit this cultural concern with memory.

Rendered anxious by questions of hitherto inadequate textual mediation, translation and commentary, humanist scholars sought to recover the spiritual and intellectual commitments of the past by returning with new eyes to the wisdom held in venerated source texts from antiquity. If, in the opening decades of the sixteenth century, Erasmus distinguished himself before an international audience for his meticulous achievements in scriptural translation and commentary, his readership revealed itself equally hungry for his own works of spiritual guidance in which the act of retrospection is often awarded pre-eminent status. This may be witnessed in the following extract from the enormously popular *Enchiridion militis christiani* (1503, English translation 1533):

> Pondre more ouer howe this lyfe vanissheth awaye faster than smoke ... Here and on this poynte it shall profyte syngularly to call to remembraunce ... lerne of another mans peryll to be more ware and cyrcumspecte. Remembre howe delycyously they lyued but howe bytterly they departed: howe late they waxed wyse howe late they beganne to hate their mortyferous and deedly pleasures. Lette come to remembraunce the sharpnesse of the extreme iudgement and the terryble lyghtenynge of that fearfull sentence neuer to be reuoked.[84]

MEMORY, HISTORY AND PEDAGOGY

The Spaniard Juan Luis Vives (1492–1540) was a correspondent of Katherine of Aragon and a visitor to the English court – indeed, so frequent were his visits to the English court in the 1520s that Erasmus branded him an 'amphibious animal'.[85] Vives was in many ways representative of many leading European humanist scholars in his sustained engagement with the long tradition of literature dating back to antiquity that had examined the faculty of memory: he famously contended in *De Tradendis Disciplinis* (1531) that 'abstract intellectual study requires knowledge in many subjects of life, experience, and a good memory'.[86] However, elsewhere in this discussion, he reflected upon the role of memory with most particular attention to the evolving cultural identity of the intellectual: 'Quintilian considers memory to be an indication of natural ability … If anyone be gifted with ability and memory, aided by his time of life and leisure, with knowledge built up by diligence and study, I would not have anything denied him.'[87] Vives advocated the practice of reading aloud for memorisation, and highlighted the importance of pictorial aids (associative remembering) and mental imaging for the strengthening of the memory. Moreover, in *De Tradendis Disciplinis* he showed himself eager to explore the roles attributed to memory in various pedagogic regimes and to formulate something approaching a conduct manual for the nurturing of the faculty:

Let the memory be exercised at an early age … For that age is not so fatigued by remembering, because it has no labour of reflexion … Memory consists of two factors: quick comprehension and faithful retention; we quickly comprehend what we understand, we retain what we have often and carefully confided to our memory.[88]

Among Vives's contemporaries, Erasmus soon emerged as one of the most dynamic and enduring influences upon memorial thinking in England, insisting that the faculty required constant care and attention: 'Like books that stick together from neglect if you do not read them, memory evaporates if not refreshed from time to time.'[89] Like Vives, Erasmus was a frequent visitor to Henry VIII's England, and in a work such as *De ratione studii* (1511) we find him acknowledging an acquaintance with the conventions of training for *memoria artificiosa* while expressing a characteristically rigorous emphasis upon intellectual apprehension:

Although I do not deny that memory is aided by 'places' and 'images', nevertheless the best memory is based on three things above all: understanding, system, and care. For memory largely consists in having thoroughly understood something. Then system sees to it that we can recall by an act of recovery even what we have once forgotten. Furthermore, care is of the highest importance, not only here but in all things. That being so you must repeatedly re-read very carefully what you want to remember.[90]

Erasmus remained determined to differentiate between knowledge acquisition and intellectual understanding; and in repeatedly returning to this concern he showed himself the worthy inheritor of anxieties voiced by his classical forebears.⁹¹ Indeed, the young Elizabeth Tudor seems to have fully appreciated this debate and remained mindful of the need to combine memorial retention with comprehension during her periods of captivity: 'I walke many times into the pleasant fieldes of the holye Scriptures; where I plucke up the goodliesome herbs of sentences by pruning, eate them by reading, chawe them by musing, and laie them up at length in the hie seate of memorie.'⁹²

More generally, the sustained textual attention devoted to rhetorical prowess down the centuries had a crucial influence upon the development of the discourse of memory and, indeed, upon evolving concepts of the intellectual and the public servant in the early modern period. As has been observed, Erasmus acknowledged, like so many of his fellow humanists, that the memory required training in order for the aspiring scholar to realise his fullest potential – for the faculty by its very nature lacked stewardship: 'Memory is a net which holds large objects and lets small things through.'⁹³ With this in mind, if Erasmus conceded that the laws of ordering and association *might be* of assistance in this undertaking, he underlined in numerous discussions that inane rote-learning could only have a damaging effect upon both the powers of apprehension and retention. Thomas More shared Erasmus's disdain for mindless exercises of mental repetition, as may be witnessed in a letter of 1515 to the theologian Martin Dorp in Louvain:

Neither will I deny that there are some in Louvain, as indeed there are everywhere, who have memorized many passages from scripture, and of these men whoever has focused his energies not only on memorizing – even illiterate monks and friars do as much – but far more on absorbing the meaning, and has gained sufficient linguistic ability to measure up to the challenge of fully understanding the works of Jerome, Augustine, Ambrose, and other men like them, such a man, in my view, has an unsurpassed right to be registered among theologians, even if he has never written a verse; yes, and even if he has not spent a whole century on … petty disputes or has even ignored them completely.⁹⁴

Interestingly, some twenty years later in his *Rhetorica elementa* (1534) the Reformist Philipp Melanchthon would go even further and banish recourse to mnemonic techniques for his students. However, as this century (characterised by wide-sweeping and often violent religious and intellectual change) wore on, memorial culture itself had to negotiate a number of assaults. The most important of these, as we have seen, was the Ramist assault. Nonetheless, this growing preoccupation with the status of logic in promoting new theories of epistemology coexisted in this intellectually diverse society with cultures of learning, religious worship, artistic performance and legal training that often continued to invest deeply in schemes of rote-learning and mnemonical teaching. This cultural emphasis is certainly made apparent at the opening of George Gascoigne's *Glasse of gouernement: A tragicall comedie* (1575) in which we are introduced to the two young protagonists in the following manner: 'The eldest being yong men of quicke capacitie, do (Parrotte like) very quickly learne the rules without booke: the yonger beeing somewhat more dull of vnderstanding, do yet engraue the same within their memories.'[95]

In publications dating from the early modern period concerning matters of pedagogy and moral instruction, it quickly becomes apparent that memory remained a theme of major interest.[96] Moreover, it is evident that the sustained periods of time spent in the company of Livy, Caesar, Sallust and Tacitus in the classroom impressed upon early modern students, if nothing else, that the commemorative business of history-writing was a legitimate occupation for those belonging to the social elite and that this was indeed supported by celebrated examples from antiquity. Nonetheless, the energetic desire to study the classical past did not only signify a willingness to cherish the wisdom and labours of the ancients. For many of the most distinguished scholars of the period, the writing of antique history articulated an aspiration to span the intervening centuries and to communicate a commonalty of experience with an enviable age of Greek and Roman achievement. These often vexed accounts of the distant past might offer an invaluable fund of *exempla* for the aspiring scholar, citizen, political servant or dignitary, as Cicero had advised. However, as Cicero had also claimed, the accounts of political trials and tribulations could offer thorny ethical and intellectual challenges with which to discipline and enrich the human spirit. This was certainly a belief that Camden underlined in the prefatory discussion to his *Britannia* where he stressed that 'in the studies of Antiquity, (which is alwaies accompanied with dignity, and hath a certaine semblance with eternity) there is a sweet food of the minde well befiting such as are of honest and noble disposition'.[97] This was also a theme upon which his contemporary's, Sir Thomas North's, translation of James Amyot's preface to Plutarch's *Lives of the noble Grecians and Romanes* (1579) dilated at some length:

And like as memorie was as a storehouse of mens conceits and deuises … So may it also be sayd, that an historie is the very treasury of mans life, whereby the notable doings and sayings of men, and the wonderfull aduentures & straunge cases (which the long continuance of time bringeth forth) are preserued from the death of forgetfulnes. Hereuppon it riseth, that Plato the wise sayth, that the name of historie was given to this recording of matters, to stay the fleting of our memorie, which otherwise would be soone lost and retaine litle.[98]

The enormous growth in interest in what we might now term historical data-collection and chronicle writing in the sixteenth century had its roots in this enduring appetite for mythologies of cultural belonging and destiny, as well as an anxiety in these changeful decades that valuable funds of experience might be swallowed up in what North's Amyot terms, 'the death of forgetfulnes'. In the early decades of the sixteenth century, such preoccupations clearly excited the imagination of John Leland, as well as that of John Bale later, to attempt a recovery of a national history, which, they felt, might well lie in the ever disintegrating (or dispersing) contents of ecclesiastical libraries across Henry VIII's kingdom. In the very midst of the turmoil of Reformation England, Leland received a warrant in 1533 'to persue and dylygentlye to searche all the lybraryes of monasteryes and collegies' so that valuable documents 'myghte be brought out of deadly darkenesse to lyvelye lyght'.[99] If his researches were never completed, this heroic undertaking clearly fired the imaginations of later generations of Tudor scholars who also wished to rival continental writers in the production of a corpus of national histories. A whole host of chronicles of varying complexions and generic affiliations emerged as the century unfolded: Edward Hall (and Richard Grafton) turned their attentions to the political crises of government in late medieval Britain in *The Union of the Two Noble and Illustre Families of Lancaster and York* (1548); the heavily moralised verse narratives of *A Mirror for Magistrates* were initially published by William Baldwin and others in 1559; John Foxe began his research for the *Acts and Monuments* during his period of exile in the 1550s on the continent; John Stow's *Summary of English Chronicles* was published initially in 1565, and then enlarged in 1580 and entitled *The Annals or General Chronicle of England*; and Raphael Holinshed's *Chronicles of England, Scotland and Ireland* was first published in 1577.

While mention has already been made of Camden's wide-ranging chorographical study *Britannia* (1586), this did not stand alone in its endeavours to unite a concern with historical change as evidenced in the British landscape with an engagement with more conventional historiography concerning regimes of political governance. And it is in this context that publications such as William Lambarde's *Perambulation of Kent* (1576), Richard Carew's *Survey of Cornwall* (1602) and a work such as the *Speculum Britanniae: Middlesex* (1593) by John Norden should clearly also be considered. Camden, like his fellow antiquarians, drew and elaborated upon Leland's findings in his own publications. Moreover, this scholarly interest continued throughout the period we are considering in this volume: apart from Ralegh's rather belated chronicle of antique peoples, *The historie of the world* (1614), the historian and cartographer John Speed published his *History of Great Britaine* (1611), Samuel Daniel *The first fowre bookes of the ciuile wars between the two houses of Lancaster and Yorke* (1595), and in his closing years Francis Bacon produced *The historie of the raigne of King Henry the Seuenth* (London, 1622). The last shaped how the opening of the Tudor century was perceived for over two hundred years, and its emphases upon human motivation, political causation and a diminished concern with providential intervention betray (belatedly in British historiography) the influences of an earlier generation of European humanist scholars, such as Machiavelli and Guicciardini. Nevertheless, whatever the scholarly ambitions of these very different narrators of the past working in England during the early modern period, it is evident that they would have shared with Sir John Hayward the sentiment addressed to James VI/I's son, Prince Charles, in his prefatory discussion to his *Liues of the III. Normans, Kings of England William the first. William the second. Henrie the first* (1613), that the parentage of memory, writing and history is both intimate and invaluable for the growth in human understanding:

> Wee are carefull to prouide costly Sepulchers, to preserue our dead liues, to preserue some memorie what wee haue bene: but there is no monument, either so durable, or so largely extending, or so liuely and faire, as that which is framed by a fortunate penne; the memory of the greatest Monuments had long since perished, had it not bene preserued by this meanes.[100]

EARLY MODERN MEMORY AND THE BODY

Lina Bolzoni has underlined in her key study *The Gallery of Memory* that one of the most important constructions of memory to be inherited from antiquity had its roots in Hippocratic medical/anatomical theorising. This intellectual system was developed further by knowledge disseminated in Galenic manuals (and notably refined by Arabic scholars such as Avicenna in later centuries) that the brain was 'at the centre of perception and the cognitive process' and, importantly, that this included memory.[101] The writings of Galen and his later commentators repeatedly stressed that the reader should think of the faculty as being located in a hollow at the rear of the brain, described as a chamber, or 'ventricle'. Bolzoni continues:

Avicenna's map is highly sophisticated; the 'inward senses' are divided into five powers or faculties corresponding to fantasy, the imagination, the *vis imaginativa* (imaginative power which operates through the forms assembled in the imagination), the *vis aestimativa* (conjecturing or surmising power), and the *vis memorativa*. Each is assigned a space that corresponds to its function and its relationship to the others. *Virtu formalis* [perception] and *sensus communis*, Avicenna writes, have their place in the first part of the brain thanks to the spirit that fills that ventricle. The reason for this is that they must supervise the other senses, which, for the most part, originate in the first part of the brain. Thought and memory have their places in the other two ventricles, but memory takes the rear so that the spirit of thought is in the middle, that is, so that it is between the treasure-house of perceptible forms and the treasure-house of abstract concepts. The space between each of them is the same so that both, together with judgment, rule in all of the brain.[102]

A vigorous fascination with the physical presence of memory has enjoyed a remarkable survival down the centuries. Indeed, this willingness to endow the faculty with somatic as well as intellectual status has remained equally attractive to contemporary critical theorising and scientific research. In textual terms, perhaps the most striking example of this kind of enquiry occurs in Hélène Cixous's *Le Troisième Corps*, where the speaker contends 'Ma mémoire est un placenta' and, as the extract from the *Independent* of 30 January 2008 (which preceded this discussion) indicates, the endeavour to site memory within the human body is far from obsolete.[103] Medieval and early modern medical theorising invested deeply in the topography of the brain as a route to understanding the processes of cognition, and the narrative of cerebral chambers or ventricles is often rehearsed as a truth *universally acknowledged*: in his *Rhetorica novissima* (completed *c*.1235) Boncompagno da Signa pauses momentarily to signal that in order 'to avoid prolixity I refrain from considering systematically the chambers of the head from a physical point of view, because it is firmly believed that the seat of the soul is in the posterior chamber, and the memorial faculty resides there'.[104] Interestingly, *The Castel of Memorie* (1562) conflates an appreciation of cerebral chambers with a meditation on the tripartite division of the soul discussed earlier, and an Aristotelian concern to link memorial prowess with humoralism and human physiology.

Memorie therefore hath his seate in the hinder part of the head in the thyrde Ventricle … There be three operations of the soule in the braine, fantasie (or imagination), reasoning (or iudgement), and Memorie (or remembraunce) … In the concauities or holownes of the brayne is frequented a liuely, small, pure, and moste cleane spirite, and suche a one is carried to the Memorie: the which surely hath neede of the clearness and subtilitie of the spirite. For if so be that that way be not opened by the whiche the spirite passeth to the hinder parte (or Puppis) of the braine, the man remembreth nothing: and contrariwise they that haue a swifte openinge of that waye, are wise, and answere spedely, as are diuers cholericke persons: and they that haue that opening slowe, are dull and slack to learne and to aunswere, and such are for the most parte flematick or melancholicke.[105]

Holofernes congratulates himself in *Love's Labour's Lost* that his own memorial gifts were 'begot in the ventricle of memory, nourished in the womb of *pia mater*' (IV.ii.63–4), and it was to this very tradition of memorial thinking that Spenser turned in the relation of the adventures of his Knight of Temperance, Sir Guyon, in the second book of *The Faerie Queene*. Already in the prologue Spenser had demonstrated a pressing concern to distinguish between 'painted forgery' and 'just memory', and this is linked directly to a discussion of legitimate human conduct – in this case, that of the writer. In contemporary theoretical debate, Gilles Deleuze and Félix Guattari have contended that

We no longer believe in the myth of the existence of fragments that, like pieces of an antique statue, are merely waiting for the last one to be turned up, so that they may all be glued back together to create a unity that is precisely the same as the original unity. We no longer believe in a primordial totality that once existed, or in a final totality that awaits us at some future date.[106]

However, as Book Two of *The Faerie Queene* unfolds, it is precisely this vexed question of recuperating an original unity (here, in terms of genealogical integrity) that Spenser addresses. Here, the consuming interest in memory soon expands to embrace wider considerations of a quest for identity and self-knowledge during the sojourn of Guyon and Arthur in Alma's castle. The visitors travel up into a tower with a tripartite structure organised symbolically in the manner in which the sensitive soul was traditionally conceived. The occupants of the first two chambers are *Phantastes* (visionary) and an unnamed representation of judgement or reason. In Spenser's vision, Phantastes is in part a melancholy dreamer of the future, but primarily one who marries information with visual imagery. The middle, unnamed resident (perhaps linked to the poet himself) appears to be devoted to the interpretation and judgement of the present. However, 'Alma thence them led to th'hindmost roome of three' and the account of the final resident, Eumnestes, a symbolic representation of Memory, is given precedence over the other two in terms of the length of his description and the narrative status of the knights' encounter with him.

In this 'hindmost' chamber, the visitors are greeted with the sight of 'an old oldman, halfe blind, | And all decrepit in his feeble corse, | Yet liuely vigour rested in his mind'. Spenser's 'man of infinite remembrance', Eumnestes, who could remember the infancies of Nestor and Methuselah, is discovered surrounded by 'old records', which 'were all worme-eated, and full of canker holes', and is attended by a young page, Anamnestes, whose role it is to retrieve lost things. 'Burning both with feruent fire', Guyon and Arthur devour their reading matter (respectively, *Antiquitie of Faerie lond* and *Briton moniments*) in their search for cultural and personal origination (II.ix.54–60). Whereas the appreciation of the cognitive abilities of Phantastes (who is shown to link knowledge acquisition with visual stimuli) is given an Aristotelian emphasis, in the case of Eumnestes's page Spenser's reader is offered the opportunity to reflect upon the Platonic theory of *anamnesis* (that human knowledge is founded upon remembrances gleaned from a prenatal existence). More generally, it soon becomes evident that Spenser's knights can only forge a knowledge of who they are with the assistance of Memory's resources, here reified into a castle library.

In the event, the information that the castle library yields is both partial and perplexing, and requires yet further labour (or 'endlesse worke') to decipher fully. However, such symbolic encounters with Memory were not unknown in the early modern period, even on the stage. In R[ichard] B[ower's?]'s *New Tragicall Comedie of Apius and Virginia* (1575), for example, the closing scene has Fame, Justice and Reward commanding the stage only to be greeted with 'Doctrina and Memorie and Virginius bring[ing] [in] a tome [tomb]' for the slain Virginia.[107] And it is equally intriguing to discover that Spenser's arresting characterisations of Memory as the aged Eumnestes with his page would be reproduced in the next century in the 'pleasant comoedie' *Lingua: or The combat of the tongue* (1607) by Thomas Tomkis. Here, at the beginning of Act Two scene four, the reader meets with

MEMORY, an old decrepit man, in a black Veluet Cassock, a Tafata Gowne furred, with white Grogaram, a white beard, Veluet slippers, a Watch, Staffe, &c. ANAMNESTES his Page, in a graue Sattin sute Purple, Buskins, a Garland of Bayes and Rosemary, a gimmall ring with one linke hanging, Ribbands and Threds tyed to some of his fingers, in his hand a paire of Table-bookes, &c.[108]

READING MEMORY IN EARLY MODERN LITERATURE

In the chapters that follow, each discussion offers an insight into a representative engagement with memorial debate in the early modern period, and aims to shed light upon the diversity of Tudor and Early Stuart reading communities. The first chapter focuses upon the poetry of Henry Howard, Earl of Surrey, and reflects most particularly upon the ways in which his textual enquiries into the faculty of memory feed into a much broader interest in the quest for cultural recognition. Howard, the last nobleman to be executed by Henry VIII, demonstrates in his poetic output that he was deeply versed in humanist concerns with textual memorialisation and with the contribution that the intellectual might make to the governance of society. This chapter engages predominantly with Surrey's erotic and elegiac lyrics not only because they have often been neglected in critical studies but because they constitute such a rich fund with which to consider the changeful and exquisitely nuanced nature of his meditations on the faculty. In his discussion of the philosophy of Heidegger, Ricoeur is timely in his contention that 'Elegies on the human condition, ranging in their modulations from lamentation to resignation, have never ceased to sing of the contrast between the time that remains and we who are merely passing. It is only the "they" that never dies? If we hold time to be infinite, is this only because we are concealing our own finitude from ourselves?'[109] It is precisely Howard's urgent and sustained investigation into the meditation of human 'finitude' that shapes this opening analysis and forms the narrative context for the succeeding chapters.

The second chapter considers the devotional writings of one of Howard's eminent contemporaries, Katherine Parr, who would survive him and continue to be a significant figure in the early, tumultuous years of Edward VI's reign. Howard's poetic scenes of self-examination and often anguished human dilemmas of desire are here counterpointed with Parr's analogous concerns with the Christian's desperate yearnings for divine grace. Her principal publications, *Prayers or medytacions* and *The lamentacion of a sinner*, interacted closely with the rapidly changing conditions of the Henrician and Edwardian religious settlements. Employing sophisticated techniques of scriptural citation, paraphrase and commentary, Henry's final consort constructs complex devotional narratives in which competing textual voices wrestle with the obligations of memory – involving spiritual, moral and, on occasions, overtly political testimonies of experience and aspiration. In the third chapter, the anxieties and obligations surrounding the business of authorship and retrospection are explored with reference to a prominent member of the next generation of Tudor religious writers, John Foxe and, most particularly, his *magnum opus*, the *Acts and Monuments*. Foxe's career as a theologian bridges the period from the Edwardian settlement and the Marian persecutions to the first half of Elizabeth's reign. His textual legacy would last much longer. The *Acts and Monuments*, as a *grand récit* of Reformist history, not only recalls 'heroic' acts of religious commitment in the face of Papal persecution, it urges the reader to ponder deeply the ways in which the labours of memory may reinvigorate the development of spiritual interiority (as Augustine had counselled) and the sobering realisation that a transcendent Godhead persists through time whose memory suffers no impairment.

In the next chapters, the emphasis not only moves chronologically to the second half of Elizabeth's reign, but the generic range of the texts under discussion and the implied readerships become much more diverse. The first of these chapters concentrates upon three very different examples of Elizabethan prose fiction in which the memorial act assumes a significant narrative function: George Gascoigne's *The Adventures of Master F. J.*, Thomas Nashe's *The Unfortunate Traveller* and Thomas Deloney's *Jack of Newbury*. In their very different ways, Gascoigne, Nashe and Deloney exploit the acts of memory rehearsed by their textual voices as key structuring devices as well as positioning them variously as vehicles for thematic emphasis, for reader seduction and as opportunities for social critique. We also encounter in each work a pressing concern with the very undertaking of authorship and the possibilities of narrative truth and self-memorialisation. Indeed, as these examples of Elizabethan prose unfold, we as readers are progressively encouraged to interrogate the exercise of memory as one of the axes through which human subjectivity may be understood.

At the heart of the great literary achievements of the late Elizabethan age lies not only the enduring work of writers whose endeavours have shaped this introductory discussion, Shakespeare and Spenser, but also the multifarious activities of the Sidneys. The mighty body of Philip Sidney's prose romance *Arcadia* is set in motion by 'that racking steward, Remembrance' as the shepherds Claius and Strephon participate in a ritualised encounter commemorating the departure of Urania.[110] However, the writing career of Mary Sidney, Countess of Pembroke, seems wholly to have been given over to the meditation of this faculty: indeed, a choleric Pembroke (at least on one occasion) reminded the King's representative, Sir Julius Caesar, in a postscript to an official letter that 'it is the Sister of Sir Philip Sidney who yow ar to right and who will worthely deserve the same'.[111] In a recent critical discussion of the faculty as a philosophical field of enquiry, Richard Sennett has proposed that 'There is no solace in the truths of memory'.[112] However, the whole of Mary Sidney's career as a published writer, both as translator and poet, reveals an indomitable fascination with retrospection and how acts of remembering may act to legitimise or enhance the status of the human subject. Most particularly in her poetic renderings of the Psalms and in her creative translations of works by Petrarch and Garnier, she carefully scrutinised the ways in which narratives of Sidneian cultural identity might be revised and rescripted with the resources of memory.

In the final chapters of this volume the chronological interest moves to the last decade of Elizabeth's reign and to the opening decades of that of her successor to the English throne, James VI of Scotland – indeed, the latter (if William Fowler is to be believed) had gained his own acquaintance with the *ars memorativa*: 'Whils I was teaching your majestie the art of me[m]orye yow instructed me in poesie and imprese.'[113] John Donne was undoubtedly profoundly aware of the Sidneian poetic achievement, both in terms of the sonnet collection *Astrophil and Stella*, which clearly influenced his own lyrical output, and of Philip and Mary's joint labours in translating the Psalms, as may be witnessed in his poem 'Upon the translation of the Psalms by Sir Philip Sidney, and the Countess of Pembroke his sister'. Donne's wide-ranging meditations upon the faculty in both his poetry and prose writing demonstrate a thorough knowledge of secular and Christian literatures upon the subject and a determination to uncover memory's links with the human construction of spiritual and erotic mythologies of belonging. While his secular verse attends to the textual scaffolding that erotic memory requires, in his devotional prose and poetic writings the promptings of memory frequently lead his poetic voices into anguished responses of loss, self-loathing, cultural revulsion, and contrition.

Chapter 7 concentrates upon the poetic output of one of Donne's eminent contemporaries, Ben Jonson. Throughout his career as a poet, Jonson remained deeply exercised by the enduring contribution that poetry might make to the *civitas*, and so, for the most part, distanced himself from the lyric conventions of erotic and spiritual confession that came to dominate so much of Donne's verse. The nature of Jonson's poetic sensibility meant that he conceived of memory primarily in terms of an ethical obligation in a fallen society gradually succumbing to the remorseless onslaught of cultural amnesia. Thus, we discover that his lyrics, odes, epigrams and satires return again and again to the need to repair the community's relationships with the past – and these are mostly viewed through the lens of the experience and literatures of antiquity. Whereas in his dramas Jonson frequently explores the potential for psychological and social trauma when individuals and communities find themselves unable to acknowledge the moral inheritance that has been bequeathed by previous ages, in his poetry he characteristically returns to the insistence that the very questions of cultural direction, moral leadership, political and literary achievement are intimately bound up with the strenuous business of recollection and memorialisation (if not, on occasions, strategic forgetfulness). Deeply versed in Ciceronian notions that a knowledge of the past enriches the spirit by furnishing our mind with a pantheon of possible human exempla, Jonson may be seen ultimately to ponder memory in many of his poetic meditations as a means of transcending an existence characterised by brutally competitive social relations.

When Fulke Greville embarked upon the *Life* of his late friend, Philip Sidney, he confessed that 'although with *Socrates*, I professe to know nothing for the present; yet with *Nestor* I am delighted in repeating old newes of the ages past; and will therefore stir up my drooping memory'.[114] Such 'delight' was widely in evidence across early modern intellectual society and presented one of the most resolute challenges to the intellectual programme of Francis Bacon. Yet Bacon remained unshaken in the belief that the human potential for growth lay with energetic and innovative intellectual enquiry: 'For there is no power on earth which setteth up a throne or chair of estate in the spirits and souls of men, and in their cogitations, imaginations, opinions, and beliefs, but knowledge and learning.'[115] In this final chapter we return to preoccupations which began this introductory discussion concerning the cultural formulations of memory: memory's place within changing theories of epistemology (*theoria* and *phronesis*). Fernando Bouza underlines that while the communication of higher knowledge in the early modern period might be associated with 'divine revelation, prophecies (expressed often in dreams), inspiration, and … divination … only memory would have been seen as characteristically human, joined by reason and the senses'.[116] This emphasis upon the invaluable material resources of memory would continue to be of recurring interest to Bacon. The natural philosopher's anxieties concerning the development of human understanding and, indeed, the roles that memory might have to play in the future reception of his own voluminous textual legacies remain abiding features of his work.

Bacon expressed profound disaffection for the centuries-old traditions of scholastic learning that had shaped pervasive habits of thinking and learning in his society: indeed, he felt that they had engendered the Age's fondness for bearing witness to the inevitability of human cultural decay. His own imagination was excited by the potential prospect of humanity continuing to expand its knowledge and exploration of the material world, and thus he may be seen to look forward to the fruition of human (and divine) designs, rather than pondering the seventeenth century's distance from the first Edenic state, like so many of his contemporaries. At many points throughout his writing career he urged his readers to rethink the status and functions of memory in order to embrace radically different theories of epistemology – to rethink the potential pathways to knowledge that the past had failed to acknowledge. And, as such, his writings constitute not only a landmark contribution to early modern cultural debate on the nature of memory that look forward to achievements in the later Stuart and Georgian periods, they also form a natural terminus for the span of this study.

As will become apparent in the unfolding of the final chapter, even if Bacon appears to advocate relentlessly the strategic importance of experimentation, observation, data-collection and 'plain' language for the careful reporting of human endeavours to extend the bounds of knowledge, he was not above drawing upon ancient theories of *memoria* when it served his purposes. If his thinking did shape for many the ways in which scientific and historical truth might be conceived for centuries to come, his published interventions did not wholly silence dissenting voices or stifle ideas on a subject that had been surrounded by controversy since antiquity. When Giambattista Vico's *Principi di Scienza Nuova* was published for the first time, in 1725, he might still draw attention to the *varietas* of memory:

And since naturally the discovery of invention of things comes before criticism of them, it was fitting that the infancy of the world should concern itself with the first operation of the human mind, for the world then had need of all inventions for the necessities and utilities of life, all of which had been provided before the philosophers appeared, as we shall fully show in the Discovery of the True Homer. With reason, then, did the theological poets call Memory the mother of the Muses; that is, of the arts of humanity … Memory thus has three different aspects: memory when it remembers things, imagination when it alters or imitates them, and inventions when it gives them a new turn or puts them into proper arrrangement and relationship. For these reasons the theological poets call Memory the mother of the Muses.[117]

CHAPTER I

'To seke the place where I my self hadd lost': acts of memory in the poetry of Henry Howard, Earl of Surrey

> There is nothing in man of all the potential parts of his mind (reason and will except) more noble or more necessary to the actiue life then memory: because it maketh most to a sound iudgement and perfect worldly wisedome, examining and comparing the times past with the present, and by them both considering the time to come, concludeth with a stedfast resolution, what is the best course to be taken in all his actions and aduices in this world: it came vpon this reson, experience to be so highly commended in all consultations of importance, and preferred before any learning or science, and yet experience is no more than a masse of memories assembled, that is, such trials as man hath made in time before.
>
> George Puttenham, *The Arte of English Poesie* (1589), I.xix[1]

In his *Arte of English Poesie* (1589) George Puttenham left his reader in no doubt of the privileged status he wished to attribute to the resources of memory. From this perspective, the faculty enabled the human mind to engage with personal and collective histories of origination and belonging, to assimilate the fruits of others' epistemological enquiries and to legitimise (through recourse to precedent) given paths of cultural interaction. In developing such arguments, Puttenham was following in the steps of generations of humanist scholars. Indeed, earlier in the century, during the reign of Henry VIII, Juan Luis Vives had stressed in *De Tradendis Disciplinis* (Antwerp, 1531) that the erudition of the ideal teacher should be 'ample, accurate, diligent, [and] careful' and that 'His memory for words and things must be good and rich, and he must keep it sound by carefulness and constant devotion to learning'.[2]

This chapter focuses upon some of the ways in which the promptings of memory, as articulated in Surrey's poetry,[3] may be perceived as belonging to a much larger matrix of cultural concerns with legacies of the past and the paradigms they might establish for present courses of action during what Greg Walker has persuasively described as 'the gathering crisis of Henry's latter years'.[4] Assuming a host of different guises, the acts of memory evoked by Surrey can offer a complex lens through which both poetic voice and reader are invited to reflect upon the ideological pressures at work in Henrician England. Surrey refrains from soothing or reassuring his readers with beguiling appeals for nostalgia: he is most often found to deploy highly selective acts of memory as a tactical resource for cultural critique. Indeed, his poetry expresses an inexhaustible fascination with controlling our access to the past, with the *production* of the past, and nowhere is this more apparent than in his poetic anatomies of political and erotic desire.

REMEMBERING 'A FOLISHE PROWDE BOY' AND A POET

Where scholarship has been devoted to Surrey, it is much involved in the discussion of 'the most folishe prowde boye that is in Englande'.[5] This celebrated comment is attributed to John Barlow, Dean of Westbury, in August 1539, and it recurs unfailingly throughout the criticism surrounding the aristocrat. In his own edition of Surrey's poetry, Dennis Keene observes that

> historians usually refer to Surrey, if at all, as an anachronism, a man with no grasp of how contemporary politics worked, possessing outmoded ideas of chivalry and honour, and an excessive belief in his own worth. For someone of his social rank, however, a belief in one's own worth was an inevitable part of life, and it seems truer to think of him as a virtuous man living in evil times.[6]

Elsewhere, Alastair Fowler draws attention to Surrey's 'gently declining esteem', and, latterly, Surrey's political career has continued to excite considerably more interest than his poetry – indeed, to such an extent that it surfaces frequently not only as a critical *point de départ*, but also as a terminus of interest and meaning.[7] In his illuminating discussion of sixteenth-century military politics, for example, Rory Rapple unveils 'the epitome of aristocratic chivalry, a gallant soldier, the lieutenant general of all England's Continental possessions and an enthusiast for Henry VIII's expansionist ambitions', but no pause is given to ponder the political power of intervention that writing might have afforded this patrician commander.[8] Interestingly, the sustained nature of this selective remembering of Surrey led C. W. Jentoft in the 1960s to lament that he 'is one of those poets who has in the twentieth century been more read about than read, the critical reaction is usually one of only nominal interest, or worse, complete disdain. This situation requires not only pedagogy, but also a degree of evangelism'.[9]

Critical neglect of, or dissatisfaction with, Surrey's poetry is closely related to the fact that its stylistic conventions and its often smooth continuities of narrative have failed to appeal to the tastes of twentieth-century readers who were encouraged to value the staccato rhythms and dramatic disharmonies of Donne's verse. This critical appetite (stimulated by Herbert J. C. Grierson and T. S. Eliot, among others, in the opening decades of the twentieth century) led in many ways to the rehabilitation of Surrey's contemporary, Wyatt, as a poet of major interest. Nonetheless, if J. W. Lever argued that Surrey's 'lyrics are for the most part awkward and uninteresting',[10] his assessment seems to have been largely influenced by C. S. Lewis's formulation of 'Drab Age' writing that was apparently in evidence from the reign of Henry VIII to the late 1570s:

Drab is not used as a dyslogistic term. It marks a period in which, for good or ill, poetry has little richness either of sound or images. The good work is neat and temperate, the bad flat and dry. There is more bad than good ... with [Surrey] the Drab Age is fully established ... Nearly all that is good, and some things that are bad, in the Drab Age, can be found in Surrey's poetry.[11]

And there seems to be no end in modern times to the number of hurdles the reader must negotiate on the path to Surrey's texts, as Elizabeth Heale has underlined: 'Surrey's poetry has attracted less twentieth-century attention, perhaps because of modern, meritocratic discomfort with his princely social status.'[12] As cultural fixations with rank (social *and* literary) transform radically from one generation to the next, one of the most striking aspects to emerge concerning Surrey's life and work is the way in which they have been subjected to successive discourses of memorialisation down the centuries. If, as Heale proposes, Surrey's output has suffered neglect owing to contemporary distaste with noble status, it would appear that it was for this very reason that Philip Sidney included him (rather than Wyatt) in his account of the development of English verse in the *Apology for Poetry*: 'I account ... in the Earl of Surrey's lyrics many things tasting of a noble birth, and worthy of a noble mind.'[13] Moreover, if, in our anxiety-ridden attempts to penetrate the alien-ness of the past, we shape a Surrey according to our desires and appetites (just as the later sixteenth century did), we are being offered at the same time a valuable opportunity to interrogate the construction of our own literary and historical narratives.

SURREY AND HUMANISM

The Introduction mapped out the very diverse ways in which early modern scholars and readers scrutinised their culture's perceived relations to its past(s). In many ways, one of the dominant intellectual movements of the period, humanism, was anti-historical in its emphasis that historical experience might be regained and rearticulated for the present. Agnes Heller went so far as to claim that 'the Renaissance was the first era which chose for itself a past', and W. A. Sessions adds that it is 'by no accident, therefore, Surrey in his own time was perceived as a humanist, one who specifically used the language of poetry in one more act of recovery and discovery'.[14] Erasmus's appeal 'ad fontes' was indicative of a widespread concern among early modern scholars that contact with the glories of classical civilisations and, indeed, those with scripture had become impoverished by inadequate mediation. At the beginning of his discussion in his *Book named the gouernour* (1531), Surrey's fellow countryman Sir Thomas Elyot felt it necessary to reflect upon the reasons why 'in our tyme noble men be nat as excellent in lernyng as they were in olde tyme among the Romanes and grekes', whereas, in *De Tradendis Disciplinis*, Vives asserted that 'it is not to be doubted that our minds are now less powerful than they were before that first transgression. Now, we are more crafty in our wickedness'.[15] The ever-increasing demand was to renew the encounter with antiquity by means of scrupulous textual analysis and commentary.

At the very beginning of the early modern period, Petrarch had passionately advocated a thorough engagement with the textual remains of the past in order for the human spirit to realise its greatest potential. He argued that there was a need

to devote oneself to reading and writing, alternately finding employment and relief in each, to read what our forerunners have written and to write what later generations may wish to read ... finally, by cherishing, remembering, and celebrating [our forerunners'] fame in every way, to pay them the homage that is due to their genius even though it is not commensurate with their greatness.[16]

In his turn, Surrey proceeds with the utmost care in his own construction of poetic dialogues with the past. The rigorously selective strategies he deploys clearly serve to foreground his preferred modes of cultural narrativisation and critique:

> Marshall, the things for to attayne
> The happy life be thes, I finde:
> The riches left, not got with payne;
> The frutfull grownd, the quyet mynde;
> The equall frend ...
>   (Martial's epigram 10.47, ll. 1–5)

If Jentoft affirms that 'as a result of his education … the Renaissance poet concerned himself not with the expression of personal experience, but with logical and rhetorical persuasion', in this poetic address to Martial the humanist Surrey wishes to emphasise the possible recovery of a classical heritage and to persuade us of the critical importance of our engagement with it.[17] Clearly relying upon the erudition of his readers, he allows this address to unfold without undue preamble and to encode, like his Roman predecessor, an analysis of the *vita civile* by celebrating the pleasures of the *vita contemplativa*. Readers down the ages of one of Surrey's most celebrated memorial acts, the sonnet on the death of Sardanapalus, have often interpreted it in terms of a covert depiction of his ageing Tudor sovereign: 'Th' Assyryans king in peas, with fowle desire | And filthye luste that staynd his regall harte' (ll. 1–2). However, while Sessions persuasively identifies here 'the roles of war and peace in a drama of the disintegrating self', in this poetic snapshot we are also clearly being urged to consider the very nature of sovereignty in both affective and political terms.[18] This careful act of cultural recollection inevitably tempts readers to look beyond the parameters of the Orientalised court for wider possibilities of analogy, without reducing it necessarily to a *poème-à-clé*. The powerful evocation of the waning of cultural integrity ('The dent of swordes from kysses semed straunge, | And harder then hys ladyes syde his targe' ('Th' Assyryans king', ll. 5–6)) feeds a much larger debate concerning the limitations of human authority that deeply preoccupied Henrician England; and its theme must clearly have had currency within the circles of Surrey's manuscript readers, which included, as Greg Walker has argued, 'a cross section of the aristocrats, gentlemen, and civil servants at the heart of the court'.[19] Indeed, more generally, throughout his career as a poet, Surrey experimented with the resources of critique afforded by the textual choices of recollection (in terms of translation, paraphrase and *imitatio*) in order to locate otherwise silenced speaking positions in his culture.

The emotional and collective crises frequently being enacted in Surrey's texts are involved in interpreting, revising and/or contesting meanings that clearly had significant purchase in the opening decades of the sixteenth century. Comparison may be drawn, for example, with the anthology of *sententiae* from classical literature and scripture entitled *The bankette of sapience* (1539) where Elyot drew together some carefully focused angles of vision on the disciplinary regimes required in the early modern polity, as we witness in the following quotation attributed to St Gregory: 'He that is in auctoritie, let hym consider howe he commeth to it: and commyng wel to it, howe he ought to lyue well in it: and lyuyng well in it, howe he muste gouerne: and gouernyng wysely, he must oft call to remembraunce his owne infiyrmitie.'[20] If Surrey's sonnet on Sardanapalus has often been critically analysed as a meditation upon political, erotic and military misgovernment, Walter R. Davis makes the telling point that the Assyrian king had 'been long considered an example of degeneracy, and had been presented as such, along with countless other examples from antiquity, by Gower and Lydgate among others'.[21] Indeed, decades later, at the beginning of the seventeenth century, John Willis's *Mnemonica* (1618, complete English translation 1661) was still at pains to observe that 'to forgoe manhood through effeminate delicacy, may be fitly accommodated to *Sardanapalus* ... [who] led a Womanish life'.[22]

Within the confined space of his sonnet, Surrey is thus able to draw upon a widely available referent among his educated readership and to renew its reading for contemporary purposes. Here, once again, his poetic voice has its authority enhanced as it travels magisterially across the centuries and highlights, on this occasion, the decline of *virtus*: 'Drenched in slouthe and womanishe delight, | Feble of sprete, unpacyent of payne' ('Th' Assyryans king', ll. 9–10). A culturally debilitating hedonism, formulated in this instance as 'womanish delight', is thus shown to spawn a counter-culture where expectations of royal government and self-government are irrevocably violated:

> When he hadd lost his honor and hys right,
> Prowde tyme of welthe, in stormes appawld with drede,
> Murdred hymselfe to shew some manfull dede.
> ('Th' Assyryans king', ll. 12–14)

In returning to a *locus classicus* of cultural decay in this way, Surrey excites enquiries into the nature of ethical obligation and rehearses for the reader the political possibilities of reading the past. As Greg Walker emphasises in his discussion of the Surrey's paraphrases of the Psalms (but with equal relevance to the present discussion), Surrey's 'theme is not the constant revolution of history but the reappearance in his own time of all the worst excesses of injustice witnessed in the ancient past'.[23] The critical significance of such undertakings was also forcefully argued by Elyot in *The Book named the governour*, where, after reaffirming Cicero's dictum that history is 'the life of memorie', he responds to 'suche persones as do contemne aunciente historie, reputing them amonge leasinges and fantises', and argues:

it may be sayd, that in contemnynge histories, they frustrate Experience: whiche (as the said Tulli saith) is the light of vertue, whiche they wolde be sene so moche to fauour, all thoughe they do seldome embrace it. And that shall they perceyue manifestly, if they will a litle while laye a part their accustomed obstinacie, & suffre to be distilled in to their eares two or thre dropes of the sweete oyle of remembraunce.[24]

THE POETICS OF MEMORY

When Surrey turns his attention to the poetic analysis of erotic defeat, he maintains many similar emphases to those in evidence in the lyrics examined above. 'In Winter's just returne, when Boreas 'gan his reign' is interested in dramatising affective crises in both the courtly lover *and* the speaker. This narrative is rendered complex with the arresting juxtaposition of contrasting time frames, and the cycles of experience being related are all communicated through the filters of the speaker's controlling memory. Luxuriating in accounts of heightened male sensibilities, the rather courtly shepherd describing this pastoral scene frames and elevates his own personal recollection of a 'misty morning darke' with the resources of mythic referencing – 'when Boreas 'gan his reign' (l. 1). Wyatt, in lyrics like the riddling Epigram XLVIII 'Vulcan begat me. Minerva me taught', had frequently explored the (mock-)aggrandising effects that myth could offer poetic narrative. Surrey is clearly exercised by such possibilities here as he seeks to evoke an antique world in which the heroics of passion may be enacted. In this lyric, the speaker assumes the role of critical onlooker to a forsaken but unnamed figure and, more importantly, operates as an authoritative editor of the past. The ensuing narrative provides an intriguing analysis of *amour courtois* under homosocial if not, on occasions, homoerotic terms. In a manner familiar from Petrarchan poetics, the emotional life of this male *voyeur* serves to magnify the status of male anguish; and in this pastoral scene (unfolding, in this case, in winter) readers are urged to shadow the movements of the shepherd in their responses to the bereft lover:

> Under a palm I heard one crye as he had lost hys wyttes.
> Whose voice did ring so shrill in uttering of his plaint,
> That I amazed was to hear how love could hym attaint.
> ('In Winter's just returne', ll. 6–8)

The varied techniques of retrospection in Surrey's verse are clearly designed to consolidate the authority of his poetic voices, and we are often compelled to attend to the unfailing sensitivity of the latter. Much more than Wyatt, Surrey is eager to reflect upon the multiple ways in which given moments of superlative human experience may be refracted and recollected through the eyes of onlookers. If, as so often in Surrey's meditations upon the nature of human desire, the narrator emerges as a political and erotic *surveillant*, this highly sensualised form of *theoria* affords no protection from affective crisis.

As was witnessed above in the poetic address to Martial, Surrey can invest deeply in the classical motif of *otium*, of cultural withdrawal, for the sophisticated purposes of critique, retrospection and narrative texture. However, if the temptations of cultural excentricity are often celebrated in his more overtly political poems, they are articulated equally expansively in his erotic lyrics. Here, his socially marginalised poetic voices repeatedly betray their Petrarchan genealogy. At the very beginning of the growth in humanist scholarship in the fourteenth century, Petrarch had demonstrated in such works as *De Vita Solitaria* (1345–47) a consuming interest in the textual productions of *otium* from antiquity, and also in their strategic importance for the intellectual in his own times:

> But when some need compels me to dwell in the city, I have learned to create a solitude among people and a haven of refuge in the midst of a tempest, using a device, not generally known, of so controlling the senses that they do not perceive what they perceive. Long after I had developed it into a habit by my own experimentation, I discovered that it was also the advice of a very brilliant and learned writer, and I committed it to memory all the more eagerly because of my joy at finding that a practice of mine was supported by the authority of antiquity.[25]

In a poem such as 'In Winter's just returne', Surrey's reader is presented with a pastoralised scene in which the isolated self recalls from his retreat the emotional turmoil of an abandoned lover. The narrative progressively unveils a tantalising dynamic whereby the mind of the *voyeur* not only anatomises the courtly lover's distress, but is profoundly stimulated by it. Indeed, it soon becomes apparent that the suicidal lover only becomes poetically significant in as much as he is a theme for the remembered sympathies of the shepherd:

> Had ben my heart of flint, it must have melted tho;
> For in my life I never saw a man so full of wo.
> With teares, for his redresse, I rashly to him ran,
> And in my arms I caught him fast, and thus I spake hym than:
> 'What wofull wight art thou, that in such heavy case
> Tormentes thy selfe with such despite, here in this desert place?'
> ('In Winter's just returne', ll. 25–30)

The memorial life of the shepherd is thus shown to equal, nay to exceed, in intensity the lover's anguish. Moreover, as the poem unfolds, the collapse in mutual feeling between the lover and the *cruel fair* becomes increasingly obscured by the effusive empathy of the shepherd and ultimately, the reader may feel, subordinated to the heroic drama of bearing witness:

> And little knoweth his lady what a lover she hath lost.
> Whose death when I beheld, no marvail was it, right
> For pitie though my heart did blede, to see so piteous sight.
> … long it was ere I could call to minde what I did there.
> But as eche thing hath end, so had these paynes of mine:
> The furies past, and I my wits restord by length of time.
> Then, as I could devise, to seke I thought it best
> Where I might finde some worthy place for such a corse to rest.
> And in my mind it came, from thence not farre away,
> Where Chreseids love, king Priams sonne, the worthy Troilus lay.
> By him I made his tomb …
> ('In Winter's just returne', ll. 66–8, 72–9)

The evocation of the lover's last moments and the shepherd's recollection of his feelings are absorbed (once again) into the heroics of myth, as the speaker relocates himself within a landscape of Trojan princes of not too distant memory. The resources of classical mythology are being exploited here not only to secure an exalted status for the speaker's personal experience but also to integrate it into a much larger scheme of cultural retrospection. Furthermore, at the close of this narrative, the tensions are not relaxed between the lover's death wish to erase memory and the speaker's retrieval of an enriched self *through* memory. Indeed, in the final tableau, the lasting emotional investment of the shepherd is shown to eclipse any legacy of betrayal bequeathed by the mistress.

In the rather different poetic environment of 'When Windsor walles sustained my wearied arme', the initial emphasis is upon natural detail that is exploited in order to colour more vividly the larger drama of the speaker's melancholia: 'The flowerd meades, the weddyd birds so late | Myne eyes discovered' (ll. 4–5). The formal meditative pose assumed on the castle ramparts ('My hand my chyn, to ease my restless hedd' (l. 2)) recalls the celebrated image of Surrey himself at the age of twenty-nine in a painting that has in the past been attributed to William Scrots (see Figure 2). And, more generally, the performance of this formal attitude may be widely identified in European erotic poetics in this period. Surrey's Spanish contemporary, Garcilaso de la Vega (1501?–36), for example, was also attracted to such lyrical stagings: 'Cuando me paro a contemplar mi estado, | y a ver los pasos por do me ha traído' ['When I stand and

Figure 2. Henry Howard, Earl of Surrey by unknown artist © National Portrait Gallery, London. Oil on canvas, c.1546.

contemplate my state, | and look back at the path that brought me here'].[26] However, in Surrey's poem, this meditative scene operates as a prelude to the exploration of irrepressible natural activity and to the staging of an act of memory – 'mine heavy charge of care' (l. 9). Here, the jarring contrast of former insouciance with present sorrow leads to a final rupture in the narrative with the articulation of the death wish: 'My vapored eyes such drery teares distill | The tender spring to quicken wher thei fall, | And I half bent to throwe me down withall' (ll. 12–14). The thrust of this poetic resolution is made all the more arresting with Surrey's favoured rhetorical technique of the delayed sentiment. Convincingly, in this context, Stephen Foley proposes that suicide itself, it might be argued, is a conventional amatory pose. If so, it is important even as a pose, for the theme of self-destruction seems central to Surrey's sonnets. Suicide is the terrifying inverse of the kind of cultivated selfhood Surrey attempts to project … Considering suicide from another point of view, it may be that this final act takes selfhood to its limit: suicide may be the last gesture of a self-consciously created identity.[27]

The rhythmic progression in this lyric towards the prospect of self-destruction is driven by the urgent need to conclude a seemingly endless cycle of thwarted desire and emotional inertia. The closing lines, drawn into the dynamic present, point to a final (potentially heroic) attempt through the *vita contemplativa* to recover a controlling sense of personal integrity. Importantly, the speaker's meditations, locked in a memorial narrative, generate chronological as well as spatial distances and thus enable the poet to animate an expansive drama of intense emotion. In such lyrics, the speaker is not only paralysed by the burden of memory but, equally significantly, seduced by death's power to erase the debilitating knowledge of the past.

More generally, Surrey's *œuvre* compels the reader to consider the recurring vision of a fragmenting society populated by estranged, suicidal or disillusioned voices, and 'When Windesor walles' is not the only instance of Surrey securing an alternative speaking position to that conventionally adopted by the courtly lover. In 'To dearely had I bought my grene and youthfull yeres' the keen contrast between a past narrative of erotic alienation and that of the present voiced by a powerfully affected onlooker is, if anything, more starkly drawn. The poetic argument and authority of the narrator are constructed out of the span from 'my grene and youthfull yeres' to those of 'mine age' (ll. 1–2). The status of the speaker is rendered ambivalent by the intimacy of his knowledge about the lovers and, in this instance, it is the affectation and sexual duplicity at work in the court that operate as the backdrop for the erotic agonies of the forsaken friend. If the speaker excites the anguish of the lover with confidences about the sexual *doings* of the mistress, the reader is also given pause by his seemingly insatiable appetite for recollection and reconnaissance work: 'I se her pleasant chere in chiefest of thy suit; | When thou art gone I se him come, that gathers up the fruite' (ll. 17–18). Here, we may again be reminded of Petrarch's insistence in *De Vita Solitaria* upon creating meditative space for the mind in the very midst of life in society. However, later in that same work, Petrarch stipulated in a revealing manner that, 'I never persuaded those for whom I said solitude was advantageous that in their desire for solitude they should despise the laws of friendship. I bade them fly from crowds and not from friends'.[28] Reviewing more generally the formulation of *otium* in early modern writing, Brian Vickers has underlined that 'absolute solitude is a state difficult to achieve and harder to maintain. In fact, once one examines the arguments in favour of solitude one discovers that they sometimes involve another person, a *solitude à deux*'.²⁹

If the powerful emotional drama frequently evoked by Surrey between narrator and courtly lover has, on occasions, clear homoerotic emphases, these potential dimensions of male friendship had preoccupied writers since antiquity. In 'To dearely had I bought', Surrey foregrounds the profound emotional commitment and empathy that the speaker feels for his abandoned friend: 'And for thy sake I burne so in my secret brest | That till thou know my hole disseyse my hart can have no rest' (ll. 9–10). He stresses the affective harmony between speaker and lover ('I se, what would you more?') with evidence of their intimate confidences: 'in thy respect I se the base degree | Of him to whom she gave the hart that promised was to the' (ll. 19–21). Ultimately, in his need to stress the absolute understanding that exists between them, the speaker reduces the mistress to a controllable stereotype of cruel promiscuity ('I se thee fed with fayned wordes' (l. 14)), and rescripts the past and the very discourse of desire in heroic terms of male fidelity.

SURREY, LANDSCAPE AND MEMORY

Surrey's poetry frequently encourages his readers to associate growth in emotional intelligence and the movement towards cultural withdrawal with the performance of acts of memory. Indeed, the recurrent and incremental evocation of the natural landscape in his lyrics invariably acts as a prelude to a mode of retrospection. If C. S. Lewis quipped that '[Surrey] takes every opportunity of bringing in external nature, or narrative, as if to take a holiday from the erotic treadmill', more recently Alicia Ostriker has argued persuasively that 'Surrey writes some of his best poetry when he can assimilate the yearning self to a background'.³⁰ This poetic reflex clearly looks back to an analogous emphasis in Petrarch's *Canzoniere* where the lover confesses, 'Per alti monti e per selve aspre trovo | qualche riposo: ogni abitato loco | è nemico mortal degli occhi miei' ['Among high mountains and wild woods I find | some rest, but every haunt of man | becomes an enemy that my eyes abhor'].³¹ Furthermore, in lyrics such as 'Stand whoso list upon the slipper top', Wyatt had also given a similar stress to the desire of his socially elevated speaker for cultural seclusion: here, the ambition is to be 'unknown in court' and to resort to some 'hidden place'. Yet, in the more explicit erotic environment of Surrey's 'If care do cause men cry, why do not I complaine?', the remembering voice is located strategically at the point of contact between the sorrows of erotic victimisation and the healing balm of recollection. If in this lyric we witness a crisis in the subject's erotic identity filtered through an evocation of the natural landscape, such poetic manoeuvres come to have an increasingly important status in Surrey's construction of dialogues between the worlds of the experience and anticipation.

> With thoughtes that for the time do much appease my paine.
> But yet they cause a farther fere and brede my woe agayne.
> Me thinke within my thought I se right plain appere
> My hartes delight, my sorrow's leche, mine earthly goddesse here,
> With every sondry grace that I have sene her have
> ('If care do cause men cry', ll. 27–31)

The keen juxtaposition in verse of these two mental planes had indeed become familiar in early modern Europe through an increasing acquaintance with narratives of affective dilemma in Petrarchan poetics: 'e 'l rimembrare et l'aspettar m'accora. | or quinci or quindi, sì che 'n veritate, | se non ch'i' ò di me steso pietate, | i' sarei già di questi pensier fora' ['forethought and memory bring such dismay, | now one and now the other, that at last, | but for self-pity that still holds me fast, | I would already from these thoughts be free'].³² However, more frequently than Petrarch, Surrey describes the contours and creatures of a given environment, the vibrant details of natural life, not only to draw a dramatic contrast with the mental landscape of his speakers but also to establish the all-encompassing quality of their solitude within the larger society.

Thus, the 'vital' presence of Nature is repeatedly seen to stimulate retrospection in Surrey's poetics and his emphasis on the associative and sequential (which characterises so much of the classical debate surrounding the faculty of memory from Aristotle onwards) is, of course, nowhere more apparent than in the *accumulatio* of his most famous sonnet 'The soote season, that bud and blome furth bringes':

> The swift swallow pursueth the flyes smale;
> The busy bee her honye now she minges:
> Winter is worne, that was the flowers bale.
>   And thus I see among these pleasant thinges
>   Eche care decayes, and yet my sorow springs.
> ('The soote season', ll. 10–14)

In this instance, the very deliberate deployment of the rhetorical trope of *hirmus*, or periodic sentence, vividly dramatises the essential plight of the forsaken speaker as he rehearses the multifarious activities of the natural world from his place of meditative isolation. If H. A. Mason argued that 'It is an alarming symptom of incapacity to find in the small number of Surrey's poems so many instances of verbal repetition', it might be countered that Surrey is *precisely* (and endlessly) fascinated with the implications of repetition (as both a linguistic and affective practice), recollection and the politics of retreat.[33] In his key study of elegiac writing and its duplicating strategies, Peter M. Sacks is timely in his stress that

> Repetition creates a sense of continuity, of an unbroken pattern such as one may oppose to the extreme discontinuity of death. Time itself is thereby structured to appear as a familiar, filled-in medium rather than as an open-ended source of possible catastrophe. Repetition is, moreover, one of the psychological responses to trauma ... By ... repetitions, the mind seeks retroactively to create the kind of protective barrier that, had it been present at the actual event, might have prevented or softened the disruptive shock that initially caused the trauma.[34]

In 'The soote season' the kaleidoscope of feverish natural activity emerges as a skilful meditation upon the human terms of change and experience: it gradually engenders an awareness, as Alastair Fowler has proposed, that 'the bee "mings" (remembers) the new season's task but at the same time, by implication, remembers the honey of the past seasons'.[35] The whole narrative of loss and marginalisation is held authoritatively in the lens of the speaker's eyes, serving to enhance cumulatively his own protesting sense of alienation from the natural cycle of desire and consummation. The erotic despair, in this writing exacerbated by the collapse in affective synchronicity between speaker and environment, is given shape and substance by the vital forces of the creaturely world; and this clearly should not be confused with the later Romantic yearning for communion with the primal forces of Nature. Nature provides rhetorically in this instance an authority that Surrey's speaker can exploit in order to communicate the lover's distress to a larger world – a world in which the organising principles of resemblance have decayed.

SURREY AND THE GENDERING OF MEMORY

In his cross-gendered poems Surrey gravitates to a more generalised account of human experience in terms of female passivity and mental torment occasioned by male absence – 'when I find the lack, Lord how I mourn'. C. S. Lewis submitted wryly that 'Oddly enough, the only two poems in which we are really moved by the theme of love are both put into the mouth of a woman; and of these women one certainly is, and the other may be, a wife in love with her husband'.[36] Down the centuries, readers have clearly searched (rather energetically on occasions) for an autobiographical key to such lyrics and have associated them with a *tableau vivant* of Lady Surrey awaiting the return of her husband from a military campaign. (Given Surrey's repeated poetic memorialisation of homosocial relations in a host of different contexts, it is perhaps noteworthy at this point to recall the recorded response of Henry VIII to Surrey's request for his wife to accompany him on the military campaign to Boulogne in 1545: the monarch reportedly threw it out, declaring that such an engagement was 'unmeet for women's imbecilities'.[37]) In general, when Surrey formulates a female voice in his poetry, he does so by training attention on latter-day Penelopes: their identities are shaped predominantly by their painfully acute powers of memory and their unfailing chastity. In 'O happy dames, that may embrace', the female voice is ventriloquised through a Petrarchan diction conventionally attributed to the male lover. The Neoplatonic emphases ('Those eyes that were my food') much associated with ideas elaborated upon in the Platonic commentaries of Ficino (with whom Surrey's contemporary, the humanist John Colet, corresponded) are drawn into a vividly realised narrative governed by the figurative language of seafaring: 'Drowned in tears to mourn my loss'. The poetic analogy between desiring and voyaging had become by this time a staple of European *Petrarchismo*, and had been developed (often rather extravagantly) upon leads given in the *Canzoniere* by such lyrics as 'Passa la nave mia colma d'oblio | per aspro mare, a mezza notte il verno' ['Fraught with oblivion, in a winter sea, | My ship sails on at midnight through the strait'] and 'La vita fugge, e non s'arresta un'ora' ['Life flees before, not stopping on the way'].[38]

> In ship, freight with remembrance
> Of thoughts and pleasures past,
> He sails, that hath in governance
> My life, while it will last;
> With scalding sighs, for lack of gale,
> Furthering his hope, that is his sail
> Toward me, the sweet port of his avail.
> ('O happy dames', ll. 8–14)[39]

Such figurative language is widely in evidence throughout Surrey's verse (voiced by both male and female narrators) and serves to highlight the fragility of all erotic undertakings in the punitive world of his poetics.

The lover as seafarer reappears, for example, in the male-voiced 'When ragyng love with extreme payne'. Here, the force of the metaphor is, if anything, more arresting as the moment of emotional collapse is carefully rehearsed and positioned within the cultural memory of Iphigenia's sacrifice and the subsequent Trojan conflict:

> I call to minde the navye greate
> That the Grekes brought to Troye towne,
> And how the boysteous windes did beate
> Their shyps, and rente their sayles adowne,
> Till Agamemnons daughters bloode
> Appeasde the goddes that them withstode.
> ('When ragyng love with extreme payne',
> ll. 7–12)

This narrative alternation (which recurs frequently in Surrey's poetry) between mythic referencing and growth in self-knowledge on the part of the speaker may also be witnessed in the work of his European contemporaries. Pierre de Ronsard, for example, would exploit exactly the same technique in his poem 'Narssis': 'Ceste belle saison me remet en memoire | Le printans que Jason époinçonné de gloire | Esleut la fleur de Grece' ['This lovely season recalls to my mind the Spring when Jason, spurred on by love of glory, selected the flower of Greek heroes'].[40] In both cases it appears that the experience of unreciprocated desire and the possibilities of human endurance can only be fully apprehended through recourse to the larger cultural memory of heroics shaped by Hector, Achilles and Odysseus. In the narrative recesses of myth, the speaker finds not only precedent, and thus legitimacy, for his own desperate encounters with adversity and defeat, he also identifies in the final 'winning' of Helen a discursive strategy for survival in a profoundly antagonistic environment.

Unlike the erotic lyrics voiced by male narrators, the female complaints in Surrey's poetry stress the fracturing of intimate relationships and the desire for alternative configurations of time and space. A. C. Spearing makes the rather striking claim that 'Surrey, *on his small scale*, more effectively expresses sympathy with women than any other English poet since Chaucer – more effectively, because his sympathy, like Chaucer's, is based on a shrewd understanding of the motives and interests of men as well as women' (italics mine).[41] However, more persuasively, it might be argued that the cross-gendering strategies of such lyrics appear to offer Surrey wider possibilities for exploring questions of cultural excentricity and silencing, rather than any convincing endeavour at psychological portraiture. In this context Elizabeth Heale is timely in her emphasis upon contemporary modes of textual transmission: 'Whether composed by men or by women, in a system of manuscript copying, appropriation and adaptation the question is less one of the name or gender of an originating author than of the kinds of voices and gestures the available discourses make possible to copiers and readers of both sexes.'[42] In Surrey's cross-gendered lyrics, we move strategically away from the histrionics of thwarted male ambition ('O viva morte, o dilettoso male' ['O living death, o exquisite anguish'] (canzone 132)) familiar from Petrarchan poetics to the mental traumas associated with more permanent forms of cultural and emotional marginality. While the commitment of male friendship is celebrated in almost grandiloquent terms in 'To dearely had I bought' and 'In Winter's just returne', in the company of Surrey's female speakers the emphasis falls squarely upon the collapse of social communion and the resulting need for the reconstruction of a specifically gendered audience: 'Good ladies, help me to fill my mourning voice' (l. 7).

Nonetheless, if the speaking female lover is much less often heard in the European poetics of the *amor de lonh*, Surrey does not seek to challenge the ideological assumptions surrounding female chastity, obedience and piety that were promoted in the instructional literatures of the period. Such discourses were clearly in evidence in the advice of Vives's *De institutione foeminae christianae* (1523, English translation 1529), for example, whereby a woman 'should apply herself to virtue, and be content with a little, and take in worth that she hath, nor seek for other that she hath not, nor for other folks, whereof riseth envy, hate, or curiosity of other folks' matters'.[43] Interestingly, if Surrey depicts his female speakers in terms of acute sensitivities, their faculties of memory mostly serve to intensify their propensity for emotional alarm: 'of ech thought a dout doth growe, | Now he comes, will he come? alas, no, no!' (ll. 41–2). The corrosive effects of remembering upon the female speakers enable his readers repeatedly to contrast the motifs of *otium*, *amicitia* and *pathos* being explored in the male-voiced complaints with the *locus remotus* to which their impotent female counterparts are consigned.

SURREY AND TROJAN RETROSPECTION

Perhaps one of the most celebrated ways in which Surrey chose to remember the past was through his translation of scriptural and classical works. In his *History of English Poetry* (1781), Thomas Warton concluded that 'Surrey, for his justness of thought, correctness of style, and purity of expression, may justly be pronounced the first English classical poet'.[44]

Uppermost in Warton's mind at this point was the question of poetic diction, but Surrey's notable foray into the area of classical translation with his rendering of Books II and IV of the *Aeneid* came to mean that he was associated with this epithet in a number of contexts. As recent criticism has taken care to stress, translation was perceived as no less creative than any other mode at the disposal of the Renaissance poet. Indeed, from antiquity there had been an emphasis upon the formative mental discipline and textual achievement of translation for the aspiring intellectual. In the *Ars Poetica*, Horace had argued, 'It is hard to treat in your own way what is common: and you are doing better in spinning into acts a song of Troy than if, for the first time, you were giving the world a theme unknown and unsung.'[45]

If translation played a key role in early modern theories of pedagogy, it also provided the ambitious translator with legitimate opportunities for conspicuous composition, intellectual development and contact with an educated elite – for Virgil's *Aeneid* remained at the very centre of the scholarly curricula across early modern Europe. In the preface to his unfinished epic *La Franciade* (1572), for example, Ronsard pronounced 'Virgile plus excellent et plus rond, plus serré, et plus parfaict que tous les autres' ['Virgil, more excellent and more accomplished, more erudite, and more perfect than all the others'] and confessed he might be found 'portant tousjours son livre en la main' ['always carrying his book in my hand'].[46] In choosing the *Aeneid* as his focus, Surrey was able to demonstrate both his veneration for classical literature and its wisdom, *and* his desire to renew them for a later age.[47]

Throughout his writing career, Surrey was clearly attracted by the opportunity to join his voice to those of the distant past and, in the process, to generate a creative space within the parent text in which parities of theme and critique might be explored.[48] A. C. Spearing promotes Surrey's classicism not only in terms of his elegance and clarity of diction, but also in terms of 'his historical sense': 'The imitation of Virgilian style is itself an example of that sense of the difference and distance of the past, accompanied by the attempt to reconstruct a past culture imaginatively from within, that marks the Renaissance.'[49] Nonetheless, the ways in which his rendering of the *Aeneid* was construed culturally by subsequent generations proved to be considerably more complex than the creative coupling of Virgil's and Surrey's voices. Patricia Thomson notes that the later humanist Roger Ascham, for example, performed a highly selective, if not flawed, act of memorial praise when he hailed Surrey as the 'first of all English men, in translating the fourth booke of

Virgill' in *The Scholemaster* (1570). Ascham made no account of Caxton's prose version of the *Aeneid*, which appeared at the end of the fifteenth century, nor that of the Scottish poet Gavin Douglas's rendering of the epic in rhyming couplets. Tellingly, Thomson underlines that 'Surrey himself sits down with a copy of Douglas alongside his Virgil, so that, according to an authoritative reckoning, 40% of his lines show debts to Douglas's wording'.⁵⁰

The textual *mise en abîme* organised around memorial acts by Aeneas, Dido, Virgil, Douglas, Surrey and the reader, among others, necessarily engenders a complex meditation on the status and function of attempting to recuperate the past. Moreover, these endeavours in translation not only permitted Surrey to engage in textual dialogues with valued classical narratives, they also allowed him to retrieve and to reconfigure a heroic discourse closely associated with noble rank. As historians and literary critics focusing on the career of Surrey have repeatedly underlined, this military commander was keenly aware of the emergent schemes of patronage, precedence and reward at work in the Henrician court culture where the administrative services of commoners were increasingly likely to attract royal attention rather than recognition of the obligations traditionally owed to the aristocracy. It is reported that the twenty-three-year-old Earl rejoiced at the news of the execution of Thomas Cromwell: 'Now is that foul churl dead, so ambitious of other's blood … now is he stricken with his own staff … these new erected men would by their wills leave no nobleman on life.'⁵¹ Ultimately, of course, the very public manner in which he revived memories of a former age of aristocratic pre-eminence would lead him to the scaffold, when in 1546 he included the royal arms and those of Edward the Confessor on his escutcheon.⁵² The gravity of the act was repeatedly underlined as the time of the Earl's execution drew closer, as Susan Brigden has highlighted, 'On 12 January, the night before Surrey's trial, his father confessed: "I have concealed high treason in keeping secret the false and traiterous act … committed by my son … in using the arms of St Edward the Confessor".'⁵³

> 'Never shall I denie, quene, thy deserte
> Greater than thou in wordes may well expresse.
> To thinke on thee ne irke me aye it shall
> Whiles of my selfe I shall have memory,
> And whiles the spirit these limmes of mine shal rule.
> For present purpose somwhat shal I say … '
>   (*Aeneid*, IV: 432–7)

Given the level of Surrey's metrical innovation, poetic ambition and his strategic evocation of a lost world of heroism, Emrys Jones would seem rather wide of the mark in his glum contention that 'the bulk of Surrey's important work was translation or adaptation. His powers of invention and of forming independent structures were small'.[54] As has been appreciated, modern expectations involving 'innovative' and 'independent' creativity must be carefully rescripted for a sixteenth-century culture whose habits of thinking yoked together the business of writing with *imitatio* in an almost indissoluble union.[55] In an age that was obsessed with the recoverability of wisdom from classical writing and which valued deeply all that the human faculty of memory could yield, the documents that survived from the past continued to offer intellectuals across Europe access to enduring discourses of subjectivity formation and to vindicate their own endeavours in the field of scholarship. In the later years of Elizabeth's reign, Puttenham had no hesitation in stating that 'without any repugnancie at all, a Poet may in some sort be said a follower or imitator ... both a maker and a counterfaitor'.[56] Like many of his contemporaries, Surrey was pursuing enquiries into the ways in which the self might be constituted from the past and be seen to depend upon memory for its sense of coherence. Moreover, in direct comparison with Mary Sidney's poetic undertakings discussed in Chapter 5, Surrey's choices of translation were clearly strategic, enabling him to conjure up for his readers a decisive moment of heroic engagement in the fates and narratives of nations performed by the members of ruling élites:

> And loe, moist night now from the welkin falles,
> And sterres declining counsel us to rest.
> But sins so great is thy delight to here
> Of our mishaps and Troyès last decay,
> Though to record the same my minde abhorres
> And plaint eschues, yet thus wil I begyn.
> (*Aeneid*, II: 12–17)

It is in this way, with a seemingly enforced act of memory on the part of Aeneas, that Surrey begins his translation of Book Two. In this instance the journeying into the past is profoundly ambiguous. The replaying of cultural destruction and Trojan defeat is, in fact, here at one level an act of courtesy to an enamoured Queen Dido. The latter, like the rest of the company, has her desires excited paradoxically by the prospect of listening to a 'woe [that] cannot be told'. Moreover, the anachronies, or repeated chronological ruptures, of Aeneas's narrative serve to multiply possibilities for contemplating further the loss of a world of heroism that has disappeared not only in cultural but also in economic terms: 'There stands in sight an isle hight Tenedon, | Rich and of fame while Priams kingdom stood: | Now but a bay, and rode unsure for ship' (*Aeneid*, II: 29–31).

In this powerful imaginative repossession of Troy, Surrey is eager to convey Aeneas's anguished act of memory, finely poised between a compulsive appetite for rhetorical display and a profound and unresolved grief that the relation of the events revives. The Trojan prince wishes to promote and participate within a cultural narrative of male heroism in which the high-ranking are allowed to express their multiple identities as warrior, orator, politician, lover – in short, to become men of destiny. Nevertheless, Aeneas's new-found role as epic bard before his Carthaginian audience irrevocably establishes his distance in time and space from the events he celebrates. Trapped by and absorbed within multiplying narratives of a city's collapse, memory clearly emerges for the Trojan as a symbolic, indeed apotropaic practice – a means of keeping death, and thus forgetfulness, at bay. As a consequence, we find that the accounts of the Fall of Troy by the displaced hero are riddled strategically with fissures designed to create space for self-assertion and for self-justification:

> Ye Troyan ashes, and last flames of mine,
> I cal in witnesse, that at your last fall
> I fled no stroke of any Grekish swerd,
> And if the fates wold I had fallen in fight,
> That with my hand I did deserve it wel.
> (*Aeneid*, II: 554–8)

If, in returning attention to the Trojan war, Surrey reconstructs textually a heroic arena in which to rehearse tales of cultural longing, he also engages with communal myths of belonging inherited from traditions of genealogical composition dating back centuries. Prior to Surrey, Wyatt's 'Tagus, farewell, that westward with thy streams' had also acknowledged the strength of such mythologies for the early Tudor readership: 'With spur and sail I go seek the Thames, | ... to the town which Brutus sought by dreams.'[57] And the (legendary) founding of the British race might be traced back, it was argued, to Brute, son of Sylvius, grandson of Ascanius, great-grandson of Aeneas. However, by the beginning of seventeenth century, if Camden might still include such narrativisation in his *Britain, or A chorographicall description* (1610), he could not suppress, like an ever-increasing number of his contemporaries, his deep misgivings: 'For mine owne part, let Brutus be taken for the father, and founder of the British nation; I will not be of a contrarie minde ... Let Antiquitie heerein be pardoned, if by entermingling falsities and truthes … it make the first beginnings of nations and cities more noble, sacred, and of greater maiesties.'[58]

This nation, which Virgil had hailed in his First Eclogue as 'penitus toto divisos orbe Britannos' ['the Britons, wholly sundered from all the world'],[59] required founding myths to legitimise itself and secured one of them in this consecrated space of classical textuality. The remembering of Troy throughout the literature of the English Renaissance remained intimately linked to cultural ideals of military heroism, political legitimacy, male descent and inheritance, and national identity-construction. If the concept of the political nation was being realised in this period at least in part through *textual* production, Surrey's renderings of the *Aeneid* into English participated fully in this highly strategic memorial commitment.

SURREY AND THE ELEGY

Surrey's ongoing interrogations of the power of memory engender poetic narratives fixated with the problems of recovery and lament, and nowhere is this more apparent than in his elegies. Elizabeth Heale argues that 'The elegy … voices nostalgia and alienation, bewailing loss and disempowerment in the present while looking back to a former happiness identified in Surrey's poems with an idealized, and in many respects conservative, social and moral order'.[60] The conservatism of Surrey's poetic enquiries into the status and function of political sovereignty and court culture and into the possibilities of human transcendence remains surely a moot point, but, as he pays tribute to a Wyatt, a Richmond or a Clere, he is clearly once again probing the difficulties associated with the burden of memory and the desire to fashion something permanent from its legacies. Indeed, his contemporary Ronsard also acknowledged an analogous undertaking 'sur l'autel de Memoire' ['on the altar of Memory'] in his own elegiac 'Odes':

> C'est un travail de bon-heur
> Chanter les hommes louables,
> Et leur bastir un honneur
> Seul veinqueur des ans muables …[61]

[It is a labour of pleasure | To sing of worthy men | And to erect a tribute to them | Lone victor over the changing years.]

The poetic encounters that Surrey established with Martial, Virgil or the Psalmist in his explorations of a desire for a world that had passed differ qualitatively from his verse meditations on figures such as Richmond or Clere whom he knew personally. In such poems he creates a historical consciousness that not only records the affective potential of the speaker but also offers a stage upon which he may disclose his detailed knowledge of an ennobling phase of human experience in which he himself has participated.

This desire to praise is deeply rooted in the early modern concept of poetic composition and, in his elegies, Surrey determines that his poetry of praise should expand beyond the figure of the deceased. His constant poetic reflex is to celebrate the cultural environment in which human greatness was still possible, whether it be that of youthful aspiration, poetic creativity, or aristocratic heroism. Inevitably, in such writing, the memorial impulse serves to underline the alienation of the bereft speaker and the mediocrity of the spectacle of cultural process and decline to which he is compelled to bear witness. In 'So crewell prison how could betyde, alas', the death of Henry VIII's illegitimate son, the Duke of Richmond, emerges as the axis for the unfolding poetic drama. In this context, Windsor Castle becomes once again an affective locus rather than an architectural space – 'Where eche swete place retournes a tast full sowre' (l. 5). Returning to the familiar resources of mythic referencing, Surrey's speaker recollects that in his youth he 'with a Kinges soon [his] childishe yeres did passe, | In greater feast then Priams sonnes of Troye' (ll. 3–4). The vivid evocation of the intimate relationship between these high-ranking boyhood companions is starkly contrasted with the demeaning circumstances of adult imprisonment: in this instance, physical confinement and political marginalisation have stimulated a memorial appetite for personal narratives of cultural and emotional liberty:

> Eache stone, alas, that dothe my sorowe rewe,
> Retournes therto a hollowe sound of playnt.
> Thus I, alone, where all my fredome grew,
> In pryson pyne with bondage and restraynt,
> And with remembraunce of the greater greif
> To banisshe the lesse, I fynde my chief releif.
> ('So crewell prison how could betyde, alas', 49–54)

The childhood experiences of these latter-day sons of Priam are vividly replayed over the course of this poetic narrative. Surrey creates a painterly effect with close details of the natural landscape that give substance and space to his unfolding account of loss. Yet the evocation of the 'quyet bedd of rest' where 'the frendshipp sworne, eche promyse (was) kept so just' (ll. 36, 39) is ruptured in the present when the liberty of his memory is placed in harsh relief with his physical captivity. If the environs of the castle 'where all my fredome grew' (l. 51) inevitably quicken his awareness of the pains of imprisonment, this knowledge is occluded by the 'great greif' (l. 53) that the dead Richmond now only has life at all in the confines of his (textualised) memory.

In turning to the death of Wyatt, Surrey self-consciously formulates poetic tributes that both confirm the exalted status of the late poet and vindicate the undertaking of his successor. The careers of poet, mourner and lover had been, of course, thoroughly intertwined in Petrarchan poetics, and defeat in one of these undertakings was often counterpointed in the speakers' minds by success elsewhere, as Petrarch himself underlined in canzone 74:

> e che' pie' miei non son fiaccati e lassi
> a seguir l'orme vostre in ogni parte
> perdendo inutilmente tanti passi;
>
> et onde vien l'enchiostro, onde le carte
> ch'i' vo empiendo di voi; se 'n ciò fallassi,
> colpa d'Amor, non già defetto d'arte.[62]

[and how, upon your track, I still travail | to follow you with firm untired feet, | wasting so many steps to no avail; | and whence comes ink, and whence come all the sheets | I fill with you; if doing so I fail, | Love is to blame, there is no fault in art.]

Throughout the *Canzoniere* Petrarch continued to reflect upon the poet's relations to his textual offspring that must endure beyond the span of mortal lives: 'Canzone, oltra quell'alpe, | là dove il ciel è più sereno e lieto, | mi rivedrai' ['My song, beyond the Alps, | where skies are happier and clear above, | you'll find me'].[63] This 'eternizing' movement in Petrarch's verse was taken up much more vigorously by his poetic successors who often retrace his journey in their own work from thwarted lover to elegist. In his epitaph for Montmorency, for example, Ronsard intones ceremoniously, 'Une coulonne à la fin est moisie, | Et les tombeaux par l'âge sont dontez, | Non pas les vers que la Muse a chantez' ['A column will in time be moss-eaten, | And tombs through age decay | But not the verses which the Muse has sung'].[64] Surrey's own 'monumentalising' tributes to Wyatt have won a good measure of critical praise down the centuries, and the restorative qualities of memory are particularly emphasised throughout his elegiac writing. In 'Dyvers thy death doo diverslye bemone' he draws upon the resources of classical history and myth once again to anchor his subject firmly in the reader's mind with narratives from the larger cultural memory. Petrarch had made reference to the authority of the Caesars, for example, in his poetic account of Italy's former glories and present woes in canzone 128: 'Cesare taccio, che per ogni piaggia | fece l'erbe sanguigne | di lor vene, ove 'l nostro ferro mise' ['Of Caesar I speak not who near and far | dyed the plains red with blood | drawn from their veins in which he plunged our steel'].[65] More famously for readers of Wyatt's 'Whoso list to hunt, I know where is an hind', in canzone 190 Petrarch had stressed the competition in erotic possession when the lover finally approaches 'una candida cerva'.[66] In his own sonnet 'Caesar, when that the traitor of Egypt' Wyatt combined a more even emphasis upon political and erotic desire. However, when Surrey takes up these themes, they are given a backdrop of political duplicity: some 'Weape envyous teares to here thy fame so good' (l. 7). Indeed, all too often in such lyrics we are encouraged to believe that the flexing of memory, the renewal of an engagement with the past, is the redemptive path by which order and meaning may be returned to the unheroic present: 'But I that knewe what harbourd in that hedd, | ... Honour the place that such a iewel bredd' (ll. 9, 11).

There are clear thematic continuities of emphasis between Surrey's elegiac writing and his erotic lyrics. He returns repeatedly in both modes to the anxieties surrounding excess of memory. In 'Dyvers thy death' the speaker's mind becomes the site for competing details of power relationships that determined the past. The grieving speaker honours the dead and transforms his own profound sense of disempowerment through funeral oration.[67] More generally, Jentoft is timely in his reminder that 'the principal motivation for the funeral elegy in the sixteenth century was praise for the life of the deceased rather than lament for his death ... In short, the occasional epitaph was part of the main tradition of Renaissance epideictic poetry'.[68] To a great extent, 'Dyvers thy death' records a textual endeavour to reverse the meagre social recognition hitherto afforded Wyatt by promoting him as a figure worthy of elegiac poetry. Indeed, the main reversal in Wyatt's fortunes begins as the poetic voice himself secures enhanced authority at the *volta* with the privileged positioning of 'But I'. As prime poetic mourner, Surrey's speaker attempts through a sequence of poems to map out and to regenerate the personal and political aspirations of those who have been lost. Sessions points out that 'If the poem evokes the Roman *epicedium* in which the mourner stands over the corpse of the beloved, looking at the beauties of body that reveal deeper glories of virtue, here the catalogue of the poem centers on the work of that body'.[69] We might add that in this final movement of the sonnet Surrey chooses intriguingly to *reverse* the mythological bodies of Pyramus and Thisbe, of lover and beloved, rendering the latter the victim of the ravenous lion.

> And kysse the ground where as thy coorse doth rest,
> With vaporde eyes; from whence suche streames avayle
> As Pyramus did on Thisbes brest bewayle.
> ('Dyvers thy death', ll. 12–14)

More generally, in such poems Surrey envisages the redemptive power of memory – the manner in which it can constitute an outlet in which the possibilities of solace and critique may be restored and re-storied. In 'W. resteth here, that quick could neuer rest', he selectively organises his material in order to highlight most particularly the cultural influence of the poet. Importantly, Dennis Kay underlines that 'the humanist cult of the individual, which informed the vogue for verisimilitude in portraiture, perhaps explains a poem like Surrey's lament "Wyatt resteth here", which appears to embrace particularity … Surrey is an exception. Most Tudor public poets responded to an important event like their predecessors: by generalizing'.[70] In addition, it is interesting to note that in a very unusual action for an aristocrat of the time, Surrey's elegies for Wyatt entered the public domain by means of print culture: they appeared in John Leland's *Naeniae in mortem Thomae Viati equitis incomparabilis* (a collection dedicated to Surrey) within weeks of Wyatt's death in October 1542.

SURREY REMEMBERED

Perhaps Surrey's very poetic *œuvre* should be construed as a collective act of memorial construction. If the 'melodious tears' offered to Wyatt were published quickly after the latter's death, more generally the full range of his poetic output only became known to a wider audience through its entry into print culture after his own death. Tottel's *Miscellany*, entitled *Songes and Sonettes, written by the ryght honorable Lorde Henry Howard, late Earle of Surrey, and other*, was published in 1557: the fact that the *late Earle* was given pride of place may be explained at least in part through his rank and his existing reputation as the translator of books from the *Aeneid*, which had also appeared in the 1550s. The *Miscellany* was to go through five editions by 1587. Given this state of affairs, it is not surprising, as Sessions asserts, that 'for the later Renaissance, Surrey is, of course, the chief survivor of the Henrician period'.⁷¹ Indeed, Surrey quickly became a model in early Tudor society for poetic composition: as early as the 1540s, the musician Thomas Whythorne was transcribing 'songs and sonets' of 'þe erll of Surrey [and] sir Thomas Wiatt þe elder' among others for his employer John Heywood: 'I afterward gav my self to imitat and follow þeir trads and devyses in wryting az okkazions moved me.'⁷² In addition, Puttenham's *Arte of English Poesie* (1589) became instrumental in privileging and romanticising the figures of Surrey and Wyatt:

> In the latter end of the same kings raigne sprong vp a new company of courtly makers, of whom Sir *Thomas Wyat* th'elder & *Henry* Earle of Surrey were the two chieftaines, who hauing trauailed into Italie, and there tasted the sweete and stately measures and stile of the Italian Poesie.⁷³

In the same way that a complex and evolving engagement with the faculty of memory allowed Surrey to formulate human experience in a host of different ways, successive generations of his readers have delighted in his favoured practices of revising, erasing, supplementing and editing in dealing with the Henrician past. Puttenham, for example, promoted Surrey erroneously as the close travelling companion of Wyatt in Italy. Elsewhere, Sir John Cheke, humanist scholar and tutor to the future Edward VI, wrote an elegy in which he chose to celebrate 'natures device … thie headd she made of witt, a paragon'.⁷⁴ By 1591, in the prefatory material to his translation of *Orlando Furioso*, Sir John Harington hailed 'the Earle of Surrey, and *Sir Thomas Wiat*, that are yet called the first refiners of the English tong', whereas his contemporary, Thomas Nashe, as we shall see, depicted 'a poet without peer': Nashe's Geraldine instructs her courtly lover Surrey wistfully, 'Aye, *pete Italiam*, go and seek Italy with Aeneas, but be more true than Aeneas'.⁷⁵

Surrey's poems trace a variety of routes, establish a host of cultural genealogies, with which to map the past: however, if memory is one of the instruments that Surrey most frequently deploys, it is ultimately shown to be profoundly insecure and ungovernable. By way of conclusion, we might add that as his poems, one by one, meditate the implications of chronological dislocation between the past and the hostile realities of the present, it becomes increasingly evident that his poetic undertaking is metaphorical in nature: pasts and presents are brought together to generate textual frictions, to stimulate a broader range of voices for cultural critique and an enriched spectrum of interpretative strategies.

> For then, as one that hath the light in haat,
> I wishe for night, more covertlye to playne,

And me withdrawe from everie haunted place,
Lest in my chere my chaunce should pere to playne;
And with my mynd I measure paas by paas,
To seke the place where I my self hadd lost ...
('The sonne hath twyse brought forthe the
tender grene', ll. 30–5)

CHAPTER 2

'Remembre not (lorde) myne offences':
Katherine Parr and the politics of recollection

> O heavenly Father, God almighty, I praie and beseeche thy mercy, benignely to heold me thy unworthy servaunt, that I maie by gefte of thy holy spirite fervently desire they kyngedome, that I maie knowe thy wil and worke theraftwer ... Keepe me, lord, from the sleighty invasion of the olde wily serpente. Defende me from the counsailes and cursynges of yvell tungues. Leat thy mighty arme be my shielde against all the malignity of this wicked worlde.
>
> Remembre not (lorde) myne offences. Instructe, prepare me to repent, to be sorie for my synnes. Make me to love Justice and hate wronge, to dooe good and absteyne from all yvels, that I maie be worthy to be called thy chylde. To the bee honour and glorie for ever and ever. Amen.
>
> Catharine [Katherine] Parr, Prayers or medytacions,
sig. D5^v–D6^{v1}

In June 1545, two years after becoming queen, there appeared *Prayers or medytacions, wherin the mind is stirred paciently to suffre all afflictions here, to sette at naught the vaine prosperitee of this worlde, and alwaie to long for the everlasting felicitee: collected out of certayne holy workes by the moste vertuous and gracious Princes Catharine, Quene of Englande, France and Irelande*. In the event, the collection only included two concluding prayers.[2] Later in November of that same year, an expanded edition was published that was now brought to a close with five prayers – and the extract above, which probes the relationships between sin, repentance and memory, is taken from 'An other praier' in this collection.[3]

Half a century later, in 1592, Mary Sidney would emerge for the first time as a published author with *A Discourse of Life and Death. Written in French by Ph. Mornay. Antonius, A Tragædie written also in French by Ro. Garnier. Both done in English by the Countesse of Pembroke*. Thus, Parr and Mary Sidney both made their debuts in print culture with a title page that proclaimed their authorial identities in terms of their sex *and* their elevated rank. In such undertakings, both women may have had in mind the cultural prejudices that Richard Younge was to bemoan in the next century that, 'alas! most men regard not what is written, but who writes: valew not the mettall, but the Stampe which is upon it'.⁴ Whatever the case, in 1545, Parr was memorialised in print as the king's consort and seemingly with her husband's blessing: *Prayers or medytacions* rolled from the presses of the royal printer, Thomas Berthelet. And in December of that year her stepdaughter, Princess Elizabeth, offered her father a New Year's gift in the shape of French, Italian and Latin translations of the collection.⁵

PRAYERS OR MEDYTACIONS

The first section of *Prayers or medytacions* was ordered into 188 short verses and clearly drew substantially upon material from Richard Whitford's translation of the *Imitatio Christi* by Thomas à Kempis.⁶ As Greg Walker has underlined, 'The repackaging of … late-medieval texts for Tudor audiences was part of a wider strategic agenda on the part of the reformers'.⁷ It clearly testified to a widespread need among this new generation of religious writers to connect with the meditative literatures of the past, in part at least, in order to establish the authenticity of their own enquiries and the ancestry of their spiritual commitment. Among the 're-packaging' printing projects in the early Tudor period, Caxton brought out the *Horologium Sapientiae* of the fourteenth-century German mystic Henry Suso (Amandus) in 1491, and, three years later, the *Scala perfectionis* of the fourteenth-century Augustinian mystic Walter Hilton was published by Wynken de Worde. Indeed, it is clear from the records detailing the contents of her library at the end of her life that Parr herself owned published copies of Sir Thomas Elyot's translation of *A swete & devoute sermon of holy saynct Ciprian of mortalitie of man* (1539) and various productions by Thomas Lupset, which included *Here be the Gathered Covnsailes of Saynct Isodorie* (1539) and *A sermon of Saint Chrysostome* (1542).⁸ The latter invited the reader to ponder that 'he that hath his mynde redy and bent to resyste synne, and well remembreth hym selfe, can not only take none hurt of men, but also tourneth from him the angre and vengeance of god, being at the poynt to punyshe hym'.⁹ In the context of Parr's own undertakings as an author, the gravitational pull of these pre-Reformation meditational legacies continued to have enormous influence upon her writing. Indeed, Richard Whitford's translation of the *Imitatio Christi* appeared under the title *The folowing of Christe with the Golden epistel of saynt Barnard* (1531); and Parr duly concentrated her attention upon Book Three (chapters 15–50) of Kempis's narrative in which a contemplative's communion with Christ is enacted.[10]

There were, of course, examples from the late medieval period of explicitly female-authored devotional writing in English, such as Julian of Norwich's *Revelations of Divine Love* from the later fourteenth century, and the dictated meditations of the illiterate Margery Kempe from the 1430s. However, in contrast to these authorities, Parr proposed a paradigm of female devotional authorship governed by a Reformist commitment that necessitated engagement with the larger community with a view to social and spiritual reform. Furthermore, by 1543, when Parr became queen, there were already precedents for intervention in print culture signalled by the actions of earlier Tudor women from both the Catholic and Reformist faith communities. Henry VIII's grandmother, Lady Margaret Beaufort, and indeed his wives, Katherine of Aragon and Anne Boleyn, had either acted as patronesses for, or in Beaufort's case engaged in, the translation of pious works. In 1504, Beaufort was the dedicatee of William Atkinson's published translation of Jean Gerson's *full deuoute and gostely treatyse of the imytacyon and folowynge the blessed lyfe of our moste mercyfull Sauyour cryste*, which celebrated in its prefatory address 'the most excelle[n]t pri[n]ces Margarete'.[11] And in 1507 Beaufort's own translation from a French version of Dionysius Carthusianus's *Speculum arrum anime peccatricia a quodam cartusiense* (1480) was published anonymously as *The Mirror of Gold to the Sinful Soul*. (Interestingly, its account of the sinner endeavouring to transcend the burdens of a world full of vanities has clear parallels with Parr's later work.) Katherine of Aragon's piety and interest in religious literature became well known during the lengthy period of her marriage to Henry; and Erasmus, for example, addressed more correspondence to her than to any other woman. Juan Luis Vives (1492–1540) acted as a spiritual counsellor to the queen during the 1520s and during his visits to England in this decade made the acquaintances of Thomas More, Cuthbert Tunstall and William Linacre, among a number of leading scholars. With reference to Anne Boleyn's engagement with the Reformist cause, Susan Wabuda has argued energetically that 'much early credit [should go to her] for being a tireless promoter of the English Bible … She even put an English Bible on a desk for members of the court to read'.[12] In addition, James Kelsey McConica has pointed to a 'conspicuous production of treatises' in the early 1540s (which is to say the period immediately preceding Parr's marriage to Henry VIII) focusing upon the positive re-evaluation of female cultural profiles, noting particularly Christopher Goodwin's *Maydens dreame* (1542), Edward Gosynhill's *Prayse of all women* (1542), Robert Vaughan's *Dyalogue defensyue for women agaynst malycyous detractoures* (1542) and David Clapham's translation of Cornelius Agrippa's treatise, *Of the nobilitie of woman kynde* (1542).[13]

The 'prayers' of *Prayers or medytacions* were clearly given precedence in the title of Parr's first publication, and among these prayers numbered 'A praier for the kynge' and 'A praier for men to saie entring into bataille'. It is indeed persuasive to think that at least significant sections of this collection date from her three-month regency in 1544 (12 July to 30 September) occasioned by Henry's unfruitful military campaign in France. Certainly, Parr took up the theme of the combative nature of all temporal existence at several reprises in this collection: 'And it is tedious to me, to liue in suche battaile, all be it I perceyue that suche battaile is not unprofitable unto me. For therby I knowe the better my selfe and myne owne infirmities' (*Prayers or medytacions*, sig. A6^r). Thus, *Prayers or medytacions*, like Surrey's verse paraphrases of scripture, belongs to the very last, stress-ridden years of Henry's reign when the textual business of remembering was a potentially dangerous undertaking for anyone in the kingdom, most especially those close to the ageing and unfailingly irascible sovereign. As we have seen, these were the years of Surrey's disgrace, trial and execution; and his poetic writings (many of which had already been circulating in manuscript for years at court) had demonstrated through religious, secular and erotic narratives the highly politicised nature that recollection might assume in the precarious climate of Henrician England.

THE TEXTUAL CULTURES OF KATHERINE PARR

Parr's own textual explorations of the status and function of memory would be influenced by writings reflecting a wide spectrum of religious confession. Parr was born *c.*1512, yet even prior to the reshaping of Europe by religious schism and indeed of the political landscape of England brought about by the king's 'Great Matter', a consuming interest in religious reform had preoccupied many of the greatest minds of the age. With his sustained emphasis on moral improvement, lay piety and institutional reform, Erasmus had been a notable voice for the promotion of scriptural translation into the vernacular, most notably articulated in *Paraclesis* (1516) where he submitted (here in the 1529 translation) that

> Paraventure it were moste expedient that the councels of kinges shuld be kept secret, but Christ wold that his councelles and misteries shuld be sprede abrode

as moch as is possible. I wold desire that all women shuld reade the gospell and Paules epistles, and I wold to god they were translated in to the tonges of all men, So that they might not only be read, and knowne, of the scotes and yryrshmen, But also of the Turkes and sarracenes … I wold to god, ye plowman wold singe a texte of the scripture at his plowbeme, And that the wever at his lowme, with this wold drive away the tediousnes of tyme. I wold the wayfaringe man with this pastyme wold expelle the werynes of his iorney.[14]

Moreover, as was appreciated in the Introduction, Erasmus returned on many occasions to the subject of memory. Throughout his career, he remained eager to affirm the status of understanding (rather than facile recognition) in the training of the mind. In *De Conscribendi Epistolis* (1522), for example, he found space to reflect upon

Plato's conception of souls descending to earth whose knowledge here is nothing but a dreamlike memory of what they once saw, free from their bodies, in the presence of God. These and many other proclaim a degree of divine nature in the mind. It is proclaimed too by the fact that a single mind, shut up in a small body, embraces so many and such varied and difficult subjects in its understanding and retains them in its memory. It will seem miraculous, if one considers it, that the man who has learned only one language knows so many names of men and things, and far more miraculous that Mithradates had a knowledge of twenty-one languages. Yet memory is the smallest part of the human mind. One must add what Plato refused to admit, that the body forms part of man's nature, that it is the instrument, habitation, or vehicle of the soul, and that the soul is the whole of what we call man … Some people's primary and almost sole anxiety is to learn things by heart, word for word. I do not approve of this as it involves much work and is practically useless … But if there is some saying, maxim, old proverb, anecdote, story, apt comparison, or anything that strikes you as being phrased with brevity, point, or in some other clever way, consider it a treasure to be stored carefully in the mind for use and imitation.[15]

As will become evident, Parr's acquaintance with the writings of Erasmus was far from superficial. Indeed, it appears that at the beginning of Edward VI's reign she purchased an English translation of Erasmus's popular *Enchiridion militis Christiani* entitled *Preparation to deathe* in which the reader is on a number of occasions invited to reflect upon the commitment to faith and the devotion to divine worship in distinctively memorial terms:

The church can not be pore, which is ioyned to so ryche an heed … The tender loue and bountyfulnes of the heed towarde vs, principally wytnesseth the crosse taken for to redeme vs. The memorie and power of these thynges we do renew vnto vs, as oft as with feith and due reuerence we do eate the fleshe of the lorde, and drynke the blud … Wherefore who soo euer, that in his lyfe is diligently exercised, in the contemplation of these thynges, at his deathe, they shall brynge vnto him more comforte. For than euen of theyr owne accorde, they shall renne into his memorie, as thinges famyliar vnto the mynd and soule.¹⁶

As the 1520s progressed, the translation of scripture into vernacular languages came increasingly to be aligned with the Lutheran cause. The earliest evidence in Britain for the appearance of Lutheran ideas is with the sale of his books in 1520 and at the end of that year there was a public burning of his publications in Cambridge; yet informal groups were to meet in the city throughout the subsequent decade to debate his ideas. By 1521, in a letter to Wolsey, Archbishop Warham was clearly taking note of the great number of Lutheran books entering England, and wrote to the cardinal: 'it is a sorrowful thing to see how gredyly inconstaunt men and specyally inexpert youthe, falleth to new doctrynes be they never so pestilent'.¹⁷ In this context, David Scott Kastan underlines that 'As early as 1524, booksellers in London were forbidden by Cardinal Wolsey from trading in books that promoted Lutheranism, and ordered to obtain ecclesiastical approval for all imported books offered for sale'.¹⁸ If Reformation theology often radically rescripted the practices of spiritual worship and the status of recollection in its soteriology, this should in no way detract attention from the fact that the business of remembering had had an integral and strategic role to play in the meditative life of pre-Reformation England. Before the break with Rome, the observances in chantries, the veneration of saints and the celebration of holy days, for example, all marked the endeavours of those eager to retain a spiritual link with the observances and commitments of those who had gone before. In a work that Parr herself owned, Thomas Lupset's *A compendious and a very fruteful treatyse, teachynge the waye of dyenge well* (1534), she might encounter with great frequency the age-old adage of the medieval *ars moriendi* tradition 'that death is not to be feared, and that by contynuall remembraunce of death, you shall prepayre your selfe to dye gladlye with a good wyll' – this was a sentiment that would prove to have powerful resonances in her own writings.¹⁹

Among her contemporaries, of direct relevance to Parr's own upbringing was the influence of the theologian and future bishop of Durham, Cuthbert Tunstall, a close family friend. This humanist scholar, who became part of the intellectual circles of More, Erasmus, Colet and Lupset, was her father's cousin, one of the executors of her father's will and the principal executor of her mother's. One of Parr's biographers, Susan James, speculates that Tunstall had a strategic role to play in the educational programme of all the Parr children; and the role that memory specifically had to perform in his own vision of Christian life is repeatedly underlined in his surviving religious writings.²⁰ His collection *Certaine godly and deuout prayers*, for example, appeared in 1558 in the final months of his life, but here again we may witness ample evidence of Augustinian thinking on the privileged status of memory circulating in early modern print culture. Tunstall not only powerfully evokes the dejected state of a sinning humanity, he also promotes memory as crucial to understanding the very constitution of the soul and the true progress of faith:

> we thanke the, that hast vouchsaued to create and to make vs like vnto thy owne symilitude & image, that we throughe memorye, vnderstandyng and wil, shuld be made lyke vnto y͏ͤ. We perceue these thre powers of the soule to be in vs: by the whych we remember, contemplate, and desyre the. By the memorye (whych is the parent of vnderstanding) … we represent thy image. By vnderstandyng (the whych is the chylde of memory) thy Image … doth shyne in vs. By the wil … thy Image is knowen in vs.²¹

During her time as queen in the mid-1540s, Parr would come to be seen as centrally associated with the Reformist parties at work in Henry's court. Nonetheless, it is clearly erroneous to see her as self-consciously distancing herself from the influences of the Catholic piety that shaped her formative years and early adulthood. Her personal reading matter through this decade maintained a considerable level of diversity, and it even included varying treatments of such key matters as the sacrament of the Eucharist. Whereas Erasmus urged his reader that the 'memorie and power of [divine goodness] we do renew vnto vs, as oft as with feith and due reuerence we do eate the fleshe of the lorde, and drynke the blud', in one of her other volumes published in her final years, *A Declaration of the ten holy co[m]maundments*, John Hooper insisted 'Let those vntractable men iudge what they list of the Sacrament and holye supper of the lord. Beliue thow with the Scripture that it is but a memorie of Christ deathe'.²²

In keeping with traditions of patronage established by earlier Tudor women, Parr assumed an active role in sponsoring translation, notably that of the first volume into English of Erasmus's *Paraphrases of the New Testament*. Nicholas Udall was given a supervisory role for the project, and in the prefatory material he shows himself fully aware that in the mid-sixteenth century there were those who 'bee enemies to Erasmus wryting'. Nonetheless, he insisted that the responses of the narrow-minded 'procedeth more of their enuie, of their vnquietnes of minde … then of any faute or iust deserte in Erasmus'.²³ Parr's stepdaughter, the future Mary I, was persuaded to translate the paraphrase of St John's Gospel. Ultimately, owing to ill health, she would be prevented from completing it, but Susan

James savours the irony that '[Mary] began to translate a book that later as queen she would order destroyed as heretical'.[24] Udall translated the gospel of St Luke and Thomas Key that of St Mark; and, indeed, critical speculation dates back at least to the eighteenth century that Parr herself composed the English translation of Matthew's gospel.[25]

In their instructions concerning bidding prayers, the Edwardian Injunctions of 1547 specified that the young king's new subjects should be led to pray

> for the whole congregacion of Christes churche, & specially for this Churche of England and Ireland, wherin first I commende to your deuoute praiers, the kynges most excellent Maiestie, supreme head immediately vnder God, of the spiritualitie and temporaltie of the same Churche: and for Quene katharine dowagier, and also for my lady Mary & my lady Elizabeth, the kynges susters.[26]

The clergy was also duly informed that it was to provide

> within thre monethes next after this visitation, one boke of the whole Bible, of the largest volume in Englishe. And within one twelue monethes, next after the sayd visitation, the *Paraphrasis* of Erasmus also in Englishe upon the gospelles, and the same set vp in some conuenient place, within the sayd Churche, that they haue cure of, whereas their Parishioners may moste commodiously resort vnto the same and read the same.[27]

HENRICIAN POLITICAL CULTURES

Henry VIII's break with Rome in the 1530s was finally brought about by the Papal refusal to annul his marriage to Katherine of Aragon that had failed to produce a male heir. This breach clearly responded at least in part to a more widely felt desire by many of those at court, in government circles and among the landed gentry to circumscribe the existing powers and possessions in the realm of the Catholic Church. However, the case for radical ecclesiastical reform had long been been vigorously argued. The emphases of the humanists upon the re-evaluation of religious and moral commitments of the exemplary Christian, founded upon close analysis of writings from scripture and antiquity, had led to an ongoing debate across Europe upon the failings of the clergy and the duties of the laity. Nevertheless, if Henry VIII (who had received the title of 'Defensor Fidei' for his anti-Lutheran treatise of 1521) eventually broke with Rome, it was not to embrace the Protestant creed with any palpable zeal.

The first formal decrees against publications affirming anticlerical or Protestant beliefs date from 1530 and 1531 and targeted many individual works such as Simon Fish's *Supplication of the poore commons*, Frith's

Disputacion of Purgatorye and Tyndale's *Newe Testament* in English. The proscription of such tomes clearly points to ongoing sources of anxiety for the Henrician administration. In Fish's *Supplication*, for example, the Tudor monarch was reminded that although some voices insist that his law should be observed as 'the lawe of God geuen by Moyses', if these same laws 'dissent from or be contrary to anye one iote of the scripture, we muste with Jhon & Peter say. Acts. iiii Iudge you whether it be better for vs to obeye God or man'.[28] In the case of Tyndale's translation of the New Testament, despite open hostility on the part of the authorities, tens of thousands of copies had been circulating secretly since its publication in Germany in 1526. Interestingly, in his prefatory discussion, Tyndale would attribute a particularly significant role to the faculty of memory in the lives of the faithful, urging his readers:

let vs arme oure selues w^t this remembraunce that as christes workes iustifie from synne & set vs in ye fauoure of god[,] so oure awne dedes thorow workynge of ye spirite of God helpe vs to co[n]tynew in ye fauoure & ye grace into which christ hath brought vs & that we can no lenger co[n]tynew in fauoure & grace then oure hertes are to kepe the lawe.[29]

However, from the point of view of Henry's closest counsellors, Tyndale and his followers were corrupting all human faculties, not just that of memory. In his *Confutacyon of Tyndales answere* (1532–3), Thomas More thundered that 'Tyndales translacyon of the new testament was well worthy to be burned bycause it well shewed in y^t selfe y^t he had an euyll mynde translated y^t in such manner of wyse'.[30] More, like so many humanist scholars, viewed the business of cultural intervention as intimately bound up with a duty to remember in carefully delineated ways: as Greg Walker has justly stressed, such men 'looked to the past, as their education and training had taught them to do, for authentic models through which they could seek to redress the ills of the present'.[31] In the event, irrevocable political and religious upheaval would ultimately be driven by the changeful sexual career of the ageing Tudor monarch, rather than the long years of thorny theological debate.

The Act in Restraint of Appeals in 1533 endowed the realm with its own legal integrity subordinate to none, and clearly brought with it a widespread sense of foreboding. Thomas Elyot wrote in that very year to the ambassador Sir John Hackett in the Low Countries, 'I would that I had some comfortable news to send you out of these parts, but the world is all otherwise. I beseech our lord amend it. We have hanging over us a great cloud which is likely to be a great storm when it falleth.'[32] Elsewhere, the humanist scholar Thomas Lupset (who, as we have seen, was an author familiar to Parr and an intimate of one of Parr's close relatives, Cuthbert Tunstall) counselled one of his students two years later in 1535 against entering the fray of religious debate:

You falle in to presumption, when you grudge agaynste your rulers, though they be worthy of all disprayses. You presume, when you meddel with them, that be not vnder you ... Leue, therfore, my good Edmond, al maner of medlynge, and praye to god to accepte your obedience. Praye also bitterly, that his wyll may be fulfilled in this worlde among vs, as the angels fulfille it in heuen. Thus pray, and meddille no further.[33]

The medieval law prohibiting biblical translation was reversed in 1534, and in the following years English Bibles started to appear (albeit erratically) in churches. Among others, the question of women reading the Bible keenly exercised the minds of the authorities, with St Jerome, St Paul and Erasmus being frequently invoked in the debate. Tyndale's rendering of the Pentateuch and the New Testament would eventually be complemented by Miles Coverdale's translation of the remaining parts of the Old Testament to form what came to be known as the Great Bible, published officially in 1538–9. However, even with this Bible's appearance, the authorities were eager to specify that it was not to be read 'with loud and high voices, in time of the celebration of the holy mass', nor were laypersons to 'presume to take upon them any common disputation, argument, or exposition of the mysteries therein contained'.[34] In this context, it is interesting to note that, if Thomas Becon is to be believed, the diffusion of scripture in the vernacular at the end of the 1530s did not, in fact, require such rigorous regulation: 'But how many read it? Verily a many may come into some churches and see the Bible so enclosed and wrapped with dust ... that with his finger he may write upon the Bible this epitaph: *ecce nunc in pulvere dormio*, that is to say "behold I sleep now in the dust".'[35] Indeed, in her later publication *The Lamentacion of a synner* (1548) Parr herself is found to confess that 'it is a lamentable thing to heare howe there be many in yͤ worlde, that do not wel digest the reading of scripture, & doo commende and prayse Ignoraunce' (sig. F2ᵛ). Nonetheless, by May 1543, the 'Act for the Advancement of True Religion and for the Abolishment of the Contrary' decreed that unofficial translation of the Bible was illegal and a reading hierarchy was firmly established: noblemen might read to their families; well-to-do merchants and women of gentle birth could read it but not aloud within earshot of others for fear that they should be thought to teach; commoners were forbidden to read the Bible in English altogether. The Act of 1543 would have to wait for the accession of Henry's son to be reversed. Until that time, the unregulated 'Englishing' of the Bible was thought by the relevant authorities to be a threat to the prevailing practices of worship and indeed to public order: yet the greatest fear, it seems, was that the interpretative community for scripture would become so extensive owing to enhanced access to the Word of God that the very authority of those who held the temporal keys of the kingdom would be challenged.

PARR, AUTHORSHIP AND MEMORY

Such was the evolving religio-political climate that Parr negotiated in the period preceding her marriage to a Tudor monarch who was already approaching the final years of his life. During her earlier marital career she had encountered the committed Reformist beliefs of her first husband's father, Sir Thomas Borough (who would be appointed Anne Boleyn's chamberlain), and the distinctly conservative religious persuasions of her second husband, John Neville, Lord Latimer, who would be regarded with continuing suspicion by Henry VIII and Thomas Cromwell for his ambivalent role as hostage/spokesman among the rebels during the Pilgrimage of Grace in 1536. A little less than a decade later, when Parr published *Prayers or medytacions*, cultural anxiety surrounding religious debate had hardly abated.

In this collection Parr was concerned to preserve the powerful meditation upon human sinfulness and the stress upon humility that readers of the *Imitatio Christi* have found so penetrating down the centuries. If Parr's reader was reminded of the elevated status of the author on the title page of *Prayers or medytacions*, the text itself constantly points to the experiences of abjection to which the speaker is condemned and, more generally, to the vanity of all worldly things: 'And thoughe some haue mo geftes than other, yet they all procede from the' (*Prayers*, sig. B1^r). Dispensing with Kempis's dialogue structure involving Christ and the 'son', Parr turns in her own collection to a prose account that emphasises the inclusiveness and universalism of the human yearning for spiritual redemption. The first section of the *Prayers or medytacions* is organised for the most part around the outpourings of the sinning 'I' to a 'Moste benigne lorde Jesu': 'Yea whan I thynke my selfe to be sure and stronge, and that (as it semeth). I have the upper hande: sodeynly I feele my selfe readie to fall with a littell blaste of temptacion' (sig. A5^v); and, as the collection unfolds, it becomes increasingly evident that memory is called upon at regular intervals to fulfil a multiplicity of different roles. One of the notable ways in which Parr engages with the collective memory is through a strategy of dense scriptural referencing, which also underpins her source text, the *Imitatio*: 'And now what shal I say: but that thy will be done in me?' (*Prayers*, sig. B4ʳ–B4ᵛ). This proves to be a key narrative technique and aligns her with textual undertakings of a host of Reformist writers in the mid-sixteenth century. Her individuated account of spiritual reflection and painful retrospection is thus imbricated at almost every turn with scriptural memories of one kind or another. The importance of this emphasis in the textual consumption of scripture (and, by implication, the production of religious writing and commentary) had been underlined by William Tyndale himself for years in 'A prologe shewinge the vse of scripture' (1530), where he affirmed to his readers that, 'As thou readeste therfore thinke that every sillable pertayneth to thyne awne silf and sucke out the pithe of the scripture and arme thy silf ageynst all assaultes'.[36]

The strategic deployment of scriptural *topoi* in *Prayers or medytacions* operates at the level both of direct quotation and of paraphrase: 'For nothyng under the sonne maie longe abide, but all is vanitee and affliction of spirite' (Eccles. 1:14); 'to us pilgrims in earthe, [the everlasting day] shyneth obscurely, and as through a mirrour or glasse' (2 Pet. 1:19) (*Prayers*, respectively, sig. B3ᵛ, C1ʳ). As so often in Reformation literature, we are being urged in *Prayers or medytacions* to configure the spiritual journeying of the human soul through the lens of biblical narratives. More generally, if the internalisation of scriptural diction and narrative in the textual staging of spiritual travails was in evidence from the earliest productions of Reformist writers, it is clear that this undertaking is also intimately connected to the more secular concept of participation in the *civitas* inherited from antiquity whereby the speaking self was rhetorically constituted through vital acts of *memoria*: 'If thou vouchesafe to comforte me, be thou highly blessed: if thou wilte I live in trouble, and withoute comforte, be thou lykewyse euer blessed' (Job 1:21) (*Prayers*, sig. A3ᵛ). Scriptural diction and theology are thus carefully recalled in a sustained manner throughout Parr's 'medytacions', assisting the readers' own powers of memorial reflection. Yet the kind of intertextuality at work in this collection is not limited to the lifting of proofs from the Bible. In a meditative exercise closely associated with earlier practices of Catholic piety (and, indeed, with the thematic emphases of her later composition, *The lamentacion of a sinner*), Parr's speaker is drawn in the 'medytacions' to the climactic scene of the crucifixion as a narrative axis not only for spiritual self-scrutiny but also for pondering the obligation to remember incumbent upon those wishing to be saved: 'O what thankes ought I to geue unto the, whiche haste suffered the greuouse deathe of the Crosse, to delyuer me from my synnes, and to obteyne euerlastyng life for me?' (*Prayers*, sig. A4ʳ). Indeed, upon closer inspection, such sentiments emerge as an arresting leitmotif within the larger body of the text, articulating the central role that memory performs in the soul's search for spiritual healing: 'Make me to knowe and folowe thy wille, and to haue alwaies in my remembraunce thy manyfolde benefyttes' (sig. A8ᵛ).

While the narratives of *Prayers or medytacions* are constantly focused upon the need 'to purge awaie the ruste of sinne' (sig. C8ʳ) and upon the redemptive ethical power of memory for sinning souls (lumped together as 'we outlawes, the chyldren of Eve', sig. C1ʳ), her speaker remains haunted by a past riddled with failure and thwarted ambition in a manner distinctly reminiscent of narrative strategies adopted in Augustine's *Confessions*: 'Howe often haue I been dispoynted, where I thought I should haue founde frendshyp?' (sig. B8ʳ). Moreover, drawing upon a motif familiar from the Psalms that would speak so powerfully to the preacher Donne at the beginning of the next century, Parr's speaker confesses the sin of forgetfulness and submits, 'Pardon me and forgeue me, as oft as in my praier my minde is not surely fixed on the. For many tymes I am not there where I stande or syt: but rather there, whither my thoughtes carie me' (Ps. 139) (sig. C3ʳ–C3ᵛ). If the dominant focus of this collection remains very much upon the Christian's quest for spiritual self-knowledge, when appeals are voiced to the divine confessor, they are frequently accompanied by the painful recognition that the speaker's past is ever-present to heavenly scrutiny. At the very close of the 'medytacions', it is this very feature of celestial omniscience that is specifically privileged in the representation of the Godhead: 'Teache me, lorde, to fulfyll thy wyll … [for] thou arte he, that knowest me as I am, that knewest me before the worlde was made, and before I was borne or brought into this life' (Ps. 139) (sig. D1ʳ–D1ᵛ).

Throughout the *Prayers or medytacions* God is solicited implicitly, and then, finally, explicitly, to 'remembre thy mercyes' (sig. D1ʳ).[37] Counterpointing this promotion of divine recollection is an equally striking thematic interest in the cravings of the soul to be purged of its inclinations towards, and memories of, sinfulness – a narrative emphasis that (as will be explored in Chapter 6) looks back to the pervasive influence of the writings of St Bernard of Clairvaux in this period. Indeed, Richard Whitford's translation of the *Imitatio Christi*, which had such a preponderant influence upon Parr's collection, was published in 1531 as *The folowing of Christe with the Golden epistel of saynt Barnard*. In 1496 had appeared the first of three publications in early Tudor England of *The Meditations of Saint Bernard* in which the reader was reminded of the Augustinian division of the soul:

> I fynde thre thynges in my soule wherby I remembre[,] beholde & desyre my lorde god[.] The whiche ben. ye mynde. ye vndersto[n]dynge & wyl or loue. By the mynde I remember him ... Whan I remember god I fynde in hym in my mynde. & fele therin in him swetnesse & plesyre of hym. lyke as he vouchesaufe to gyue me.[38]

As was appreciated in the Introduction, Augustine's *Confessions* had on occasions envisaged memorial operations in terms of the motions of the body: 'just as food is brought from the stomach in the process of rumination, so also by recollection these things are brought up from the memory'.[39] This analogy would be drawn upon at length in Bernard's *De Conversione*[40] and clearly circulated widely in early modern print culture. Erasmus drew upon it, for example, in the *Enchiridion* ('thy memory the stomacke of thy soule'[41]), as did Donne.[42] However, in a dramatic image towards the close of her own 'medytacions', Parr has the body cleansed of such digestions and welcomes God the Physician as 'the heuenly leache of mannes soule, whiche strikest and healest, whiche bryngest a man nygh unto deathe, and after restorest hym to lyfe againe' (sig. c7^r). Interestingly, this redemptive vision of spiritual purgation is developed elsewhere into an active yearning on the part of the speaker for celestial oblivion: 'Sende foorthe the hotte flames of thy loue, to bourne and consume the cloudie fantasies of my mynde' (*Prayers*, sig. c3^r).

In general terms John N. King has argued persuasively that 'Reformation literature presupposes a major shift in mimetic theory. In opposition to the artistic externalization of religious feelings, Protestant subjectivity demands inner faith predicated upon spiritual understanding'.[43] The often obsessive depiction in Reformist writing of a fallen humanity frequently led to urgent appeals to the readership to return to the memory of personal sin in order to prepare the way for contrition and vigorous self-government in future conduct. In his preaching, Hugh Latimer continued to represent human life as an arduous combat against temptation, and the faculty of memory is often deployed in his perorations as a key weapon in the Christian's armoury:

> As for an ensample, I see a fayre woman, I like her very wel, I wish in my heart to haue her. Now withstand, this is a temptation. Shal I folow my affections?

No, no, call to remembraunce what the deuill is: call god to remembraunce and his lawes, consider what he hath commanded thee: say vnto god: Lord leade vs not into [damnation], but deliuer vs from euyll.⁴⁴

And in the prefatory verse to the second book of his *treatise of morall phylosophie contaynyng the sayinges of the wyse* (1547), another of Parr's contemporaries, William Baldwin, in turn viewed the exercise of memory as integral to the Christian's growth in spiritual knowledge about the very nature of mortality: 'Death the dissoluer of eche mortall bodye, | Dryueth all agayne to theyr fyrst matter dust. | Whiche whyle we lyue shulde put vs in memory | Fro whence we came, & hence, to what we must.'⁴⁵

This textual paradigm may be found widely in evidence elsewhere in meditative writing published in the period: in Henry Brinkelow's *The lamentacyon of a Christe[n] agai[n]st the citye of London for some certaine greate vyces vsed theri[n]* (1542) the Tudor capital itself presents a panorama of fallen humanity.⁴⁶ The Reformist tract ponders the flawed nature of the citizens repeatedly in the context of those abiding memories that circulated in the community concerning the practices and observances of the Catholic faith: 'Oh Lorde God how blind be these Cityzens, whych take so great care to prouyde for yᵉ deade, whych thynge is not commaunded them, nor avayleth the deade, no more then the pissing of a wrenne helpeth to cause the see to flowe at an extreme ebbe.'⁴⁷ Most signficantly in this instance, a narrative stress upon the doctrine of memorialism (which came to be centrally associated with the Swiss theologian Ulrich Zwingli) underpins many of Brinkelow's spiritual reflections:

the Sacrament of thankes geuinge, is to vs a signe, a token, a spyrituall memorye of our spirituall deliueraunce ... the same faith which saueth vs, saued the olde fathers: for they beleued throughe yᵗ outwarde sygne that a redeamer shulde come, and we through the memory of thys holy Sacrament of thanckes geuynge beleue yᵗ he is come, and hath fullfylled all that was of him prophecied ... thys holy sygne putteth vs in remembrance for the same to be thanckefull to the Lorde.⁴⁸

THE LAMENTACION OF A SINNER

On 5 November 1547, some ten months after Henry VIII's death, Parr (now newly married to Thomas Seymour) published *The lamentacion of a sinner, made by yᵉ most vertuous Ladie, Quene Caterin, bewayling the ignoraunce of her blind life; set furth and put in print at the instaunt delite of the righte gracious ladie Caterin Duchesse of Suffolke, & the earnest requeste of the right honourable Lord, William Parre, Marquesse of Northampton*.

In many ways this whole collection would seek to privilege spiritual undertakings in terms of both painful retrospection and the expression of contrite humility, and it remains difficult to believe that this ambitious publication dates wholly from the Edwardian period. Janel Mueller has persuasively linked its early circulation to surviving correspondence from the later years of Henry's reign: in 1545, Sir William Paget, one of the royal secretaries, sent a package to Stephen Gardiner, Bishop of Winchester, containing a number of other works that may plausibly have included both a version of Parr's *The lamentacion of a sinner* and also Brinkelow's recently published tract.[49] In a reply dated November of that same year, Gardiner (who had officiated at the royal marriage in 1543) betrays his outrage at the content of the writings sent to him and reserves some special comments for some of the reading matter: 'Mary, to the books of Lamentacion which your sent me, I wyl oonly answer lamentably to youe, and, lamentyng with youe, counforte myself; digesting in thiese letters so moch displeasour as I receyved in reding of this most abhominable booke.'[50] Indeed, it remains all too possible that Gardiner's rage would have been triggered by the reading of a 'Lamentacion' such as Parr's in which the speaker is repeatedly found to demonise the Catholic religion and to revisit the past only to uncover more evidence of her own fallen ways when she was prey to the practices of the 'old faith':

> I forsoke the spirituall honoryng of ye true liuyng god, & worshipped visible idoles, and ymages made of mennes handes, beleuing by them to haue gotten heauen, yea to say ye truthe, I made a great ydol of my selfe: for I loved my selfe better then god … but the children of light … are led by the spirite of god to the knowledge of the truthe, & therfore they discerne and iudge all thinges right, and knowe from whence they cum, euen from the bishop of Rome, & his membres, the headspring of al pride, vainglorie, ambicion, hipocrisie, and faired holynes.[51]

The narrative of the ways in which the religious conservatives at court came to focus their disaffection upon Henry's last queen would be memorialised later in the century in Foxe's *Acts and Monuments*.[52] As queen, Parr discovered that the main lines of attack which her enemies chose were to associate her with the alleged heretic Anne Askew and with the possession of prohibited books.[53] By February 1546, such was Parr's anxiety surrounding her parlous state as Henry's consort that, as Susan E. James observes, 'she ordered new coffers for her chamber, with new locks, metal hinges, corner bands and handles with nails'.[54] Given this context, it is perhaps unsurprising that Parr would delay the publication of her most important devotional work *The lamentacion of a sinner* until after the death of

Henry, whose Protestant sympathies (where they existed) were of a much more restrained and opportunistic nature than those of his last wife.

It is all too likely that *The lamentacion of a sinner*'s explicitly Lutheran character, with its acknowledgement of the doctrine of Justification by Faith and its commitment to scripture available in the vernacular, would have met with rather more than short shrift in the mid-1540s as the king retreated increasingly into religious conservatism. Parr's speaker in *The lamentacion of a sinner* confesses:

> Saynt Paule sayeth, we be iustified by the fayth in Christe, & not by the deades of the lawe. For if rightwisenes cum by the lawe, then Christ died in vayne … This dignitie of fayth is no derogacion to good workes, for oute of this fayth springeth all good workes. Yet we may not impute to the worthines of fayth or workes, our Iustification before god.⁵⁵

Luther's *Liberty of a Christian Man* (1520) had stated that 'as the Soule hathe neede of the only word, to obteyne reighteousnesse and life, euen so it is iustifyed by onely faith, and no workes'.⁵⁶ However, this doctrine was to prove a persistent stumbling-block for Henry VIII after his break with Rome. At the end of May 1543, *The King's Book or A Necessary Doctrine and Erudition for Any Christian Man* clearly rejected Justification by Faith among other Reformist commitments, such as the discarding of masses for the dead. Nonetheless, in the later 1547 *Book of Homilies*, promulgated at the beginning of his son's reign, the doctrine would be firmly readopted by the authorities: 'thei whiche glister and shine in good workes, without faithe in God, be like dead men, whiche haue goodly & precious tombes, and yet it availeth them nothyng'.⁵⁷

REMEMBERING ONESELF: PARR AND CONTROVERSY

Apart from Thomas Bentley's anthology *The monument of matrones* (1582), which collected together Parr's writings with those of a number of other eminent Tudor women (including those of the dedicatee herself, Elizabeth I), Foxe's *Acts and Monuments* proved to be one of the key resources that was generally available to the wider population for the memorialisation of Parr's political career. In this narrative it was in 1546 that Parr incurred the disfavour of Henry for being perceived to lecture him with her forthright Reformist views during one of their more public audiences. Stephen Gardiner, Bishop of Winchester, is then seen by Foxe to lead the conspiracy against Parr. This involved the attempted indictment of some ladies-in-waiting and the queen for ownership of forbidden books, and the violent interrogation of Askew. The Bill of Articles drawn up against her by the conspirators fortuitously came into Parr's hands, and the extent of the conspiracy was confirmed by the royal physician, one Dr Wendy, in whom Henry had (strategically?) confided. After a due period of agitation, Parr stages her submission to Henry and it is recorded by Foxe in the following manner:

> Your Maiestie (quoth she) doth right well know, neither I my self am ignoraunt, what great imperfection & weakenes by our first creation, is alotted vnto vs women, to be ordeyned and appoynted as inferiour and subiect vnto man as our head, from whiche head all our direction ought to procede … how then commeth it now to passe that your Maiestie in such diffuse causes of Religion, will seme to require my Iudgement? Whiche when I haue vttered and sayd what I can, yet must I and will I referre my Iudgement in this and all other cases to your Maiesties wisedome, as my onely anker, supreme head, and gouerner here in earth next vnder God, to leane vnto.[58]

In Foxe's text Parr's submission is primarily significant as an enabling factor for the continuing evolution of the Protestant Church in the British Isles, but it is also significant in textually enacting the ritual of a woman being called upon to 'remember herself' – the labour in this instance is to reconstitute with circumspection that which had been 'undone' with forgetfulness. Here, Parr is shown to belittle her own intellectual potential in terms of physical weakness: by the end of Foxe's narrative, the survival of the Reformist cause *and* radically imbalanced gender relations have been assured.

The whole question of access to and the interpretation of scripture by the laity of whatever sex or rank remained, as we have seen, a highly contentious issue throughout the century – a period in which, as A. G. Dickens pointed out, 'all English books, even the more innocent-seeming *Prick of Conscience* and the *Shepherd's Calendar*, tended to bring suspicion upon proletarian owners'.[59] The laity had always been allowed access to the Latin Vulgate, but its ability to engage with it on any but the most superficial of levels was questioned by the Reformers: indeed, the preface to the first Edwardian Prayer Book (1549) lamented later that 'the seruice in this Churche of England (these many yeares) hath been read in Latin to the people, whiche they understoode not; so that they haue heard with theyr eares onely; and their hartes, spirite, and minde, haue not been edified thereby'.[60] However, church law passed in 1408 (and supported by subsequent anti-Wycliffite statutes) prohibited the translation of scripture into English unless permitted by bishops. Allied to the cultural obstacles faced by the woman writer in the sixteenth century must be those associated with the Protestant anxieties surrounding the very act of putting pen to paper. Protestant subjectivity had grave misgivings about textual creativity, about the Sidneian clash between 'the erected wit' and 'the infected will': might writing itself not constitute a temptation away from the all-important business of scriptural study? might it not deliver the would-be writer into a state of falseness, self-assertion and ungodliness? Later in the century, Sidney would lament, 'mine own writings like bad servants show | My wits, quick in vain thoughts, in virtue lame' (*Astrophil and Stella*, xxi, 3–4). However, the Reformist writer in the early Tudor period frequently sought cultural legitimation through the explicit and sustained referencing of scripture. In *De instituendis ministris* (1523), Luther had submitted importantly for his followers that 'Nos puram et germanam divinis literis praescriptam rationem quaerimus, parum solliciti quid usus, quid Patres in hac re vel dederint vel fecerint' ['We seek the pure and genuine system, prescribed in holy scripture, and are little concerned about what custom or the Fathers have given us or done in this matter'].[61] Such declarations would indeed give added weight to the widespread assertion in early modern faith communities that the cycles of experience detailed in biblical narrative were played out in microcosm in the everyday lives of the present *as through a glass darkly*.

REMEMBERING PARR

In the event, Parr's *The lamentacion of a sinner* would not enjoy the popularity of its predecessor in terms of re-publication, with only four editions during the sixteenth century rolling from the presses. However, there are a host of stylistic and thematic continuities in evidence between it and the *Prayers or medytacions*. In direct comparison with the earlier collection, Parr is found to return repeatedly to a memorial staging of the crucifixion as the dominant theatre through which the individual's relationship with the divine might be articulated:

Sainct Paule desired to knowe nothing but Christ crucified after he had ben rapt into the thirde heauen ... Truly it maye be most iustely verified y^t to behold Christ crucified, in spirite, is the best meditacion that can be. I certeynlye neuer knewe myne own miseries, and wretchednes so wel, by booke, admonicion, or learnyng, as I haue doen by lokyng into the spirituall booke of the crucifix. I lamente muche I haue passed so many yeares, not regardyng the diuine booke, but I iudged, and thought my self to be well instructed in the same: whereas nowe, I am of this opinion, that y^f God woulde suffre me to lyue here a M.yeare, and should studye continually in the same diuine booke, I should not be fylled with the contemplacion therof.[62]

More generally, if the lamentations of Parr's speaker often gravitate towards vividly realised expressions of abjection ('for in my selfe I fynde nothing to saue me, but a donghill of wyckednes, to condemne me', sig. B1^r), spiritual weakness ('for I am so ignorant, blinde, weake & feble, that I cannot bring my selfe out of this intangled & weyward mase', sig. B1^r) and frail humanity ('I can not aske forgeuenes nor be repentante or sory for [my sins]. There is no man can auowe that Christe is the only Sauiour of the world: but by the holy ghost', sig. B1^v), such accounts are consistently bound up with the textual revelation of a remembering self: 'What cause nowe haue I to lament, mourne, sigh & wepe for my life, & time so evil spent?' (sig. A7^v).

Inevitably, the more sophisticated range of narrative demands that this continuous prose account places upon its reader means that *The lamentacion of a sinner* has attracted more scholarly attention than the *Prayers or medytacions*. For the first edition of *The lamentacion of a sinner*, a prefatory letter by William Cecil, Elizabeth's future Lord Burghley and at this time secretary to the Protector Somerset, introduced the dowager queen's meditations and memorialised her for future generations: here, the 'moste gentle & Christian reader' is encouraged to recall that the author is no ordinary woman, but 'a woman of highe estate … refusing the worlde wherin she was loste, to obteyne heauen wherin she maye be saued'. Sixteenth-century readers were thus invited not only to attend to the writings of this eminent personage but to celebrate her deliverance from Catholic 'supersticion, wherwith she was smothered, to enbrace trew Religion, wherewith she may reuiue'. Interestingly, at the close of his prefatory address, Cecil configures Parr as a universal role model for future ages: 'see thou her confession, that thou maist lerne her repentaunce: practyse her perseueraunce, that thou mayest haue like amendemente: displease thy selfe, in eschewing vice, that thou mayste please god in askynge grace'.[63] She becomes in this way both a paragon of Christian virtue and of especial value as an example to women of rank in Tudor society:

> let us therefore now fede by thys gracious quenes example, and be not ashamed to become in confession publicanes, since thys noble lady wyll be no Pharesie. And to all ladies of estate I wish as ernest minde to folowe our quene in vertue, as in honour: that they might ones appere to prefer god before the worlde: and be honorable in religion, whiche nowe be honorable in vanyties: so shall they (as in some vertuouse ladies of right high estate it is with greate comforte seen) taste of this fredome of remission of the euerlastyng blisse.[64]

In *The lamentacion of a sinner* Parr departs significantly from the prevailing conventions of patronage and translation inherited from previous

Tudor female luminaries, adopting a meditative prose narrative of spiritual journeying for which her main textual models would have been predominantly male-authored.[65] As we have seen, towards the end of the reign of an increasingly conservative Henry VIII, the queen was finding herself under attack from conspiracies at court and from speculation that her husband might readopt Anne of Cleves or choose a seventh wife. It is thus highly unlikely that she would have wished to draw undue attention to herself as a devotional writer and a committed Lutheran by publicly voicing the sentiments contained in *The lamentacion of a sinner*: 'And euen as much talke of the worde of God, without practicing the same in our lyuing is euill and destestable in the sight of god, so it is a lamentable thyng to heare howe there by manye in ye worlde, that do not wel digest the reading of scripture, & doo commende and prayse Ignoraunce' (sig. F2ᵛ).

Susan James has argued that 'the uncompromising androgyny of the text is underscored by [Parr's] description of Christ as one who impersonated virtues commonly bestowed upon women'.[66] Nonetheless, if Parr's speaker remains for the most part ungendered, it is characterised by much greater individuation than is the case in the *Prayers or medytacions* – and this individuation is articulated in terms of vivid powers of recollection, most particularly in the opening sections of *The lamentacion of a sinner*. Indeed, the opening address is wholly devoted to the business of retrospection and how the dissection of the past may be seen to have shaped the present state of spiritual awakening:

When I considre, in the bethinking of myne euill, & wretched former life, myne obstynate, stony, and untractable herte, to haue so much exceded in euilnes, yt it hath not only neglected, yea contemned, & dispised goddes holy preceptes & commaundementes: But also enbraced, receyved, and estemed vayne, folish and feyned trifles: I am partely by the hate I owe to sinne, who hath reygned in me, partely by the loue I owe to all Christians whom I am contente to edifye, euen with thexample of mine owne shame, forced and constrayned with my harte and wordes, to confesse and declare to the world, howe ingrate, negligent, unkynde, and stubberne I haue bene to god my Creatour: and howe beneficiall, mercyfull, and gentill, he hath ben always to me his creature, beyng suche a miserable and wretched sinner.[67]

As the narrative unfolds, the dissolute past is returned to compulsively ('I lamente muche I haue passed so many yeares, not regardyng that diuine boke', sig. D2ᵛ–D3ʳ) as the scene of a crime from which enhanced knowledge of the self may be pieced together: 'I called supersticion, godly meaning, and true holynes, erroure. The lord did speake many pleasant and swete wordes vnto me, and I woulde not heare' (sig. A2ᵛ–A3ʳ). The speaker recounts that, in an unredeemed past,

> the bloud of Christe was not reputed by me, sufficient for to wassh me from the fylth of my sinnes: neyther suche wayes he hath appoynted by his word. But I sought for suche rifraf as the bishoppe of Rome hath planted in his tyranny and kingdom, trusting with greate confidence by the vertue & holynes of them, to receyue full remission of my sinnes.[68]

In this way, Parr invests in a narrative tableau whereby a contrite speaker offers up a sinful past to the scrutiny of an omnipotent, if not forbidding, Godhead: 'Tourne not thy face from me, deferre not thy visityng of me, ne withdraw not thy comfortes, lest happely my soule be made as drie earthe without the water of grace' (*Prayers or medytacions*, sig. DI'). This kind of textual paradigm is clearly in evidence at regular intervals throughout the *Prayers or medytacions*, but Parr chooses to re-present it in much less abstract terms for the opening sections of the *lamentacion*. In this more ambitious, multivocal text, the insights relating to the speaker's failings are played off against accounts of the erring ways of those still trapped in the practices of the faith of the past. The speaker thus wishes to distance him- or herself from those who continue to believe 'theyr dead, human, historical faith, & knowlage (which thei haue learned in their scholastical bokes)', while acknowledging that all of God's creatures are called to bear the memory of sin and that this together with the soul's agonised yearning for grace must ultimately be surrendered up to divine scrutiny: 'And although the dregges of Adam doe remayne, that is our concupiscences, which in dede be sinnes: neuertheless they be not Imputed for sinnes, yf we be truly planted in Christe' (*The lamentacion of a sinner*, sig. B6ᵛ, C4ᵛ). The sophisticated intertextual nature of the *lamentacion* is becoming increasingly evident as the work itself succumbs to a succession of detailed and illuminating critical analyses.[69] Apart from scriptural influences (most notably those of the Psalms) upon this narrative collection, the textual voices of Erasmus, John Fisher, Bishop of Rochester, William Tyndale, Thomas Cranmer, Hugh Latimer and St John Chrysostom (among others) have been identified as significant sources for Parr's wide-ranging narrative. Yet in addition to this gathering together of a host of voices from the present and the past Parr endows her meditation with a much greater specificity of utterance than is to be found in the *Prayers or medytacions*. Interestingly, this has prompted Janel Mueller to claim *The lamentacion of a sinner* as 'the first conversion narrative in English'.[70] During Edward VI's reign, the business of government was managed initially by his uncle, Edward Seymour, Duke of Somerset and Protector of the Realm, and subsequently by John Dudley, Duke of Northumberland and President of the Privy Council. As John N. King has pointed out, the Protectorate saw an enormous widening in toleration in terms of Reformist affiliations and publications in evidence in England: 'three out of four books printed under Seymour dealt with religion. Only during the Puritan Revolution did the proportion of religious publications exceed that of the Reformation press.'[71]

Developing Parr's profile further as a politically committed writer, Susan Wabuda contends that 'when Parliament assembled in the autumn of [1547], the old Act for the Advancement of True Religion was under fire, with Katherine Parr and the godly Duchess of Suffolk leading a propaganda campaign against it. The printing of Katherine's *The lamentacion of a sinner* was timed to coincide with Parliament's meeting'.[72] However, the case for Parr's role as a politically militant voice in Edwardian print culture has still to be made convincingly. Unsurprisingly, the newly formed administration was eager not to have the dowager queen aligned with any powerful magnate (Seymour was one of the king's uncles), and most especially in the months immediately following Henry's death when there still might be a possibility that she was pregnant. Nevertheless, in January 1547 Parr married Thomas Seymour in private. In the early years of Edward's reign, Parr could not escape the political fall-out surrounding her secret marriage, nor was her situation helped by embittered wrangles with the Protector's wife over questions of social precedence and the government's refusal to return jewels that Henry had apparently promised her on his deathbed. Furthermore, her religious persuasions continued to attract attention from an international audience. Dakota L. Hamilton notes that the Reformist Heinrich Bullinger received word from a correspondent that Parr continued to sympathise with the Protestant creed. Elsewhere, a report from the Imperial ambassador suggested that Parr was encouraged in her Reformist faith by the Duchess of Suffolk, the Countess of Dorset and Lady Lisle. By the end of 1547, the Imperial ambassador reported that mass was no longer being celebrated in her household or those of the Protector and the Earl of Warwick.[73] As the following year wore on, much of Parr's time was focused upon her forthcoming confinement. In the event, in September 1548, she died of a puerperal fever five days after giving birth to a daughter Mary. Miles Coverdale, who had been appointed as her almoner after the death of Henry VIII, preached her funeral sermon.

One of the primary ways in which Parr has been memorialised in the popular imagination is as the only one of Henry's wives to survive him.

However, even this abiding belief is erroneous. In fact, Anne of Cleves outlived Parr and travelled to the coronation of Mary in a state coach. More generally reflecting upon Parr's profile as an Edwardian author, Susan James stresses that during the summer of 1547, 'so ribald were the jests made at her expense that Seymour had attempted to get an Act of Parliament passed condemning public slander against the queen. Royal lamentations by [Parr] in November 1547 over sins she had committed would have had all too specific an interpretation for the backbiters at court and the wags in city taverns'.[74] The distressed sinner in *The lamentacion of a sinner* would plead, 'Beholde lorde howe I come to the, a sinner, sycke, & greuously wounded: I aske not breade, but the crummes that fall from the children's table' (sig. B1^r). Carole Levin has attributed Parr's ability to survive the anxiety-ridden final years of the Henrician era to her willingness to play 'a traditionally submissive and sexually chaste role'; and in the sixteenth century Foxe had invited his reader to arrive at a somewhat similar conclusion that, 'besides the vertues of the mynd, [Parr] was endued with very rare giftes of nature, as singular beautie, fauour, and comely personage, beyng thinges wherin the king was greatly delighted: and so enioyed she ye kynges fauour'.[75] Subsequently, he chose to inscribe the beleaguered Parr in a much more heroic discourse:

But, see what ye Lord God (who fro[m] his eternall throne of wisdome, seeth and dispatcheth al the inuentions of Archithophel, and comprehe[n]deth the wyly beg[u]ily, themselues) dyd for hys poore handmaiden, in rescuing her from the pyt of ruine, whereunto she was ready to fall vnawares.[76]

Nonetheless, the memorialisation of Parr even within critical scholarship remains unresolved. In Roland H. Bainton's study of Reformation women, for example, she must count herself fortunate indeed not be included under the heading of 'The negligible Wives of Henry VIII': in this fold, Anne of Cleves and the 'docile' Jane Seymour are joined by Catherine Howard, who is censured as 'an imprudent minx' for her promiscuity: it appears, however, their husband's sexual career does not merit censure. Parr has an equally diminutive status in David Loades's most recent review of Tudor queens in which she emerges from her first widowhood as 'passably good looking and sexually frustrated' – for good measure, he also notes that as a published author she 'attracted rather more praise and attention from humanist scholars and ecclesiastics than she strictly deserved'.[77] In direct contrast, Susan James hails 'the first Queen of England to write and publish her own books and to become a recognized author during her lifetime, and the first Englishwoman to publish a work of prose in the sixteenth century'; and Janel Mueller invites her reader to reflect that, 'if the categories of the compilation and the familiar letter are excluded, Katherine Parr is the first certain instance in English of a woman writer'.[78] Interestingly, in the decades that followed the publications of *Prayers or medytacions* and *The lamentacion of a sinner*, these textual accounts of the arduous but urgent duties of spiritual recollection tended to be displaced by larger cultural appetites for narratives recalling her as a political player. Many of those looking back to the records and testimonies of the 1540s would follow in Foxe's footsteps and cast her with a modest, but noteworthy role in the history of the nation's 'Reformation'. With reference to the early modern reception of her memory, Parr appears to have been chiefly characterised in terms of her Reformist piety and her persecution at the hands of others.

By way of conclusion, it might be added that the posthumous publication of George Sandys's *Anglorum speculum, or, The worthies of England in church and state* (1684) would not appear unrepresentative in seeking to limn her for future ages by attributing to her a discreet heroism – it seems that the strategic recuperation of her memory for wider consumption would concentrate for centuries not upon her authoring identity but upon her spiritual commitments and, most significantly, upon her marital career.

She was a great Favourer of the Gospel, and would earnestly argue for it. Once politick *Gardiner* had almost got her into his Clutches, had not Divine Providence delivered her. Yet a *Jesuit* (who was neither Confessor nor Privy-Councellour to the King) tells us, that the King intended, if longer surviving, to behead her for an Heretick – She was afterwards Married to Sir *Thomas Seymour* Baron of *Sudeley*, and Lord Admiral, and dyed in Child-bed of a Daughter 1548.[79]

CHAPTER 3

'Better a few things well pondered, than to trouble the memory with too much': troubling memory and martyr in Foxe's Acts and Monuments

> Better a few thinges well pondered, then to trouble ye memory with to much, you shall preuayle more with praying, the[n] with studying, though mixture be best. For so one shall alleuiate the tediousnes of the other. I entend not to contend much with them in wordes, after a reasonable account of my fayth geuen: for it shall be but in vayne. They will say, as theyr fathers sayd, when they haue no more to say. We haue a law, and by our law he ought to dye. Be ye steadfast and vnmoueable sayeth Saynt Paule, and agayne, *persistito*, stand fast. And how oft is this repeated, if ye abide, if ye abide. &c. But we shall be called obstinate, sturdy, ignorant, heady, and what not? So that a man hath need of much pacience, hauing to do with such men.
>
> John Foxe, *Acts and Monuments* (1583), p. 1718[1]

This is just one of a number of interventions that John Foxe attributed to Hugh Latimer in his extended discussions with his fellow prisoner Nicholas Ridley in the year 1555.[2] The ordeals of Latimer and Ridley in their journeys towards trial and execution number among the most famous and most often cited narratives of Foxe's *magnum opus* described in the 1583 edition as the *Acts and monuments of matters most speciall and memorable, happenyng in the Church with an vniuersall history of the same, wherein is set forth at large the whole race and course of the Church, from the primitiue age to these latter tymes of ours, with the bloudy times, horrible troubles, and great persecutions agaynst the true martyrs of Christ, sought and wrought as well by heathen emperours, as nowe lately practised by Romish prelates, especially in this realme of England and Scotland*.[3] In their exchanges both Latimer and Ridley not only seek to defend their doctrinal position in opposition to that of their Catholic persecutors, we also find them centrally concerned with diverse forms of remembering, and pondering the act of being remembered. Furthermore, in this, they are representative of a whole host of different martyrs portrayed throughout the huge collection. In direct comparison with many other

Foxean 'worthies', Latimer is seen to subscribe to an Augustinian position whereby recollection may facilitate access to a higher spiritual truth and a renewed commitment to faith.

More broadly, throughout *The Acts and Monuments* it is made repeatedly apparent that the faculty of memory not only yields valuable insights into any understanding of human epistemology, it also constitutes an indispensable resource for true Christian worship. In the depiction above of his captivity, Latimer is discovered drawing upon his rhetorical training as a scholar: by recalling select fragments from scriptural apophthegms, the divine is seen to formulate an appropriate *ethos*, to shape a legitimate and authoritative self, with which to confront his accusers. Repeatedly exploiting such arresting images of the faithful beset by enemies, Foxe hailed both Latimer and Ridley as 'two … speciall & singuler Captaines, & principall pillers of Christes Churche … of whose famous doinges & memorable learning, & incomparable ornaments & giftes of grace, ioyned with no lesse co[m]mendable sincerity of lyfe, as all the Realme canne witnes sufficiently' (*Acts* [1583], p. 1717). The chronicler not only retraced with his sources the doings and sayings of such martyrs, he framed accounts with his own narrative emphases upon remembering as a crucial obligation for his readers that would inevitably lead onto their own personal acts of spiritual witness.[4] Indeed, he insisted that 'the tragical story and life of Dr. Ridley, I thought good to commend to chronicle, and leave to perpetual memory; beseeching thee (gentle reader) with care and study well to peruse, diligently to consider, and deeply to print the same in thy brest' (*Acts* [1583], p. 1717).[5] At the beginning of the sixteenth century, Juan Luis Vives had cautioned that

> We be framed and facioned by these three things, knowledge, wit, & Memory, & the diligence whiche we use to the atteyning of them, is called study. Wit is quickened by exercise and memory encreased by diligent tillinge and occupienge thereof: delicate handelynge weakeneth them both … Whether thou rede or here ani thing, do it with attention and effectuously, let not thy mind wander, but constraine it to be there, and to do that thyng, whych is in hande, and none other.[6]

Such attentive preoccupation with the nursing and cherishing of the precious faculty figured prominently in intellectual debate across the length and breadth of the early modern period. At the very end of the sixteenth century, A.P.'s prefatory discussion to Sir John Hayward's ill-timed *first part of the life and raigne of King Henrie the IV* (1599) also invested in Augustinian analogy, proclaiming, 'who are to be better accompted then they whose memory is as it were a rich storehouse, of the experiences not of one age or Country, but of all times and of all nations'.[7]

More generally, the central position of memorial training in pedagogic theories of the sixteenth century (and indeed later) is widely apparent in the documents of the period, and is regularly reaffirmed in the course of *The Acts and Monuments*. This may be exemplified in Foxe's record of 'The report of the Princes [Edward VI's] Scholemaister, in commendation of his towardnes to the Archb.'. Here, the exceptional nature of this future sovereign committed to the 'true faith' is demonstrated in no uncertain terms with an account of his extraordinary powers of recollection:

[Edward] hath learned almoste foure bookes of Cato to construe, to parse, and to say wythout booke. And of his owne courage nowe in the latter Booke hee will needes haue at one time 14. Verses which he konneth pleasantly and perfectly, besides things of the Bible, *Satellitium Viuis*, Æsops Fables, and Latin making, whereof he hath sent your Grace a little tast.[8]

However, it quickly becomes evident that the young prince is far from being the sole model of memorial prowess in Foxe's huge textual gallery of extraordinary specimens of humanity.

THE PRODUCTION OF MEMORY

The cultural undertaking of commemoration continued to preoccupy Foxe in a variety of ways throughout his publishing career. In some prefatory remarks to the *Pandectae locurum communium* (1572), he had enquired, 'what can poets, what can historians, what can rhetoricians, and orators … provide by their art without memory?'[9] In *The Acts and Monuments* memory lay once again at the very heart of his authorial motivations, and, as the project grew in magnitude, every effort was made to ensure that no precious detail of Catholic persecution down the ages would be allowed to slip the attention of his pen. The preliminary versions of the work were published in Latin on the Continent in 1554 and 1558 during the reign of Mary I, and then expanded to twice the original length into English in 1563 when her half-sister Elizabeth was on the throne. The next edition of *The Acts and Monuments* was reworked for 1570 and expanded significantly once again: from 1,471 folio pages in 1563 to 2,314 in 1570. (The later editions in Foxe's lifetime in 1576 and 1583 also underwent further revisions.) In the editions of 1563 and 1583, Foxe appended to the main body of text a 'Kalender of Martyrs' in which Tudor Protestants who had been burnt at the stake jostled for position with New Testament figures to be commemorated on an annual basis. This additional document, together with a series of woodcut images dispersed throughout the volume (expanded in number from 53 in 1563 to over 150 in the 1570 edition) established the publication as the preeminent vehicle in English for celebrating the martyrs of the Reformed faith.[10] Both the 'Kalender' and the woodcut images constituted supplementary memorial devices, an explicitly Reformist expression of the *ars memorativa*, which was deployed to signal momentous scenes of persecution. Given the enormous complexity of the operations at the presses to bring the work into the public domain, it is little wonder that John N. King terms this 'The largest and most complicated English printing venture of its age'.[11] Indeed, *The Acts and Monuments* continued to be published on into the seventeenth century and it has been estimated that by the ninth edition in 1684 there were some ten thousand copies in circulation.[12] Clearly, the early career of the volume could only have been enhanced when a meeting of Convocation in 1571 decided that 'Euery Archbishop and bishop shall haue in hys house The holy Bible in the largest volume, as it was lately printed at London, and also that full and perfect history, which is intituled Monumentes of Martyres', in addition to copies being 'bestowed in … Cathedrall Church[es], in such conuenient place, that the vicares … and other ministers of the Church, as also straungers and forieners may easelie come vnto them, and read thereon'.[13] By 1577, William Harrison observed of Elizabeth's court that

everye offyce hath eyther a Byble, or the bookes of the Actes and monumentes of the Church of Englande, or both, beside some hystoryes and Chronicles lying therin … whereby the straunger that entereth into the court of Englande vpon the sodeine, shall rather imagine himselfe to come into some publicke schoole of ye vniuersities … than into a Princes Pallace.[14]

In the compiling of his work Foxe was unsurprisingly indebted to a host of earlier scholars who had worked upon the history of the Christian Church, most notably to the fourth-century bishop Eusebius of Caesarea's *Ecclesiastical History* for the accounts of the sufferings of the Early Church martyrs.[15] Beginning his project during the period of Marian exile, Foxe found himself confronting the thorny question of how an enquiry (which extended across a chronological span from the travails of the Early Church to the final persecutions during the reign of Mary I) might resist the all too evident forces of social amnesia and neglect, and renew itself effectively for succeeding generations of Reformist readers. Certainly, one of the strategies he adopted was to represent the resistance to persecution by Catholics and tyrants and the bearing of spiritual witness (most especially that of Reformists) in magnificently *heroic* terms.[16] Elsewhere, he frequently attended specifically to the eternal nature of God's truth and the continuities of human experience across the centuries to the Tudor present. With this great work, Foxe wished to fashion the still lively memories of the Tudor martyrs into a prosthetic collective memory, a supplementary sacred space of collective commemoration. Thus, we are greeted with a grand birthing narrative for the Reformist faith in which the extraordinary actions and the written records of the martyrs become 'precious monuments' and constitute things 'meet to be recorded … [rather than] buried vnder the darkenes of obliuion' (*Acts* [1583], sig. *vi^r). In his address to 'Christian Protestantes, Professours of the Gospell', his readers are instructed, as they subsequently leaf through the volume, that they are to consider 'the times that haue bene, the times that bee, and the times that may come, how we stand, and by whom we stand' (sig. ¶ii^v).

Foxe's authorial ambitions for the *Acts and Monuments* met with a great measure of success.[17] Sharon Achinstein has stressed that 'Aside from the Bible, this work was the key printed text that shaped English Protestantism', and Richard Helgerson has argued equally energetically that 'No books, with the obvious exception of the English Bible and the Book of Common Prayer, have had a greater part in shaping England's religious self-understanding than Foxe's *Acts* and Hooker's *Laws*'.[18] Therefore, it is all the more interesting to ponder the frequency with which Foxe's protagonists themselves examine the very various spiritual, intellectual and political obligations that the cultural pressures of remembering may impose. They are repeatedly discovered reflecting upon the figures that they will assume in the society after their executions. Even apparently minor actions committed by the martyrs are often related to anxieties concerning their subsequent memorialisation. In the case of Thomas Cranmer such actions are given a characteristically moral emphasis: 'In the smal tyme of respite betwene Kynge Edwardes deathe, and hys owne imprisonment, he solde hys plate, and payed all hys debtes, so that no ma[n] could ask him a grote, althoughe thereby, and by the spoyle of hys goodes, after hys attainder he left hys wyfe and chyldren vnprouided' (*Acts* [1563], pp. 1478–9). Elsewhere, as was witnessed above in the account of the young Edward VI, descriptions of the extraordinary powers of recollection can be seen actively to feed into the ongoing celebration of the Foxean 'worthy'. Thomas Cromwell's exceptional intellectual ability, for example, is clearly highlighted by way of preparing the reader for his singular spiritual commitment:

such was the actiuitie and forward rypenes of nature in him so pregnau[n]t in witte … he could not be long vnespied … Nothyng was so hard which with witte and industrie he could not co[m]passe. Neyther was his capacitie so good but his memorie was as greate in reteining whatsoeuer he had atteined. Which well appeared in connyng the text of the whole new Testament of Erasmus translation without booke, in his iourney going and comming from Rome.[19]

As the collection unfolds, both the highly literate and the illiterate of society are regularly described as 'connyng' texts by rote in order to demonstrate both their mental prowess and their ethical powers of self-government. In this way, Foxe shows himself determined to showcase the heroic mind of the martyr before unveiling the heroic body that endures torture and execution – and one of the principal ways he does this is through an insistence upon the subject's powers of memory. Indeed, any indication of forgetfulness would constitute a moral, as well as an intellectual, deterioration for the martyr – and, it should be stressed, for the reader too.

At the beginning of his account of Cranmer we learn that, like so many of his fellow scholars in the early modern period, 'He neuer came to any writers booke without penne and inke, but yet so, y^t he exercised his memorie no lesse than his penne'. Indeed, Cranmer emerges as the very model of intellectual diligence:

Whatsoeuer controuersie came, he gathered euery autors sente[n]ce briefly, & the diuersitie of their iudgeme[n]tes in to common places, whiche he hadde prepared for that purpose. Or els, if the matter were too longe to wryte out, he noted the place of the autor and the nomber of the leafe, whereby he might haue the more helpe for his memorye.[20]

Where possible, the intellectual achievements of the martyrs are often chronicled at an early stage and married to a humanist emphasis upon the crucial importance of learning and mental industry in the pursuit of human perfectibility. In this particular case, the account of meticulous mental and textual commonplacing on Cranmer's part enables the theologian to be viewed specifically as one whose thoughtful intelligence leads him inevitably to invest in the labours of memory. A recurring narrative thrust in *The Acts and Monuments* is not only upon the valour and faith of the martyrs but also often upon their humble beginnings, their domestic arrangements or their personal writings in order to establish reader intimacy and identification with these extraordinary individuals: as readers, we must be convinced of the authenticity of their participation in a shared humanity before we can assent to their subsequent apotheoses. Ridley, for example, 'was passingly well learned, his memorye was greate, and he of suche reading withall, that of right he deserued to be comparable to the best of this our age' (*Acts* [1583], p. 1717). Such praise is supplemented later by an account of the domestic community of this *pater familias*:

> Being at his manor at Fulha[m], as diuers times he vsed to be, he read daily a lecture to his family at the commo[n] prayer, beginning at the acts of the apostles, & so going throughout all the Epistles of S. Paul, geuing to euery man that could read a new Testament, hyring the[m] besides with mony to learne by hart certayne principall Chapters, but especially the xiii. chapter of the Actes, reading also vnto his housholde oftentimes the 101. Psalme, being maruellous carefull ouer his family, that they might be a spectacle of all vertue & honesty to other. To be short, as he was godly & vertuous himselfe, so nothing but virtue and godliness reigned in his house, feeding them with the food of our sauiour Iesus Christ.[21]

The virtuous regime of paternalism characteristic of life at Ridley's Fulham manor is intimately connected here with the patriarch's profile as a scholar and, equally importantly, with his ability to inspire others in his scholarly ambitions – extending as far as to 'hire' others to rote-learn biblical texts. The spiritual and moral dimensions of the well-tempered memory of this moral paragon are thus clearly in evidence for the members of the Fulham household, and indeed for readers to appreciate and to emulate. Nor should we lose sight of the fact that Foxe is conspicuously reserving for himself, as well as for his virtuous subjects and readers, the honours that his society awarded to those who exercised their memories publicly for the good of the polity.

MEMORY AND HEROIC RESISTANCE

From a more general perspective, absolutely central to the Foxean project of commemoration was, of course, the depiction of the monstrous violence of a *corrupt, greedy and conspiratorial* Catholic Church that had persecuted the faithful down the generations: 'what is there almost in the pope's church, but either it is mingled, or depraved, or altered, or corrupted, either by some additions interlaced, or by some diminution mangled and mutilated, or by some gloss adulterate, or with manifest lies contaminate?' (*Acts* [1583], p. 584). In the wider context of post-Reformation politics in England, R. Malcolm Smuts has justly underlined that

> Religious conflict not only posed immediate threats to the kingdom's peace. It also disrupted Elizabethans' relations to their own past and the moral authority that the past conveyed. All across Europe the ideological underpinnings of political authority were being subjected to searching examination and polemical assault by confessional adversaries. Appeals to history had become double-edged

weapons, used to attack government as well as to defend it. Protestants especially needed to reinvent the past, to justify what might otherwise appear an arrogant break with ancestral customs.[22]

Thus, the ideological 'scramble' for the past in evidence across the Continent opened up equally difficult questions regarding the epistemological status of memory and the faculty's role in the recovery or formulation of spiritual history. Interestingly, Foxe's own troubled account of religious persecution down the ages was prepared for those who resisted the national Church as well as for those who counted themselves among the faithful. In the prefatory text to the 1563 edition 'To the Persecutors of Gods Truth, commonlye called Papistes', these particular readers were forced to embark upon a very specific journey of remembrance, for they had to 'consider the number almost out of nomber of so many, silly & symple lambes of Christ, whose bloud you haue sought and suckt, whose lyues you haue vexed, whose bodies you haue slayne, racked, and tormented, some also you haue cast on dunghils, to be deuoured by Foules and Dogges, wythout mercy, wythout measure, without al sense of humanity' (sig. B4ᵛ).

Interestingly, if Foxe responded enthusiastically to the call of earlier generations of humanists to scrutinise the sources anew, he appears nonetheless to have become increasingly aware of the limitations of his textual legacies he had inherited, and indeed of the fragile powers of the human memory itself.[23] When dealing with religious fugitives during the reign of Richard II, for example, he was able to cite eight names from his source material, but lamented

> many more did forsake the Realme, but what they were or what kinde of punishement they suffred [the source] left no mention. But we will not suffre their names to be blotted out with silence, which we might by any meanes pick out: But sure we are greatly sorye that there came nothing els into our handes but only their bare names. Wold to God that the constant diligence of our predicessours had preserued in memory for vs the whole order of their life, the forme of their proces and iudgement, and what was to be obserued in their aduersaries, or to be co[m]mended in them.[24]

Elsewhere, as in the account of the execution of Henry Howard, Earl of Surrey, Foxe (as a historian in receipt of insufficient data or — more persuasively — giving way to some strategic ignorance of arbitrary government by a Tudor monarch) deferred to an omniscient Godhead, confident in His knowledge and memory of all human actions:

After or about the deth therfore of king He[n]ry, the Duke of Northfolk the same time being committed in to the tower, and his sonne the Erl of Surry shortly after behedded, for what offence, because as yet it is vnknowen to me I commit it vnto the lorde, who as knoweth all things perfectly, so shal iudge al things rightuously. God graunt that the doinges of al men may be such, that eyther they may stand in his iudgment through vprightnes, or els may obtein mercy, thrugh repe[n]ta[n]ce.'[25]

In this manner throughout *The Acts and Monuments* the reader is brought to witness the contrary pressures at work within Foxe's various narratives. From one perspective, the remorseless accounts of religious persecution are being marshalled in order to establish the virtuous ancestry of resistance to Catholic hegemony. However, the humanist in Foxe clearly also wishes to involve readers thoroughly in his deliberations as a commentator (and indeed editor) of the past, and to expose for wider consideration the great difficulties associated with the perplexing business of historiography. Even taking into account the profoundly partisan axis upon which this huge undertaking was built, the seemingly inexhaustible energies that Foxe employed in order to bring it to fruition should not be underestimated. Importantly, John N. King has stressed that the 'Collation of extant letters and documents by an extraordinary number of different hands in eleven massive volumes of Foxe papers shows that where a source survives, *Actes and Monuments* contains an accurate transcript'.[26] Nevertheless, the chronicler remains on occasions profoundly aware of the parlous nature of the information he has at his disposal. This is clearly evident, for example, in the life of William Tyndale related in the 1563 edition where, as David Daniell argues, 'Though [he] is our prime source of information about the life of Tyndale, what we are told over 18 columns is in fact pretty meagre – Foxe is cleverly making bricks without straw, as any biographer must do at times.'[27]

Whatever the persisting difficulties for more recent critics concerning his methodologies as a historian, his remorselessly driven sense of historical selection and interpretation, Foxe found himself in no difficulties whatsoever in identifying the true villain of his chronicles. In his painstaking engagement with the labours of earlier historians and the details of surviving documents he showed himself determined to throw back upon Catholics the familiar accusation levelled at Reformists, who were thought by their enemies to have no past in which to anchor their faith: 'I aske here of the Romane Clergie, where was this Churche of theirs which now is, in the old aunciente tyme of the primitiue Church of Rome, with this pompe and pride, with this riches and superfluitie, with this *gloria mundi* [?]' (*Acts* [1583], p. 3). Given the context of his profound outrage at the Papacy as an ungodly foreign force polluting the spiritual development of Christendom, Foxe is found unsurprisingly to insist that in the doings of the Inquisition, 'all is done in hugger-mugger, & in close corners, by ambages, by couert waies, and secret counselles. The accuser secret, the crime secret, the witness secret: whatsoeuer is done, is secret, neither is the poore Prisoner euer advertised of any thing' (*Acts* [1583], p. 931). Indeed, accounts of Catholic wrongdoings and Papal malefactors are even seasoned with a reference to Pope Joan as 'a mery and comycall spectacle' for the 'gentle Reader' among 'a great number of lamentable and bloudy tragedies' (*Acts* [1563], p. 625).

Equally importantly, as his enterprise progresses, Foxe endeavours to guide even his Catholic readers in Britain to cherish their native culture as an inviolable spiritual and political 'home' from which to challenge Papal claims of allegiance: 'let other countryes passe, let vs turne now to the peaceable gouernment in this realme of England, vnder this our so milde & gracious Queene now presently reigning. Vnder whome you see howe gently you are suffered, what mercy is shewed vnto you: how quietly ye lieu' (*Acts* [1583], sig. ¶i[r]).[28] Given the explicit political investment of his narratives, the gravitational pull towards British, and most especially English, martyrs becomes increasingly evident. Initially in these sections of *The Acts and Monuments* treating instances of native persecution, Foxe goes to great lengths to conjure up powerful evocations of the ways in which the contagion of Catholicism infected the land. Anthony Low has highlighted persuasively how 'the Reformation brought contempt for certain forms of communal life into England', and clearly one of these *forms* that was repeatedly vilified in Foxe's narratives was monasticism.[29] A more charitably minded William Camden in his *Britannia* submitted for the next generation of early modern readers that

> There are certaine, as I heare who take it impatiently that I have mentioned some of the most famous Monasteries and their founders. I am sory to heare it, and with their good favour will say thus much, They may take it as impatiently, and peradventure would have us forget that our ancestoures were, and we are of the Christian profession when as there are not extant any other more conspicuous, and certaine Monuments, of their piety, and zealous devotion toward God. Neither were there any other seed-gardens from when Christian Religion, and good learning were propagated over this ile, howbeit in corrupt ages some weeds grew out over ranckly.[30]

However, Foxe was temperamentally less disposed to appreciate any manifestation of Catholic culture, and summoned up the vision of a malignant spirit of monasticism feeding on the lifeblood of the nation with a creative skill that bears witness to the imaginative resources with which his prose is frequently suffused: 'first began to creepe from the cold field into warme townes and cloysters: from townes, then into cities, and at length from their close cellers and citties, vnto Cathedrall Churches … where, not onely they did abound in wealth and riches (especially these Monkes of our latter tyme), but much more did swimme in superstition and Pharisaicall hipocrisie' (*Acts* [1583], p. 154).[31]

As one century gave way to the next in this breathtaking panorama of European persecutions, Foxe turned to every available textual source to support his thesis that the See of Rome was the Antagonist for those wishing to proclaim their faith according to the models established by the Early Church.[32] Indeed, this familiar Reformist commitment proved to be an abiding concern throughout Foxe's career, as his 1570 'Sermon of Christ Crucified' testifies: 'England neuer fared better then when ye Pope did most curse it.'[33] Jane Facey argues convincingly that 'Wherever Foxe found criticism of either the claims of the Pope or of popish religious practice on the one hand, and persecution by the Church of Rome on the other, there he claimed to discern the true church'.[34] In the course of these labours of recuperation, both Dante and Petrarch were enlisted to the cause and cited as referring to the Pope as 'the whore of Babylon'; and Petrarch was also recorded as describing the See of Rome as 'the schole and mother of error, the temple of heresy, the nest of traichery growing and increasing by ye oppressing of others' (*Acts* [1583], p. 390). More generally, one of the very reasons why *The Acts and Monuments* appears to have captured the imaginations of so many Elizabethans resides in the fact that Foxe excited his cornucopian text with a psychomachic struggle between the forces of the true faith and its persecutors on earth. In this discussion, Alec Ryrie is timely in his emphasis that for many early Protestants 'martyrdom was an apocalyptic event, and to write a martyr-narrative was to make an apocalyptic statement. This reflects the generally apocalyptic mindset of early Protestantism: it was a deeply confrontational movement, with rigidly separated mental categories of good and evil, or the true and the false church, of Christ and Antichrist'.[35] Given this context, it is clear that Foxe sought to channel memories of all textual, and indeed personal, accounts of persecution into a larger, transhistorical schema in which bloodthirsty forces conspire against all those who resist 'Romanist' doctrine.

MEMORY, SACRAMENT AND TEXT

Given the sources of violent contention regarding doctrinal interpretation that characterised and sustained schismatic forces in Reformation

Europe, it was inevitable that the status of the Eucharist together with the authority of the Papacy would come to dominate many of the more recent narratives of *The Acts and Monuments*. Indeed, there appears no end to the anxious unravelling of the story of 'how and by whome this popish or rather apish Masse became so clampered and patched together with so many dyuers and sondry additions …' (*Acts* [1583], p. 1401). In the extended discussion upon the doctrine of transubstantiation during his account of the Henrician period, Foxe concluded:

And thus I suppose, it standeth cleare & euidently prooved by course of al these ages afore recited, from the time of Tertullian and Au[gu]stine vnto the daies of this Elfricus aboue mencioned, and after him, that this newcome miracle of transubstantiation was not yet crept into the heades of men, nor almost came in any question among learned me[n] nor was admitted for any doctrine in the Churche, at least for any general doctrine of all men to be receiued, til a M. yeare complete after Christe, that is, till Sathan began to be set at large.[36]

Almost half of the 1563 edition is devoted to the sufferings of the Marian martyrs, and vigorous accounts of their verbal interrogations are often starkly juxtaposed with their bodily sufferings for the edification of the readership. Again and again, those held in captivity are discovered affirming the commemorative, symbolic status of the sacrament in opposition to their antagonists who subscribe to the doctrine of transubstantiation. Ridley, for example, protests that in a world governed by such Catholic dogma, 'The signe is seruilely worshipped, for ye thing signified' (*Acts* [1583], p. 1718). Elsewhere, Foxe records that a few days before her execution in February 1554, Lady Jane Grey received one Master Fecknam, sent by Queen Mary to convert her to the Catholic faith:

FECKNAM Why? what doe you receiue in that Sacrament? Doe you not receiue the very body and bloud of Christ?
GREY No surely, I doe not so beleeue. I thinke that at the Supper I neyther receiue flesh nor bloude, but bread and wine: Which bread when it is broken, and the wine when it is dronken, putteth mee in remembraunce howe that for my sinnes the body of Christ was broken, & his bloudshed on the Crosse, and with that breade and wine I receiue the benefites that come by the breaking of his body, & sheding of his bloud for our sinnes on the Crosse.[37]

And as Foxe's narrative of the reign of Mary I unfolds, there emerges a swelling number of voices reiterating precisely these sentiments. John Webbe affirms in the presence of his accusers that

I do beleeue … [the sacrament] to be left vnto hys Churche (wyth thankes geuyng) in commemoration of hys death & passion, vntill his commyng agayne.

So that it is left in remembrance of hys body, and not by the wordes of consecration to be made his body, really, substantially, and the same body that was borne of the virgin Mary: I vtterly do deny that.³⁸

The Eucharist thus constitutes not only a sacrament, but a superlative act of memory on the part of these Reformists in their endeavours to make public their spiritual allegiance. The beleaguered Dr Rowland Taylor proclaims that 'Christ ordayned the holy communion in the remembraunce of his death and passion', and cites St John Chrysostome during his interrogation conducted by Bishop Gardiner: '"Our Sacrifice is only memoratiue, in the remembrance of Christes death and passion"' (*Acts* [1583], pp. 1520–1).³⁹

However, if, like a true humanist, Foxe never really divorces the practices of reading from remembering in his *magnum opus*, the persisting concerns embedded in Protestant subjectivities relating to textual consumption and production meant that these crucial activities could never pass unmonitored, even among great ones. Foxe remained painfully aware that the work in which he was investing so much time and energy might have to compete for its position against other forms of reading matter, even at the highest echelons of Tudor society:

In consideration whereof, me thinkes I haue good cause to wish, that lyke as other men, euen so the heroical wittes of kinges and princes, which for the most part are delited with heroicall stories, would carye about with them such monumentes of Martyrs as this is, and lay them alwaies in sight, not alonely to reade, but to follow, and would paint them vpon their walles, cuppes, ringes and gates. For undoubtedly these martyrs are much more worthy of this honor, then, 600 Alexanders, Hectors, Scipioes, and warring Iulies.⁴⁰

There was one particular kind of production from which Foxe wished to distinguish his work completely: his own 'monumental' work had much in common with Catholic hagiographies and religious publications circulating in the opening decades of the sixteenth century. As was appreciated in the Introduction, many of the prevailing discourses of memory at work in early modern Europe were often heavily influenced by Aristotelian thinking – thinking that nourished the belief that (the recalling of) material objects might be the focal point for the triggering of memory. Apart from areas of early modern cultural expression such as pedagogy and the visual arts, such beliefs had clearly found expression down the centuries in Catholic observances of worship. In turn, as *The Acts and Monuments* rolled from the printing presses of Elizabeth's England in great folio editions, the very materiality of Foxe's accounts of violent religious persecution meant that they also came to assume a status worthy of veneration: in post-Reformation England, Book (rather than Relic) might easily be promoted as a conduit for the collective exercise of memory and spiritual reflection.[41]

In the context of pre-Reformation print culture, the most notable comparison for Foxe's work would be with the enormously popular thirteenth-century martyrology the *Legenda Aurea* of Jacobus de Voragine. The English translation of the *Legenda* was published by Caxton in 1483 and enjoyed numerous reprintings prior to the Reformation.[42] Despite the sustained emphasis in Voragine's text upon miracles, revelations and visions, Foxe remained richly sensitive to the possibility that his own collection might be perceived as harking back to such earlier forms of reading experience: 'I wish this history were "not" so true as it is, were really like their golden legend and their other lying stories. These miseries were inflicted by you, not feigned by me; we have more witness to them than we would choose.'[43] Thus alarmed at the persistence of reading appetites inherited from earlier generations reared in the 'old faith', the chronicler remained at pains to differentiate his own ambitions from those expressed in Catholic hagiographies. Indeed, his narratorial voices become increasingly shrill in their insistence that readers should refrain from any form of worship that relates to the heroic mortals described in the volume. When he turned to the Church Fathers, for example, he affirmed strenuously that, 'though this cannot be denied, but that holy *Cyprian* and other blessed Martyrs were holy men, yet notwithstanding they were men: that is, such as might haue, & hath their falles & faultes, men I say & not aungels, nor gods, saued by God, not sauiours of men, nor patrons of grace' (*Acts* [1583], p. 70). Elsewhere, there is the notable example of the response to Bede's account of St Alban's miracles:

> of drying vp the Riuer, as *Alban* went to the place of his execution: then of making a welspring in the top of the hill, and of the falling out of the eyes of him that did behead him (with such other prodigious miracles me[n]tioned in his story) because they seem more lege[n]dlike than truthlike: againe, because I see no great profit, nor necessitie in the relation thereof, I leaue them to the free iudgement of the Reader, to thinke of them, as cause shall moue him.[44]

Unsurprisingly, such accounts were dismissed as 'Monkish miracles and grosse fables, wherewith these Abbey Monkes were wont in time past to deceaue the Church of God, and to beguile the whole world for their own adua[n]tage' (*Acts* [1583], p. 89). Nonetheless, it is revealing that later in his descriptions of the Marian persecutors Foxe clearly found himself in very great difficulties indeed in recording the visions of those such as the reformist Cutbert Symson:

> Some, I see, will not beleue it, some will deride the same, some also will be offended with setting forth things of that sorte incertayne, esteeming all thinges to be incertayne and incredible, whatsoeuer is straunge from the common order of Nature ... Agayne, neyther am I ignorant that the papistes, in their bookes and legendes of saintes haue theyr prodigious visions and apparitions of Aungelles of our Lady: of Christ and other sayncts: which ... I wil not admit to be beleeued for true ... [I] onely reporte it as it hath bene heard of persons knowne, naming also yᵉ parties who were the hearers there of, leauing the iudgement there of, notwithstanding free vnto the arbitremente of the reader.[45]

Despite his protestations that martyrdom relied solely upon divine intervention rather than upon any other agency, Foxe was compelled to stress the exceptionalism and exemplarity of the individuals he treated and, as a consequence, he often ran the risk of imitating earlier traditions of sacred biography rather too closely. There are, for example, the prophetic dream visions of the martyr John Rough (1558) who wakes from his sleep with images that his deacon Symson is being led away by guards and that he himself is persecuted by the bishop (*Acts* [1583], pp. 2031–2). As Ridley and Latimer leave their final prison for the journey to the stake in Oxford in 1555, 'Some plucked the pointes off [Ridley's] hose. Happy was he that might get any rag of hym' (*Acts* [1583], p. 1769). In an earlier case of the arraignment and burning of one Joan Boughton (1494), Foxe recorded that 'My author sayth, she was a Disciple of Wickliffe ... The night following that she was burnt, the most parte of her ashes were had away by suche as had a loue vnto the doctrine that she dyed for' (*Acts* [1583], p. 731).[46] In this context, David Daniell is all too persuasive in his conclusion that 'In a crude sense, Foxe's colossal volumes are Protestant saints' lives with documentation'.[47]

MEMORY AND VIOLENCE

In general terms the awe-inspiring peripeteia that the Foxean worthies endure and render them wholly remarkable are inextricably linked to detailed presentations of spectacular violence. Narrative expectations involving dire conditions of captivity, blood-curdling torture and harrowing scenes of execution build incrementally as the work unfolds, so that by the time we arrive at the sixteenth-century persecutions the responses of fear, pity and admiration (conventionally associated with the genre of Tragedy in this period) are fully established in our repertoire of reading strategies. There is the notable example of Anne Askew. As we have seen, this woman was demonised by the authorities for disseminating heretical teaching during the reign of Henry VIII: the consequent regime of torture to which she was forced to submit was so vigorous that for her execution in 1546 she 'was brought into Smithfield in a chayre, because she could not goe on her feet, by meanes of her great tormentes' (*Acts* [1583], p. 1240). Later, in the accounts of the Marian martyrs, we encounter John Fetty lying in prison, 'by the space of xv dayes, hanging in the stockes, sometyme by the one legge, and the one arme, sometyme by the other, and otherwhiles by both'; or the 'blessed Deacon and Martyr of god Cutbert Symson, [who] after his painful racking' at the Tower of London was to be found on the day before his burning in March 1558 in 'the Bishops colehouse there in the stockes' (*Acts* [1583], pp. 2056, 2033). In Norwich in 1555 the preacher Robert Samuel

> was chained bolte vpright to a greate post, in such sort, that standing only in tip-toe, he was faine to stay vp the whole paise or waight of his bodye thereby. And [was kept] without meate and drinke … O worthy constancie of the Martyr! O pitilesse hearts of papistes, worthy to be complained of, and to be accused before God and nature![48]

The rigours of these torments were then counterpointed elsewhere in Foxe's narratives with the mental fortitude required of the martyrs under the duress of interrogation. Interestingly, as the accounts of Marian inquisitions proliferate, the more erudite martyrs frequently remonstrate with their accusers for depriving them of all intellectual sustenance as well as their liberty. Latimer turns on his interrogator, the Bishop of Gloucester, thundering, 'Lo, you looke for learnyng at my handes, whiche haue gone so longe to the school of obliuion, makynge the bare walles my Librarie, keepyng me so long in prison without booke or penne and inke: and nowe you let me lo[o]se to come and aunsweare to Articles' (*Acts* [1583], p. 1763). Elsewhere in the 'examination' of John Philpot, former archdeacon of Winchester under Edward VI, there is a comparable emphasis upon textual deprivation as one of the most keenly felt hardships of the captivity.

> LONDON Loe, what a Varlet is this! Besides this (my Lordes) euen yesterday hee procured hys man to bryng a bladder of blacke Pouder, I can not tell for what purposes, I.
> PHILPOT Your lordship needeth not to mistrust the matter: it is nothing but to make inke withall, for lacke of inke, as I had it before in the kings Bench, when my keeper tooke away my inkhorne.
> LONDON And why shouldst thou go about any such thing vnknowyng vnto me beyng thy keeper? for I am thy keeper in this house I tell thee.
> PHILPOT My L[ord]. because you haue caused my penner and inkhorne to bee taken from mee, I woulde yet faine that my friends might vnderstand what I lacke.[49]

Again and again, in order to combat the distress of the privation of mental and social activity, recourse is taken to the faculty of memory to maintain a spiritual and moral integrity in the face of persecution. In her treatment of religious culture in the earlier medieval period, Catherine Cubitt has emphasised that 'Both memory and the production of written texts are vital activities in the process of political change'; and it is evident throughout *The Acts and Monuments* that the power to write and to remember are perceived as key resources at the disposal of the martyrs who wish to recover their powers of cultural intervention and to resist the ideological pressures that aim to shape their identities in terms of loss, denial and submission.[50] At every opportunity, Foxe was eager to bring before his readers textual proof in terms of letters and messages from the prisoners themselves on the nature of their imprisonment and their unfailing willingness to remain true to their beliefs. At such moments, martyr, author and reader are perceived as bound together in a Foxean undertaking to record for others (through published text or memorial account) the defining nature of their spiritual calling.

I. Ross Bartlett has rightly emphasised that 'Foxe, like many others, was clearly not content to restrict himself to the role of a compiler. He was much more interested in what his readers wanted and needed than in the troublesome quest for some abstract concept which modern historical studies might label as "truth" divorced from the real life of his reader'.[51] Moreover, Foxe's reader is repeatedly urged to view the faculty of memory in terms of responsibility, obligation and vocation. In opposition to the martyrs who are shown to divest themselves and to be divested of temporal concerns, we are encouraged to possess and to cherish these heroic narratives of earthly endurance – to become the religious custodians of such texts and to continue the martyrs' commitment to the 'true' faith and to cultural reform.[52]

THE PERFORMANCE OF MEMORY

Given the overarching narrative emphases of *The Acts and Monuments* treated thus far, it comes as no surprise that the martyrs themselves highlight to those around them the spiritual importance of recollection. In his history of the Early Church, for example, Foxe exploits his source Eusebius for a striking account of St Peter who, 'seeing his wife going to her Martirdome (belike as he was yet hanging upon the crosse), was greatly ioyous & glad thereof. Who crying unto her with a loude voyce, and calling her by her name, bad her remember yͤ Lorde Iesus' (*Acts* [1570], pp. 54–5; corrected pagination).⁵³ Much later, the Marian martyr John Philpot writes rather imperiously from his place of imprisonment to his 'faithful brethren': 'Let them reme[m]ber that in the Apocalips the fearfull be excluded the kingdome', and in another letter to 'certaine godlye women' that he 'wryteth this to be as a perpetual memorial betwixt you and [I], vntil our meeting together before God, where we shall ioy that we have here louingly put one another in memory of our duetie to performe it' (*Acts* [1583], pp. 1833, 1834). In turning to the celebrated account of John Frith, Foxe focused most particular attention upon the redemptive power of memory early in the narrative when the future martyr is taken for a vagabond during a stay in the town of Reading:

> the simple man whiche coulde not craftily enough colour him selfe, was set in the stockes. Where after he had sitten there a lo[n]g time, and was almost pined with hunger, and woulde not for all that declare what he was, at last hee desired that the Scholemaister of the towne might be brought to hym, which at that time was one Leonard Coxe, a ma[n] very wel learned. As soon as he came vnto hym, Frith by and by began in the Latine tongue to bewaile his captiuitie.
>
> The Schoolemaister, by and by, beinge ouercome wyth his eloquence, did not only take pitie and compassion vppon him, but also began to loue and embrace such an excellent witte and disposition vnlooked for, especially in such a state & miserie. Afterward, conferring more together upon many things as touching the Vniuersities, scholes, and tongues, they fell from the Latin into the Greeke, Wherein Frith dyd so inflame the loue of that Schoolemaister towardes him, that he brought him into a maruellous admiration, especiallye when the Schoolemaister hearde him so promptly by hart, rehearse Homers verses out of his first book of the *Iliades*. Whereupon the Schoolemaister we[n]t with all speede, vnto the Magistrates, greeuously complaining of the iniurie which they did shew vnto so excellent and innocent a young man.
>
> Thus Frith, through the helpe of the schoolemaister, was freely dimitted out of the stockes, & set at libertie without punishment. Albeit this safetie continued not lo[n]g, thorow the great hatred and deadly pursuit of sir Tho[mas]. More, who at that time being Chauncelour of Englande, persecuted him both by land and sea, besetting all the waies and hauens, yea & promising great rewardes, if any ma[n] could bryng him any newes or tydings of him.⁵⁴

Once again, in this instance, we find the protagonist's intellectual prowess being strategically privileged above and beyond more conventional heroic tropes of physical endurance. Foxe is clearly exciting his narrative with the leitmotif of remorseless conflict between the forces of the true faith and those of persecution. Thomas More is consigned to the role of 'a bitter persecuter of good men … and a wretched enemie against the truth of the Gospel' (*Acts* [1583], p. 1069). Alternatively, Frith, with his felicitous display of classical learning and assisted by a seemingly virtuoso performance of memory, is feted for his mental and spiritual commitment.

However, Foxe does not only encourage his readers to reserve admiration for an elite community of erudite scholars. One of the favourite tales from *The Acts and Monuments* for readers down the generations has been that of the illiterate Welsh fisherman, Rawlins White, who sent his child to school to learn to read English: 'Now after the little boy could read indifferently wel, his father euery night after supper, sommer and winter, would haue the boy to read a piece of the holy scripture, & now and then of some other good booke.' After subsequently discovering his vocation as a preacher, Foxe's reader is duly informed that for White

> God did … adde in him a singular gyft of memory, so that by the benefite therof he would & could do that in vouching and rehersing of the text, which men of riper and more profound knowlege, by their notes and other helpe of memory, could very hardly accomplish. In so much that he vpon the alledging of scripture, very often would cite the booke, the leafe, yea and very sentence: such as the wonderfull working of God in this simply and vnlearned father.[55]

If William Haller emphasised that 'persecution gave its victims the opportunity to dramatize their faith in the Word by embracing martyrdom, and its survivors the opportunity to exploit the testimony of the martyrs by the classic device of a martyrology', it is evident that Foxe repeatedly deploys the martyr's memorial performances within his narratives in order to demonstrate their exceptional status even among the faithful.[56] More generally, if the tireless chronicler endeavours to convert cultural trauma into a corpus of spiritual knowledge, he remains adamant that the establishment of this 'collective memory', this fund of exemplary conduct, can be to no avail if it is greeted with spiritual lethargy by subsequent generations. Without equally emphatic commitment to spiritual witness from his readers, this huge work would constitute little more than an extended lament. Indeed, in this instance we may wish to identify once again continuities with the Catholic cultural inheritance from the pre-Reformation period: for, as Catherine Cubitt has argued, in medieval culture 'Saints were not … passive figures for remembrance … but active figures since, through their exemplary power, their actions and words informed the lives of others'.[57] If, as some critics have argued, we are witnessing here the possibility of a shared communal identity being shaped with narratives of heroic individuals to whom the spiritual origins of this society belong, it is evident that we should not lose sight of the fact, as Ernest Renan famously declared, that 'l'essence d'une nation est que tous individus aient beaucoup de chose en commun, et aussi que tous aient oublié bien des choses' ['the essential quality of a nation is that all the members have a great many things in common, and equally that they have all forgotten a great many things'].[58] In turning to 'this my countrey Church of England', Foxe affirmed that 'There hathe beene no region or country more fertil or fruteful for martirs' (*Acts* [1570], sig. 2ᵛ; [1563], p. 347). Nonetheless, like every writer of history, Foxe placed carefully shaped lenses on the past; and his readers are only ever allowed a restricted viewing of the events he described. At certain points the historian-as-editor emerges clearly. When he chronicled the doings of Henry V, for example, he concluded that the subject of the monarch's

> vertues, and great victories gotten in Fraunce, I haue not greatly to intermeddle: Especially, seing the memory of hys worthy prowesse, being sufficiently described in other writers in this our time, may both content the reader, and vnburden my labor herein. Especially, seing these latter troubles and perturbations of the Churche offer me so much, that vnneth any vacant laisure shalbe left, to intermeddle wyth matters prophane.[59]

Elsewhere, this process is distinctly more covert. In his illuminating study of early modern drama, Garrett Sullivan Jr submits that 'forgetting [is] more than a mere failure of memory',[60] and while Foxe repeatedly demonstrates his commitment to draw the narratives of martyrs from humbler origins into the public domain, he was in no doubt that others would [or should] be displaced, or 'forgotten', in the process. One such figure earmarked for relegation was Thomas Becket: 'If the cause make a Martyr (as is said) I see not why we should esteeme Tho[mas] Becket to dye a martyr, more than any other whome the Princes sword doth here temporally punish for their temporall desertes' (*Acts* [1583], p. 205).

In his *Sermon of Christ Crucified* (1570), Foxe had voiced a widely held sentiment among Reformists facing Catholic persecution that there was a continuous theory of power extending from the divine patriarch to temporal princes: 'Briefly, if the wrath of a terrene kyng in this earth, bee death (as the wyse kyng speaketh in the scripture): what is it then to bee vnder the wrath of the almighty kyng of all kynges, and GOD of all creatures.'[61] The role of the earthly ruler as potential protector of those whose beliefs brought them into conflict with the Papacy was never underestimated by the Reformists; and repeatedly *The Acts and Monuments* accuses malignant advisers and Catholic representatives for wrongdoings and deflects moral condemnation from the monarchs themselves, as was witnessed in the previous chapter with Foxe's account of the conspiracy against Katherine Parr. More generally, the presiding force of divine memory is an all-important factor in the Foxean cosmology.

Its authority might prove terrifying and/or reassuring to the Reformist mind, as Foxe stressed in his *Sermon preached at the Christening of a certaine Iew* (1578):

> accordyng to Saint Paules aduertisement … wee shoulde duely, and with carefull consideration, exactly examine the seueritie of God: and not his seueritie onely, but his bountyfull goodnesse withall: That so through the often remembrance of the one, wee myght bee restrayned in a couenable feare, and through the dayly recordyng of the other, wee myght be raysed to thankefulnesse and duetyfull loue towardes God.[62]

This subject had also been treated in his earlier *Sermon of Christ Crucified* (1570) where Foxe pondered the infinite expanse and the infinite mercy held *in potentia* within the divine memory for those who repent:

> God promiseth neuer to remember, not to impute our sinnes any more for Christes sake. Ieremy. 31. And hereof springeth the fountaine of perpetuall remission, promised in the xiii. Chapter of the Prophet Zachary: where hee sayth: *In that day shall be open to the house of Dauid, and to the dwellers of Ierusalem, a fountaine to the cleansing away of sinne, & monstrui. &c*.[63]

Like many Reformist writers of the age, Foxe exploited age-old practices of typology and summoned up a vision of history in which present experience might be seen as replaying familiar narratives from scripture: 'Thus the poore Christians (as ye see) like to the seely Israelites vnder the tyranny of Pharoa, were infested and oppressed in euery place, but especially heere in England' (*Acts* [1583], p. 554).[64] In this way, the biblical past became an interpretative lexicon for the present; and, as Sharon Achinstein has justly emphasised, 'Whether reformers looked forward to a future of apocalyptic bloodshed or messianic peace, or glanced backward to a repudiated past of superstition and idolatry, time was a central coordinate to their world view. Stories of the Jews mattered in a construction of a reformed time-line'.[65]

Early on in *The Acts and Monuments* Foxe's reader is reassured by the narrator that 'Such is the wisdome and prouidence of God, that the bloud of his deare Saints (like good seede) neuer falleth in vaine to the grounde, but it bringeth some increase' (*Acts* [1583], p. 72). We are thus brought to conclude that such is the foresight and indeed providential nature of the ways of God that no deed or declaration goes unrecorded in the divine memory:

> neither chaunce nor fortune, nor disposition of man, hath had any place: but onely the forecou[n]sail and determination of the Lorde hath so gouerned & disposed the same. Who not onely did suffer them to fal, & foresee those persecutions

before they fel: but also appointed the times and yeares how long they shoulde last, and when to haue an ende.[66]

THE TEXTUAL LEGACIES OF FOXE

Michael S. Pucci has proposed that 'it is a mark of [Foxe's] genius that he was able to treat history covering nearly 1600 years as if it were part and parcel of [the] personal memory of persecution'.[67] The great work had clearly attracted a national, nay international, audience; and, as a consequence, his historical vision had become a vigorous site of contestation. Clearly feeling smitten in hip and thigh, Foxe himself recorded that 'no English Papist almost in all the Realme, thoght himselfe a perfect Catholike vnless he had cast out some word or other to geue that book a blow' (*Acts* [1583], sig. §6ʳ). Perhaps of greater concern to the Elizabethan regime as one edition of *The Acts and Monuments* succeeded another was that this volume might also be raising a question whether there remained a political need for radical intervention in the present to resolve crises in the practice of the true faith.[68] If the fruits of Foxe's labours would be embraced by the Elizabethan authorities as an important line of defence against the nation's Catholic antagonists, the theologian himself remained fully cognisant of the radical implications of memorial endeavour. Indeed, like so many Elizabethan Reformists, he did not refrain from looking back to an earlier reign of Elizabeth's half-brother in which the faithful might think themselves secure within the fold of a Church Militant: 'how much then are we Englishe men bound, not to forget our duetie to kyng *Edward* … I see but few to whom he may not be equall, so agayne I see not many, to whom he may not iustly be preferred' (*Acts* [1570], p. 1483).[69]

Warren W. Wooden has concluded that 'Few of the ingredients of Foxe's grand design were original with him; his genius lay rather in his enormous devotion to the project and capacity for work (in a word, his zeal), his power of synthesis, and his extraordinary narrative gifts'.[70] And, indeed, despite the remorseless promotion of his Reformist thesis, Foxe's narrative skills can on occasions take the reader by surprise, as in his account of the martyrdom of St Lawrence in the third century AD when his 'gentle reader' is invited to 'draw neare to the fire of Martyred Laurence, that our colde heartes may be warmed thereby' (*Acts* [1583], p. 71). Even more arrestingly, he anthologises St Jerome's example of a soldier who would not relinquish his Christian faith and so is forced to negotiate an ordeal that allows him to 'remember himself' in a spectacular manner:

> the souldiour [was] layd vpon a soft bed in a pleasant garden among the floorishing Lillies and redde Roses, which done, all other beyng remoued awaye, and himselfe there left alone, a beautifull harlot came to him, who embracing him, and with al other incitementes of an harlot, laboured to prouoke hym to her naughtynes. But the godlye souldiour fearing God more, then obeying flesh, byt of his own tong with hys own teeth, and spit it in the face of the harlot, as she was kissing him, and so got he the victory, by the co[n]stant grace of the Lord assisting him.[71]

Drawing upon a multitude of different sources and different generic expectations, Foxe brought to fruition an enormous venture that shaped historical understanding and spiritual experience for generations of readers. He offered *The Acts and Monuments* as the dominant point of contact with the history of the Christian Church for his national audience: 'that we beyng instructed by their examples, might be the more prompt and ready in the policies of those warres, to stand more stoutly in battaile agaynst our aduersaries, & learne the more easily to contemne & despise this world' (*Acts* [1570], p. 1541).[72] However, as has become increasingly apparent in critical studies, the vigorous prosecution of such arguments may provoke no small crises of interpretation for latter-day readers: tellingly, Claire McEachern enquires, 'What, for instance, are we to make of a state religion that demanded passive obedience and yet honoured as martyrs those slaughtered for disobeying the combined authority of Crown and Church?'[73]

Foxe's successive, almost ritualistic, narratives of martyrdom arrested time, sought to bridge the gap with a heroic past, and responded to the desires of his readership for a site of cultural permanence and belonging. Yet the success of this project relied entirely upon a prospective commitment to memory, and this faculty, as Ben Jonson would later lament in his commonplace book *Timber, or Discoveries*, was 'of all the *powers* of the mind … the most *delicate* and *fraile*'.[74]

CHAPTER 4

Text, recollection and Elizabethan Fiction: Nashe, Deloney, Gascoigne

> some alleadge, they trauell to learn wit, but I am of this opinion, that as it is not possible for anie man to learne the Arte of Memorie, whereof *Tully*, *Quintillian*, *Seneca*, and *Hermannus Buschius* haue written so manie bookes, except he haue a naturall memorie before: so is it not possible for anie man to attaine anie great wit by trauell, except he haue the grounds of it rooted in him before.
>
> Thomas Nashe, *The vnfortunate traueller. Or, The life of Iacke Wilton* (1594)[1]

Drawing upon the heritage of Roman and Augustinian intellectual traditions, Thomas Nashe's Jack Wilton, hero of *The vnfortunate traueller* (1594), offers in the midst of his frenzied peregrinations across Reformation Europe his own contributions to the lively cultural debate concerning the status and function of memory. In the interjection above, Wilton both acknowledges the pervasive legacy of rhetorical training at work within his society and promotes with his usual suasive tones his own innate ability to retrieve and exploit narratives of past experience – an ability that may allow him (and his readers) to apprehend sensitively and intelligently the multifariousness of the challenges that the present imposes. As we have seen, making their voices heard across the length and breath of Tudor society, those in spiritual and temporal authority focused remorselessly upon the business of 'remembering oneself', and starkly contrasted legitimate 'place' and 'station' with roving rebelliousness. As Nashe's prose narrative unfolds, his protagonist fails to know his *place* in more ways than one and often expertly scrambles the readers' own historical powers of recall as we are pulled from pillar to post, back and forth across decades and national borders on a continent being torn apart by religious schism. In his *Arte of Rhetorique* (1553), Thomas Wilson had railed 'shall not an Oratour have in store good matter, in the cheste of his memorie, to vse and bestowe in tyme of necessitee?'; and Wilton is similarly determined to drain his own memorial fund of 'good matter' to its very limits to provide the frame for his seemingly endless cycle of adventures in early sixteenth-century Europe.[2]

In his influential essay, 'Epic and Novel: Toward a Methodology for the Study of the Novel', Mikhail Bakhtin argued authoritatively that 'The plane of comic (humorous) representation is a specific plane in its spatial as well as its temporal aspect. Here the role of memory is minimal; in the comic world there is nothing for memory and tradition to do. One ridicules in order to forget'.[3] And, indeed, it may appear initially that Nashe's troublesome page, first discovered malingering in the dark corners of Henry VIII's court, salvages little of note from his own, very particular Grand Tour of Europe. However, while comic representation may indeed rely heavily upon the narrative resources of erasure, ellipsis and reduction (when in Rome, Wilton notoriously confides, 'I was at *Pontius Pilat's* house and pist against it'[4]), Nashe's textual ambitions clearly have little interest in amnesia. The successive moves to Wittenberg, Hampton Court, Florence, Venice and Rome chronicled in this prose narrative do not simply constitute a sequence of geographical displacements: they serve as memorial prompts with which to reflect upon the cultural roots of Elizabethan England, the genealogies of its religious, political and artistic formation. Moreover, these courtly and urban spaces are newly performed and apprehended through Wilton's textual adventures: his various sojourns are a participation in, rather than a re-enactment of, the past. Yet the Nashean March of History, the unveiling of Wilton's very own 'acts and monuments', is profoundly disorderly, protean rather than providential. Like Foxe, Nashe furiously couples his own fictions with those on loan from others, in this case a Lanquet or a Holinshed; but for Wilton the very business of chronicling has more often than not to do with the relation of opportunistic hedonism and unharnessed social critique, rather than a bid to enhance the cultural legitimacy of a faith community. Arthur Kinney argues persuasively that 'at first … Jack undermines order from within, but as his travels continue he finds the outer world even more chaotic – and more alien. He attempts to search the past for counsel, returning to the time of Henry VIII, at the first dawn of humanism'.[5] Ultimately, in *The vnfortunate traueller*, the authority of history, of universal experience and heroic example, is found progressively to collapse and the reader is left with the dynamic, but disturbingly shivered lens that Wilton places upon the past.

The cultural theorist Richard Terdiman contends that 'To understand what we have made, we have to be able to *remember* it',[6] and *The vnfortunate traueller* (1594) (like all the Elizabethan prose texts examined in this chapter) subjects the composition of memory and fiction to vigorous scrutiny. In very different ways, each of the texts under discussion in this chapter questions the seemingly indomitable cultural reflex to confirm the processes of identity-formation rooted in fictions of the past; and each, in their different ways, ponders the fraught difficulties involved in reconstituting the past on the page.[7] Indeed, this anxiety would still haunt the writing of fiction into the next century, as Cervantes's *Don Quixote* (English translation 1612) indicates. Quixote's own seemingly inexhaustible library of prose romances is swiftly transformed into a bonfire of the vanities and a walled (thus impenetrable) closet by the local priest and barber. The hapless knight errant even assures his restive squire Sancho Panza 'que no hay memoria a quien el tiempo no acabe' ['that there is no memory which time does not efface'],[8] but the whole of Cervantes's narrative of 'El Caballero de la Triste Figura' ['The Knight of the Sad Countenance'][9] meditates at length upon the ways in which subjectivity may be the incremental effect of recollected textual consumption: Quixote is unable, or unwilling, to rid himself of the tales of the abductions, seductions, deliverances and trials by combat related in his variously lost, burned or secreted volumes that have shaped his rich imaginative world – and, in turn, we, as *his* readers, are irrevocably drawn to the conclusion that the unending stream of characters described by Cervantes who repeatedly insist that the hero is 'falto de juicio' ['out of his wits'][10] are trapped themselves, but within a lesser, more meagre reality.

Among Nashe's contemporaries, in *Jack of Newbury* (1597), Thomas Deloney strategically 'retrieves' from the Henrician past a romance of social mobility for the final years of economic crisis in Elizabeth's reign, and, more broadly, the fictive editor G.T. in Gascoigne's *Pleasant discourse of the aduentures passed by Master F. J.* (1573) draws attention to the abiding anxieties surrounding any narrativisation of human experience. G.T. leaves the reader in no uncertainty of the profound human appetite to draw sustenance from the practices of recollection, and to preserve such nourishment textually for what Bakhtin terms 'the future memory of a past'. Indeed, Bakhtin was at pains to train attention upon the subversion potentially at work in such acts devoted to 'future memory': 'a broadening of the world of the absolute past, an enriching of it with new images (at the expense of contemporaneity) – a world that is always opposed in principle to any *merely transitory* past'.[11] Locked in an erotic tale of detection unfolding in an Elizabethan Great House, Gascoigne's G.T. compels us to reflect upon the means we employ to recuperate the past: how can such narratives be composed legitimately? Might they not *de-compose*, or suffer debasement, as they circulate among a wider readership? How secure is the human memory as a foundation for textual record? And to what extent is the history we receive a narrative of competing memories?

The vexed nature of the hermeneutic circle that Elizabethan prose fictions generate is rendered even more acute by the realisation that our textual encounters with the past are repeatedly shown to have been tactically edited. In this instance, there is no 'distanced plane of memory', which Bakhtin associated with narrative from the antique epic, where the 'past is distanced, finished and closed like a circle'.[12] Instead, in these fictions the labours of selective retrospection remain both a cultural necessity and resolutely in process. During his account of the eternal city, for example, Wilton underlines that his 'chronicles' have been carefully fashioned, nay governed by some strategic *forgetting*:

> These are but the shop dust of the sights that I saw, and in truth I dyd not beholde with anie care hereafter to report, but contented my eie for the present, and so let them passe. Should I memorize halfe the myracles which they there tolde me had beene done about martyres tombes, or the operations of the earth of the sepulchre, and other reliques brought from Ierusalem, I should bee counted the [most] monstrous lier that ever came in print ... Let mee be a Historiographer of my owne misfortunes, and not meddle with the continued Trophees of so olde a triumphing Citie.[13]

NASHE: REMEMBERING FROM THE MARGINS

Paradoxically, in the prefatory address to *The vnfortunate traueller*, directed to '*the right Honorable Lord* Henrie Wriothesley, *Earle of Southhampton, and Baron of Tichfeeld*', we are urged to query the 'blinde custome methodicall antiquity hath thrust vpon vs', which causes writers 'to dedicate such books as we publish, to one great man or other' (sig. A2ʳ). Even at the outset, Nashe's narrative thus problematises the supposed epistemological certainties that textual transmission may yield – most especially those communicated via the devices and desires of print culture. From this initial intervention (which places in question its own legitimacy), we are duly introduced to 'the terror of the world, and feauer quartan of the french, *Henrie* the eight, (the onely true subiect of Chronicles)' and to one '*Iacke Wilton*, (a Gentleman at lest)' – who is found to be, 'a certaine kinde of an appendix or page, belonging or appertaining in or vnto the confines of the English court'. In the earlier 'Induction to the Dapper Monsieur Pages of the Court', preparations had been made not for a Bakhtinian *festa stultorum*, but for a 'Chronicle of the King of Pages'

(*The vnfortunate traueller*, sig. B1ʳ). In the event, the door is not closed on either possibility.

If Walter R. Davis proposes that Elizabethan fiction should be viewed primarily in terms of the interrogation of inherited political ideologies – 'the testing of ideas of order by experience' – it becomes increasingly evident that *The vnfortunate traueller* is constantly dissecting the ways in which memory (historic, heroic, erotic or religious) surfaces as an ontological site of absolute privilege.[14] In the politically charged and highly volatile world of Nashe's prose fiction, any received notions of social hierarchy and decorum (to which we have hitherto given succour) may be subjected to a vigorous process of revision:

> It was concluded betwixt vs, that I shoulde bee the Earle of Surrie, and hee my man, onely because in his owne person, which hee would not have reproched, he meant to take more libertie of behauiour, As for my carryage hee knew hee was to tune it at a key, eyther high or low, or as hee list.[15]

The revisiting of experience, admittedly fictive in *The vnfortunate traueller*, brings with it the inevitable realisation that we are locked in a differential relationship with the past and are forced to occlude and to supplement its silences and legacies with our own narrative creativity – most especially, if our own powers of intervention are to be rendered conspicuous to future audiences. Davis argues that 'when the page adopts the manners of his betters, as he frequently does, he does so with the kind of self-conscious parody typical of a little girl wearing her mother's high heels – as we see in Jack's impersonation of Surrey or in his exaggerated Hampton Court foppery'.[16] Nevertheless, despite the obvious comic effects that the twists and turns of Nashe's narrative engender, he never allows the possibility to exceed his grasp of exploiting the evocation of an inverted and/or reversible social order (held in a not-too-distant past) for the purposes of incisive critique. A rather disoriented Surrey is not only transported (unhistorically) into a morally chequered Italy and forced to negotiate a series of picaresque capers, he is simultaneously trapped within the paralysing discourses of Petrarchan desire lifted from his own lyrics: his Geraldine declares, 'Aye, *pete Italiam*, go and seeke Italie with *Aeneas*, but bee more true than *Aeneas*, I hope that kinde wit-cherishing climate will work no change in so wittie a breast' (*The vnfortunate traueller*, sig. E4ʳ). As was appreciated in Chapter 1, the pre-eminent status of Virgil's epic as a focus for cultural veneration remained unassailed in scholarly environments across early modern Europe. Indeed, during the reign of Elizabeth, Philip Sidney urged the reader of *An Apology for*

Poetry, 'Only let Aeneas be worn in the tablet of your memory', and later in Jonson's *Haddington Masque* (1608), Hymen proclaimed to his august audience: 'Thinke on thy lou'd ÆNEAS, and what name, | MARO, the golden trumpet of his fame, | Gaue him, read thou in this'.[17] However, in Nashe's satirical account of Surrey, the poet is matched (unhistorically) with a Petrarchan *donna angelicata* of his own age and amorous inclination. In her brief appearances in the narrative she is afforded the physical and moral beauty of Petrarch's Laura ('uno spirito celeste, un vivo sole' ['a heavenly spirit, a living sun'] (canzone 90)[18]) and, interestingly, from the point of view of the fiction's gender politics, is not permitted to evade the conventional materiality of the Petrarchan *descriptio pulchritudinis*. Surrey, on the other hand, has a number of opportunities to enter a world of more multifarious experience (frequently as the butt of Wilton's pranks), even if he is not endowed with much emotional intelligence. The feats of this knight errant are generally overshadowed by the actions of the quick-witted servant: the latter's disarming powers of lucidity mean that he is able to decipher the histrionics of the earl's 'passion vpon passion' without too much effort: 'I perswade my self he was more in loue with his owne curious forming fancie than her face' (*The vnfortunate traueller*, sig. G4ʳ). Indeed, the master is left with cold cuts when he finds himself unexpectedly competing against the dynamic sexual initiatives of his page for a mistress: 'My master beate the bush and kept a coyle and a pratling, but I caught the birde' (sig. F3ᵛ). Such expert cunning is as much in evidence in Wilton's seduction of the voluptuous Diamante as it is in his cross-dressing ruse when he adopts the shape of 'a half a crown wench' for a 'Swi[t]zer Captaine that was farre gone for want of the wench'. And when push comes to shove, Wilton 'fained an impregnable excuse to be gone, and neuer came at him after' (sig. C4ʳ).

It is certainly no accident that Nashe chose to locate the historical figure of Surrey so centrally in his highly heterogeneous narrative. As was appreciated in the first chapter, W. A. Sessions has argued that, 'for the later Renaissance, Surrey [was], of course, the chief survivor of the Henrician period'.[19] Nashe takes such bodies of received thinking and inscribes them within the precarious spaces of his fictive worlds; and, it should be noted, such was the potency of the fictions he constructs that his account of Surrey in Italy as *preux chevalier* and/or lovesick pilgrim (Surrey never in fact visited Italy) became accepted as common fact for some 200 years after the publication of *The vnfortunate traueller*. Moreover, Wilton and Surrey are not alone as questers in *The vnfortunate traueller*: Nashe summons a throng of characters from the past who are variously seeking validation, plenitude and/or control through beguiling forms of self-drama, mostly involving violence. These techniques of creative memorialisation are noticeably more subversive when Nashe turns his attention to the thorny issues of temporal authority, theological justification and human autonomy. Nashe can quicken our pulses with expert rhetorical flourishes: 'Prepare your eares and your teares, for neuer till this thrust I anie tragicall matter vpon you. Strange and wonderfull are Gods iudgements, heere shine they in their glory'(*The vnfortunate traueller*, sig. N4^v). However, all too often our responses to such textual displays of virtuosity have already been rendered problematic by earlier comments by the same voice who confided to us, '[the] Heauens will not always come to witnes when they are cald' (sig. G2^r). So profound are the effects of liberating history from its usual tethers that this writer, who was engaged as a polemicist against Puritan pamphleteers by the Church ascendancy in the 1590s, can even find opportunity in *The vnfortunate traueller* for compassion for 'those ouermatcht vngratious' Anabaptists slaughtered at Münster. And, when in Rome, Wilton bedevils the ruminations of the Elizabethan reader even further with the claim, 'Yet this I must say to the shame of vs Protestants, if good workes may merit heauen, they doo them, we talke of them' (sig. E2^r, K2^r). In this way, rather than simply mediating accounts of historical record, it is clear that *The vnfortunate traueller* excites its audiences with the prospect of more multifarious possibilities of cultural enquiry than those habitually on offer under the Elizabethan regime of the 1590s.

Readers may be initially seduced by the effects of comic *bonhomie*, of Bakhtinian *billingsgate*, generated in the company of the 'sole king of the cans and black iackes, prince of the pigmeis, countie pall[at]ine of cleane strawe and prouant … Lord high regent of rashers of the coles and red herring cobs' (*The vnfortunate traueller*, sig. B1^r). Nonetheless, Nashe's quarry becomes apparent as his narrative concentrates increasingly upon how historical narratives are coded for ideological purposes, and how the constructedness of these discourses may be unmasked. Ann Rosalind Jones has underlined persuasively that '*The vnfortunate traueller* makes clear that the world it constructs is a jarring confrontation of contemporary discourses, not the mirror of a world that rises above them'; and it should be added that, at its very outset, a gauntlet is quickly thrown down before Nashe's reader: 'well, to the purpose. What stratagemicall actes and monuments do you thinke an ingenious infant of my age might enact?'[20] The burlesque referencing of Foxe's providential narrative creates just one of a whole host of hermeneutic frames that will be dismantled and placed under interrogation. Nashe's textualised pasts are as anxiety ridden and devoid of cultural direction as the present may seem to a late Elizabethan reader; and, in the face of such challenges, his characters frequently try to make sense of their cycles of experience with vain fictions of heroic endeavour: 'Some courtiers to wearie out time would tell vs further tales of *Cornelius Agrippa*, and how when sir *Thomas Moore* our countrie man was there, hee shewed him the whole destruction of Troy in a dreame' (*The vnfortunate traueller*, sig. F4ʳ).

The large canvas of sixteenth-century European history emerges as increasingly threadbare as Nashe teases out one narrative strand after another with the resources of parody, sarcasm, inversion, bathos and satire. Urged on by the promise of Wilton's very own 'stratagemicall actes and monuments', the reader embarks in 1513 on a journey to Henry's sieges of Tournai and Térouanne, and then Nashe's century undergoes a disorienting process of revision as we are made to zigzag back and forth across the decades dropping in to join, among other events, the Field of the Cloth of Gold in 1520 in the company of François Iᵉʳ, a freak-show rendering of the sweating sickness in London in 1517, Luther's debate with Carlstadt at Wittenberg in 1519, Leiden's Anabaptist uprising in 1535 elided with the battle of Frankenhausen in 1525, the battle of Marignano in 1515, implausible adventures involving Surrey sometime in the 1530s and so on and so forth. Yet Wilton's frantic itinerary back and forth across Europe offers him strategic opportunities to reflect upon abiding faultlines and sources of disaffection in Tudor society. The routes he selects initially appear baffling; and they inevitably trigger experiences of textual discontinuity and reader harassment that the narrative explicitly acknowledges:

> sleepe an houre or two, and dreame that Turney and Turwin is wonne, that the King is ship't againe into England, and that I am close at harde meate at Windsore or at Hampton court. What will you in your indifferent opinions allow me for my trauell, no more seigniorie ouer the Pages than I had before? yes, whether you will parte with so much probable friendly suppose or no, Ile haue it in spite of your heartes.[21]

If we discover Wilton is in fact travelling from the 'Munsterian conflict' to Italy via Rotterdam, for example, Nashe is collapsing familiar schemes of chronology and geography in order to excite vigorous reader engagement. Wilton's journeys emerge as a kind of narrative shorthand that enables his reader to juxtapose in swift succession formative sites of cultural self-definition for Elizabethan England. And we should remain mindful that even in the most desperate of scrapes that Wilton endures, Nashe is keen to allow all narrative lines of enquiry to converge upon a study of English political culture. So that even when contemplating the interior of an Italian prison, an exiled English earl is brought forward to remind Wilton and Surrey of the risks they are running:

> Countriman, tell mee what is the occasion of thy straying so farre out of *England* to visit this strange Nation. If it bee languages, thou maist learne them at home, nought but lasciuiousness is to be learned here … wee had rather liue as slaues in another land, crouch and cap, and bee seruile to euerie iealous Italians and proude Spaniards humor, where wee may neyther speake look nor doo anie thing, but what pleaseth them: than liue as free-men and Lords in our owne country.[22]

While the exiled earl is underlining the sins of forgetfulness and unruly desire to his captive compatriots, he is also asking the larger community of auditors to reflect upon native myths of belonging constructed across time and space. Ultimately, *The vnfortunate traueller* unpicks the defining past of the Elizabethans and suggests that his society's urgent quest for cultural rootedness and security must acknowledge that a myriad of discourses of history may be invoked and adopted – and none may be greeted uniformly with unwavering awe. The religiously and politically charged *loci* that Wilton inhabits during the course of *The vnfortunate traueller* indicate that he is not simply being deployed as textual witness: he is also uncovering epistemological uncertainties and his adventures gesture towards a multitude of pasts that might have come to fruition.

DELONEY, MEMORY AND LABOUR

John Carey has argued that '[Deloney's] fiction for the working classes was immensely popular, supplying what its readers wished to believe: that foreigners are funny, that apprentices marry rich widows, and serving-maids, courtiers, that nobles talk Euphuism, that Henry VIII rubbed shoulders with artisans and "laughed heartily" when they smeared his jester with dog droppings'.[23] Rather than submit without demur to such an unnuanced reading of Deloney's work as an act of nostalgic recuperation, it may be more fruitful to rely less upon such bodies of received thinking and entertain the possibility that we may renew our textual dialogues with the unfinished past in order to access the cultural power of intervention. Part of Deloney's re-membering of the Henrician past, with its celebration in heroic strains of the social mobility of an artisan employer, must inevitably serve to unsettle the rigid ideology of rank and civic subjectivity in evidence during the reign of the last Tudor monarch.

Indeed, the conventional aristocratic *habitus* (of paternalism, hospitality, military service, fealty to the Crown and so on) is made freely available to the successful merchant in his fictions.

If *Jack of Newbury* (1597) does not take issue with the cultural markers of rank and hierarchy as strategic structuring devices for the social order, Deloney does attend to the possibilities of new projects of selfhood emerging in the late Elizabethan period in which lineage and royal favour no longer function as the sole organising principles in this particular *chain of being*. The inherited discourses of aristocratic magnanimity (*magnus animus*) and magnificence (*magnus facere*) are textually superseded by the ethical and cultural initiative of the propertied merchant as the most significant manifestation of Tudor citizenship. Strikingly, the courtiers are progressively silenced in the power relations imagined in Deloney's Henrician past, and their economic inertia makes them appear destructive and/or superfluous to the well-being of the nation. Indeed, it would seem that the aristocrats are paradoxly condemned to the margins of the narrative by accidents of birth.[24] This may be exemplified from the manner in which Jack showcases his talents for moral policing: he is frequently discovered discharging the responsibilities of the *grand seigneur* and, indeed, a nobleman is asked to account for his erotic dallying with one of the maidservants. In the latter phases of the narrative, Sir George is made to stoop while Jack conquers, and the merchant hero dons the garb of magistrate as well as that of a stage manager when he has his maid disguised as a rich heiress in order to gull Sir George and to manoeuvre him back into the moral order of romance:

> Came you to my table to make my maide your strumpet? had you no mans house to dishonour but mine? Sir, I would you should well know, that I account the poorest wench in my house to good to bee your whore, were you ten knights: and seeing you tooke pleasure to make her your wanton, take it no scorne to make her your wife: and vse her well too, or you shall heare of it. And hold thee *Ioane* (quoth hee) there is a hundred pounds for thee: And let him not say thou camest to him a begger ... And thus they liued afterward in great ioy: and our King hearing how *Iacke* had matcht sir *George*, laughing heartily thereat, gaue him a liuing for euer, the better to maintaine my Lady his Wife.[25]

And now that Jack has brought his aristocratic betters to order, his wife curtsies to her former maid who is now become a Lady – and thus, the whole community pays homage to the ethical power that has been restored to the social structure and that radiates from the master clothier. No longer, it seems, can the feckless aristocrat be trusted with duties of social government. The Tudor ascendancy (which Deloney fantastically conjures up in his fictive world of early sixteenth-century England) comes into being by relying upon values of paternalism and ownership, rather than those of custom and lineage. It is, however, worth pondering at greater length how Deloney justifies the power assertions of the socially mobile Jack by drawing upon a well-established discourse of lordly munificence. When royalty is entertained in Newbury there is no evidence of mercantile parsimony, every detail of hospitality is expressed in the grand style of noble country houses – but if Jack refuses a knighthood as a reward for the peerless services he has rendered, the court finds alternative means to bind this powerful subject to its authority through the power of gift-exchange and preferment: Henry and his courtiers adopt weavers' children to act as servants in their households, and Queen Katherine, 'taking her leaue of the good wife with a Princely kisse, gaue her in token of remembrance a most precious and rich Diamond set in gold, about the which was also curiously set sixe Rubies, and sixe Emeralds in one peece, valued at nine hundred Markes: and so her Grace departed' (*Jack of Newbury*, sig. G2ᵛ). In his study of early modern drama, Garrett Sullivan Jr importantly draws attention to the fact that 'Memory disciplines and interpellates the subject into the social order', and memory is materially communicated in Deloney's textual world yoking subject and sovereign together, as we see above in the queen's 'token of remembrance'.[26] However, if Jack of Newbury's acts of loyalty and largesse are regularly confirmed by the sovereign (as in the case of Sir George's marriage), it is the merchant's, rather than Henry's, dynamic form of patronage that is repeatedly proposed as a moral yardstick by which to adjudge all actions in the narrative.

Deloney's fiction taps into accounts of the Tudor past in order to promote alternative paradigms of labour relations to those operational in Elizabethan England. Those critical studies that devote any attention to Deloney's work have made much of the fact that in 1595 Deloney was one of the weavers arrested for drawing up a complaint to the authorities, detailing injustices that foreign weavers were not subject to the same trading regulations as native English ones. Such knowledge certainly contextualises the supplication of Jack and his fellow clothiers to the king, which spells out that, in this society, 'the poore hate the rich because they will not set them on worke; and the rich hate the poore, because they seeme burdenous; so both are offended for want of gaine' (*Jack of Newbury*, sig. H2ʳ). Moreover, in Strype's edition of Stow's *Survey of London* (1720) it is recorded that the Mayor of London came across one of Deloney's ballads in 1596,

containing a Complaint of great Want and Scarcity of Corn within the Realm. And forasmuch as it contained in it certain vain and presumptuous matters, bringing in the Queen, speaking with People Dialogue-wise in fond and undecent sort ... and prescribing Order for the remedying of this Dearth of Corn ... done in that Vain and indiscreet manner, as that thereby the Poor might aggravate their Grief, and take occasion of some Discontentment.[27]

Given this broader context of social unease, the possibility that *Jack of Newbury* may be transporting its readers back to Henrician England to scrutinise issues of mercantile dissatisfaction and government unresponsiveness in the 1590s appears less remote. In Deloney's textual vision, early sixteenth-century England is clearly a place where Henry VIII does not hesitate to attend to the distresses of his merchant subjects. If Deloney is thought to be constructing some kind of Socratic dialogue with an idealised past in which an alternative (indeed, inverted) matrix of cultural interactions between a (male?) sovereign and artisans is rewritten in the service of the present, we are nonetheless left in no doubt what kind of readership is being targeted for most particular attention. Deloney dedicates his prose fiction 'To all famous Cloth-Workers in England, I wish all happinesse of life, prosperity and *brotherly affection*'. Indeed, in this prefatory discussion, the author confides strategically that he has rooted around in 'the dust of Forgetfulnesse' and discovered 'a most famous and worthie man, whose name was *Iohn Winchcombe*, alias *Iacke* of *Newberie*, of whose life and loue I have briefly written, and in a plaine and humble manner, that it may be the better vnderstood of those for whose sake I took pains to compile it, that is, for the well minded Clothiers' (*Jack of Newbury*, sig. A2^r–A2^v).

Given our prior knowledge of the king's erotic career, it is all too clear that even this benign court presided over by Henry and Katherine of Aragon is a fragile, illusory and, ultimately, transient cultural construct. Moreover, Henry's absence on (what the Elizabethan reader knew to be) fruitless continental wars and Jack's prominent involvement in levying forces during Katherine's regency to resist the army of James IV of Scotland in the north of the country equally point to an imperfect exercise of sovereignty. In this particular instance, these political crises can only be remedied by an expression of Jack's superlative loyalty to the Crown in the recruitment of forces; and this debt to the premier Tudor subject is recognised extravagantly in the amount of royal (and textual) attention he is awarded in this prose narrative. Drawing explicitly upon the resources of romance, Deloney blurs the distinctions for his Elizabethan readers between imaginative possibility and observable fact by exploiting the notion of festive labour. At this point, we may be reminded of Bakhtin's 'carnivalesque crowd', which appears (and only 'appears') to be 'the people as a whole', but 'outside of and contrary to all existing forms of the coercive socioeconomic and political organization, which is suspended for the time of the festivity'.[28] Indeed, when Henry and Katherine choose to view Jack's weavers at their looms in the workshop, they are treated to a lyrical outburst from the shop floor:

> When *Hercules* did vse to spin,
> and *Pallas* wrought vpon the Loome,
> Our trade to flourish did begin,
> while Conscience went not selling Broomes.
> Then loue and friendship did agree,
> To keep the band of vnitie.
> (*Jack of Newbury*, sig. F1ᵛ)

This is just one of a myriad of responses in Deloney's text to the seductive myth of a heroic past that is being summoned up in order to legitimise models of economic success. Jane M. Kinney contends that 'in *Jack of Newbury* what Deloney in essence creates is a mercantile utopia: a happy monarch and a happy merchant class working together to make a happy and prosperous England'.[29] Nonetheless, before we succumb effortlessly to a 'heroic' fiction of master-and-worker harmony, it might be more valuable to scratch away at the textual appetites of his readership for nostalgia. David Margolies is surely timely in his emphasis that 'it is easy to overlook Deloney's role as a propagandist because he presents his values as valid … But his attitudes are no more natural than Sir Philip Sidney's and his excursions into history, no less than Sidney's chivalry, are value-laden. In such figures as John Winchcomb Deloney "discovers" bourgeois values in the past'.[30] As the narrative unfolds, Deloney's reader might also be inclined to put pressure upon the notion of the common-man-made-good through his own industry. Judith Broome Mesa-Pelly argues justly that, 'despite Jack's worthy character and prudent bookkeeping, he gets ahead, not by his superior craftsmanship, but through his pure good fortune: he marries the master's widow. We never actually see Jack weaving. Jack's ability as a weaver – or his lack of it – is not the only thing suppressed in Deloney's nearly seamless fantasy of social mobility'.[31] (It is surely worth underlining that such fantasies of miraculous possession and social climbing were viewed in quite a different light by Webster, some ten years later, when he came to dramatise Antonio in *The Duchess of Malfi*.)

At several reprises we are encouraged to fête the *doings* of a new breed of gentlemen, a new order of worthies – chivalric merchants who are no longer stigmatised with vulgarity for their involvement in trade and money-dealing. In this area, for Laura Stevenson, there is a clear contrast between Deloney's undertaking and those of earlier generations of Tudor writers: 'Before Elizabeth's reign, merchants and craftsmen appeared only in negative literary contexts – in sermons condemning avarice, in estates satires exposing greed and dishonesty, and in chronicles lamenting the fickleness of the commonalty.'[32] Clearly, in prose narratives such as *Jack of Newbury* and the later *Thomas of Reading* (1600) (which unfolds in an England of another Henry – Henry I) we are urged to bear witness to the matchless authority of a sovereign who enjoyed continued popular support – it should, however, be observed that such popular support is locked in an oblique past and is subjected to highly variable ratios of intelligibility. In *Thomas of Reading*, the legitimacy of Henry I is challenged by his marginalised elder brother Duke Robert. While this intrigue focusing on the pretender's relationship with the disguised daughter of the Earl of Shrewsbury is largely confined within the generic expectations of romance, Henry I is deployed textually as the *blessed* recipient of merchant approval. His kingship is thus duly celebrated as he demonstrates his capacity to honour the material prosperity created by some of his most strategic political allies, the master clothiers. Furthermore, the narrative begins with the king as spectator to the endless caravans of cloth-bearing carts wending their way to market. In the earlier *Jack of Newbury*, Henry VIII is shown to be acutely sensitive to the swelling coffers of the fortunate merchants; and, if anything, the king functions primarily in order to confirm the worth of the hero's mercantile energy and largesse. Thus, the Tudor patriarch is more significant as audience and intercessor than cultural magistrate: indeed, he is seen primarily to enjoy the benefits of an ascending theory of power. Interestingly, Deloney's Henry VIII is shown to be so impressed by the economic and cultural leadership expressed in Jack's conduct that he offers to legitimise his meteoric rise through the ranks of society with a knighthood. Jack, however, prefers to have his status articulated solely in economic terms.

In chapter 5 of *Jack of Newbury* Deloney's reader is treated to a *through-the-keyhole* experience of the hero's household with a tour of his personal gallery of fifteen portraits. Norman Jones is persuasive in his emphasis that such galleries supplanted the cloister in the new architectural spaces of Reformist England:

> As the City companies were recasting their customs they, like all other organizations which sought benefactions, reinvented the purposes and memorialization of benefactions ... In hall after hall, portraits, in paint or glass, memorialised the great donors and leaders, creating a secular genealogy to replace the connection

to the saints. At the same time, a rising tide of historical enthusiasm created a new collective memory for organizations, one that discounted the religious connection and celebrated the communal virtues.³³

Moreover, in this context, it is interesting to note that Bakhtin highlighted that 'Greatness always makes itself known only to descendants, for whom such a quality is always located in the past (it turns into a distanced image); it has become an object of memory and not a living object that one can see and touch ... One may, and in fact one must, memorialize with artistic language only that which is worthy of being remembered'.³⁴ And thus the inheritor of greatness must indicate for all eyes his close proximity to a heroic past. In Sidney's *Arcadia*, for example, the munificence of the *seigneur* Kalander is amply communicated when Musidorus is led to 'a house of pleasure built for a Sommer retiring place; whither *Kalander* leading him, he found a square roome full of delightfull pictures made by the moste excellent workman of Greece'.³⁵ As the romance unfolds, this grand architectural statement of rank, privilege and ownership becomes intimately bound up with the erotic ambitions of the indomitably patrician heroes: 'Cousin (said [Pyrocles]) then began the fatal ouerthrow of all my libertie ... walking among the pictures in Kalander's house ... there were mine eyes infected.'³⁶

In Deloney's narrative, as we perambulate textually along this gallery, we discover domestic space being deployed politically by the master employer as a site to rival aristocratic promotions of coats of arms or genealogies. This instance is one among many in the prose fictions under consideration where we are asked not only to attend primarily to the motivations at work behind individual stimuli of memory but, equally importantly, to the ambitions of the protagonist to control our angle of vision upon the grand narrative of History itself. Here, Jack is seen to stage for a select audience of 'friends and servants' a heroic lineage for the upwardly mobile artisan. Chiming together the names of Diocletian, Marcus Aurelius, Pope John XXII and so on, Jack raids celebrated accounts from the past in order to confirm his own performance of social ascent:

In a faire large Parlour which was wainscotted about, *Iack of Newburie* had fifteene fair Pictures hanging, which were couered with curtains of greene silke, fringed with gold, which hee would often shew to his friends and seruants. In the first was the Picture of a shepheard, before whom kneeled a great King named *Viriat*, who sometime gouerned the people of *Portugall*. See here, quoth *Iacke*, the father a shepheard, the sonne a Soueraigne. This man ruled in *Portugall*, and made great warres against the Romanes, and after that inuaded *Spaine*, yet in the end was traitorously slaine.

   The next was the Portraiture of *Agathocles*, which for his surpassing wisdome and manhood was created King of *Sicilia*, and maintained battaile against the people of *Carthage*. His father was a poore Potter, before whom he also kneeled. And it was the vse of this King, that whensoeuer he made a banquet, he would haue as well vessells of earth as of gold set vpon the Table, to the intent he might alwaies bear in minde the place of his beginning, his Fathers house and family.[37]

The gallery in Jack's house is significant not only for its investment in a fantasy of feudal ownership conventionally associated with baronial dwellings, it is also a memory theatre in which the images of Jack's adopted ancestors allow everyone present to reacquaint themselves in a spectacular manner with successful endeavours at social mobility 'in the daies of King *Henrie* the eight, that most noble and victorious Prince' (sig. A3ʳ).

GASCOIGNE AND ARTFUL RETROSPECTION

Such was the wider level of anxiety in some quarters that appears to have greeted Gascoigne's anonymously published miscellany *A Hundreth Sundrie Flowers* (1573) that he swiftly brought out a revised collection, *The Posies of George Gascoigne*, in 1575 in which he confessed, 'I heare that ["sundrie wanton speeches and lascivious phrases"] have been doubtfully construed'.[38] From the sketchy evidence that survives it seems that there may have been those in high places who recognised that the novella might be a *roman-à-clé*, and thus sought to suppress it after the first publication.[39] When the revised text, *The Posies*, appeared in 1575, the dedicatees now turned out to be 'the reuerende Diuines'. Interestingly, the 1575 publication estranges the Elizabethan reader even further by identifying the protagonists of 'A Pleasant discourse of the aduentures of Master F. J.' as residing within 'The Fable of *Ferdinando Jeronimi*, and *Leonora de Valasco*' ('translated out of the Italian Riding Tales of Bartello').[40] This later miscellany, *The Posies*, is now organised into sections, and that of Master F.J. is not ranged among those entitled 'Flowers' or 'Herbs', but consigned to the rear of the publication among the 'Weeds'.[41] Whatever the labours may have been on Gascoigne's part to address the concerns of those who censured him, they were clearly insufficient – for some fifty copies of the new miscellany were seized in 1576.

   As its narrative unfolds, Gascoigne's original 1573 text makes possible multiple points of contact between different time frames, and in each case the stress falls upon flawed human achievement. Indeed, at the very outset, G.T.'s letter to H.W. partakes of a Sidneian sorrow in bearing witness to the inadequacy of any attempt to formulate a grand narrative for the nation's literary output:

> our natiue countrimen … [have not] (translations excepted) deliuered vnto vs any such notable volume, as haue bene by Poets of antiquitie, left vnto the posteritie. And the more pitie, that amongst so many toward wittes no one hath bene hitherto encouraged to followe the trace of that worthy and famous Knight Sir Geffrey Chaucer.[42]

In his own account of sixteenth-century poetics, *A discourse of English poetrie Together with the author's iudgment, touching the reformation of our English verse* (1586), William Webbe had asserted authoritatively that 'The ende of Poetry is to wryte pleasant thinges, and profitable. Pleasant it is which delighteth by beeing not too long, or vneasy to be kept in memory, and which is somewhat likelie, and not altogether forged'.[43] This appetite for harmonious, uplifting, highly moralised writing which might be held conveniently in the memory was widely articulated by almost every Tudor author who bothered to afford any attention at all to questions of literary theory, yet it is conclusively thwarted in Gascoigne's 'Pleasant discourse'. Laments (both in poetry and prose) relating to literary, erotic and/or moral inadequacy, frequently punctuate the account of F.J.'s adventures, and serve to puncture any desire the reader might have to attribute some measure of heroic commitment to an earlier age. And yet this fictional world constantly strives to dignify the desire to revisit the past and reaffirms the privileges of the *vita contemplativa* to which this desire belongs:

> And yet for a man to record vnto him selfe in the inward contemplation of his mynde the often remembrance of his late receiued ioyes, doth as it were ease the hart of burden, and ad vnto the mynd a fresh supplie of delight, yea and in verse principally (as I conceyue) a man may best contriue this way of comforte in him selfe.[44]

In the event, few if any of the voices in Gascoigne's textual world of earthly delights choose to invest very deeply in a meditative calling. It is, of course, all the more ironic that the narrator G.T. should value the cultural performance of private reflection so highly when he is textually deployed as an agent of disclosure – bringing together documents chronicling erotic subterfuge and moral collapse in a country house community. Ultimately, it proves impossible to rectify the poor mediation of the past by returning to the close analysis and commentary of the sources. All narrative enquiries in Gascoigne's text constantly succumb to misprisions imposed by the competing ambitions of the various participants: while F.J. chooses to bewail his erotic frustration in verse, the prurient Dame Frances (initially at least) looks forward to the 'due triall of the experiment long desired' ('Pleasant discourse', p. 220), but is equally stimulated by the delays that intervene; the changeful Elinor appears to take equal pleasure in intrigue and adultery; and G.T. endeavours to assume a choric status with a seemingly endless fund of speculations, and so on and so forth. In this way, the hermeneutic horizon of the narrative is already crowded even before Gascoigne's readers try to make space for their own speculations. We are drawn successively in contrary directions, most especially by G.T.'s often terse revelations that: communications supposedly by Elinor have been penned by her secretary; Dame Frances's and Dame Pergo's interpretative missions are intimately related to their desires; and that F.J. is thoroughly unable to identify his own departures from his adopted and progressively implausible persona as courtly lover. F.J's desires of bedding (and then raping) the 'cruel fair' involve him in 'un-manning' the lord of the Great House and recovering a medievalised fantasy of the *droit de seigneur*. Indeed, the dissolution of Petrarchan suit and feudal service is held in keen tension with the violent expression of erotic appetite throughout the narrative.

Interestingly, the 'cruel fair', Dame Elinor, in Gascoigne's 'Pleasant discourse' is initially very reluctant to enter any interpretive community: '*For that I vnderstand not* (quoth shee) *th'intent of your letters, I pray you take them here againe, and bestow them at your pleasure.* The which done and sayde, shee passed by without change either of pace or countenance' (p. 207). Nevertheless, a tangled matrix of hermeneutic possibilities has already been opened up by Gascoigne before the account of F.J.'s erotic career has even begun. Like Thomas More at the beginning of his *Utopia*, Gascoigne stresses the difficulties of establishing any authoritative access to the past by generating a number of competing paratexts drawing attention to: the printer A.B.; how G.T. collated the various documents of his friend F.J.; how G.T. provided a commentary on them; how G.T. gave sight to H.W. of these documents belonging to their mutual friend F.J.; how H.W. encouraged the printer to publish them despite the fact that G.T. had insisted that H.W. should 'by no means make the same common' (p. 204).[45] As these varying bids for authorship jostle for position and authority, readers are furnished with multiple points of contact with F.J.'s youth; and, as a consequence, they are clearly frustrated (seemingly, the default position for all human experience in Gascoigne's fictional world) in any ambitions they may foster to locate in definitive terms a narrative beginning or a finalised past. Hemmed in by a cluster of disclaimers, preambles and prefatory discussions of uncertain provenance, each of Gascoigne's readers is thus left to fend for him- or herself, and to pick the bones of F.J.'s poetic 'confessions' and memorial fragments.

Gillian Austen argues that 'Gascoigne's intrusive narrator is … a disloyal confidant, a poor editor, an inept critic', yet, more generally, it becomes increasingly difficult to contextualise disloyalty, astute interpretation and vain human achievement in a fiction riddled with examples of interpretative failure.[46] In this context, we may be reminded of G.T.'s conclusions after a lyrical outburst to 'Helen' from F.J. Seemingly unable to decipher a rather tired poetic analogy between the *cruel fair* and Helen of Troy, the stunted mind of G.T. leads him to entertain the possibility that there is a real-life Helen in F.J.'s affections:

I haue heard him declare, [Elinor] grew in ieolosie, that the same were not written by hir, because hir name was *Elynor* and not *Hellen* … And some haue attributed this prayse vnto a *Hellen*, who deserued not so well as this dame *Elynor* should seeme to deserue by the relation of *F. I.* and yet neuer a ba[rr]ell of good herring betwene them both: But that other *Hellen*, bycause she was and is of so base condicion, as may deserue no maner commendacion in any honest iudgement, therfore I will excuse my friend *F. I.* and aduenture my penne in his behalfe, that he would neuer bestow verse of so meane a subiect. An[d] yet some of his acquayntance, being also acquainted (better then I,) that *F. I.* was sometimes acquaynted with *Hellene*, haue stoode in argument with mee, that it was written by *Hellene* and not by *Elynor*.[47]

Such a tangle of fruitless speculation resembles that of some of the early critics of the 'Pleasant discourse' who were drawn obsessively to the belief that Gascoigne's text might be a lightly disguised fragment of very precise memory work. Felix E. Schelling, for one, lamented that 'It was probably during this earlier period of his life at Court that Gascoigne indulged in those questionable amours, of which he has had the bad taste to leave us a careful, if somewhat mystical account' and, in turn, R. S. White also identified 'the emotional pressure of a thinly disguised autobiographical element'.[48] Interestingly, in Book Two of Spenser's epic *The Faerie Queene* we are similarly introduced to an 'vnlucky Squire' who, it appears, has 'Falne into mischiefe through intemperaunce', and he is solemnly exhorted to 'take heede of that thou now hast past, | And guyde thy waies with wane gouernaunce, | Least worse betide thee by some later chaunce' (II.iv.36). However, it is noteworthy that none of the Elizabethan prose fictions under discussion here invites anyone to endure sustained periods of rueful meditation. Foucault proposed that 'If one controls people's memory, one controls their dynamism ... It is vital to have possession of this memory'.⁴⁹ One of the reasons why none of the prose fictions indulges in the Spenserian moral solemnity of retrospection (nor even the abstracted variety communicated by Ophelia – 'There's rosemary, that's for remembrance') may be that relatively little narrative time or space is devoted to the portrayal of contrition. It appears to warrant minimal interest in comparison with erotic or economic speculation. In the case of the 'Pleasant discourse' no conclusive enquiries may be performed by Gascoigne's reader. Both editor and characters continue to puzzle over the nature of all human experience unfolding at the country house in the north of England: in fact, the text stages a crisis of interpretation for everyone attempting to decode its meanings.

Despite the Petrarchan rhetoric of having 'a continuall frost, in ... most feruent fire', it is interesting that the two dominant time frames in this text (of F.J.'s youth and G.T.'s commentary) are increasingly shown to demonstrate less nuanced schemes of gender expectation ('Pleasant discourse', p. 206). The sympathy expressed by G.T. at several reprises for the youthful F.J. and the shared interest in masculinist power assertion lead effortlessly to the denigration of any obstacles on the path to self-gratification – as is the case when a rival presents himself for Elinor's affections in the shape of her secretary: 'Hee was in height, the proportion of twoo pigmies, in breadth the thicknesse of two bacon hogges, of presumption a *Gyant*, of power a Gnat, Apishly wytted, Knauishly mannerd & crabbedly faurd ... This manling, this minion, this slaue, this secretary' ('Pleasant discourse', pp. 215–16). F.J. is not content, it appears, to restrict himself to the customary role of relying solely upon lyrical outbursts as responses to experiences of sexual humiliation and frustration. Even more revealing is the way in which Gascoigne's text obsessively gravitates towards an insatiable interest in F.J.'s experience as erotic victim – an interest that must be mitigated for the reader by the hero's violation of the body of the intermittently *cruel fair* Elinor, of the hospitality offered by Elinor's husband, and F.J.'s distinctly unheroic gloating during the hunting expedition of having reduced the husband to a cuckold. The reader is never allowed to lose sight of the fact that both protagonist and narrator remain conspicuous in choosing to define themselves in relation to the discursive paradox of a sexually promiscuous and intriguingly histrionic mistress: 'the first thing which he felt, was that his good mistres lay pressing his breast wᵗ the whole weight of hir body, and biting his lips with hir friendly teeth' ('Pleasant discourse', p. 269). In such instances the critic Lynette McGrath declares no difficulty in identifying how reader sympathies are directed: 'Elinor, who has no time for codes, understands precisely what F.J.'s motives are, but, without an ethical code of action, she denies herself, her lovers and her husband, the possibility of any other than physical love.'[50] However, rather than limiting Elinor's textual meaning to that of transgressor, it may be more productive in the context of the markedly volatile society of this country house to view her as creatively experimenting with a more varied number of erotic *personae* than Petrarchan discourses would conventionally allow. In fact, as Gascoigne's narrative unfolds, an increasing number of textual voices is found to be interested in the multiple ways in which human identity may be configured:

> but his Mistres could not be quiet vntil shee heard him repeat the *Tyntarnell* which he vsed ouer night, the which F. J. refused not; at end whereof his Mistres … fell to flat playn dealing, and walking to the window, called her seruaunt apart vnto hir, of whom she demaunded secretly & in sad earnest who deuised this *Tyntarnell*? My fathers Sisters brothers sonne (quod F. J.) His Mistresse laughing right hartely, demaunded yit again, by whom the same was figured: by a niece to an Aunt of yours, Mistres (quod he). Well then seruaunt (quod she) I sweare vnto you here by my fathers soule, that my mothers youngest daughter, doth loue your father's eldest son aboue any creature liuing.[51]

The past is thus a place in which the subject's sense of self is as fractured and as irresolvable as in the editor's, G.T.'s, present. Sifting through F.J.'s texts at the distance of some time after the event, it becomes all too obvious that G.T. learns nothing from his own experience or his endeavours at textual praxis. The past does not contain the present in embryonic form: to all intents and purposes, its creatures exist in a parallel state of imperfect knowledge. Indeed, such consuming interests were not confined to prose writers of the early modern period. In his *Sonnets* Shakespeare proposed that his reader might like to 'look what thy memory cannot contain', and that through a reappropriation of the 'waste blanks' of pages, the lines would 'take a new acquaintance of thy mind' (sonnet 77, ll. 9–10, 12). Here, Shakespeare points to the creative power that the operations of textual and memorial labours can assume: how meaning may be endlessly spawned in our composition, reading and re-reading of experience across the 'waste blanks' of the page. The past may be ordered, enriched and endlessly supplemented through the act of writing.

The refusal of the ludic mistress to be contained within the period's prevailing discourses of the feminine (in terms of silence, obedience, piety and chastity) enables Gascoigne to expose the implications of the ideological formulation of male desire in terms of control and ownership.

Clearly, Elinor's protean cultural meaning is a decisive obstacle to F.J.'s ambitions of erotic success, which is to say in narrative terms, desire for self-completion. Whether Elinor is designated by F.J. and G.T. as 'cruel fair', *femme fatale* or sexual prey, she is always for these men a barely legible, corrupt text rather than a transparent, resolvable one. Surrounded by a bewildering accumulation of documents spinning out yarns of erotic gaming, Gascoigne's textually/sexually inexperienced editor/narrator G.T. confesses his own sense of vulnerability in trying to tease order from chaos:

> But why hold I so long discourse in discribing the ioyes which (for lacke of like experience) I cannot set out to ye full? Were it not that I knowe to whom I write, I would the more beware what I write. F. I. was a man, and neither of vs are sencelesse, and therfore I shold slaunder him, (ouer and besides a greater obloquie to the whole genealogie of Aeneas) if I should imagine that of tender hart he would forbeare to express hir more tender limbes against the hard floore. Suffised that of hir curteouse nature she was content to accept bords for a bed of downe, mattes for Camerike sheetes, and the night gowne of F. I. for a counterpoynt to couer them.[52]

Tellingly, by the final phases of the affair, G.T. makes no attempt to finesse the record of his mental reflexes for subsequent reader consumption. Indeed, he permits himself the following peroration, coloured by his own well-tested inclinations for psychological projection and elision: 'I doubt not, but shee slept quietly the rest of the night' (p. 271).[53]

In this way, Elinor becomes a valuable specular agent for editor and protagonist, refracting in a highly selective manner what they perceive to be the effects of their power. Nonetheless, F.J.'s and G.T.'s fantasies of a sympathetic erotic economy in the Great House have only a provisional reality, if they have any reality at all. More generally, at such points, it is clearly worth questioning how much Gascoigne allows his reader to disengage from the epistemological discomfort and voyeuristic speculation of G.T. The multiplicities of intrigues and the partial nature of textual transmissions in this *récit* reveal evidence of human limitation at every interpretative level. In direct comparison with *The vnfortunate traueller* and *Jack of Newbury*, the 'Pleasant discourse' explicitly focuses upon the ways in which the past may be *produced* for succeeding generations. Yet, ultimately, what can such productions hope to achieve? Stimulate reader identification? Generate a realm of vicarious human experience? Formulate an enquiry leading to moral edification? Demonstrate the wisdom that may be gained from studious application to documents of the past? All of these metanarratives are foiled as Gascoigne's complex text unfolds. Unable to secure sufficient data with which to arrive at persuasive conclusions, the beleaguered G.T. falls back on his fund of prejudices, anxieties and tentative recollections in the attempt to assert control over this profoundly intriguing and unwieldy narrative.

Each of the texts under discussion in this chapter reveals itself as being equally eager to expose the selective and transformative nature of our engagements with historical narrative – a contribution that Bakhtin would attribute to the later novelisation of literature: the introduction of 'an indeterminacy, a certain semantic openendedness, a living contact with unfinished, still-evolving contemporary reality (the openended present)'.[54] The fictional worlds of Gascoigne, Nashe and Deloney worry away at the motives behind a culture's need to remember; and they each speculate about its desire to exploit the authority of both collective and individual memorial discourses in order to validate ideological value-systems in the present. Nonetheless, the ambition to configure the past during the early modern period is never simply about memorial excavation and textual editing; as has been witnessed in earlier chapters, it all too frequently discloses the urgent desire for reassuring myths of belonging from the perspective of a seemingly volatile or hostile present.

RECALLING ELIZABETHAN FICTION

In general terms, Elizabethan fiction has continued to present its readers with enormous difficulties regarding taxonomy. C. S. Lewis had to content himself with identifying 'the romantic, the realistic, and one other for which I can find no satisfactory name. Its characteristic is that it subordinates narrative to rhetoric'.[55] John Carey proposed that '[Elizabethan] fiction is thoroughly and (with the exception of Nashe's *vnfortunate traueller*) deservedly dead. This is not just because it has been superseded by the novel, but also because it was meticulously superficial'.[56] However, a less solemn A. C. Hamilton has asked his readers to consider 'Elizabethan prose fiction [as] the Harlequin romance of the late sixteenth century'; and, more recently, Andrew Hadfield has submitted that, 'like so many genres or kinds of literature produced in the Renaissance it is hard to underestimate the experimental nature of these works. Moreover, we do not really know that the writers themselves realized what they were doing and were basing their efforts on tried and tested models that were commonly understood'.[57]

Nonetheless, in their very different ways, Gascoigne, Nashe and Deloney may be seen to be reinvestigating cultural narratives of origination, reopening old scenes of cultural antagonism and conflict, in order to delineate the selves we might have been. The reason why such narratives may be attractive to contemporary readers at the beginning of the twenty-first century is all too apparent, as R. Malcolm Smuts underlines: 'The history of Elizabethan and Stuart political culture has perhaps reached ... a juncture. Old ways of unifying the subject, rooted in Whig, Marxist and other teleologies, no longer appear convincing, but adequate alternatives have not yet emerged to replace them.'[58] If these narratives invest an extravagant amount of energy in restaging the past, we might like to view them as engaging keenly with pervasive anxiety-ridden Elizabethan obsessions with recollection, affiliation and legitimacy. Indeed, Andrew Hadfield suggests that 'profound paranoia' is 'arguably the definitive mood of the early English novel'.[59]

There seem to have been few pairs of eyes to acknowledge the achievement of Gascoigne's prose text in the 1570s, and only in the latter decades of the twentieth century has the 'Pleasant discourse' been thought to deserve scholarly attention. Despite being registered in 1597, the earliest copies that survive of *Jack of Newbury* are from the 1619 imprint. Thus, it is all too possible that editions of Deloney's texts were read by contemporaries to the point of disintegration, but it was only F. O. Mann's edition of his works at the beginning of the twentieth century that renewed critical interest in him. In *The vnfortunate traueller*, Nashe offers the 'conueyance of historie & varietie of mirth' (sig. A2r). However, despite his declared intentions to 'canonise' Henry Wriothesley for 'posterity' in the prefatory material, the text of *The vnfortunate traueller* appears not to have been printed between 1594 and Grosart's edition in 1883.

The constant shuttling back and forth between time frames in Gascoigne's, Nashe's and Deloney's prose narratives raises questions about the textual intervention of these works in our own times. Thomas Healy has argued that 'Renaissance texts are exciting both as repositories of vanished cultural practices and as empowered writing which can help us to clarify and more clearly address our own cultural needs'.[60] The past can clearly be configured in an endless number of different ways – for Nashe, even through the puffs of smoke of Cornelius Agrippa at the Emperor's court. In summoning up Erasmus, More, Luther, the Earl of Surrey, Henry VIII, François Ier and so on during the course of his narrative, Nashe asks us to reflect upon a geography of religious and political space that is not monopolised by cultural elites: one in which Wilton, Diamante, Heraclide, Zadoch have by far the most significant and dynamic textual presences. The conventional heroes of history become framing devices for discussion in all the texts under discussion: 'And so as my Storie began with the king at Turnay and Turwin, I thinke meet heere to end it with the king at Ardes & Guines' (*The vnfortunate traueller*, sig. O4ʳ). Gascoigne, Nashe and Deloney each urge readers to reflect upon the undisciplined faculty of memory. Ultimately ridiculing Elizabethan taste for didacticism, Gascoigne draws his narrative proceedings to a close, confiding that 'it is now time to make an end of this thriftlesse Historie, wherein although I could wade much further ... Yet I will cease, as one that had rather leaue it vnperfect than make it to plaine' ('Pleasant discourse', p. 292).

In his obsessive concern with the cultural benefits to be reaped from a study of mercantile empire-building, Deloney sought to generate alternative narratives of social order to those proposed by the Tudor authorities. Nashe and Gascoigne uncover such frictional energies at work in any interpretation of the past that their readers are more often confronted with textual aporia than alternative modes of cultural narrativisation. The cultural theorist Elizabeth Tonkin has proposed that 'We live in other people's pasts whether we know it or not and whether we want to do so or not';[61] and it becomes increasingly apparent that all three writers under consideration in this chapter reflect upon how their prose narratives, embedded in earlier Tudor pasts, may be digested by their Elizabethan readers – and, in so doing, Nashe, for one, meditates not only upon an endlessly producible past, but also upon the parlous nature of all textual commitments:

A proper fellow page of yours called Iack Wilton, by me commends him vnto you, and hath bequeathed for wast paper here amongst you certaine pages of his misfortunes. In anie case keep them preciously as a priuie token of his goodwill towards you. If there bee some better than other, he craues you would honour them in theyr death so much, as to drie & kindle Tobacco with them ... All the conclusiue Epilogue I will make is this; that if herein I haue pleased any, it shall animate me to more paynes in this kind. Otherwise I will sweare vpon an English Chronicle, neuer to bee out-landish Chronicler more while I liue. Farewell as manie as wish me well. Iune 27, 1593.[62]

CHAPTER 5

The Doleful Clorinda? Mary Sidney, Countess of Pembroke, and the vocation of memory

> For what is it that enables us to remember, or what character has it, or what is its origin?
>
> Cicero, *Tusculan Disputations*, I.xxiv.59[1]

But lett your Ladyship take what course y^t shall please you with me, this shalbee myne with you [that] you may repent you of so many ill spent yeares of so vaine a book and that you may redeeme the tym with writing as large a volume of heavenly layes and holy love as you have of lascivious tales and amorous toyes that at the last you may followe the rare, and pious example of your vertuous and learned Aunt, who translated so many godly books and especially the holly psalmes of David, that no doubt now shee sings in the quier of Heaven those devine meditations which shee so sweetly tuned heer belowe, and which being left to us heer on earth will begett hir dayly more and more glory in heaven as others by [them] shalbe enlightened, who as so many trophies shall appear to her further exaltation in gods favour, with which prayer for you I end and rest
 Your most wellwishing frend

Edward Denny[2]

While much has been made critically of the ways in which writers such as Katherine Philips in the second half of the seventeenth century were held up to succeeding generations of women as potential role models for female engagement with print culture, the processes of cultural remembering surrounding Mary Sidney, Countess of Pembroke, are equally instructive in their insights into early modern society's relations with its (textual) pasts. The extract above concludes a vigorous letter of complaint to Pembroke's niece, Lady Mary Wroth, from Sir Edward Denny, who believed that he had been satirised (as appears to have been the case) in Wroth's prose romance *The Countess of Montgomery's Urania* (1621). On its title page, *Urania* proclaims itself to be written by the 'neece to the ever famous, and renowned Sr. Phillips Sidney knight. And to the most exele[n]t Lady

Mary Countesse of Pembroke late deceased', and indeed many critics have speculated that Pembroke herself is figured forth in the prose romance as the Queen of Naples. Nonetheless, the ranting Denny insists that if Wroth must violate cultural proprieties by taking up the pen in the first place, then she should acknowledge the full weight of her Sidneian past and be controlled (rather than empowered) by the 'pious example' of her aunt. However, there remain intriguing questions surrounding Pembroke's own participation in the ongoing Tudor commitment to the textual projects of *imitatio*, memorialisation and heroic narrative.

MEMORY AND MOURNING

The cultural productions of Pembroke in the 1590s were intimately related to those of another in which she was fully implicated – those of her brother, Philip Sidney, who had died as a result of wounds received at the battle of Zutphen in 1586. To all intents and purposes, Pembroke's writing career appears to have been substantially triggered through responses to the death of her brother. Nor, it must be added, was she by any means alone in shaping her own authorial identity for public consumption in this way. Recalling his close friendship with the fallen knight in his own *Life of Sir Philip Sidney* (1652), for example, Fulke Greville submitted, 'although with *Socrates*, I professe to know nothing for the present; yet with *Nestor* I am delighted in repeating old newes of the ages past; and will therefore stir up my drooping memory touching this mans worth, powers, wayes and designes'.[3]

One of the ways in which the sister's cultural profile was significantly articulated in the 1590s was through the editing and publication of the writings of her dead brother. Sidney had dedicated his prose romance *Arcadia* to her, and acknowledged in a prefatory letter that it was composed 'most of it in your presence, the rest by sheetes, sent vnto you, as fast as they were done'.[4] In response to Greville's 1591 publication of the *Arcadia*, Pembroke brought out a revised and edited version in 1593: Hugh Sanford, secretary to the Pembrokes, specified that 'The disfigured face … wherewith this worke not long since appeared to the common view, moued that noble Lady to whose honour consecrated, to whose protection it was committed … to take in hand the wiping away those spottes wherewith the beauties thereof were vnworthely blemished'.[5] Sidney's prose romance is itself suffused with 'ouer-busie Remembrance, Remembrance, restlesse Remembrance', and, in a host of different ways, the publications of Sidney's *œuvre* and the praise lavished upon his writing in this period not only celebrated (for contemporaries) the possibilities of human achievement, they also gave added voice to the enduring cultural desire to resist the wasting powers of Time.[6] Furthermore, as literary executor, writer and indeed as patroness, Pembroke was not only frequently being seen to remember her dead brother for succeeding generations, she was also memorialising herself into the bargain.

In his *Catechism* (1564), Thomas Becon proved not unrepresentative of his Age in the contention that 'Except the gravity of some matter do require that she should speak, or else an answer is to be made to such things as are demanded of her: let her keep silence. For there is nothing that doth so much commend, avaunce, set forth, adorn, deck, trim and garnish a maid, as silence'.[7] The girl born Mary Sidney in 1561 was extraordinarily well placed in the newly minted Elizabethan society as granddaughter of the Duke of Northumberland, as niece of the queen's favourite Robert Dudley, Earl of Leicester, and as daughter to parents who had served at court under Edward VI, Mary I and Elizabeth herself. Nonetheless, she could not but be aware of the normative pressures at work in her society seeking to circumscribe the activities of any would-be woman writer. In the event, if Pembroke's writing career appears to have spanned the relatively short period of 1588–1601, it did, however, extend to dedicatory and elegiac poems, pastoral dialogue, translations of Petrarch, Philippe de Mornay, Robert Garnier and the Psalms. Her powerful cultural investment in her family and the business of writing were to be formulated and reformulated for wider recognition both during and after her life. What becomes increasingly apparent concerning the memorialisation of Pembroke are the ways in which differing cultural voices compete to promote her as a role model. Simon de Passe's famous engraving of her (see Figure 3) when she was nearing sixty years of age unveils the author as an intellectual, a reader and as a pious poet, surrounded by the paraphernalia of her rank and Sidney dynasty. While Mary Ellen Lamb is undoubtedly just in her assertion that 'The Countess of Pembroke's patronage has been especially exaggerated', it is clear that the figures whom she did attract into her affinity, such as Samuel Daniel, Abraham Fraunce and Nicholas Breton, served to *fix* her, like de Passe's engraving, as a significant source of textual and cultural interest for her contemporaries.[8]

By the beginning of the 1590s, the number of dedications and referencings of Pembroke indicate that she, rather than Sidney's widow, Frances Walsingham, was being perceived as her brother's representative and literary heir. In one of the dedicatory sonnets of *The Faerie Queene* Spenser

Memory and mourning 141

Figure 3. Mary Herbert, Countess of Pembroke. Early seventeenth-century engraving by Simon de Passe © National Portrait Gallery, London.

proposes to the Countess of Pembroke that Philip Sidney's 'goodly image [is] liuing euermore, | In the diuine resemblaunce of your face'.⁹ In the dedication to *The Ruins of Time* to 'the right Noble and beautifull Ladie, the La. Marie Countesse of Pembrooke', Spenser gave public expression once again to 'his most entire loue & humble affection vnto … your noble brother deceased'.[10] Elsewhere, in her *Salue deus rex iudaeorum* (1611), Aemilia Lanyer celebrated one of her dedicatees, 'the Ladie Marie, the Countesse Dowager of Pembrooke', in Olympian surroundings as one 'great Pembrooke hight by name, | Sister to valiant Sidney'; and Lanyer's persona resolves to present the countess 'with the fruits of idle houres; | Thogh many Books she writes that are more rare' (sig. D1^v, D3^r). A good deal of Pembroke's work circulated during her lifetime in manuscript. However, as recent scholarship on early modern reading practices has shown, this is not to assert that her output was reserved for a small inner circle of readers.[11] The Sidneys had access potentially to a readership among the highest ranks of Elizabethan society, and indeed in time attracted a large community of both readers and imitators.

MEMORY AND THE WRITING OF DEVOTION

Sidney had begun English translations of the Psalms and had finished versions of the first forty-three by the time of his death. In the years that followed, his sister continued with the project, revising his work and completing the translation of the 150 Psalms. In general terms, Elizabeth van Houts has argued that 'The facility to produce memories and the human instinct to wish to recall events make sense only if there are people to whom one can relate one's memories and who, in turn, can interpret them within the same referential system'.[12] Pembroke was clearly intent upon preserving such an interpretive community for the circulation of Sidney's memory. Indeed, she composed two dedicatory poems that were appended to the complete version of the Psalm translations to be offered to Elizabeth I on the occasion of a 1599 visit to the Pembroke estate at Wilton House. Despite the fact that the visit never took place, these poems are clearly an energetic bid to maintain the cultural currency of her brother in late Elizabethan political culture by renewing his (textual) participation in that society's shared political goals and commitments. Later in the seventeenth century, in his *The Victory of Patience and benefit of Affliction*, Richard Younge would submit that 'All publique actions are subject to diverse, and uncertaine Interpretations; for a great many heads judge of them, and mens censures are as various as their palats'.[13] Similarly aware of the imponderables surrounding the politics of commemoration, Pembroke believed that she needed to consolidate a Sidney 'knowledge base' within her culture not only to ensure public recognition of her brother's achievements but also to legitimise her own authorial ambitions.

While Margaret P. Hannay insists that the dedicatory poems 'prepare the reader to hear a personal voice in her *Psalmes*, one that comments on female experience and reveals a desire to use poetic composition to soar above the confinement of gender restrictions', Pembroke's readers may not necessarily be compelled to characterise her poetic interventions solely in terms of the personal and the gendered.[14] It is all too possible to inscribe these texts within a wider cultural forum of debate centring, for example, upon early modern discourses of memory, grief and history. Florio's Montaigne was adamant that '*Plato* hath reason to name [memory] *A great and mighty Goddesse* … In my countrie, if a man will imply that one hath no sense, he will say, such a one hath no memorie'.[15] The very real anxieties surrounding the strategic business of remembering for the Elizabethans and Jacobeans are all too evident from the productions of contemporary print culture. One need only think of the thematic emphases of Foxe's *Acts and Monuments*, Holinshed's *Chronicles*, Shakespeare's *Richard II* and *Hamlet*, or indeed the fact that Greville's dramatic version of the Antony and Cleopatra narrative never survived because he believed that 'many members in that creature (by the opinion of those few eyes which saw it) [had] some childish wantonness in them apt enough to be construed or strained to a personating of vices in the present governors and government'.[16]

It becomes increasingly apparent from her writings during the 1590s that when Pembroke reviews the immediate past, which is to say the life span of her brother, this chronology is constructed as the defining paradigm for human experience in her culture. In *Time and Narrative* Paul Ricoeur has argued that 'time becomes human time to the extent that it is organised after the manner of a narrative',[17] and this concern with memory's appetite for narrativisation has remained an ongoing preoccupation in contemporary theoretical debate. Paul Antze, for example, has invited his readers to resist constructing the past in terms of 'frozen events', but instead to negotiate it 'on the same footing with the present. This makes the past into something that, at least in principle, can be reencountered … and reappropriated'.[18] Such enquiries look back to the very origins of the theorising of memory in antiquity. In *De Memoria et Reminiscentia* Aristotle had pondered how the memory, driven by spiritual yearnings, may seek to supplement the insufficiencies of the material world, to engage emotionally with that which is absent, and to appropriate that which remains locked in the past in the desire to complete psychic narratives.[19] In the Psalm translations, Pembroke is clearly reconfiguring and refreshing the Sidney 'imprint', or cultural memory, for her audience. The dedicatory poem 'To the Angell spirit of the most excellent Sir Phillip Sidney' not only invokes the heroic potential of the deceased courtier, soldier, scholar – it also revives importantly for public attention Sidney the writer. In fact, this lyric stresses that it is the dynamic inspiration of the brother, rather than that of the Old Testament David, which has excited the sister's pen into action.

> To thee pure sprite, to thee alone's addres't
>   this coupled worke, by double int'rest thine:
>   First rais'de by thy blest hand, and what is mine
> inspir'd by thee, thy secrett power imprest.
>   So dar'd my Muse with thine it selfe combine,
>   as mortall stuffe with that which is devine,
> Thy lightning beames give lustre to the rest ...
> ('To the Angell spirit of the most excellent Sir Phillip Sidney', ll. 1–7)[20]

Suzanne Trill is persuasive in her contention that here Pembroke 'oscillates between an idealised representation of her brother, which demands her own self-abnegation, and an assertion of her sorrow ... by so doing, [she] places her brother in a position analogous to that of the idealised lady in sonnet sequences, or, indeed, in the conventionally female role of muse'.[21] Furthermore, in the effusive celebration of Sidney's spirit, Pembroke's speaker positions herself strategically as the memorialiser, indeed the unifier, of her brother's *dismembered* text, and of his artistic undertaking as a whole:

> Oh, had that soule which honor brought to rest
>   too soone not left and reft the world of all
>   what man could showe, which wee perfection call
> This halfe maim'd peece had sorted with the best.
>   Deepe wounds enlarg'd, long festred in their gall
>   fresh bleeding smart; not eie but hart teares fall.
> Ah memorie what needs this new arrest?
> ('To the Angell spirit of the most excellent Sir Phillip Sidney', ll. 15–21)

Elizabeth Mary Tilyou extends Trill's emphasis upon the exaltation of the loved one and is eager to view this particular lyric as 'an excellent example of Fician metaphysics and the idealistic spiritual concept of Platonic love'.[22] It is certainly possible here to identify significant Fician leitmotifs, such as the progressive ascent of human desire towards the world of the spirit, the celebration of human dignity and the immortal soul. However, all of these emphases, in a poem designed for presentation to a reigning monarch, feed a very real political investment in the cultural capital of Sidney and serve as confirmation of Pembroke's own artistic project. Her contemporary, Richard Hooker, stressed that 'The care of the living both to liue and to dy well must needs be somwhat increased when they knowe that their departure shal not be folded vp in silence but the eares of many bee made acquainted with it',[23] and when Pembroke reacquaints her readers with a heroic yet deceased brother, she employs a memorial discourse that frequently relies upon the lexis of obligation and debt: 'Oh! When to this Accompt, this cast upp Summe, | this Reckoning made, this Audit of my woe, | I call my thoughts, whence so strange passions flowe' (ll. 43–5).

MEMORY AND HEROISM

Michael Neill argues persuasively that '"death" is not something that can be imagined once and for all, but an idea that has to be constantly re-imagined across cultures and through time; which is to say that, like most human experiences that we think of as "natural", it is culturally defined'.[24] Clearly, Pembroke is particularly exercised by the idea that cultural inflections of death are always in process, and such considerations may indeed have served to stimulate her interest in translating Robert Garnier's neoclassical tragedy *Marc Antoine*, which she completed in 1590. Interestingly, Anne Dowriche had published her verse translation *The French History* in the previous year. In the preface to her own interesting amalgam of historical narratives by Jean de Serres and François Hotman, Dowriche submitted to her reader, 'That my onelie purpose in collecting & framing this Worke, was to edifie, comfort, and stirre up the godlie mindes vnto care, watchfulnesse, Zeale, & feruentnesse in the cause of Gods truth'.[25] However, whereas Pembroke's spiritual commitment is in evidence in much of her writing, in turning to Garnier she is most concerned with the rather more earth-bound political spectacle of the *ars moriendi*, the art of dying well. In this highly stylised tragic narrative, the plangent sentiments of the classical heroes confronting their doom are expertly crafted into English by Pembroke:

> CHORUS Our plaints no limits stay,
>   Nor more then doo our woes:
>   Both infinitely straie
>   And neither measure knowes.
>   *In measure let them plaine:*
>   *Who measur'd griefes sustaine.*
>   (*Antonius*, 11.386–91)

Garnier's work is wholly preoccupied with the protagonists' reflections upon the most worthy manner in which to resolve in a disaffecting present the unfinished commitments of a heroic past. As the narrative unfolds, the exploitation of memory becomes the strategic means of self-promotion for the cornered heroes as they hesitate between competing versions of their histories described in rhetorically charged monologues. Pembroke's translation is extremely faithful to the original and her rendering in English carefully conveys Garnier's thematic emphases upon the ills of political amnesia and the prospect of an iron age in the wake of the heroes' deaths. Mary Ellen Lamb has contended that 'A woman who translated a male-authored work was, presumably, less vulnerable to accusations of circulating her words inappropriately; after all, they were not, strictly speaking, her words at all'.[26] Despite John Florio's much-cited comment that 'all translations are reputed femalls', it is nonetheless clear that early modern intellectual society attributed considerable cultural and political significance and status to the business of translation.[27] When the poet Nicholas Grimald, for example, introduced his *Marcus Tullius Ciceroes thre bookes of duties* (1558), he drew particular attention to the fact that he had made 'this latin writer, english: & ... [had] caused an auncient writing to becomme in a maner, new againe'.[28] Indeed, Nicholas Udall in the dedicatory address to Edward VI in his translation of Erasmus's *Paraphrase upon the Newe Testamente* (1549 – a project that, as we have seen, enjoyed Parr's patronage) had affirmed that 'a translatour trauaileth not to hys own priuate commoditie, but to the behoufe & publique use of his countrey'.[29] Thus, as became apparent in the earlier discussion of Surrey's poetics, the cultural potential of the translator's undertaking and indeed the very concept of creative authorship should not be circumscribed too narrowly in our reading practices for the early modern period – most especially when engaging with writing from a culture that was wholly committed to the renewal of textual legacies of the past. The decisions to translate, the choice of translation and the manner of translation frequently constituted strategic forms of cultural and textual intervention in this period. Moreover, the gravitational pull within Pembroke's writing towards a privileging of memorial performance and the arts of *imitatio* is in evidence throughout her career. Most interestingly, the abiding textual emphasis upon retrospection and nostalgia forms a dominant thematic thrust that runs the length of her translation of *Marc Antoine*:

> ANTONIUS In watch, in sleepe, her Image follow'd thee:
> Not dreaming but of her, repenting still

> That thou for warre hadst such a Goddes still.
> (*Antonius*, 1.105–7)

> Veillant ou sommeillant, son idole te suit.
> Tu ne songes qu'en elle, et te repens sans cesse
> D'avoir pour guerroyer laissé telle Déesse.

Pembroke is a meticulous translator of Garnier and the extract above is not unrepresentative of her careful rendering of *Marc Antoine*'s 1,999 lines into 2,000 lines of English. Garnier clearly designed his drama of 1578 to be at least in part a meditation upon the excessively volatile nature of French political life in the second half of the sixteenth century. In the play's dedicatory letter to Monseigneur de Pibrac, he stresses: 'Mais sur tout, à qui mieux qu'à vous se doivent addresser les représentations tragiques des guerres civiles de Rome, qui avez en telle horreur nos dissentions domestiques et les malheureux troubles de ce Royaume' ['But above all, to whom better than yourself should the tragic narratives of the Roman civil wars be dedicated, you who have beheld our internal divisions and the unfortunate upheavals of this realm in such horror'].[30] The potential of the translated narrative to elide great expanses of time and space yielded thus not only opportunities for political critique, as Garnier indicates explicitly, but also allowed for a significant diversification of access to cultural debate. When William Fulwood, for example, published his translation of Guglielmo Gratarolo's text as *The Castel of Memorie* (1562), he was at pains to highlight both the pedagogic and politicised dimensions to this undertaking to his readership:

> Among other there bee twoo seuerall causes instigated me to enterprise and publishe the translation hereof. Partly, because of myne own exercise and commoditie. But chiefly and especially, for the common utililitie and profite of my natiue countrey … and for that purpose to distribute accordynge to the greatnes or smalnes of the talent ministred & lent vnto him: to the end that same (be it neuer so lytle) yf it maye in any wise profite, doe not remaine in him as dead and frustrate: but rather that it be bestowed forthe to encrease and fructifie.[31]

The deliberate decision not to allow narratives from the past to lie 'dead and frustrate' clearly governed Pembroke's commitment as writer, and this is in evidence both in her texts that circulated in manuscript and in those destined for wider consumption through publication. Throughout her own *Antonius*, Pembroke maintains Garnier's detailed analysis of the political evils of hesitation, division and inactivity. Moreover, in the course of the play all of these themes are intimately linked to inadequate responses to the obligations of the past: indeed, her Antony confesses, 'Nay, as the fatted swine in filthy mire | With glutted heart I wallow'd in delights, | All thoughts of honor trodden under foote. | So I me lost' (III.1166–9). There has been a good measure of critical speculation that Shakespeare probably knew Pembroke's translation, given some details of comparable phrasing in his own later tragedy.[32] While *Antony and Cleopatra*, unlike *Antonius*, was written for performance in the public playhouse, each of these dramas offers poignant meditations upon failed human transcendence and neither permits its audiences to forget that the actions of the protagonists have profound and abiding repercussions for the political communities that depend upon them: 'With Souldiers, strangers, horrible in armes | Our land is hidde, our people drown'd in teares' (II.266–7).[33] In her study of *Antonius*, Karen Raber argues persuasively that

> Neo-Senecan closet drama's deliberate rejection of the place, the institution, and the practices of theater appears to return its reader to the timeless arcadian landscape of the aristocratic estate and the noble gentility of classical style ... *Antonius*, however, offers its illusions at a price. Its readership, while lulled into forgetting the troubling conditions of aristocratic power, is simultaneously invited to ponder the limits and contingencies of monarchical power, and made complicit in a project that asserts the value of a woman's voice.[34]

In *Antonius* the desirability of cultural codes of heroic expectation in the interests of the welfare of the polity is affirmed ceaselessly, and the political capital and potential of the patriciate remain intimately linked to such expectations. Moreover, in works such as *Antonius* the narrative inheritance from antiquity becomes an endlessly fertile resource for reflecting upon the political mores of later cultures. Indeed, Pembroke remains faithful to the emphases in Garnier's tragedy upon crucial acts of communal remembering and upon the ways in which recollection may be seen to invest in larger shared discourses of political idealism.

> CHORUS OF ROMAN SOLDIERS Olde Memorie doth there
> Painted on forhead weare
> Our Fathers praise: thence torne
> Our triumphes baies have worne:
> Therby our matchles Rome
> Whilome of Shepeheards come
> Rais'd to this greatnes stands,
> The Queene of forraine lands.
> (*Antonius*, IV.1795–1802)

MEMORY AND THE *ARS MORIENDI*

In 1592, Pembroke appeared for the first time in print with *A discourse of life and death. Written in French by Ph. Mornay. Antonius, a tragædie written also in French by Ro. Garnier. Both done in English by the Countesse of Pembroke*. In *Antonius* Pembroke had chosen a work that focused not only upon late sixteenth-century culture's relations with the past, but also upon the political evocation of those who appeared to be living on borrowed time. Analogous enquiries characterised the accompanying translation of a French author. Earlier in the century in his *compendious and a very fruteful treatyse, teachynge the waye of dyenge well* (1534), Thomas Lupset had drawn deeply upon the tropes of *ars moriendi* literature and had argued powerfully, 'one mynde shulde be in vs, as well to remember we shall not be, as to remember we ones were not. It is no newe thyng to dye, our fathers our grandfathers, our great foresiers be gone the way, that both we shal go, and al that folow vs must come the same'.[35] In her rendering of Philippe de Mornay's *Discourse*, one of her own contributions to late Elizabethan *ars moriendi* literature, Pembroke is called upon to interrogate at length the status and functions of memory: how does the examination of memory prompt us to negotiate questions of ontology and epistemology? how might people and ideas from one time frame be translated to another so that we may reflect anew upon the destiny of humanity? and what are the implications of resurrection – textual resurrection in the present and spiritual resurrection in the future?

This life is but a *Penelopes* web, wherein we are always doing and vndoing: a sea open to all windes, which sometime within, sometime without neuer cease to torment vs: a weary iorney through extreame heates, and coldes, over high mountaynes, steepe rockes, and theeuish deserts.[36]

The translation of Mornay's *Excellent Discours de la vie et de la mort* (1576) has been integrated into a larger political undertaking by a number of leading European scholars in the later decades of the sixteenth century supporting the Protestant cause. It is supposed that Sidney himself had had a hand in the 1587 translation of Mornay's *De la vérité de la religion Chrestienne* (1581).[37] Mornay had befriended Sidney in France during the latter's participation in a diplomatic mission in 1572, and the French intellectual clearly became a welcome visitor in the Sidney circle on the occasion of various visits to Britain. Indeed, Victor Skretkowicz speculates that '[Pembroke] probably entertained Mornay and his wife at Wilton or at Baynard's Castle during Mornay's diplomatic mission to England in 1577–78 on behalf of the Huguenots'.[38]

The narrative in the *Excellent Discours* of the journey of the human spirit as it ponders the implications of mortality and the possibility of redemption is not gender-specific. Mornay's sustained meditation upon human mortality is designed to prompt readers to ponder anew their commitments to ethical self-government and to spiritual witness, and to interrogate the ultimate nature of human achievement – a textual undertaking that would clearly have been sympathetic to someone questing to reaffirm Sidney's legacy. Certainly, Pembroke's contemporary, Elizabeth Grymeston, explored these very sentiments at length in her own *Miscelanea, Meditations, Memoratiues* (1604): 'Miserable man, why doest thou not dispose thy selfe to death, since thou art sure thou canst not liue? *Nostrum viuere, è vita transire*: our best life is to die well.'[39] However, in her own textual evocations of human and literary pasts for an Elizabethan present, Pembroke's output responds to a persisting anxiety, which Donne later spelled out in his sermons, that flawed humanity might be finally drawn in death into a void without degree: 'the *ambitious* man shall have *no satisfaction*, if the *poorest alive* tread upon him, nor the *poorest* receive any *contentment* in being made *equall to Princes*, for they *shall bee equall* but in dust.[40] For her own part, Pembroke remains richly sensitive to the Augustinian strains in Mornay's reflections ('And what else I pray you is the beginning of youth, but the death of infancy? … the beginning of to-morow, but the death of to day?'; 'The past is no more, the future is not yet, the present is, and no more is')[41] and indeed to the underlying Lutheran contention that the conflicted human spirit can be neither reconciled to nor divorced from the body. From this premiss of interminable struggle, Pembroke's rendering of Mornay's meditations strikes some sobering notes:

> But the worst is, when we are out of these externall warres and troubles, we finde greater ciuill warre within our selues: the flesh against the spirite, passion against reason, earth against heauen, the worlde within vs fighting for the world, evermore so lodged in the botome of our owne hearts, that on no side we can flie from it … Conclude I say, that life is but a wishing for the future, and a bewailing of the past: a loathing of what wee haue tasted, and a longing for that wee haue not tasted, a vaine memorie of the state past, and a doubtfull expectation of the state to come: finally, that in all our life there is nothing certaine, nothing assured, but the certaintie and uncertaintie of death.[42]

With no good works to ease our way through to the hereafter, Pembroke's Mornay summons up a familiar Reformist image of humanity in a state of absolute vulnerability, racked by endless vicissitudes in mortal life. Interestingly, in this context, the role of memory remains equivocal in that it may respond either to vain and base appetites or to the promptings of spiritual need.

The art of dying well, or *ars moriendi*, may well have been particularly associated with the Sidney name for a number of reasons. There were not only the thematic emphases in Pembroke's writing and the rather spectacular demise of the chivalrous Sir Philip, but Holinshed's *Chronicles* (1587) had also drawn attention to another deathbed scene, that of their mother Mary Sidney. Here, the reader is presented with a subject of intense veneration, for

During the whole course of hir sicknesse and speciallie a little before it pleased almightie God to call hir hense to his mercie, she vsed such godlie speeches, earnest and effectuall persuasions to all those about hir, and vnto such others as came of freendlie courtesie to visit hir, to exhort them to repentance and amendment of life, and dehort them from all sinne and lewdnesse, as wounded the consciences and inwardlie pearsed the hearts of manie that heard hir.[43]

In this manner, as we move from the textual markers of Holinshed, Denny, Lanyer, Spenser, Daniel and Pembroke herself, we uncover a proliferating matrix of memorial narratives revealing a pantheon of Sidneian worthies guiding us through this fallen world. Interestingly, Peter Sherlock has argued that the Reformation, rather than loosening the ties between the living and dead, transformed the cultural expression of memory, replacing the anxious desire for saintly intercessors for the departed and the diverse traditions of *memento mori* with a more confident formulation of the dead as 'exemplars for the living to copy … on account of their virtuous deeds and good deaths'.[44] In her translation of Petrarch's *Trionfo della Morte* (undated but transcribed onto a surviving manuscript in 1600), Pembroke would revisit these considerations, selecting a narrative that once again problematises the status and functions of retrospection:

> There saw I, whom their times did happie calle,
>   Popes, Emperors, and kings, but stranglie growen,
>   All naked now, all needie, beggars all.
> Where is that wealth? Where are those honors gonne?
>   (*The Triumph of Death*, 1.79–82)

Unlike Mornay's *Excellent Discours*, this textual investigation unfolds specifically within an amatory context, weaving together familiar themes from Petrarchan poetics (in terms of dynamic stagings of erotic and spiritual desire) and is informed by the conventions of *ubi sunt* literature. Petrarch's *Trionfi* remained key sites in the development of artistic production throughout early modern Europe, influencing the visual arts and political spectacle as much as literary composition.[45] Elizabeth I herself had translated part of the *Trionfo della castità*; yet, in the case of Pembroke's renderings of Garnier's and Petrarch's narratives, Lamb contends that

> Both Cleopatra and Laura are, finally, models of negation. Each model defines women as important solely in terms of their relationships with men, even in the most private and solitary act of death … These negative aspects of the constant heroine remind us that the Countess was a translator, not an author in her own right. In both the literal and the broad sense, she translated a male perspective on women.[46]

However, this would seem unhelpfully to circumscribe the ways in which texts might be valued by early modern reading culture, especially given that Pembroke's own brother had underlined that 'Poesie … is an art of imitation, for so Aristotle termeth it in the word [mimesis] – that is to say, a representing, counterfeiting, or figuring forth'.[47] In her rendering of the *Trionfo della Morte*, Pembroke is drawn to focus upon both the erotic and spiritual imperatives that may accompany the flexing of memory as the dead Laura emerges for the first time as the speaking female, sharing her reflections upon the past with her Petrarchan suitor: 'A thousand times wrath in my face did flame, | My heart meane-while with love did inlie burne, | But never will, my reason overcame' (II.100–2).

Aristotle had asserted in his *De Memoria et Reminiscentia* that 'it is not possible to think without an image'.[48] *The Castel of Memorie* (1562) argued that 'Memorye is a retaynyng of the Images or symilitudes first perceyued of the soule, the which neuertheles is vnprofitable except it both retayne all, and also restore theym in the same order wherein it conceyued theym. And it belongeth not to present thinges nor thinges to come, but onlye to thynges paste, as Aristotle saith'.[49] In her translation of Petrarch, more than in those of Garnier or Mornay, Pembroke found herself confronted with a text that sought to stress the visual, and indeed visionary, dimensions of recollection. Rather than being construed dismissively as the mental residue of former experience, the narrative arc of *The Triumph of Death* supports a whole panoramic spectacle of memory that serves to monumentalise both the dead and the living.

> That gallant Ladie, gloriouslie bright,
> The statelie piller once of worthinesse,

> And now a little dust, a naked spright:
> Turn'd from hir warres a ioyefull Conqueresse:
> > Hir warres, where had foyl'd the mightie foe,
> > whose wylie stratagems the world distresse,
> And foyl'd him, not with sword, with speare or bowe,
> > But with chaste heart, faire visage, upright thought,
> > wise speache, which did with honor linked goe:
> > > (*The Triumph of Death*, 1.1–9)

Interestingly, this drama of remembrance figuring the speaking woman is reproduced in a much more intimate context in another lyric associated with Pembroke. The attribution to her of the original poem 'The Dolefull Lay of Clorinda', which was included in Spenser's collection *Astrophel: A Pastorall Elegie upon the Death of the Most Noble and Valorous Knight, Sir Philip Sidney* (1595), is the source of some lively critical dispute.[50] This is not the place to rehearse the energetic arguments that have been put forward to challenge or support the attribution. For the purposes of this discussion I wish to concentrate upon the textual promotion here of a memory-laden Pembroke, whether or not it was she who composed it. In the collection *Astrophel*, Spenser introduces the 'Lay' mourning the death of Sidney as being voiced by 'his sister ... most resembling both in shape and spright | Her brother deare'.[51] In this way, we are asked to link the dependent subjectivity of the lamenting sister directly with the development of artistic creativity and, as Peter M. Sacks has underlined more generally, 'the elegist's need to draw attention, consolingly, to [his or her] own surviving powers'.[52] To all intents and purposes, Pembroke's public identity is being shaped once again through this narrativisation of personal grief: memory is shown to constitute a resource with which to challenge the limitations of human action and indeed the provisionality of human experience. However, in clear contrast to the more postmodern sensibilities whereby the past may never be sufficiently lost, Clorinda's lay communicates a vision in which grief and remembrance are constant burdens, nay organising principles in the fashioning of an enduring self. Angelica Goodden has argued persuasively that 'It is because memory fixes the ways we interpret that it settles what we will become quite as much as what we have been. One image applied to memory over the ages reflects the notion that it digests experience and, as it were, supplies fuel to sustain subsequent life'.[53] And certainly such formulations of memory look back notably to the writings of the Church Fathers, as we shall see in the next chapter, with their many and varied emphases upon both *soma* and *psyche* drawing sustenance from the faculty.

It is clear that in Grymeston's *Miscelanea, Meditations, Memoratiues* early modern readers were left in no uncertainty regarding the urgency with which this memorial regime should be addressed: 'Thinke, ô thinke, and bethinke thy selfe, from whence thou camest, where thou art, and whither thou goest, for thou art here in an obscure land, gouerned by the prince of darkenesse, where vice is aduaunced, vertue scorned, where pleasures are few, paines infinite.'[54] The importance of what might be called the prospective commitment of memory is central to Pembroke's writing, and indeed to this particular textual portrait of her as Clorinda: 'The woods, the hills, the rivers shall resound | The mournfull accent of my sorrowes ground' (23–4). While Sidney is seen in a host of different ways to achieve a kind of apotheosis in Pembroke's cultural undertakings as writer, patron and translator, Clorinda's future in this instance does not undergo any rebirthing narrative. She is indeed 'fixed' psychologically and temporally by the experience of bereavement.

> Ay me, can so divine a thing be dead?
>
> Ah no: it is not dead, ne can it die,
> But lives for aie, in blisfull Paradise:
> Where like a new-borne babe it soft doth lie,
> In bed of lillies wrapt in tender wise …
> ('Dolefull Lay', ll. 66–70)

At the beginning of the modern period, Freud returned attention repeatedly to the ways in which the experience of loss might be pathologised, noting that while self-loathing may frequently constitute the defining characteristic of melancholia, 'The disturbance of self-regard is absent in mourning'.[55] In the 'Dolefull Lay' it remains apparent throughout that mourner and mourned compete vigorously for reader attention. Moreover, the fusion of textual voices of prayer, lament and hopefulness that characterises this poem contributes to the more general project of *Astrophel* to accommodate and extend existing ceremonies of public commemoration. Dennis Kay has specifically linked the growth in elegiac writing in the sixteenth century to the rise of Protestant culture in Britain: 'With the Reformation the Requiem Mass, with its potential for infinite repetition, endless accumulation, disappeared … The focus of funeral observances shifted radically towards the secular. Ceremonies became, on the one hand, representations of the status of the deceased at the time of death and, on the other, expressions of the reaction of the survivors.'[56] Clearly, these changeful modes of recollection must encourage us to attend more broadly to the growing diversification in the status and functions of memory in the early modern period. Ricoeur's formulation is timely in this context that what we inherit from the past are 'traces' (in terms of testimonials, documents, oral narratives and memories) and that these supplement and narrativise our relations with a perished field of experience – 'a past that is abolished yet preserved in its traces'.[57] Indeed, one of Sidney's intimates, Fulke Greville, found that his very powers of memory were able, as Cicero and later Petrarch had counselled, to compensate for the insufficiencies that he identified in the present:

> The difference which I have found between times, and consequently the changes of life into which their natural vicissitudes doe violently carry men, as they have made deep furrowes of impressions into my heart, so the same wheeles caused me to retire my thoughts from free traffique with the world, and rather seek comfortable ease or employment in the safe memory of dead men, then disquiet in a doubtfull conversation amongst the living.[58]

ELEGY, MEMORY AND THE SACRED PAST

Contemporary critical debate focusing upon the elegy has frequently viewed the lyric form as seeking to generate an aporetic space of unceasing grief and to frame and privilege trauma within achronological narratives. Indeed, at such junctures, we may be reminded of the celebrated utterance of Virgil's memory-laden Aeneas, *forsan et haec olim meminisse iuvabit* (perhaps some day remembering even this will be a pleasure).[59] However, the 'melodious tears' of elegies may not only serve to present a fine-grained sensibility surrendering the fruits of memory, they may also here reintroduce for a contemporary Elizabethan audience the discursive possibility of a heroic mourner, familiar from the poetics of antiquity, and indeed from the lyrics of Surrey as discussed in Chapter 1. In his study of the early modern elegy, Dennis Kay has explored the ways in which the form emerged as 'a means of learning about decorum, of investigating, exploring, representing, analysing, anatomising social relationships on the occasion of the subject's death'.[60] In the staging of Clorinda's grief in the 'Dolefull Lay' textual emphasis remains resolutely upon the need for a figurehead who can act as voice and conduit for a broader performance of public commemoration. Thomas Wilson had stressed in his *Arte of Rhetorique* (1553) that 'all extreme heaviness and vehement sorrows cannot abide comfort, but rather seek a mourner that would take part with them'.[61] In the context of what modern theorising has often communicated as the psychic ruptures enacted in mourning, one of the purposes of the elegiac mode might be apotropaic in tenor, a means of keeping Death at bay, or alternatively an endeavour to rebuild a social network from which to confront the enormity of death. Whatever the case, it is noteworthy that a redemptive movement in either direction is not figured forth in the mental journeyings of Astrophel's Clorinda.[62]

> To men? Ah they alas like wretched bee,
> And subject to the heavens ordinance:
> Bound to abide what ever they decree.
> Their best redresse, is their best sufferance.
>   How then can they like wretched comfort mee,
>   The which no lesse, need comforted to bee?
>   ('Dolefull Lay', ll. 13–18)

The poetic emphasis upon the desire for an empathetic community, witnessed earlier also in Surrey's cross-gendered lyrics, has less to do with resolving the problems surrounding dependent subjectivity as a defining condition of existence, than with securing an audience of sufficient magnitude for commemorative performance: 'Ay me, to whom shall I my case complaine, | That may compassion my impatient griefe?' (ll. 1–2). With the past thus suffused with the seemingly hyperbolic identity of the dead brother, Clorinda can secure no source of adequate selfhood or cultural direction without the resources of memory. In this context, Kate Chedgzoy is illuminating in her analyses of the ways in which 'traumatic memory' may be seen to surge up 'unbidden to disrupt the subject's relation to the social';[63] and, interestingly, Pembroke would extend this discussion of the highly political relations forged between memory and identity-construction in her other dedicatory poem to the Sidney Psalm translations, 'Even now that Care which in thy Crowne attends'. Here, in a lyric positioning Elizabeth herself as prime reader, Pembroke concentrates once again upon the image of a heroic, but beleaguered, woman who may now, it seems, be in need of some timely counsel. In direct comparison with examples of devotional literature evoking Elizabeth's father during the Reformation, Pembroke reformulates the last Tudor monarch as a latter-day David, highlighting Elizabeth's own political and religious commitments: 'One whom in chiefe dependeth to dispose | what Europe acts in theise most active times?' (ll. 7–8).

This stress upon the obligations of Protestant leadership incumbent upon England's monarch is closely aligned with the illustrious example of the Protestant knight Sidney who conspicuously failed to achieve the great favour at court to which he aspired during his lifetime: 'How can I name whom sighing sighes extend, | and not unstopp my teares eternall spring? | but hee did warpe, I weav'd this webb to end' (ll. 25–7). Thus, even in this lyric, the most energetic encomium is reserved for the dead Sidney rather than the Old Testament monarch. Of course, in life Sidney himself had never refrained from inviting the queen to exercise her memorial powers and to attend to the counsel of History. When the possibility of a royal match with the duc d'Alençon threatened, Sidney wrote to her insisting that Alençon was 'the son of the Jezebel of our age' and to be resisted as one of the leading 'Papists' among whom there were 'many thinking you an usurper; many thinking the right you had, disannulled by the Pope's excommunication'.[64] In 'Even now that Care which in thy Crowne attends', Pembroke's engagement with her implied reader is unsurprisingly rather less forthright even if it does compare thematically with many of the emphases of her brother's letter dated some twenty years earlier. As Elizabeth was drawing towards the final years of her life, she would have been reminded by Pembroke's dedicatory lyrics (had the 1599 Wilton visit taken place) that her political identity and legacies were not in her gift, but were continually in process and resided with those who memorialise her.[65] Pembroke seeks deliberately to repair any faultiness of memory or 'strategic forgetting' to which the queen and her court may be subject, and to emphasise that the axis of her own authorial identity is centrally related to the Protestant and Sidneian legacies which she is invoking.

More generally, the articulation of discourses of memory in relation to mourning, trauma and cultural control are, of course, nowhere more apparent in Pembroke's textual output than in the paraphrases of the Psalms. In a wide-ranging discussion of sixteenth-century cultural interest in *imitatio*, Angelica Goodden has stressed that 'It is easy to see how over-reliance on memory may make man unduly subject to the authority of others, and so prevent him from living his life as an autonomous creature'.[66] Indeed, one of the principal challenges for Pembroke (and, it should be added, for her readers) in this project was to identify the degree to which she was going to depart from the very familiar existing translations that formed such a cornerstone of early modern patterns of worship. Down the centuries, the Psalms have constantly invited their readers to reflect upon the status of human epistemology. The crises of interpretations contained within these densely allusive texts for successive generations of readers should not deflect attention from their emphases that: memory is promoted as a key resource with which to invigorate spiritual vocation; that the past irrevocably shapes and impresses itself as an obligation upon the present; and that present models of political and religious subjectivity may be radically questioned as a consequence.

> Indeed to you the stile I gave
>   of gods, and sonnes of god, to have:
> but err not princes you as men must dy:
> you that sitt high,
> must fall, and low, as others ly.
>
> (Ps. 82:21–5)

Sidney's, and subsequently Pembroke's, 'Englishing' of the Psalms into metrical settings for private contemplation would have had a good number of rivals vying for attention by the time manuscript versions of them were circulating at the end of the century. Rivkah Zim has estimated that in the period 1530–1600 alone there were more than 'seventy different new versions' of the Psalms printed in English.[67] Pembroke's own Dudley uncles, John, Earl of Warwick and Robert, Earl of Leicester, had also turned their attentions to the Psalms of vengeance when imprisoned in the Tower in the aftermath of the failed political coup supporting the cause of Lady Jane Grey.[68] The widespread familiarity with the Psalms and the cultural predisposition to allegorise them for the purposes of political critique rendered them an obvious choice for aspiring poets and political subjects seeking an enhanced voice in that society.

As has been appreciated above, Pembroke took up this project at the death of her brother who had completed versions of the first forty-three Psalms. Wendy Wall proposes that 'The *Psalms* were a particularly appropriate text for [her] because they both signalled an allegiance to her brother and provided a religious version of similar literary forms associated with the Sidney family'.[69] Certainly, the textual influences upon the composition of Sidneian Psalms are very extensive and include: the Great Bible (1539); the Coverdale psalter in the Book of Common Prayer; *Al such Psalmes of David* by Thomas Sternhold, John Hopkins and others (1549); the Geneva Bible (1560); the Vulgate; the Marot-Beza psalter (1562 – of which the Latin and English edition in 1580 was dedicated to Pembroke's aunt and uncle, the Earl and Countess of Huntingdon); Anthony Gilby's translation of Beza's prose paraphrases, *The Psalmes of David truely opened and explaned by Paraphrasis* (1580) – quite apart from the stylistic emphases of Sidney's own verse and the religious poetry of Anne Vaughan Lok. When turning to the Psalms, Pembroke departed from the mode of close translation that she had practised in the cases of Garnier and Petrarch, and thus acknowledged, as Zim stresses, an existing early modern convention of creative *paraphrasis*, rather than a more literal rendering of the texts from scripture. Erasmus had specified earlier in the century that 'the purpose of studying the basic disciplines, of studying philosophy, of studying eloquence, [is] to know Christ, to celebrate the glory of Christ. This is the goal of all learning and all eloquence', and this humanist determination to fuse artistic and rhetorical creativity with the commitment of faith clearly lies at the heart of this collaborative Sidneian project.[70]

> My harte endites an argument of worth,
>   the praise of him that doth the Scepter swaie:
> My tongue the pen to paynt his praises forth,
>   shall write as swift, as swiftest writer maie.
>   (Ps. 45:1–4)

The Psalms were put to a multitude of uses in Elizabethan culture as texts for personal meditation and expression, public worship, scriptural instruction, exercises in translation and composition and hymn singing. Fernando Bouza has persuasively argued how memory might be sustained (indeed, 'created') in the early modern period through visual and aural achievements in the arts as well as through the writing: 'one could claim that reading, writing, seeing, and hearing waged a kind of battle on memory's behalf in the sixteenth and seventeenth centuries.'[71] In his 1627 sermon 'of Commemoration of the Lady Danvers' Donne drew attention to the late mother of the poet George Herbert who 'with her whole family, (as a *Church* in that *elect Ladies* house, to whom *Iohn* writ his second *Epistle*) did, every Sabbath, shut up the day, at night, with a generall, with a cheerfull *singing of Psalmes*'.[72] However, it should be underlined in the case of the Sidneian Psalm collection, as Hannibal Hamlin rightly stresses, that 'it was as a book of poems, rather than as a psalter with any sort of liturgical or devotional purpose … that the Sidney Psalter had its greatest impact'.[73]

Arthur Golding's translation of Calvin's commentaries on the Psalms had specified that, 'Bycause they discover all the inner thoughtes, [the Psalms] do call or drawe every one of us to the peculiar examinatien of himself, so as no whit of all the infirmities to which wee are subject … may abyde hidden'.[74] In *An Apology for Poetry* Sidney himself had celebrated their pre-eminent importance, for in them the Psalmist 'sheweth himselfe a passionate lover of that unspeakable and everlasting beautie to be scene by the eyes of the minde, onely cleered by fayth'.[75] The rich discursive formulations of memory in the Sidneian Psalms constantly invite the reader to reflect upon the multifariousness and multivalency of retrospection. Some of the most common articulations of the memorial impulse in Pembroke's settings are the arresting scenes in which the pathetically vulnerable voice of humanity implores the Godhead to recollect the desperate plight of the faithful:

> Now that age hath me attainted,
> ages snow my hed hath painted,
>   leave me not my god forlorn.
>   (Ps. 71:55–7)

>   From depth of grief
>   Where droun'd I ly
>   lord for relief
>   to thee I cry
> my ernest, vehement, crying, prayeng,
> graunt quick, attentive, heering, waighing.
>   (Ps. 130:1–6)

Danielle Clarke justly stresses that 'Religion was a master-discourse in this period, and we should not let our post-Christian sensibilities occlude the fact that devotion was central to ideology and culture: hence, women's engagement with this area, while it undoubtedly is connected to ideas of virtue, is also mainstream, and often directly political'.[76] The powerful cultural appetite down the centuries for the destruction of political and religious adversaries is vividly expressed in these Psalm translations and, on occasions, Pembroke does not shrink from reproducing the dynamic, impassioned railing of the Psalmist who urges Jehovah to embrace vigorously his former undertaking to vanquish the enemies of the chosen people and to sweep them from the face of the earth:

>   Their teeth, Lord, where they stand
>   Crack in their mouths: crush with thy bruising hand
>   These lions jawes; as water in dry ground
>   So make them sink …
>   (Ps. 58 variant: 21–4)

In a variant of Psalm 50 Pembroke's equally percussive textual voice admonishes those whose understanding of spiritual direction is so feeble that they exist within a memorial vacuum: 'Mark this all you, whose crazed holely braine | Cannot one thought of God in you contain' (ll. 61–2). By Psalm 105 the narrative thrust is upon the need for 'Abrahams progeny | you Jacobs sonnes, whome he doth chosen save' (ll. 11–12) to establish a communal record of divine workings to counteract the inevitable failings of human memory: 'Record I say in speciall memory | the miracles he wrought, the lawes he gave' (ll. 9–10). Such spectacular interventions, however, must be keenly contrasted with the more reflective moments when Pembroke's Psalmist foregrounds the importance of memory and the assistance it may offer in the face of cultural trauma. Possibly the most affecting in this context are the scenes of Pembroke's Psalmist resisting the collapse of faith and spiritual defeat with profound meditative enquiry:

> At length with turned thought
>   a new I fell to thinck
>   uppon the auncient tymes
>   uppon the yeares of old:
>   yea to my mynd was brought,
>   and in my hart did sinck,
>   what in my former Rimes
>   my self of thee had told.
>   (Ps. 77:25–32)

> Grave deeply in remembring mind
>   my trust, thy promise true:
> this only joy in griefe I find,
>   thy words my life renue.
>   (Ps. 119, 'G':1–4)

REMEMBERING PEMBROKE

The Sidneian Psalms would not be published until 1823, and then only in inaccurate format. Pembroke's revisions to the Psalms were completed by the time of her husband's death in 1601, but there is critical speculation that a draft existed as early as 1594. Nonetheless, we should in no way underestimate the significance that their manuscript circulation had upon the literary culture of the seventeenth century despite their long neglect after 1700.[77] It has been calculated that there are over 150 different stanzaic forms and over ninety different distinct metres in the collection, and even during Pembroke's lifetime, these metrical translations won significant acclaim. John Donne celebrated 'this Moses and this Miriam' – 'Two, by their bloods, and by thy spirit one'. He insisted that the Sidneian Psalms 'show us Islanders our joy, our King, | They tell us why and how to sing'.[78] Sir John Harington, Elizabeth's godson, confessed, 'meethinke it is pitty they are unpublyshed, but lye still inclosed within those walls lyke prisoners, though many have made great suyt for theyr liberty'.[79] Nonetheless, as Gary Waller has underlined, 'the Sidneian spirit is as much tempered by Calvin as by Castiglione',[80] and Nicholas Breton must indeed have been most mindful of Castiglione's idealisations of court culture when he turned in his *Pilgrimage to*

Paradise (1592) to compare Pembroke to Elizabetta Gonzaga, Duchess of Urbino:

> who hath redde of the Duchesse of Vrbino, may saie, the Italians wrote wel: but who knowes the Countesse of Penbrooke, I thinke hath cause to write better: and if she had many followers? haue not you mo seruants? And if they were so mindfull of their fauours: shall we be forgetfull of our dueties? ... and if shee haue receiued her right in remembrance, you must not haue wrong in being forgotten.[81]

In the course of her career Pembroke adopted a number of cultural personae, and had a number of others imposed upon her. In Abraham Fraunce's transposition of Torquato Tasso's *Aminta* to the Wiltshire countryside in *The Countess of Pembroke's Ivychurch* (1591): readers were greeted by the unexpected addition of the regal Pembrokiana who seems quite adept at bear hunting. However, the most leaden textual evocation of Pembroke by her contemporaries must surely have been in the poetic offering *Sir Philip Sidney's Ourania* (1606) by one (impoverished) Nathaniel Baxter who has Sidney's ghost insist: 'Yet Cinthia shall afford thee maintenance. | My dearest Sister keepe my Tutor well, | For in his element he doth excell' (sig. N1ᵛ). If Samuel Daniel was not only the most talented of the writers to receive Pembroke's patronage, he would be one of the very few to dedicate work to her after she was widowed – when she had thus lost her position of power overseeing the Pembroke estate and the exercise of patronage that accompanied it: he dedicated the 1609 edition of *The ciuile wars betweene the howses of Lancaster and Yorke* to 'The Right Noble Lady, the Lady Marie, Countesse Dowager of Pembrooke'.[82]

As the variety of her output is reviewed, it becomes increasingly evident that Pembroke did not promote the inviolable authority of memory, rather there emerges a persistent acknowledgement that bids for cultural narrativisation are vigorously competitive, always in process and painfully subject to amnesiac social pressures. This realisation becomes most explicit in one of the final textual productions of her career again in preparation for the projected 1599 royal visit to Wilton. Pembroke's 'Dialogue betweene two shepheards, *Thenot* and *Piers*, in praise of Astrea' was published in Francis Davison's *A Poeticall Rhapsody* (1602). This binary vision upon the conditions of human achievement had exercised minds since antiquity and remained a lively debate throughout the early modern period. Her brother's courtly entertainment *The Lady of May* clearly ponders this enquiry and, in a very different context, Francis Bacon, for example, was drawn in *The Advancement of Learning* (1605) to investigate 'the two estates, the contemplative state and the active state'.[83]

Steven W. May concludes that 'The countess's verse entertainment may be a trifle, yet it is also one of the most enjoyable and clever instances of dramatic praise offered to the queen'.[84] The pastoral became an enormously accommodating and flexible medium for early modern writers, and her brother Philip clearly had no hesitation in ascribing important work to this genre for his own times: 'under the pretty tales of wolves and sheep, can include the whole considerations of wrong-doing and patience'.[85] In her own 'dialogue' Pembroke combines some of the generic expectations of the pastoral with (now well-established) conventions of Elizabethan panegyric:

> THENOT ASTREA is our chiefest joy,
>   Our chiefest guarde against annoy,
>   Our chiefest wealth, our treasure.
> PIERS Where chiefest are, there others bee,
>   To us none else but only shee;
>   When wilt thou speak in measure?
>   ('Dialogue betweene
>   two shepheards', ll. 31–6)

In this way, Pembroke exploits dialogue as a means with which to reflect upon the politicising of memory: while Thenot makes a passionate, Neoplatonic investment in the ability of human expression to praise Astraea, Piers punctures this endeavour with his suspicion of the deceit and flaws inherent in all such undertakings. Designed as an encomium to Elizabeth, it is sobering to reflect that ultimately the readers of this dialogue may find themselves concentrating upon the very impermanence of all claims to cultural status and political heroism.

This chapter began by analysing how Pembroke herself was memorialised by some of her contemporaries and indeed by succeeding generations. When Sir John Harington wrote to Lucy, Countess of Bedford, enclosing some copies of Pembroke's Psalms, he lauded 'the mirroir of our Age'.[86] However, when we consider her epitaph by William Browne in Salisbury Cathedral, Pembroke's identity is effectively collapsed between that of her male relatives: 'UNDERNEATH this sable herse | Lies the subject of all verse: | Sidney's sister, Pembroke's mother'.[87]

The authenticity of Pembroke's investment in her brother's cultural and textual investments has never been questioned by generations of readers and critics, but the complex narratives of her own textual (rather than biographical) achievements should not be erased as a consequence. As an author, Pembroke intervened strategically in the present to redress the inadequate narratives inherited from the past. Wendy Wall has argued that '[Pembroke's] legacy for women writers was, finally, an elegiac poetic corpus created from within sanctioned religious meditations and predicated on the absent and therefore representable male body'.[88] Elsewhere, Tina Krontiris has unveiled another Pembroke persona: 'Extremely reluctant to display her talents, she usually worked from behind curtains, using men as protective shields. Significant men in her life became surrogate figures, public substitutes of her own creative self.'[89] While Denny conjured up a pious Pembroke for the wayward niece and William Browne's epitaph fashioned a famous 'sister' and 'mother', modern criticism has repeatedly sought and produced in Pembroke the image of insecure and/or covert authorship. As one fictive identity of Pembroke collapses with the arrival of another critical construct, we may be reminded of Ricoeur's thesis that 'on the one hand, history in some way makes use of fiction to refigure time and, on the other hand, fiction makes use of history for the same ends'.[90] This discursive imbrication of memory, fiction and experience was equally apparent to Freud in his own enquiries into the unconscious: 'The way in which the memory behaves in dreams is undoubtedly of the greatest importance for any theory of memory in general … what we remember of a dream and what we exercise our interpretative arts upon has been mutilated by the untrustworthiness of our memory.'[91]

Pembroke died in 1621, but her consuming interest in the cultural status of memory continued to exercise many of the philosophical enquiries of her age. Indeed, voices such as that of Sir Thomas Browne in the succeeding generation despaired of humanity's ambition to make a lasting contribution (or even a difference) to this sublunary world. Instead, he counselled that, rather than training our attentions upon the narratives of the past, it was now most timely to submit to the higher memory of 'the register of God', and it is to this subject that we shall turn in the next chapter.

'Tis too late to be ambitious: the great mutations of the world are acted, or time may be too short for our designs. To extend our memories by monuments, whose death we daily pray for (and whose duration we cannot hope without injury to our expectations) in the advent of the last day, were a contradiction to our beliefs … But the iniquity of oblivion blindly scattereth her poppy, and deals with the memory of men without distinction to merit of perpetuity … Oblivion is not to be hired: The greater part must be content to be as though they had not been, to be found in the register of God, not in the record of man.[92]

CHAPTER 6

'*Tell me where all past yeares are*': John Donne and the obligations of memory

> SIR, – Every Tuesday I make account that I turn a great hour-glass, and consider that a week's life is run out since I writ. But if I ask myself what I have done in the last watch, or would do in the next, I can say nothing; if I say that I have passed it without hurting any, so may the spider in my window ... to this hour I am nothing, or so little, that I am scarce subject and argument good enough for one of mine own letters.
>
> Addressed 'To Sir Henry Goodyer'[1]

This letter, signed rather unexpectedly 'Your hearty true friend, J. DONNE', amply demonstrates the abiding anxieties in evidence throughout Donne's writing career concerning the pressures of memory and the limits of human achievement. Here, in 1608, during one of the most frustrating periods of his life when he was denied public preferment in the aftermath of his illicit union with Ann More, Donne was continually haunted by the prospect of his unrealised potential and prolonged social ostracisation.[2] Indeed, his aspirations for political promotion appear in large measure to have been stifled in the opening decade of the seventeenth century by those who continued to remember the circumstances surrounding his marriage to his employer's ward. In later years, as a preacher, he would console his congregations with the lifting of a favourite proof from Hebrews 12:6, 'whome the Lord loveth hee chasteneth', and this would emerge as a recurring theme in his sermons, as in 1625 where he confided to the assembled company, 'All our life is a continuall burden, yet we must not groane; A continuall squeasing, yet we must not pant' (*Sermons*, vii.1.54).[3] Nonetheless, Donne himself was not always equal to the demands of such counsel in the early years of James VI/I's reign as he lingered year after year on the margins of a society in which he sought advancement.

Despite the profound melancholia clearly being exhibited in his letter, Donne is ironically giving proof of a vexed enquiry that would be taken up by succeeding generations of his own readers: how would his life's work be remembered by future ages? In fact, even during his lifetime this appears not to have been an unknown preoccupation. Ben Jonson, a notably competitive contemporary, observed archly in 1619 to Drummond of Hawthornden (if the latter's memory can be relied upon) that 'he esteemeth John Done the first poet in the World in some things'. Leaving his listener teasingly to hesitate between questions of hierarchy and chronology, Jonson nevertheless reverenced Donne with his *own* powers of memory. He informed Drummond that '[Donne's] verses of the Lost Chaine, he heth by Heart and that passage of the calme, that dust and feathers doe not stirr, all was so quiet'. Ultimately, however, Jonson would respond uncannily to his fellow poet's acute fears concerning loss, absence and indeed erasure with the verdict that 'Done himself for not being understood would perish'.[4] In the event, Jonson did participate in the memorialisation of his fellow poet: he is known to have assisted in the circulation of some of Donne's poems, and he celebrated 'the delight of Phoebvs, and each *Muse*' in a dedicatory lyric that was printed at the beginning of each edition of Donne's works from 1650 to 1669. Indeed, in another panegyric, he went as far as to name Donne as the sole arbiter of poetic excellence: 'if I find but one [poem] | Mark'd by thy hand, and with the better stone, | My title's seal'd'.[5]

One of the ways in which Donne became known, mediated and re-presented to succeeding generations of seventeenth-century readers was through the *Life of Donne* composed by his friend, Izaak Walton. In this narrative (which itself betrays on occasions a rather absent-minded biographer in terms of the relation and sequencing of events) Walton conjured up the figure of 'a second S. Augustine' who repeated the Church Father's cycles of experience, moving from a feckless youth to a life of piety in his later years.[6] Indeed, Walton extended this analogy to another very familiar conversion narrative in order to *fix* his heroic subject conclusively in the reader's memory: 'where he had been a *Saul*, though not to persecute Christianity, or to deride it, yet in his irregular youth to neglect the visible practise of it: there to become a *Paul*, and preach salvation to his beloved brethren.' Even so, ever alert to the manner in which Time might gnaw away at his friend's legacies, Walton submitted anxiously, 'It is observed, that a desire of glory or commendation is rooted in the very nature of man … [and] that like our radical heat it will both live and dye with us; and, many think it should do so; and, we want not sacred examples to justifie the desire of having our memory to outlive our lives.'[7]

This enterprise to figure Donne forth for future generations in terms of epiphany, conversion and religious vocation would be taken up again in Sir Richard Baker's *Chronicle of the Kings of England* (1643) in which he portrayed the youthful poet as

> not dissolute, but very neat; a great visiter of Ladies, a great frequenter of Playes, a great writer of conceited Verses; until such time as King *James* taking notice of the pregnancy of his Wit, was a meanes that he betooke him to the study of Divinity; and thereupon proceeding Doctour, was made Deane of *Paules*.[8]

Interestingly, Donne himself participated vigorously in these competing narrativisations of his identity. When he sent a personal copy of his tract *Biathanatos* in 1618 to the royal favourite Sir Robert Ker, he was at pains that his reader should 'know the date; and that it is a Book written by *Jack Donne*, and not by D. *Donne*'.[9] Indeed, in a sermon of the following year, he rehearsed this theme more generally (and at length) for the assembled company:

> First, therefore if thou wouldest be heard in *Davids* prayer; *Delicta juventutis*; O Lord remember not the sins of my youth; remember to come to this prayer, *In diebus juventutis*, in the dayes of thy youth. *Job* remembers with much sorrow, how he was in the dayes of his youth, when Gods providence was upon his Tabernacle: and it is a late, but a sad consideration, to remember with what tenderness of conscience, what scruples, what remorces we entred into sins in our youth.[10]

Tellingly, Ben Jonson also engaged in this cultural project to fracture Donne's selves, observing that 'now since he was made Doctor[, Donne] repenteth highlie & seeketh to destroy all his poems'.[11] If Donne did indeed try to call in all copies of his secular verse in order presumably to convince the larger public of his newly minted authority in the Church, he was clearly thwarted in his endeavours.

DONNE AND THE PRACTICE OF MEMORY

> I am not all here, I am here now preaching upon this text, and I am at home in my Library considering whether *S. Gregory*, or *S. Hierome*, have said best of this text, before ... You are not all here neither; you are here now, hearing me, and yet you are thinking that you have heard a better Sermon somewhere else, of this text before.[12]

Donne remained under no illusion concerning how unwieldy, contrary and morally corrosive the promptings of memory might prove. Here, in a Lincoln's Inn sermon (thought to date from 1620), he painted an arresting image of the potentially diffusive (and thus destructive) energies of the faculty. A 'right relationship' with memory would excite a precious growth in self-knowledge and a collapse in temporal ambition, but this relationship also imposed onerous obligations and labours upon the human spirit. If these challenges were not met, Donne argued in a sermon of 1626, we may all too often find ourselves diminished by surrendering to 'A memory of yesterdays pleasures, a feare of to morrows dangers, a straw under my knee, a noise in mine ear, a light in mine eye, an any thing, a nothing, a fancy, a Chimera in my braine' (*Sermons*, vii.10.264–5). Yet it becomes increasingly apparent in Donne's writings that even when the labours of memory were seen to have been truly executed they still required wider dissemination among an attentive interpretative community in order for their authority to be fully realised. Mary Sidney had acknowledged in her own textual productions of the 1590s that the true power of memory would be held partially *in potentia* if its purchase were restricted only to the meditative enquiries of the single self. As the years wore on, Donne would develop such concerns within more generalised theories of human epistemology of which he periodically gave intimations, such as those contained within a letter to his father-in-law, Sir George More: 'much of the knowledge buried in books perisheth, and becomes ineffectual, if it be not applied, and refreshed by a companion or friend.'[13]

This poet, preacher, diplomat, courtier constantly sought out cultural networks in which learning might be recalled, circulated and exchanged. Florio's Montaigne confessed, 'I am ever heer and there picking and culling, from this and that booke.'[14] Similarly endowed with an acquiring taste in matters of the intellect, Donne acknowledged in the prefatory epistle to 'Metempsychosis' that 'if I do borrow any thing, of antiquity, besides that I make account that I pay it to posterity, with as much and as good: you shall still find me to acknowledge it, and to thank not him only that hath digged out treasure for me, but that hath lighted me a candle to the place'.[15] Here, as we shall see in the next chapter devoted to Jonson, both Montaigne and Donne were responding to leads given by the authors of antiquity such as Seneca, who had advised the writer's thorough immersion in and ingestion of the literatures of the past in order to fashion an authoritative textual voice in the present. Izaak Walton affirmed that 'The latter part of [Donne's] life may be said to be a continued study', and, in direct comparison with the textual emphases concerning the peerless scholar-martyrs in Foxean accounts discussed in Chapter 3, Walton's narrative was eager to stress that the close government of memory had had a crucial role to play in his subject's intellectual development:

after his Sermon he never gave his eyes rest, till he had chosen out a new Text, and that night cast his Sermon into a form, and his Text into divisions; and the next day betook himself to consult the Fathers, and so commit his meditations to his memory, which was excellent ... all businesses that past of any publick consequence, either in this, or any of our neighbour nations, he abbreviated either in Latine, or in the Language of that Nation, and kept them by him for useful memorials.[16]

Deeply versed in Patristic writings, it is to Augustine that Donne turned most frequently among the Church Fathers in his preaching. By the beginning of his ministry in 1615, he was so familiar with the *Confessions*, *De Civitate Dei* and *De Trinitate* that the development of their arguments is often seamlessly woven into those of his own. Interestingly, as the period of his ministry progressed, Donne's facility for allowing his own memorial experience to coalesce mentally with narratives shaped by Augustine, Jerome or Paul (or, among the Pagans, by Aristotle, Plato or Cicero) quickly emerged in his sermons as one of the principal ways in which he formulated a commanding voice of spiritual leadership. In an undated sermon given at St Paul's, for example, Donne followed Plato in aligning all human knowledge with the recuperation of wisdom from a prenatal existence, and celebrated Moses in terms of exceptional memorial achievement: '*Moses was learned in all the wisedome of the Egyptians* ... he had an extraordinary education ... *Vt Reminisci potiùs videretur, quàm discere*, That whatsoever any Master proposed unto him, he rather seemed to remember it, then to learne it' (*Sermons*, ix.11.253). Most famously, in a Lincoln's Inn sermon of 1618, Donne forged an intimate link between the faculty and the ceaseless human yearning for divine grace:

The art of *salvation*, is but the art of *memory*. When God gave his people the *Law*, he proposes nothing to them, but by that way, to their memory; *I am the Lord your God, which brought you out of the land of Egypt*; Remember but that. And when we express Gods mercy to us, we attribute but that faculty to God, that he *remembers* us; *Lord, what is man, that thou art mindfull of him?* And when God works so upon us, as that *He makes his wonderfull works to be had in remembrance*, it is as great a mercy, as the very doing of those wonderfull works was before. It was a *seal* upon a *seal*, a seal of *confirmation*, it was a *sacrament* upon a *sacrament*, when in instituting the *sacrament* of his *body and his bloud*, Christ presented it so, *Doe this in remembrance of me*. *Memorare novissima*, remember the *last* things, and *fear* will keep thee from sinning; *Memorare praeterita*, remember the *first* things, what God hath done for thee.[17]

This emphasis upon the commemorative status of the sacrament assumed as important a status in Donne's theology as it had in Foxe's narratives of the martyred faithful half a century earlier. For the Reformist mind, as Malcolm Mackenzie Ross has underlined, 'The Eucharist is no longer a sacrifice but the celebration of the memory of a sacrifice',[18] and Donne would again stress this doctrinal belief at greater length in a 1622 sermon preached to the Earl of Carlisle and his company: 'Christ said, *Doe this in remembrance of mee*; which is, not onely remember me when you doe it, but doe it that you may remember me' (*Sermons*, v.13.262). At such moments Donne demonstrates that he is richly sensitive to Augustine's counsel that memory may both invigorate spiritual vocation and also enhance the performance of Christian witness.

DONNE, MEMORY, SELF

As discussions in earlier chapters have indicated, sixteenth-century authors such as Surrey, Parr and Foxe attended closely to the faculty of memory in their writings in order to promote in different ways its redemptive potential in a dangerously volatile human environment. Although the prospect of spiritual peril is rarely absent from Donne's own sermons, he did not treat the memorial impulse with quite the frequency of many of his predecessors in terms of a response to immanent trauma. However, like Foxe, Donne explored the ways in which historical and theological narrative frequently compelled readers to ponder: the challenges posed by the faculty; the manner in which we partake of the collective experience; and the mysterious operations of spiritual cognition. In a Lincoln's Inn sermon of 1618, he emphasised that

Plato plac'd *all learning* in the memory; wee may place *all Religion* in the memory too: All knowledge, that seems new today, says *Plato*, is but a remembring of *that*, which your soul knew before ... Nay, he that hears no Sermons, he that reads no scriptures, hath the Bible without book; He hath a *Genesis* in his *memory*; he cannot forget his *Creation*; he hath an *Exodus* in his memory; he cannot forget that God hath delivered him, from some kind of *Egypt*, from some oppression; He hath a *Leviticus* in his memory; hee cannot forget, that God hath proposed to him some Law, some rules to be observed. He hath *all* in his memory, even to the *Revelation*; God hath *revealed* to him, *even at midnight alone*, what shall be his portion, in the next world; And if he dare but remember that nights communication between God and him, he is well-near learned enough. There may be enough in *remembring our selves*; but sometimes, that's the hardest of all; many times we are farthest off from our selves; most forgetfull of our selves.[19]

It is at such moments that we rediscover the quicksilver intelligence and lyrical eloquence so notably in evidence in his erotic poetry. In direct comparison with the multiple and often conflicting voices that treat the nature of human desire in his secular verse, Donne's religious prose never fails to offer arresting and very diverse lines of vision upon the faculty of memory. In the extract above he clearly engages in a sympathetic and persuasive manner with the thrust of Platonic models of thinking. Turning away on this occasion from experiential authority, Donne focuses upon the wisdom gained by the soul from a prior realm of existence and the sobering consequences of our entry into flux-ridden materiality. If, in this instance, Donne expatiates upon the implications of *anamnesis*, he is also persuaded by an underlying principle of Plato's philosophy that the immutable quality of Truth means that it is only with mental and spiritual labour of some moment that it may be apprehended in a temporal environment that is subject to relentless change.[20]

Elsewhere, however, there are indeed occasions when he links his discussions of memory (and indeed human epistemology *per se*) solely to the sublunary, and thus appears particularly influenced by Aristotelian materialism (filtered for the most part through the minds of Augustine and Aquinas). In a 1619 sermon, the vicissitudes of earthly existence serve to underline the urgency with which we must apply ourselves to the spiritual imperatives of recollection: 'This is then the faculty that is excited, the memory; and this is the time, now, now whilest ye have power of election: The object is, the Creator, *Remember the Creator* ... the memory can go no farther then creation; and therefore we have no means to conceive, or apprehend any thing of God before that' (*Sermons*, ii.11.245). At such points, the memory is seen to be governed, held in check, by the motions of this lower world, and it becomes incumbent upon the minister to remind his congregations of the impermanence of this life and the emergency of spiritual decision-making. We are thus urged repeatedly to disengage from the devices and desires of our daily selves, and to exercise our thoughts wholly upon the remembrance of the blessings of God's munificence: 'what God hath done for us, is the object of our memory, not what he did before we were' (*Sermons*, ii.11.245).[21]

In the course of such enquiries into the spiritual status and functions of recollection, Donne's thinking is clearly influenced by Aristotelian distinctions that differentiated between the quotidian operations of memory and the conscious exertions of the faculty, prompted by pictorial or external stimuli. Nonetheless, Donne the preacher remains ever alert to the failing powers of the human memory, which might 'not understand all, or not remember all the Sermon'. Instead, here in 1626, he reassures the congregation, 'If thou remember that which concerned thy sin, and thy soul, if thou meditate upon that, apply that, thou hast brought away all the Sermon, all that was intended by the Holy Ghost to be preached to thee' (*Sermons*, vii.13.327, 329). More generally, in direct comparison with Augustine, Donne is most persuasive regarding this question of memorial labour when he offers up the emblematic experience of the speaking *self*. Like Augustine, Donne draws us into convincing narrative worlds, figured forth with an affecting intimacy of detail, so that no doubt may remain concerning the mental discipline to which we (like the speaker) must commit ourselves: 'yet every man hath a pocket picture about him, a manuall, a bosome book, and if he will turn over but one leaf, and remember what God hath done for him even since yesterday, he shall find even by that little branch a navigable river, to sail into that great and endless Sea of Gods mercies towards him, from the beginning of his being' (*Sermons*, ii.11.238).[22]

Clearly reminiscent of the crises vividly dramatised in his erotic verse, Donne's sermons frequently stage a whole host of compelling self-dramas, and these quickly emerge as one of the most potent weapons in his armoury as a preacher:

I impute nothing to another, that I confesse not of my selfe ... I rack no mans memory, what he did last year, last week, last night, I onely gather into my memory, and powr out in the presence of my God, and his Church, the sinfull history of mine own *youth*. (*Sermons*, ii.1.53)

Having seized our interest in this manner, Donne re-enacts the journey so often performed in the *Confessions*: his audiences are urged to forswear the ties that bind them to their earthly existence, and to acknowledge the soul's natural desire for transcendence.

MEMORY AND POETRY

From the perspective of Donne's wider textual output, memory quickly emerges not only as a pervasive theme of interest but, on occasions, as a source of vexed speculation. In the teasing and ultimately enigmatic lyric 'Goe and catche a falling starre', Donne's feverish textual voices conjure with fantasies of memory and endurance, and thrust the reader into a bewildering arena of impossible quests for knowledge. In this vision, the vain attempt to control the past and the ravages of age is intimately linked to the illusory ideal of a 'woman true, and faire'.

> Go and catch a falling star,
> Get with child a mandrake root,
> Tell me where all past years are ...

> If thou be'st borne to strange sights,
> Things invisible go see,
> Ride ten thousand days and nights,
> Till age snow white hairs on thee …
> (Goe and catche a falling starre',
> ll. 1–3, 10–13)²³

Driven on by this remorseless sequence of imperatives, we are compelled to reflect upon our own and others' incapacity to realise heroic exploits in erotic or any other contexts. Indeed, the probing of seductive, but wildly extravagant fictions of earthly achievement in this poem serves to unmask the frailty of all human faculties. The illusory desire to capture 'a falling star' or even the past is not only a ludic *and ludicrous* way of resisting a deeply flawed present, but a strategic attempt to close down any prospect of transcendence (except, perhaps, for poetry itself). In such a textual world, splintering under the strain of its contradictions, there can be no coherence, because the key to all meaning, the feckless mistress, 'Will be | False, ere I come, to two, or three' (ll. 25–6).

The possibility that human achievement might be re-membered by writing remained a source of animated interest for readers, patrons and authors alike, and by the final decade of the sixteenth century the abiding concern with the eternising powers of verse looked back not only to Petrarchan lyrics but also to emphases found in the poetics of antiquity: Horace, for example, had affirmed in his Third Ode, 'Exegi monumentum aere perennius | regalique situ pyramidum altius' (3.30.1–2) [I have achieved a monument more lasting than bronze, and loftier than the pyramids of kings].²⁴ The textual triumph of memory assumes centre-stage in many of Donne's most famous lyrics: again and again he takes the eternising ambitions of the courtly lover and transposes them to new poetic environments. In 'The Canonization', rather than the anguished articulation of male sexual frustration, Donne's speaker promotes a magnificent exemplum of mutual affection. If the lovers (whose 'legend … will be fit for verse') cannot have their memory preserved in a 'piece of chronicle', then succeeding generations may prise it from the 'pretty rooms' of sonnets. In direct comparison with the mnemonic techniques advocated by Roman theorists of rhetoric, the reader is invited at the close of this poem to visit in sequence with the mind's eye such fictional spaces as rooms, 'well-wrought urn[s]' and 'half-acre tombs' to appreciate fully the true significance of the lovers' achievement. All of these structures become echoing chambers or shrines memorialising those '*canoniz'd* for Love' (ll. 30, 32–6). The necessity for architectonic structures to house memory becomes imperative as the poetic narrative unfolds, and indeed the very identity of the lovers at this point appears to depend wholly upon such memorialisation, nay monumentalisation.

In some of the most dramatic moments of his lyrical output, Donne's poetic voices are eager to claim for the power of love the ability to control time and to hold human experience transfixed. In 'The Canonization' he plays off the energies of memory against the appetite for erotic heroism. Interestingly, in this instance, the mistress is asked primarily to be the *bearer* of memory. Even though the world may be 'elder by a year' since the lovers' first meeting and 'All other things to their destruction draw', the mistress must recollect that 'Only our love hath no decay; | This, no tomorrow hath, nor yesterday' (ll. 4–8). Here, memorial exertion enables this superlative love to defy time, to break out of the changeful sublunary and to enter a realm of eternal significance. Conversely, in the 'Farewell to Love' the resources of memory do little to contribute to a sense of human achievement, and the reader is thrust into a world in which the fulfilment of desire 'Being had, enjoying it decays', and all that remains is 'A kind of sorrowing dullness to the mind' (ll. 16, 20).

Throughout his career as a writer, the grandiloquent rhetoric deployed by Donne's speakers all too often betrays a persisting horror of diminution and disintegration. In the *Devotions Upon Emergent Occasions*, one of the most affecting examples of his meditative prose, Donne's disease-ridden speaker contends that 'Man is a *diminutive* to nothing. Man consistes of more pieces, more parts, then the world … And if those pieces were extended, and stretched out in Man, as they are in the world, Man would bee the *Gyant*, and the world the *Dwarfe*, the world but the *Map*, and the Man the *World*'.[25] This textual *mise en abîme* of an almost endlessly extending human body is but one of a whole host of examples in Donne's writing that render decay and disintegration as *points de départ* for broader ontological enquiry. In a 1621 sermon, his auditors were asked repeatedly to couple the knowledge of mortality ('when everlasting darknesse shall have an inchoation in the present dimnesse of mine eyes') with angst-ridden speculation regarding the humanly unquantifiable delay before our re-membering after death: 'God knowes, how many generations, till the Redeemer, my Redeemer, the Redeemer of all me, body, as well as soule, come againe' (*Sermons*, iv.1.56). It seems to matter little whether Donne is working in secular or religious textual modes, the profound uncertainty of the human present occasioned by crises of failing belief or fissured knowledge can often only be resolved by recourse to the restorative coherence of memory.

In some of his most famous poems, Donne allows fictions of time, imagined futures, to engender sites of heroic memory: he evokes poetic scenes in which the present is subordinated to a drama of future generations remembering. With its Catholic emphases upon survival of a precious past through ceremonial strategies of preservation and veneration, 'The Relique' clearly tests the potentially redemptive powers of memory in this way with its expert concatenation of time frames. Similarly, in 'The Funeral', new generations are asked to attend to 'That subtle wreath of hair, which crowns my arm; | The mystery, the sign, you must not touch' (ll. 3–4). This intensely fragile link with the past symbolised by ritualised burial is the only means left to memorialise, to 'control, | And keep these limbs, her provinces, from dissolution' (ll. 7–8). The ways in which such lyrics *produce* memory for audiences, as yet unborn, serve not only to amplify the status of desire in the poetic present but also compel readers to interrogate the provisionality of all other remaining narratives of human experience.

Such enquiries would haunt Donne throughout his life. In a 1609 letter to 'the *Worthiest* Lady Mrs. Bridget White', he begins by speculating if he 'could make some guess whether souls that go to heaven retain any memory of us that stay behind'. Although the letter unfolds in an increasingly playful mode, proposing that 'heaven' in this case is 'yourself, at home', Donne betrays once again his enduring fascination with strategies for survival and remembrance.[26] On a number of occasions elsewhere, Donne's poetic mistresses are also deployed as purveyors of memory. In 'Woman's Constancy', he attends closely to the implications of eroticised memory and, indeed, to the female as an ungovernable keeper of the records of desire:

> Now thou hast lov'd me one whole day.
> Tomorrow when thou leav'st, what wilt thou say?
> Wilt thou then antedate some new-made vow …
> ('Woman's Constancy', ll. 1–3)

In such lyrics we are drawn into an environment that has witnessed the collapse of memorial ties – of obligation, commitment, and of value itself. However, in this instance, the bitter, yet witty speaker determines to assume the changeful nature of the *cruel fair*, rather than the customary humiliation of the erotic victim: 'For by tomorrow, I may think so too' (l. 17). If in 'Confined Love' the 'law' is derided that insists each woman 'should but one man know' (ll. 5–6), in 'The Indifferent' a swaggering speaker exults in the prospect of a promiscuous world in which *soma*, rather than *agape*, is recalled: 'I can love both fair and brown, | Her whom abundance melts, and her whom want betrays' (ll. 1–2). Here, the male asserts his superior rights of sexual appetite and memory, and lays siege to his mistress with the sentiment 'Oh we are not [true], be not you so' (l. 14).²⁷ In the desire to gain an incremental carnal knowledge of womankind, the speaker promotes his own sexual 'craft' and closes off any possibility for the woman of independence of thought or body – a theme that is rehearsed even more forcefully and teasingly in Donne's third elegy, 'Change'.

With equal frequency, however, Donne's textual voices find themselves appalled by the impermanence of sexual achievement, and indeed by the impermanence of their place in the affections of others. In such cases, poetic creativity appears to compete with the sobering awareness of the provisionality of all erotic identities and the failing powers of recall exerted by each succeeding lover. Thus, if in the past Donne's personae believed that the mistress's body might be the means to access a heroic identity, in a chilly poetic present they are driven to shore up their dwindling status with their own memorial exertions.²⁸ Such crises of identity and ownership are clearly being articulated in the seventh elegy 'Nature's lay idiot, I taught thee to love', where the apparently unbiddable mistress is instructed, 'I planted knowledge and life's tree in thee; | Which oh, shall strangers taste?' (ll. 26–7). These performances of Donnean angst culminate in a poem such as 'The Apparition', where sexual memory is deployed as a deadly force. The powerlessness of the speaker in the present causes him to reserve his bile for a ghostly future in which the feckless and sexually unruly mistress will become a satisfying object of revenge for her erstwhile lover: 'What I will say, I will not tell thee now' (l. 14). In this elegant inversion of an *amor de lonh*, the *cruel fair* comes to represent the limits of the speaker's sexual authority that can only be reclaimed, it seems, through recourse to a future of supernatural fictions. Acknowledging the deeply seductive, but precarious nature of such *fictions*, Judith Scherer Herz convincingly locates Donne's poetics at such moments within a Baroque aesthetic, whereby 'Their subject, like Pozzo's ceilings or much of Bernini's oeuvre, is the nature of illusionism itself.'²⁹ However, the fantasies of retribution (articulated in lyrics such as 'The Apparition') are significant not only in that they may unveil a subject seeking to occlude erotic failure with the illusory prospect of retributive violence, such fantasies also point to the frequent possibility in Donne's writing that the human process of apprehension itself remains wholly subject to the fruits of memorial labour.

DONNE, MEMORY AND POETIC AUTHORITY

It remains striking that throughout his writing career Donne was excited by the stark and witty juxtaposition of contradictory, often equally extreme, positions of allegiance. In the *Paradoxes and Problems*, for example, he teasingly explores the question of woman as *le mal nécessaire*: 'I am not of that sear'd impudency that I dare defend women, or pronounce them good: yet when we see phisitians allow some vertu in every poyson, alas why should we except women? Since, certainly they are good for phisick.'³⁰ Elsewhere in the 'Nocturnall upon S. Lucies Day' he famously conjured up a haunting vision in which 'The world's whole sap is sunk' (l. 5). In this poem, woman is not associated with erotic therapy, but with completion of the male narrative of desire, albeit consigned to the past. The lover's superior rights of memory are affirmed and, like so many of Donne's poetic personae, he goes onto remind auditors that the most fulfilling moments of human desire may be construed in the Neoplatonic terms of *ecstasis*: 'absences | Withdrew our souls, and made us carcasses' (ll. 26–7). In a favoured poetic manoeuvre at the close of the poem, Donne then reconfigures the rememberer as the remembered (always a parlous relationship in his textual worlds) for the wider audience beyond the page: 'You lovers ... | Enjoy your summer' (ll. 38, 41).

In whatever context, it remains difficult to ignore Donne's concern with memory as a mechanism for control. Despite the fact that Helen Gardner famously disputed his authorship of 'Sappho to Philaenis' and classed it under 'Dubia', this 'heroical epistle' has enjoyed increasing critical attention among scholars.³¹ Sappho's narrative of affective defeat and stifled erotic appetite ultimately couples the memory of sexual belonging with an urgent interrogation of the eternising ambitions of poetry itself: 'Where is that holy fire, which Verse is said | To have? is that inchanting force decai'd?' (ll. 1–2). Firmly situated within Petrarchan conventions that linked the recollection of desire with the mental imaging of the loved one, Donne's Sappho proclaims that 'Onely thine image, in my heart, doth sit' (l. 9). Whereas Aristotle had likened the operations of memory to those of a signet ring upon wax, Donne's passionate Sappho claims that the image itself is 'wax' and the 'fires' of her heart 'environ it' (l. 10). If this bereft female speaker is ultimately left to ponder the contents of her 'irksome Memory, | Which, both to keepe, and lose, grieves equally' (ll. 13–14), the equivocal nature of the legacy that memory bequeaths remains more generally an ongoing theme of enquiry in Donne's writing. In the sermons he can be found to argue at length that this faculty operates as a stimulus to self-knowledge, yet, on other occasions, memory may also impoverish spiritually and betray the unwary Christian: 'in this survey of sin, thy first care must be, to take heed of returning too diligently to a remembrance of those delightful sins which are past; for that will endanger new' (*Sermons*, i.3.194).[32]

In her landmark study of discourses of time in the early modern period, *The Map of Time*, Achsah Guibbory persuasively advanced the thesis that, for Donne, 'Memory seems to be the faculty that has been least impaired by the Fall', and that 'Because God, once learned, is in our memory, the way to find God is through memory'.[33] Guibbory is surely just in her assertion that Donne attributes 'unusual weight' to this faculty and views it as an indispensable resource for spiritual contemplation. However, Noralyn Masselink has more recently put forward the case that in Donne's writing critics have 'overestimated Donne's trust in memory', and she contends that, in his writing, memory, like understanding and will, is also perceived as 'subject to decay'.[34] Nonetheless, at many strategic points Donne the preacher clearly does position the faculty as a dominant element in his soteriology. If, like Augustine, Donne privileges the spiritual, rather than the chronological, understanding that memory can yield, as the extracts above from the sermons have indicated, we are cautioned to remember in carefully governed ways – for former sources of temptation may entice us anew. In the third of the Holy Sonnets, Donne's reader is reminded that 'Th' hydroptic drunkard, and night-scouting thief, | The itchy lecher, and self-tickling proud | Have the remembrance of past joys, for relief | Of coming ills' (ll. 9–12). Clearly, the fund of memory must be exploited with the utmost care. Indeed, Florio's Montaigne stressed the boundless creativity of the faculty ('the Magazin of Memorie, is peradventure more stored with matter, then is the store-house of Invention'[35]), but warned that it required discipline. Another of Donne's European contemporaries, the Spanish Augustinian friar and poet, Fray Luis de León (1527–91), drew in his third Ode a direct link between the seductive creativity of music and the human spirit's succumbing to the operations of *anamnesis*: 'a cuyo son divino | mi alma, que en olvido está sumida, | torna a cobrar el tino | y memoria perdida | de su origen primera esclarecida' ['at that glorious sound divine | my soul, mired deep in all it has forgotten | regains its bearings and course, | the memory that was lost | of origins and its first, noble home'] (ll. 6–10).[36] Interestingly, this preoccupation with the creative, epiphanic resources of memory was to persist into the modern period, as may be witnessed in the contention of the philosopher F. C. Bartlett in the first half of the twentieth century that 'remembering is not the re-excitation of innumerable fixed, lifeless and fragmentary traces. It is an imaginative reconstruction, or construction'.[37]

In his sermons Donne repeatedly asserts that the narratives of memory must be strategically edited in order to amplify their powers of instruction and to keep sinfulness and despair at bay. However, towards the end of his life, in a sermon of 1629, he offered powerful solace for those in possession of an erring memory by acknowledging the immanent potential of divine intervention at such moments of waywardness: 'If ... the memory and sinfull delight of passed sinnes, the ghosts of those sinnes haunt me againe; yet there is a holy Ghost in heaven, that shall exorcise these, and shall overshadow me, the God of all Comfort and Consolation' (*Sermons*, ix.1.61).

THE LOCATION OF MEMORY

As became apparent in the Introduction, Augustine was responding to debates dating back to the writings of Plato and Aristotle at least when he famously envisaged in his *Confessions* that memory might be a voluminous storage space and, even more importantly, a governing principle for identity formation. Clearly sympathetic to Augustine's thinking, Donne can on occasions subscribe to this materialist model of memory as a container or receptacle that houses the narrative remnants of human experience. However, one of the principal ways in which the legacy of his thinking is most influential in his work is in the frequent affirmation of the Augustinian subdivision of the soul into will, understanding and memory. In Augustine's *De Trinitate* the triune soul is seen as a mortal echo of the tripartite nature of divine power; and Donne takes up and elaborates upon this theory at regular intervals during his career as a preacher.[38] An important example of this may be witnessed in a 1629 sermon that was preached before Charles I at court, where he specifies that

> in [the] first naturall faculty of the soul; the Understanding, stands the Image of the first Person, the Father, Power: and in the second faculty which is the Will, is the Image, the Attribute of the second Person, the Sonne, which is Wisdome ... And then, in the third faculty of the soul; the Memory, is the Image of the third person, the holy Ghost, that is, Goodnesse ... The wise-man places all goodnesse in this faculty, the memory.[39]

If, as Achsah Guibbory has justly argued, the figuration of triune soul was a commonplace in early modern religious writing, it is evident that Donne privileges memory in this discussion more distinctively than many of his predecessors in the Reformist tradition.[40] In the Whitsunday sermon of 1628 he insists that 'truly the Memory is oftner the Holy Ghosts Pulpit that he preaches in, then the Understanding' (*Sermons*, viii.11.261). Indeed, memory seems not only to take the Christian faithful to the origins of their own spiritual knowledge, it compels them to retrace a collective cultural narrative back to the Fall in Eden. In one of his earliest surviving sermons of 1616, Donne affirmed the absolute depravity and dependency in this postlapsarian world of the human sinner who desperately yearns for the spiritual balm of divine grace: 'as his sin is elder then himself (for *Adams* sin is his sin) so is it longer liv'd then his body, for it shall cleave everlastingly to his soul too' (*Sermons*, i.3.193).[41] Nonetheless, it should be underlined that he frequently tempered the Calvinist emphasis in his preaching upon Original Sin with an enduring concern with salvation (rather than election) and with the operations of the divine memory: 'when Man is returned to dust, God returns to the remembrance of that promise, *Awake and sing ye that dwell in the dust*' (*Sermons*, iv.1.62).[42] In a similar vein, Donne's contemporary Richard Greenham argued in *Propositions containing answers to certaine demaunds in divers spirituall matters* (1597) that 'The best art of memorie, is to bee humbled at Gods threatning, and comforted at his promises'.[43]

If in *De Inventione* Cicero had defined virtue in terms of Wisdom (*Prudentia*), Justice (*Iustitia*), Courage (*Fortitudinis*) and Temperance (*Temperantia*), this philosophical tradition of *mémoire moralisée* (witnessed in Titian's sixteenth-century rendering of *An Allegory of Prudence* – see Figure 1) clearly had an enormous influence upon Donne's intellectual development. However, rather than relying exclusively upon conceptual models derived from antiquity to explicate Donne's formulation of memory, Noralyn Masselink has argued persuasively that critics may be overlooking the crucial link of Thomist influences.[44] Like his mentor and fellow Dominican, Albertus Magnus, Aquinas wrote a commentary upon Aristotle's *De Memoria et Reminiscentia* that took into account later contributions from Roman theorists such as Cicero. Aquinas maintained the Aristotelian distinction between passive memory and deliberate recollection, but was also strongly influenced by the aligning of *memoria* with Prudence and, more generally, with the promotion of historical exemplarity in Cicero's writing. As in so many of his discussions, when Aquinas came to consider memory, his interest was upon the ways in which reason and moral knowledge may enrich a commitment to faith. Indeed, as Masselink has pointed out, Donne is significantly influenced by the Aristotelian emphasis in Thomist thinking whereby the human mind engages with the past by drawing upon mental processes of association (particularly pictorial in nature) and by recalling sensory data of the (divinely orchestrated) material world. Donne affirmed in a 1628 sermon that 'The ignorantest man that is, even he that cannot read a Picture, even a blinde man, hath a better book in himself; In his own memory he may read many a history of God's goodness to him' (*Sermons*, viii.11.261) and there are many examples of such instances in his religious writing where the recalling of personal sensory experience becomes the rock upon which to build spiritual knowledge.[45]

Yet while the influences of Augustine, Cicero and Aquinas are clearly identifiable in Donne's theological discussions of memory, his thinking can be seen to respond to the work of an enormous range of strategic figures in this centuries-old cultural debate. In this context, we might also take into account the influence of Bernard of Clairvaux. In an undated Lincoln's Inn sermon, Donne filters Augustinian formulations of memory through the lens of Bernard's rhetoric: 'as Saint *Bernard* calls it, *A trinity from the Trinity*, in those *three faculties* of the soul, the *Vnderstanding*, the *Will*, and the *Memory*' (*Sermons*, ii.2.72–3). In another sermon, of 1619, exploring the nature of true faith, Donne not only celebrates the role of memory in the communication of spiritual knowledge, he also turns to Bernard's figurative language of physiology to explain the enigmatic workings of the faculty to his congregation: 'The memory, sayes St *Bernard*, is the stomach of the soul, it receives and digests, and turns into good blood' (*Sermons*, ii.11.236). Offering up for his congregation their very own memory theatre of the soul, Donne continues in the same sermon, counselling:

go to thine own memory; for as St *Bernard* calls that the stomach of the soul, we may be bold to call it the Gallery of the soul, hang'd with so many, and so lively pictures of the goodness and mercies of thy God to thee, as that every one of them shall be a catachism to thee, to instruct thee in all thy duties to him for those mercies.[46]

Donne's meditations upon memory often seek to embed the faculty in materiality (notably the body) in order to reassure his listeners of the naturalness and the inevitability of the spirit's responses to memorial promptings. Interestingly, in the Christmas Day sermon of 1622 at St Paul's, Donne pondered the journeyings of the sinful soul by attending particularly to Bernard's close imbrication of *memoria* with *soma*: 'If thou wilt sacrifice the bloud of thy soule, (as St *Bernard* cals the will) sacrifice the fat too; If thou give over thy purpose of continuing in thy sin, give over the memory of it' (*Sermons*, iv.11.295). Janet Coleman has demonstrated in her magisterial study of the early discourses of *memoria* that Bernard was a key figure in the medieval treatment of this subject because both he and Saint Anselm 'saw themselves as expounding methods by which the practitioner might transcend the memory of sacred text and the memory of lived life, to achieve the forgetfulness of self in the contemplation of God'.[47] Whereas Donne never failed to acknowledge the urgency with which the soul must dispossess itself of the trappings of this lower world, he remained keenly alert to the intense spiritual strain which this desire for transcendence engendered. Indeed, he lamented poignantly in an early sermon (thought to date from the years 1616 or 1617) that 'Endymion loved the Moon. The sphear of our loves is sublunary, upon things naturally inferior to our selves' (*Sermons*, i.3.200).

Coleman stresses that 'Augustine's treasure house of memory [became] a sewer for Bernard. The belly of Bernard's memory [was] congested with filth',[48] and the deliberative *bleaching* of the memory (advocated by medieval thinkers such as Bernard and Anselm) was proposed as a liberation from the contamination of spiritual failure and flawed allegiances of the past. This role of the faculty to act as repository for the material experiences of the senses that must submit to the rigours of spiritual catharsis clearly exercised Donne's contemporary, Saint John of the Cross (1542–91) in his *Cántico espiritual*, and such emphases were eagerly seized upon by Donne and often articulated with extended lexical fields of cleansing, erasing, shedding. Indeed, the members of his congregation were urged to immerse themselves in 'a sea of mercie', which acts to dissolve former selves along with the stains of their sinfulness:

> as the Sea retaines no impression of the Ships that passe in it … so when we put out into the boundlesse Sea of the blood of Christ Jesus, by which onely wee have reconciliation to God, there remaines no record against us; for God hath cancelled that record which he kept … And yet here, the uncharitable man will know more, and see more, and remember more, then my God, or his devill remembers, or knowes, or sees: He will see a path in the Sea; he will see my sin, when it is drowned in the blood of my Saviour.[49]

MEMORY, DEVOTION AND THE BODY

Mary Warnock is timely in posing the question, 'What is it about memory that inevitably brings in the physiological?'[50] As we have seen, in *De Memoria et Reminiscentia*, Aristotle had forged intimate links between the operations of the body and those of the memory.[51] Later theories of the bodily humours, as explicated by Galen, extended Aristotelian premisses about human anatomy and circulated widely in the Mediterranean world and beyond for centuries. Both Albertus Magnus, in his commentary upon *De Memoria and Reminiscentia*, and Boncompagno da Signa, in his *Rhetorica Novissima* (1235), for example, would ponder the liaison between *memoria* and *melancholia*.[52] In due course, a memorial sensibility was firmly paired, as Aristotle had proposed, with melancholia: this humour was linked with dryness, and thus it was thought that the melancholic's mind would most easily receive the *imprint* or image of experience on its surface.[53] Theorists such as Galen did not reject the Aristotelian principle that the heart was the ultimate seat of government for human actions (physical and cerebral), but he devoted much more attention to the brain, which, in his writings, came to be associated not only with bodily functions but with the mental powers of *phantasia*, *cogitatio* and *memoria*. The influence of his recorded enquiries meant that melancholics were often perceived in terms of their retentiveness; and their endeavours to restore humoral balance and harmony might frequently be expressed in terms of memorial activity. Following in the footsteps of Galen, Arabic medical theoreticians such as Razes and Avicenna had paid particular attention to the functions of the brain and maintained that, although principally solid in substance, the brain had cavities or *ventricles*. *Memoria* (*virtus memorialis* or *conservativa*) was deemed to be lodged in the ventricle to the rear of the head, as was explored in the discussion of Spenser's Eumnestes at the Castle of Alma in the Introduction. Ruth E. Harvey has argued persuasively that for Avicenna 'the power *memorialis* and *reminiscibilis* ... is a power set in the hindmost ventricle of the brain. It retains what *extimativa* has apprehended, the intentions of the individual *sensibilia*, which were not perceived by the senses'.[54] During the thirteenth century, Aquinas was among the first in the West to be deeply versed in both Aristotelian and Arabic philosophical writings on this matter. He emphasised the crucial importance of the effects of the material, sensory world upon the body *and* soul of man, and thus resisted the pressures of Platonic traditions of thinking with their dualist emphases upon the contrary motions of *psyche* and *soma*. As has been witnessed above, Donne was clearly very familiar with these intellectual legacies and expected his lawyerly congregations to be similarly informed. In a sermon strategically taken from Ecclesiastes ('Remember now thy Creator in the dayes of thy Youth') and preached before his departure for Germany on a diplomatic mission in 1619, he reacquainted his listeners during a wide-ranging analysis of the spiritual efficacy of memory with its supposed anatomical placement: 'Remember therefore, and remember now, though the Memory be placed in the hindermost part of the brain, defer not thou thy remembering to the hindermost part of thy life' (*Sermons*, ii.11.235).[55]

If Donne was thoroughly concerned with the ways in which the human memory might become the means for spiritual and cognitive renewal, he never allowed his audiences to forget their existential state of desperate frailty. Florio's Montaigne confessed, 'When I religiously confesse my self unto my selfe, I finde, the best good I have hath some vicious tainte ... *Man all in all, is but a botching and party-coloured worke.*'[56] However, Donne is characteristically more eager to conduct this enquiry in terms of the Reformist doctrine of the human condition of utter dependency – that we are held tightly in a higher, divine narrative of memory: '*He remembers that we are but dust*; but dust then when we lie in the grave; and yet He remembers us. But His memory goes farther then so, He remembers that we were but dust alive, at our best' (*Sermons*, iv.2.66). These concerns with the abiding nature of divine scrutiny, the anguish of the wavering soul, the dramatic outbursts of an unruly spirit and the pained recognition of a flawed past all have determining influences upon the narrative structures of Donne's devotional verse. Roger B. Rollin contends justly that the 'Holy Sonnets' are 'public demonstrations of (in this case) spiritual malaise meant to be exemplary to disease-prone readers',[57] and thus may be seen to share continuities of theme and purpose with Donne's sermons. Indeed, Donne never allows the anxieties and tensions surrounding the agonised human yearning for redemption to slacken throughout his devotional prose or poetry. If he cautioned against making 'Religion too homely a thing' (*Sermons*, vii.12.314), this point was highlighted even more forcefully in a sermon thought to date from 1626/7 where he urged his congregation that we must not imagine 'a God of wax, whom we can melt, and mold, when, and how we will ... By terrible things, O God of our salvation, doest thou answer us in righteousnesse' (*Sermons*, vii.12.324). To the Reformist mind, the soul could never count upon the inevitability of salvation, it could only pray urgently for the advent of divine grace. Mindful of such emphases in the ninth Holy Sonnet, 'If poisonous minerals, and if that tree', Donne constructs a vigorous narrative of spiritual rebellion and ultimate submission (so widely apparent in seventeenth-century religious verse), which resolves itself in a plea that

> thine only worthy blood,
> And my tears, make a heavenly lethean flood,
> And drown in it my sin's black memory;

>   That thou remember them, some claim as debt,
>   I think it mercy, if thou wilt forget.
>   ('If poisonous minerals, and if that tree',
>   ll. 10–14)

In instances such as these, Masselink appears most convincing in her argument for the Thomist influence upon Donne's memorial thinking. Rejecting as a general principle the Platonic dualistic tension between the worlds of Being and Becoming, Aquinas had insisted upon the existential continuity of body and soul that allows physical experience to engage intimately with the promptings of the soul.[58] In this way, divine sacrifice and human penitence are played out in a larger drama of remembrance in both somatic and spiritual terms.[59]

In 'Good Friday, 1613, Riding Westward', the memory of Christ's sacrifice is directly connected both with earthly pilgrimage and with a providential sense of spiritual journeying. Here, we may discover a familiar Augustinian discursive strategy: Donne's poetic persona engages with a material and memorial landscape in order to realise the full scope of his spiritual meditation upon the nature of transcendence. In the previous century, Reformists like William Tyndale had insisted vigorously upon the *sola scriptura* position for the path to true salvation: 'As thou readest therefore thinke that every sillabe pertayneth to thine own selfe, & sucke out the pithe of the scripture.'[60] In Donne's poem the contours of the environment are construed as a decipherable text and act in the manner of a mnemonic for the soul's instruction. This habit of thinking, which maps the eschatological onto the spatial, remained in evidence throughout Donne's career as a preacher. In one of his later sermons, of 1629, for example, we are reminded that 'Christ's name is *Oriens*, the East; if we will be named by him, (called Christians) we must look to this East' (*Sermons*, ix.1.49).[61] In 'Riding Westward' the mind of the speaker moves effortlessly from the sublunary world with its changeful skies to the vision of a cosmological drama enacted every time a soul hangs in the balance:

>   … I am carried towards the west,
>   This day, when my soul's form bends to the east.
>   There I should see a Sun by rising set,
>   And by that setting endless day beget;
>   But that Christ on this Cross did rise and fall,
>   Sin had eternally benighted all.
>   …
>   Though these things as I ride be from mine eye,
>   They are present yet unto my memory,

> For that looks towards them; and thou look'st towards me,
> O Saviour, as thou hang'st upon the tree.
> ('Riding Westward', ll. 9–14, 33–6)

The mental narrative of the sun's course re-enacts a spiritual resurrection in microcosm. Armed with the precious resources of memory, the speaker is able to pass beyond the constraints of purely sensory engagement with the material world and to formulate a landscape that suggests typologically the divine figuration of death and rebirth. Here, in this lyric, memory is posited once again as the axis around which spiritual yearning may be conceived.

The most celebrated examples of Donne's meditations upon memory and transcendence are the poetic narratives on the occasion of the death of Elizabeth Drury – the 'Anniversary' poems. Interestingly, there appears not to have been any personal remembrance at work here.[62] However, he positions the account of Drury's demise as a textual surface upon which to organise an intricate enquiry into the nature of human transience and temporal decline. If the poetic bid is initially to 'eternize' Drury for subsequent generations, Donne gradually allows the commemoration of the subject to be subsumed within a larger poetic investigation into the ways in which memory itself may assist us to resist the onslaught of universal decay. This desire to 'fix' the life and legacy in verse of those warranting singular praise is in evidence at regular intervals throughout his writing career. In 'To the Countess of Bedford at New Year's Tide', for example, the speaker argues beguilingly that 'Verse embalms virtue' (l. 13); and, more generally, the formulation of the poetic voice as an expert in memory quickly became a recurrent device of his poetics. In this particular lyric, panegyric is being deployed for apotropaic purposes, as a means of keeping death at bay. The Countess of Bedford *encore vivante* is invited to contemplate her own transcendence through the textual vehicle of poetry, to contemplate a future not characterised by death but by endless renewal. In the 'Anniversary' poems, however, Donne maps out an enormously ambitious textual panorama of a change-ridden universe from which the late Elizabeth Drury is redeemed. With the resources of figurative language, the speaker illuminates with unfailing energy the temporal conditions of human existence in which each death is the intimation of a more personal fate. In a sermon of 1619, he had contended that 'The Patriarchs in the old Testament had their Summer day, long lives; we are in the Winter, short lived' (*Sermons*, ii.9.199). With Drury's demise, this ageing and 'sick world' collapses into a 'lethargy', and humanity rediscovers the memory of a particular and unresolved grief, that 'we are never well, nor can be so' (ll. 23–4, 94).

The 'Anniversary' poems began as elegiac tributes, but they quickly expanded more ambitiously to embrace the remit of a philosophical oration pondering the decline of earthly perfection, social order and epistemological cohesion. As David Lowenthal has argued more generally, 'Once predicted, decay and death could be found in every falling leaf' – even Francis Bacon would concede that 'these times are the ancient times, when the world is ancient, and not those which we account ancient *ordine retrogrado*, by a computation backward from ourselves'.[63] And this consuming interest in temporal decline was clearly preoccupying a great number of Donne's contemporaries across Europe, such as the Spanish poet Francisco de Quevedo (1580–1645), whose speaker affirms at the close of the second of his *Poemas Metafíscos*, 'En el hoy y mañana y ayer, junto | pañales y mortaja, y he quedado | presentes sucesiones de difunto' ['In my today, tomorrow, yesterday | I join swaddling and shroud, and have become | present successions of the same dead man'].[64] Nonetheless, Jonson famously baulked at the poetic undertaking of the Anniversaries, finding it 'profane and full of Blasphemies': 'if [the poems] had been written of the Virgin Marie it had been something'. Donne's alleged rejoinder on this occasion was that 'he described the Idea of a Woman and not as she was'.[65] Through the idealised Drury, Donne thus offers his readers a moral and spiritual referent with which to gauge the very multifariousness of earth's ceaseless decay, and stresses how significant it is that memory itself should be the principal resource bequeathed to the grieving world, for within it lies the seed of Man's renewal.

> … And though she have shut in all day,
> The twilight of her memory doth stay;
> Which, from the carcase of the old world, free
> Creates a new world; and new creatures be
> Produc'd …
> ('An anatomie of the world', ll. 73–7)

If in the 'Anniversary' poems Donne never ignores the enormous gulf that lies between ourselves and this extraordinary exemplum of Drury ('We seem ambitious, God's whole work to undoe' (l. 155)), she ultimately emerges in his ambitious narratives as a touchstone of spiritual enquiry and meaning: 'See, she is dead; she's dead: when thou knowest this, | Thou knowest how poor a trifling thing man is' (ll. 183–4). Indeed, her memory assumes an almost talismanic effect, renewing at each iteration of her name an intimation of transcendence for the penitents who are left behind. Here, memory is being enlisted to compete against degenerative forces, and we are urged to complete Drury's achievement by formulating our own memorial narrative of spiritual growth.

REMEMBERING DONNE

Donne's secular and religious textual voices continue to excite and seduce his audiences with their rapid alternation between potentially contradictory lines of enquiry. His particular and ongoing concerns with the faculty of memory are found repeatedly to constitute critical endeavours to make sense of temporal ambition and spiritual dilemma: 'thy business is to remember, and thy time is now; stay not till that Angel come which shall say and swear, that time shall be no more' (*Sermons*, ii.11.239). In such discourses, memory is seen to unmask all the contrary motions of sinful desire to which the self is subject, and potentially, by way of response, to excite a renewed sense of spiritual commitment. In a 1626 sermon, Donne envisaged the final Judgement when

> God shall re-compact and re-compile those atoms and graines of dust, into that Body, which was before ... the resurrection from this death, is by way of Re-collection; God shall recall and re-collect all these Atoms, and grains of dust, and re-compact that body, and re-unite that soule, and so that resurrection is accomplished.[66]

And thus Donne imparted with characteristic punning wit what had determined his lifelong investigations into the workings of the faculty.

In his *Paradoxes and Problems*, Donne responds artfully to his 'Problem' – 'Why doth Sir Walter Ralegh write the *Historie* of these times?' – by asserting that the great chronicle is being assembled 'because [Ralegh] would re-enjoye those times by the meditation of them'.[67] This very emphasis upon re-visiting, re-considering, re*membering* in Donne's output has famously exasperated the critic Stanley Fish in more recent times:

> I found [the poetry] sick, and thought that I must be missing the point so readily seen by others. I now believe that to *be* the point: Donne is sick and his poetry is sick ... Donne is bulimic, someone who gorges himself to a point beyond satiety, and then sticks his finger down his throat and throws up. The object of his desire and of his abhorrence is not food, but words, and more specifically, the power words can exert.[68]

Yet even at the turn of the seventeenth century, Florio's Montaigne remained under no illusions that memory might be reduced to banal and futile peddling of undigested experience: 'Above all, old men are dangerous, who have onelie the memorie of things past left them, and have lost the remembrance of their repetitions.'⁶⁹ Readers of the *Essayes* were thus left in no doubt how stifling the aimless representation of our past selves might be. (Indeed, renewing this enquiry more recently for contemporary audiences, the critic Susan Sontag contended that devotion to the past is 'one of the more disastrous forms of unrequited love'.⁷⁰)

Conversely, arriving at some similar conclusions to those expressed by historicist critics such as John Carey and R. C. Bald, Philipp Wolf has sought to resist arguments such as those of Fish, urging that we must negotiate Donne's *œuvre* in terms of a writer experiencing cultural rupture with the past, unable to recycle its lessons.⁷¹ The radically diverse nature of critical responses to Donne's treatment of memory in many ways pays tribute to the rich complexity of his enquiries over a number of decades. Indeed, Donne may be seen to propose, in both his secular and religious writing, a kind of counter-memory: a meditative power that allows the mind to forsake the debilitating conditions of temporality and to contemplate anew questions of human epistemology and spiritual ontology.

We began this chapter with Jonson's sobering judgement predicting neglect and oblivion for Donne. Of course, Jonson was himself compulsively drawn in both his drama and his poetry to the depiction of a society that had ceased to understand the importance of the legacies it inherited from the past. In his own satires Donne demonstrated that he too was no stranger to the anxieties of cultural loss: 'Where are those spread woods which clothed heretofore | Those bought lands? not built, nor burnt within door. | Where's th'old landlord's troops, and alms?' (Satire 2, 103–5). More characteristically, however, he constantly reflected upon the business of recovery and renewal in erotic, spiritual and memorial terms. Indeed, he pursued such enquiries with an arresting passion at the end of his life when he commissioned an image of himself in his own shroud: 'when the picture was fully finished, he caused it to be set by his bed-side, where it continued, and became his hourly object till his death.'⁷²

Unlike the majority of his more modern readers, when contemporaries chose to remember Donne, it seems that they often preferred the minister to the poet, the expert rhetorician to the erotic lyricist. This is amply demonstrated in Walton's *Life*. He himself revised his elegy for Donne many times, but in his 1658 edition of the *Life* he celebrated 'that man where language chose to stay | And shew her utmost power'.

Thomas Carew, considered by succeeding generations of readers to be the most distinguished of Donne's elegists, proclaimed in verse that he '[dared] not trust | ... with unkneaded dowe-bak't prose thy dust'.[73] However, by the beginning of the nineteenth century, Hazlitt confessed that 'Of Donne I know nothing but some beautiful verses to his wife', while Southey railed that Donne's son and editor 'would have shown himself more worthy of such a father, if he had destroyed a considerable part of [the poetry]'.[74] Donne himself had no illusions about the potency of the destructive forces that might gnaw away at any human endeavour to endure beyond the span of a mortal life. Shadowing in this instance the steps of Marcus Aurelius in his *Essays in Divinity*, he conceded:

Amongst men, all Depositaries of our Memories, all means which we have trusted with the preserving of our Names, putrifie and perish. Of the infinite numbers of the Medals of the Emperors, some one happy Antiquary, with much pain, travell, cost, and most faith, beleeves he hath recovered some one rusty piece, which deformity makes reverend to him, and yet is indeed the fresh work of an Impostor. The very places of the *Obeliscs*, and *Pyramides* are forgotten, and the purpose why they were erected.[75]

If, as we saw at the beginning of this discussion, Jonson viewed Donne's work as destined to 'perish' for not being 'understood', it is astonishing how many of his critics in succeeding generations have believed in their turn that he will be consigned to the ranks of the forgotten. T. S. Eliot, who, along with Herbert J. C. Grierson, appears to have done most to awaken the twentieth century to Donne's achievements, celebrated in the sermons what he termed 'the knowledge of the weakness of the human soul'. Nonetheless, like Jonson, he was ready to predict the collapse of this particular corner of Donne's textual edifice: 'His sermons will disappear as suddenly as they have appeared.'[76] Even the son of Donne's friend and literary executor Henry King confessed in a 1643 letter that he always thought of Donne along with another Jacobean preacher of the previous generation, Lancelot Andrewes: 'I could never conceive better of them, then as a voluntarie before a lesson to the lute, which is absolutely the best pleasing to the care; but after finished absolutely forgotten, nothing to be remembred or repeated.'[77]

Notwithstanding, with the ever-increasing critical interest in his life and work, it may just be that Donne's acute anxieties over the cultural threats of forgetfulness, loss and erasure are the very things which have ultimately ensured his survival among later generations.

Now to make up a circle, by returning to our first word, remember: As we remember God, so for his sake, let us remember one another. In my long absence, and far distance from hence, remember me, as I shall do you in the ears of that God, to whom the farthest East, and the farthest West are but as the right and left ear in one of us; we hear with both at once, and he hears in both at once; remember me, not my abilities.[78]

CHAPTER 7

'Of all the powers of the mind ... the most delicate and fraile': the poetry of Ben Jonson and the renewal of memory

> But to restore great things is sometimes not only a harder but a nobler task than to have introduced them.
>
> Erasmus, Letter 'To Leo X', 384[1]

Memory, of all the *powers* of the mind, is the most *delicate*, and *fraile*: it is the first of our *faculties*, that Age invades. *Seneca*, the father, the *Rhetorician*, confesseth of himselfe, hee had a miraculous one; not only to receive, but to hold. I my selfe could in my youth, have repeated all, that ever I had made; and so continued, till I was past fortie: Since, it is much decay'd in me. Yet I can repeat whole books that I have read, and *Poems*, of some selected friends, which I have lik'd to charge my memory with. It was wont to be faithfull to me, but shaken with *age* now, and *sloath* (which weakens the strongest abilities) it may performe somewhat, but cannot promise much. By exercise it is to be made better, and serviceable. Whatsoever I pawn'd with it, while I was young, and a boy, it offers me readily, and without stops: but what I trust to it now, or have done of later yeares, it layes up more negligently, and often times loses.[2]

In his commonplace book, *Timber, or Discoveries*, which would appear to be an accumulation of reflections dating from across the Caroline period to his death in 1637, Jonson offered a revealing portrait of what was for him the precious commodity of memory. Here, he is seen to disclose in careful detail the painful recognition of his own ageing and decline, giving particular emphasis to the *process* of memory and its powers to frame and, indeed, to unframe the self.

In the main, Jonson eschewed the spiritual exercise of memory that Donne investigated in his sermons, seeming rather to share the opinions of his friend Sir Henry Wotton, who pondered in later life, 'I read, that old Men live more by Memory than by Hope'.[3] The poet-playwright favoured an interest in the *ars memorativa* as it had been advocated in pagan antiquity – an art that affirmed that an 'artificial memory' might be trained with a regime of rigorous mental discipline. Moreover, this interest could surface in any number of unexpected places in his writings, such as in his comedy *The Case is Altered* (published 1609), where Francisco Colonnia submits, 'I will be silent, yet that I may serve | But as a decade in the art of memory, | To put you still in mind of your own virtues' (II.iii). More generally, Roman writers such as Cicero and Quintilian, who, as we have seen, conducted such influential expositions of the rhetorical practices of sequential imaging and the requirements of retrospection for public service, were among those held in particular esteem by Jonson. Indeed, a rather piqued Drummond of Hawthornden was informed by his voluble house guest in 1618 that he should turn back to Quintilian, 'who ([Jonson] said) would tell me all the faults of my Verses [as] if he had Lived with me' (i.132: 12–14).

MEMORY AND DISCRIMINATION

In the initial extract quoted above from *Timber, or Discoveries*, Jonson assumes, in part at least, an Aristotelian position that posits an indissoluble union between the operations of memory and the material world of the senses: the waxing and waning of memorial powers is thus seen to synchronise with the (progressively failing) operations of the body. Yet, whatever the vagaries of the faculty's transformations, it remained for Jonson, as for so many of his contemporaries, a fragile, but invaluable link with a former age of vigour, in terms of both personal and collective cultural experience. Furthermore, the changeful temper of Jonson's memory certainly did not affect his willingness to make authoritative pronouncements upon questions of aesthetics and the literary endeavours of others – as Drummond found out to his cost. (In this instance we may be reminded of a *maxime* coined by the rather different cultural critic La Rochefoucauld later in the century, when he proposed that 'Tout le monde se plaint de sa mémoire, et personne ne se plaint de son jugement' ['Everyone complains of their memory, and nobody complains of their powers of judgement'].[4])

At the end of the 1960s, George Parfitt highlighted that Jonson's poetic narratives often rely upon the 'exclusion of important aspects of human experience ... [and] the reduction of moral complexity to simplified clarity'.[5] This emphasis upon a self-conscious paring down or limitation of fields of enquiry also feeds an ongoing debate in Jonson's writing concerning the commitment and scope of memory. Acknowledging the precarious operations of winnowing to which the faculty submits over the passage of time, Jonson asserted that his own experience of memorial decay was all too clearly being negotiated in the wider forum of his society – and thus, the business of writing was to shore up more generally the collapsing limits of memory and to renew and extend the cultural repository of inherited knowledge. While David Norbrook is persuasive in his contention that, unlike Spenser, 'Jonson never attempted to present himself as a prophetic poet; his stance was that of a detached and ironic observer of human affairs rather than a visionary who laid claim to special prophetic insights',[6] Jonson clearly did invest much time and energy throughout his career in the belief that the past, and most particularly the Roman past, bequeathed a rich fund of paradigms of human experience, a precious fount of wisdom for future generations. Indeed, his poetic undertaking may be usefully illuminated in the context of Fernando Bouza's critical discussion of the perceived talismanic properties of language in the early modern period whereby 'there existed a relationship between signs and the realities they signified going beyond the merely expressive to the domain of the creative ... this capacity of the sign to make the signified present'.[7] In the Caroline period, Sir Robert Naunton lamented that 'We are naturally prone to applaud the times behind us and to villify the present',[8] but rather than striking this note of melancholia in a sustained fashion, Jonson promoted a more dynamic relationship with the past, resolutely asserting the inviolable right of the Roman past in particular to remain on intimate terms with the present. Thus, following in the steps of Virgil's Aeneas, we may come to the realisation that the human reflex to remember can develop into a much larger commitment through which we articulate what we are and wish to be: *nec me meminisse pigebit Elissae, | dum memor ipse mei, dum spiritus hos regit artus* [nor shall my memory of Elissa be bitter, while I have memory of myself, and while breath governs these limbs].[9]

It is everywhere apparent that Jonson's modes of praise (in many ways the master discourse of early modern poetry) cannot be divorced from his unfailing engagement with classical culture, and this may be witnessed in his eulogy of Sir Horace Vere:

> Which of thy names I take, not onely beares
> A romane sound, but romane vertue weares,
> Illustrious VERE, or HORACE; fit to be
> Sung by a HORACE, or a *Muse* as free ...
> 					viii.58: 1–4.

If, as Paul Ricoeur has argued, 'One of the functions of history ... is to lead us back to those moments of the past where the future was not yet decided, where the past was itself a space of experience open to a horizon of expectation', Jonson all too frequently returns his readers to the dawning of a new imperial age with its Roman heroes *redivivi*.¹⁰ Whereas his contemporary Francis Bacon contested that 'knowledge which is new, and foreign from opinions received, is to be delivered in another form than that that is agreeable and familiar',¹¹ Jonson repeatedly invites us to experience life in human society in terms of the poetic narratives and diction set down in antiquity. The full potential of his chosen poetic subjects, caught in the radically unstable present, can only be fully realised when thus positioned through the lens of an ancient past. Interestingly, within this wider context of Jonson's appreciation of textual and human exempla gleaned from encounters with classical cultures, he expressed an aspiration on at least one occasion to rival the achievements of those who had gone before him as 'makers' of heroic poetry. He confided during his visit to Drummond, 'that he had ane intention to perfect ane Epick poeme entitled Heroologia of the Worthies of his Country, rowsed by fame, and was to dedicate it to his Country, it is all in Couplets, for he detesteth all other Rimes' (i.132: 1–5). It remains uncertain whether this claim was a bravura performance to impress his host or a genuine undertaking on Jonson's part. However, it is evident from the surviving record of the Drummond conversations that he had found other ventures in that field by his contemporaries to be wanting: 'Spencers stanzaes pleased him not, nor his matter, the meaning of which Allegorie he had delivered in Papers to S^ir Walter Raughlie … That Michael Drayton's *PolyOlbion* (if [he] had performed what he promised to writte, the deads of all ye Worthies) had been excellent[,] his Long Verses pleased him not' (i.132–3: 20–3, 25–8).

In *Timber, or Discoveries* Jonson not only assembles and re-presents matter from his classical reading in a manner common to generations of intellectuals across Europe, he demonstrates quite explicitly that he views the ongoing cultural dialectic between the past and the present to be a key axis through which to plot the formation of subjectivity: 'Wee *praise* the things wee heare, with much more willingnesse, then those wee see: because wee envy the present, and reverence the past; thinking our selves instructed by the one, and over-laid by the other' (viii.564: 39–42).¹² His poetry returns to the referents of Ancient Rome; and by limning narratives of Roman exemplarity *and* adversity onto the Jacobean present, his readers are thus forcefully reminded of the historical continuity of human experience and indeed of the fragility of the cultural system that they inhabit. The frantic nature of the moral disorders of the late Elizabethan and Jacobean present (which Jonson communicated only too persuasively in his comic drama) tended to occlude the monitory authority of recollection, and so it became incumbent upon such a poet with a vocation to participate prominently in the *vita civile* to repair the precious links with the cultural knowledge that had survived from the past through his verse.

Sara van den Berg is timely in stressing that 'There are few personal lyrics among [Jonson's] poems, no soliloquies in his plays: his is an art of community and contest'.[13] This emphasis upon broad cultural critique and ethical interrogation in his poetry has often served to distance audiences eager to anchor their reading strategies around clearly individuated voices. At the beginning of the twentieth century, T. S. Eliot conjured up a portrait (which persists) of a formidable Jonson who has daunted students and scholars alike. Nevertheless, Jonson himself remained endlessly fascinated by the ways in which the arresting achievements of those who have gone before might be digested and reinterpreted by succeeding generations. From the saturnalia of his city comedies to the solemnities of his elegiac writing, he pours scorn remorselessly upon those who fail to exercise their powers of memory, and thus dispossess themselves of the indispensable sources of learning that the past tenders. Indeed, his obsessive enquiries into our ability and (dis)inclination to remember place him in the very midst of a whole community of scholars and intellectuals in the early modern period seeking to forge vigorous cultural relations with the past. Fully engaged, as we have seen, in this lively cultural debate, Florio's Montaigne appears artful, if not downright disingenuous in lamenting the fearfully impaired state of his own memorial powers:

> There is no man living, whom it may lesse become to speake of memorie, then myselfe, for to say truth, I have none at all: and am fullie perswaded that no-mans can be so weake and forgetfull as mine. All other partes are common and vile, but touching memorie, I thinke to carrie the prise from all-other, that have it weakest.[14]

If contemporary cultural theorists such as Raymond Tallis continue to argue that 'Sensations and memories converge to create a continuing, if interrupted, sense of a coherent self', it is evident that this preoccupation with the ways in which memory relates to larger concerns of epistemology and subjectivity weighed down heavily upon the minds of many early modern intellectuals.[15] Building upon the insights of rhetoricians down the ages who had insisted upon the strategic status of memory in the organisation of knowledge and in the staging of the speaking self in the *civitas*, writers such as Jonson decipher the present almost wholly in terms of memorial narratives. Interestingly, in his Latin verses accompanying the 1607 quarto of *Volpone*, Donne contended that Jonson warranted attention in that he might be seen to vie with, and indeed even to excel, the achievements of classical writers. No praise would have been more eagerly appreciated by the learned poet who, as Robin Sowerby points out, 'consciously turned to the classical tradition, and it is probably no exaggeration to say that he felt a greater affinity with Catullus and Horace than with his Elizabethan predecessors or early Jacobean contemporaries'.[16]

Moreover, as his career unfolded, the classical past emerged as an indispensable resource with which Jonson formulated his ideas on authorship. In his commonplace book he argued that 'the mind and the memory are more sharply exercis'd in comprehending an other mans things, then our owne; and such as accustome themselves, and are familiar with the best Authors, shall ever and anon find somewhat of them in themselves' (viii.616: 1743–7). This is most particularly the case for his collections of poetry: *Epigrams* (first published in 1612); *The Forest* (published in the 1616 Folio *Works*); and the ungathered verse of *The Underwood* (published posthumously in the 1640 Folio, edited by Sir Kenelm Digby). In these, Jonson returns again and again to the diction, themes and formal structures of classical poetics as organizing principles for the understanding of his own work: he urges his readers to (re-)gain knowledge of the rich tradition of Greco-Latin verse as they explore anew the possibilities of the elegy, ode, pastoral and satire in his own collections. This point is made explicit at the beginning of the *Epigrams* in the poetic address to his 'Mere English Censurer': 'To thee my way in *Epigrammes* seemes new, | When both it is the old way and the true' (viii.32: 1–2). Refraining in the main from an interest in erotic or religious poetic narratives, Jonson looks most frequently (and, in the process, pays homage) to such figures as Horace, Martial, Catullus and Juvenal in his ambitions to delineate the dominant power relationships in his society. In the process, his poetic *œuvre* is committed to the unveiling of a new generation of worthies *and* villains for his seventeenth-century readers. However, Jonson not only remembers earlier, classical performances in satire and encomia for new audiences, he also asks us to embark upon an epistemological journey of *anamnesis* in which we assess new and emerging figures of cultural attention against what Janet Coleman has termed in her discussion of Platonic thought a 'prior ontology' of archetypes.[17] Once such a pantheon is established, it is but a little step to associate the antique worthies with our guide, whose good offices have allowed us to refresh our acquaintance with the superlative achievements of earlier generations.

In surveying Jonson's textual galleries of extraordinary human specimens, we are clearly being asked to flex our moral, ethical and political powers of discrimination: as Kate Chedgzoy has underlined more generally, 'Memory, involving both incorporation of information from the outside world and its expression and externalization in forms of record, lends itself easily to being a dialogic, interactive process, in which both self and others may share in learning'.[18] However, in such textual negotiations we are also being prompted by Jonson to reflect upon the very act of discrimination and how it may be modified by the competing cultural matrices of rank, obligation and ownership. On repeated occasions the poet controls our reading strategies by carefully restricting our access to the past, reserving our attentions for examples of extraordinary cultural leadership and of astonishing moral delinquency. In collections such as *The Forest* and *Epigrams* as we move in alternating motion between the present and the classical past, between egregious virtue and egregious vice, we are pressed inevitably to experience the present in terms of the past and (most disturbingly in the portraits of those riddled with vice) we may be being coerced into identifying textual versions of ourselves. Thus, if his stainless heroes exceed our grasp, our uncomfortable fate may be to join the ranks of those drafted in to participate in his remorseless pageant of cultural decline.

MEMORY AND THE JONSONIAN READER

Introducing the *Epigrams* as 'the ripest of my studies', Jonson argued that 'in my Theater ... Cato, if he liu'd, might enter without scandal'.[19] Some later readers have repeatedly cast doubt upon such an assertion. Notably, Swinburne protested:

> No man can ever have been less amenable than Sir Walter Scott to the infamous charge of Puritanism or prudery; and it is he who has left on record his opinion that 'surely that coarseness of taste which tainted Ben Jonson's powerful mind is proved from his writings. Many authors of that age are indecent, but Jonson is filthy and gross in his pleasantry, and indulges himself in using the language of scavengers and night-men.' I will only add that the evidence of this is flagrant in certain pages which I never forced myself to read through till I had undertaken to give a full and fair account – to the best of my ability – of Ben Jonson's complete works. How far poetry may be permitted to go in the line of sensual pleasure or sexual emotion may be debatable between the disciples of Ariosto and the disciples of Milton; but all English readers, I trust, will agree with me that

coprology should be left to Frenchmen. It is nothing less than lamentable that so great an English writer as Ben Jonson should ever have taken the plunge of a Parisian diver into the cesspool: but it is as necessary to register as it is natural to deplore the detestable fact that he did so.[20]

Thus, rather than contemplating the 'bleaching' or cleansing of the spirit, as Donne had advocated at points in the course of his career as a preacher, Swinburne, with characteristic wit, invites us to view Jonson's narratives as luxuriating in the moral decay of society – and sullying the sensitivities of the reader in the process. Swinburne clearly had in mind productions such as 'On the Famous Voyage', which revel in oneiric allusion and caustic social critique unperturbed by any sense of queasiness. However, if Jonson remains keenly alert to the powerful temptations that vice may wield, his poems repeatedly urge us to exchange any potential delights that may reside in immorality and sensual abandon for the more lasting pleasures of remembering oneself, of virtuous self-government. (Interestingly, Swinburne later conceded in his critical discussion that 'The collection of his epigrams which bears only too noisome witness to this fact is nevertheless by no means devoid of valuable and admirable components'.[21])

In order to appreciate fully Jonson's poetic undertaking, readers must attend to continuities of narrative, theme and ethical enquiry as the collections as a whole unfold. We are often compelled to read many of the lyrics memorially – that is, to juxtapose, replay, contrast, remember earlier poetic narratives in the collection and to range them against the present one. Many of the energies generated in *Epigrams* or *The Forest* focus precisely upon the cumulative crises of reader expectation and moral response that accompany the introductions of such eminent figures as Sir Voluptuous Beast, the Court Pucelle and My Lord Ignorant: 'Thou call'st me *Poet*, as a terme of shame: | But I haue my reuenge made, in thy name' (viii.29: 1–2). Thus, it is only when we are suitably armed with *incremental* textual knowledge, gained as a consequence of a progressive reading experience, that we may fully apprehend the moral extremity of the nether worlds to which this particular company of Grand Guignol figures is consigned. Moreover, the power to name and to un-name in the presence of Roe, Camden, Sir Voluptuous Beast or the Court Pucelle is wielded with great deftness and authority in a collection such as the *Epigrams*. It signifies not only the poet's powers of authority and dominion over his subjects but also the ability to withhold detail and to transform our understanding of social existence through poetic language. When he turns to panegyric, Jonson can reveal himself all too eager to unveil the achievements of his subjects in abundant detail. He praises, for example, the various members of the Sidney clan who fulfil their obligations of rank and privilege, and thus realise their cultural potential – nevertheless, even in these instances, he never fails to interrogate what that potential should be. Elsewhere, poetic dramas may concentrate upon those whose social rank is of a much more modest nature, like the rising city merchant Roe or writers such as Beaumont, Donne and Shakespeare. Yet Jonson's thorough investment in the redemptive potential of political and moral exemplarity is most frequently expressed in terms of memorial exertion. As he indicates at the beginning of the *Epigrams* in 'To All, to Whom I Write', if ethical discrimination is established firmly as a strategic concept for the whole collection, it may be deciphered in a number of ways:

> May none whose scatter'd names honor my booke,
> For strict degrees of ranke, or title looke:
> 'Tis 'gainst the manners of an Epigram:
> And, I a *Poet* here, no Herald am.
>
> (viii.29: 1–4)

By the period that Jonson was writing it had become a major tenet of European humanist thinking that the enduring cultural fixation with lineage and descent was obscuring the more valuable cultural virtues of learning and merit. Sidney's peerless host in the *Arcadia*, the noble Kalander, proclaims, 'I am no herald to inquire of men's pedigrees, it sufficeth me if I know their vertues … God forbid, but where worthynesse is … any outward lownesse should hinder the hi[gh]est raysing'.[22] If these themes of debate (ongoing at least since the fourteenth century) did not seek wholly to unpick the prevailing social theories of hierarchy and rank, they were certainly destined to scrutinize them fiercely and to render them more problematic.

The early modern cultural theory of unending resemblance, articulated perhaps most famously in the 1559 Elizabethan homily *An Exhortation concerning Good Order and Obedience to Rulers and Magistrates*, meant that human experience was organised within a much larger, divinely ordained schema, designed to enhance the ability of all creatures and natural forces to realise their true nature: 'Almighty god hath created and appointed all things in heauen, earth and waters in a most excellente and perfect order.'[23] Locked between the familiar Augustinian helpmeets of mind and understanding, memory for the Tudor homilist remains a key consideration when formulating what the human subject could or should be: 'manne hymselfe also hath all his partes, both wythin and withoute, as soule, hearte, mynde, memorye, understandyng, reason, speache wyth all and synguler corporall members of hys bodye, in a profitable, necessarye and pleasaunte order'.[24] Clearly receptive to the pressures of such cultural expectations, Jonson also remained mindful as a poet, dramatist and writer of masques, of the human potential to renege upon these obligations of spiritual and moral development. The depraved moral subjects delineated in his verse frequently serve to embody a moral vacancy more widely in evidence in an early modern society governed by appetite rather than reflection.

MEMORY AND PANEGYRIC

Jonson's was an Age in which decades of religious conflict and political strife at home and abroad had placed the authority of the past (and thus frequently the legitimacy of those in temporal and spiritual government) under intense scrutiny. 'To Penshurst' clearly encourages its readers to re-examine received thinking about place (cultural *and* topological) and to envisage alternative possibilities of social interaction in an otherwise Iron Age given over to apolaustic pursuits. In his desire to ponder the ethical responsibilities of ownership and privilege, Jonson may be occluding the labour economies at work in this landscape (as was argued most famously by Raymond Williams, and more recently in persuasive detail by Don Wayne and Rhonda Lemke Sanford[25]), but it becomes increasingly evident that much of the poem's narrative interest is driven by a fear of cultural amnesia – an unwillingness to appreciate that to sever our links wholly with the practices of the past is to divorce ourselves from processes of moral growth and self-knowledge.

'To Penshurst' begins by thwarting schemes of narrative expectation, by informing us what it is not. As we embark upon this unexpected *via negativa*, we are asked to reverence the longevity of the 'ancient Pile', rather that its august splendour. Instead of belonging to an overripe social order, in Jonson's poem the Sidneys are discovered dwelling at the heart of a vigorous, fruitful community, living in dynamic continuity with *great creating Nature*. Luxuriating in the blessings 'of soyle, of ayre, | Of wood, of water' (viii.93: 7–8), it turns out to be the opulent landscape, rather than any temporally located authority, which proclaims initially the matchless prosperity of the Great House and its estates: in this way, a *locus amoenus* is identified that is seemingly in communion with the heavens and familiar to Pan, Bacchus and to dryads. The recuperation of mythic narratives (with all their aggrandising properties) was clearly one of the dominant strategies that Jonson employed throughout his career as a poet and writer of masques to communicate a poetic idealism to his audiences. In this particular case, we are invited to believe that this English vision of plenitude (reassuringly 'reared with no man's ruin, no man's grone') blends effortlessly with the harvesting of 'ripe Daughters' on this site of endless fertility and largesse: even the relieved epicurean speaker recalls that 'Here no man tells my cups' (viii.94–5: 46, 54, 67). The king himself resorts with his entourage to the ancestral home of the Sidneys; and the good husbandry of the Lady Sidney (formerly *a lady richly left*, the heiress Barbara Gamage) is called upon to articulate in miniature the cohesive social governance of the Sidneys themselves in this sacred place where 'thy Lord dwells' (viii.96: 102).

In a more general account of early modern representations of domesticity, Heather Dubrow argues justly that 'Early modern England … attached increased significance to the home as the place where men were protected and, more importantly, were obliged to protect'.[26] And, indeed, it is the cultural role of custodianship that is given particular prominence in Jonson's poem: in fact, 'To Penshurst' provides a model of cultural patronage that the reader is urged throughout to meditate at length. To a very great degree, the legitimacy of the Penshurst social ideal is formulated memorially through recourse to Golden Age and pastoral narratives inherited from antiquity. If this poetic vision formulates in a highly selective manner an imaginary order of harmonious social intercourse, it is noteworthy that Jonson places himself strategically at the heart of these power relations, enjoying both an intimacy of knowledge and, equally significantly, the munificence of his Sidneian patrons. Interestingly, the management of hospitality and gratitude are scripted in an analogous manner in another lyric, 'Inviting a Friend to Supper'. Here, we move away from cultural panorama to a more individuated focus upon fayre for both *soma* and *psyche*. Initially, the tastebuds of the prospective guest (and the reader) are excited by the offer of 'a short-leg'd hen, | If we can get her, full of egs, and then, | Limons, and wine for sauce' (viii.64–5: 11–13). However, the speaker is at pains to stress that this menu is thoughtfully complemented with the promise of equally sophisticated textual consumption: 'my man | Shall reade a piece of VIRGIL, TACITUS, | LIVIE, or of some better booke to vs' (viii.65: 20–2).

If the satisfying of the body in this instance operates merely as a prelude to a higher communion involving intellectual exchange and liberality of fellowship, the extravagance of this banquet is firmly locked in a narrative of anticipation. In the earlier discussion devoted to Donne, it became increasingly apparent that the faculty of memory could be aligned easily in early modern minds with a meditation upon futurity ('the art of memory is the art of salvation').[27] Indeed, William E. Engel has convincingly proposed a cautionary discourse of memory for the early modern period: 'Memory was understood to include judgment of the future as well as recollection of the past ... The admonition to remember what is to come (in particular one's passage from life to death, and then more generally some version of afterlife) requires that one project an image of oneself into the future.' However, when we turn to the case of Jonson we often encounter a rather different discourse of memory and imaginative futurity, which Engel terms, more generally, 'projective memory': '[This] calls upon a visual and rhetorical vocabulary of ideality concerning both time and space: one relies on the future tense (to facilitate being in more than one time frame) and on imaginary scenes and places that already have been encountered and explored in one's past'.[28] In 'Inviting a Friend to Supper', the lavishly evoked 'moment' of largesse and hospitality that is eagerly anticipated by Jonson's speaker, draws the reader forward into an imaginative future of sensual and intellectual feasting. Yet this is a future clearly shaped by models established in antiquity and associated with the figures of Maecenas, Marcus Valerius Messalla Corvinus and Gaius Asinius Pollio in Roman cultural narratives. Sara van den Berg contends that 'As urban man, Jonson attends to the relationships that can be chosen: friendship and love',[29] and, by constantly positioning his readers thus within *completed* narratives of these enquiries, even the future may be made to enter the fastness of memory.

If Jonson's lyrics often express the desire to impede the progress of Time (and, thus, the decline of the self) with the resources of memory, this ambition is not confined to epigrammatic or overtly classicised poetic narrative.[30] In the 'Epistle to Elizabeth, Countess of Rutland', for example, we are initially introduced to a society in which 'all vertue now is sold' and, as a consequence, a more durable offering is called for, which will not be subject to earthly corruption. If those who lived in the earliest times before writing 'lack'd the sacred pen' (viii.113, 115: 1, 56), it appears that there is now time enough to make amends to Philip Sidney's daughter:

> With you, I know, my offring will find grace.
> For what a sinne 'gainst your great fathers spirit,
> Were it to thinke, that you should not inherit
> His loue unto the *Muses*, when his skill
> Almost you haue, or may haue, when you will?
> Wherein wise *Nature* you a dowrie gaue,

> Worth an estate, treble to that you haue.
> Beautie, I know, is good, and bloud is more;
> Riches thought most: But, *Madame*, thinke what store
> The world hath seene, which all these had in trust,
> And now lye lost in their forgotten dust.
>
> (viii.113–14: 30–40)

In this tribute, which itself concludes with a collapse in textual memory 'The rest is lost', Rutland is discovered caught at the centre of a cultural dialectic governed by poetic aspiration and the knowledge of human transience. Interestingly, the countess is not defined under any terms of intrinsic merit: her cultural profile is mapped along the axes of inheritance and obligation. Most significantly, she is urged to turn her attention away from questions of ownership (economic or somatic) and to focus upon an investment in poetic memory. Indeed, the defining discourse of Rutland's identity is formulated as the offspring of Sidney: she is thus constructed textually at the convergence of the ambitions of two competing poets.

Throughout this poem, Jonson is keen to stress the redemptive powers of the pen without whose talents those whose beauties might have rivalled (or even excelled) the 'Argive Queen' would have been consigned to dust. More arresting is Jonson's decision to eulogise Sidney's daughter with a succession of memorial acts. Inasmuch as she is seen to have palpable life as the subject of this poetic tribute, her identity is pieced together with contentions that are the fruits of the labours of retrospection. Indeed, the speaker insists that in adoring his muse Lucy, 'I haue already vs'd some happy houres, | To her remembrance; which when time shall bring | To curious light, to notes, I then shall sing' (viii.115: 74–6). In an earlier epigram ('To Elizabeth, Countess of Rutland') Jonson had characteristically inscribed himself within a commemorative frame of reference, drawing attention to himself as supremely cognisant of this age of poetic achievement: 'That *Poets* are far rarer births then kings, | Your noblest father prou'd' (viii.53: 1–2). However, in the later 'Epistle' he mythologises his own poetic undertaking ('[I] Will proue old ORPHEUS act no tale to be'), and strategically monumentalises his own textual offering to Rutland ('There like a rich, and golden *pyramede*, | Born vp by statues, shall I reare your head') and to the last bard, 'the god-like SYDNEY' (viii.115–16: 77, 83–4, 91). At the close of the poem, there is a division of the spoils: the power to 'eternise' remains in the clutches of poets (past and present), whereas Rutland's creative potential is resolved in terms of her fertility – her physical, rather than her intellectual, powers to conceive.

JONSON AND SOMATIC MEMORY

As Jonson's poetic career evolved, he appears to have become increasingly preoccupied with the ways the body might fashion its own memorial narratives. As has been witnessed in earlier chapters, there was a rich fund of anatomical and physiological theorising inherited from the classical period, which linked the functioning of the memory to that of the body – and in Jonson's poetry it becomes evident that the body can be composed in scandalous, as well as virtuous, terms. The early modern period was an age with an inexhaustible appetite for anatomising the collapse of human potential, whether it was performed in the law courts, the pulpit, the playhouse or on the scaffold. Whereas Donne pondered at length in some of his sermons and poems the bleak prospect of spiritual failure linked to memory, and Bacon (as will become evident in the final chapter) remained frequently appalled by the natural philosophy inherited from the ancients, Jonson decoded human collapse in terms of moral and societal decay. An obvious example of this is Sir Voluptuous Beast, who emerges rapidly in Jonson's epigram as a morally bankrupt (and haggard) grandee. Beast's desire to redramatise (and thus memorialise) his sexual career by stage-managing the perversion of his virtuous wife means that the latter must submit progressively to all kinds of debasement ('In varied shapes, which for his lust she takes') – her only option, the speaker urges, is to 'leave to be chaste' (viii.34: 6–7). In the sequel 'On the Same Beast', tired with the constant recapitulation of his sexual fantasies, Beast takes refuge in fictions of promiscuity that his mind consummates: 'Then his chast wife, though BEAST now know no more, | He'adulters still: his thoughts lye with a whore' (viii.35: 1–2). In the equally energetic poetic vision 'On Groyne', the collapse of human aspiration is expressed in similar terms of physical ownership. Here, the reality of a squandered family inheritance is eclipsed by rival territorial claims – 'Groyne, come of age, his state sold out of hand | For 'his whore: GROYNE doth still occupy his land' (viii.75: 1–2). However, the remorseless force of human corruption is most evident in 'On Gut' where the body is found to persist, leaving no memory of itself for subsequent generations apart from its gross physicality. It simply exists in an unending cycle of provisional pleasures: 'Thus, in his belly, can he change a sin, | Lust it comes out, that gluttony went in' (viii.76: 5–6). Indeed, this theme of enquiry is probed in the company of 'Fine Lady Would-be', who seeks to control, to reformulate, to wipe the past from her body in order to compete successfully in her chosen society – 'What should the cause be? oh, you liue at court' (viii.46: 9).

Promoted thus as custodians of cultural memory and moral authority, Jonson's poetic speakers challenge us defiantly to disagree with their verdicts. If it remains for his readers to decide whether they will raise an assenting or contrary voice, silence is not an option for those who wish to participate in his poetic *civitas*.

The recurring interest in the ways in which his contemporary society sought fulfilment in a mostly passionless hedonism feeds a much larger debate in Jonson's poetry concerning our often anxiety-ridden encounters with the past, and indeed how the disjunction between memorial knowledge and moral experience leads to the flawed engagement with life in society. In this context, the body becomes a key discursive marker in Jonson's enquiries into the crazed human search for self-gratification and the contemporary cultural horror towards the process of ageing. In 'My Picture left in Scotland' the tensions between the achievements of the lover and the poet are carefully rendered and played off against each other. The consolation of verse has brought with it a commemoration of personal decline and the poignant realisation that the speaker's mistress may have been a resisting reader of his charms.

> Tell me that she hath seene
> My hundred of gray haires,
> Told seven and fortie yeares.
> Read so much wast, as she cannot imbrace
> My mountaine belly, and my rockie face,
> And all these through her eyes, have stopt her eares.
> (viii.149–50: 13–18)

If, in this instance, Jonson maintains a plangent register for a recollection of erotic defeat, elsewhere he can, on occasions, review desire under more urgent terms. In the famous *carpe diem* lyric 'Song. To Celia', the mistress is cajoled by a restive lover: 'But if once we loose this light, | 'Tis, with vs, perpetuall night. | Why should we deferre our ioyes?' In this world inhabited by spies and facile minds 'To be taken, to be seene, | These haue crimes accounted beene' (viii. 102: 7–9, 17–18). While in 'My Picture left in Scotland' the speaker reflected upon the manner in which he might be 'fixed' and diminished by memory, here, conversely, Celia is asked to repress memory and conscience and to yield to the transit of Venus.

MEMORY AND THE JUDGEMENT OF TIME

The guises that Jonson attributes to Time can be seen to vary considerably in the course of his poetic career as he invokes at various junctures: Time the destroyer, the tyrant, the devourer, the discloser, the ally of truth, the elusive patron, and the force only to be mastered by extraordinary specimens of humanity. Of course, the promotion of Time as the governing lens through which to understand mortal experience is widely in evidence as a commonplace among poets and dramatists in the early modern period, as it had been in the writings of their Roman forebears. In *Richard II*, for example, Shakespeare's Salisbury appeals 'O, call back yesterday, bid time return' (III.ii.69); indeed, an analogous appeal is made in the rather different generic context of Jonson's late play *The New Inn* (performed 1629), when Lady Frampul laments: 'O, for an engine, to keepe backe all clocks! | Or make the Sunne forget his motion!' (IV.iv.230–1).[31] In rather more desperate circumstances, Marlowe's Faustus implores, 'Stand still, you ever-moving spheres of heaven, | That time may cease and midnight never come' (V.ii.134–5), and, elsewhere, we encounter 'cormorant devouring Time' in *Love's Labours Lost* (I.i.4) and, of course, 'Time's wingèd chariot' in Marvell's 'To his Coy Mistress' (l. 22). In an intriguing paradox, Jonson's poems frequently meditate in painful detail the effects of the passing of time and simultaneously flatter his readers into believing that they are spectators to, rather than participants in, its passage. In his commendatory poem to Ralegh's *History of the World* (to which he claimed to have contributed (i.138: 199–201)), Jonson noted 'From Death, and darke oblivion, neere the same, | The Mistresse of Mans life, grave Historie | Raising the World to good and evill fame | Doth vindicate it to eternitie' (viii.175: 1–4). In this instance, History emerges with all the solemnity of a Rhadamanthine arbiter of human fortunes as Jonson returns to the well-known Ciceronian formula that it 'bears witness to the passing of the ages, sheds light upon reality, gives life to recollection, and guidance to human existence, and brings tidings of ancient days'.[32] The Reformist thinker Philipp Melanchthon had insisted half a century earlier that it was imperative for scholars to apply themselves to the calling of historiography, 'to know the counsels, utterances and deeds of great men. For the mind is roused to virtue by contemplating their example'.[33] While Jonson's ongoing preoccupation with History clearly endorsed such a sentiment, his enduring fascination with all kinds of commemoration at a personal and collective level was also intimately linked to the textual anxiety in evidence throughout his verse with cultural fixity and control. The desire to establish enduring models of superlative human achievement comes to represent not only a response to surmounting evidence of social decay (made widely available in his poetic and theatrical anatomies of contemporary society), but also an endeavour to reflect upon the possibilities of human transcendence.

Although by no means a devotional poet, Jonson can on occasions give voice to spiritual meditation in an affecting manner. In direct comparison with many of his satirical epigrammatic pieces, we find in lyrics such as 'Of Death' that he explores vigorously the relationships between human commitment (social and spiritual) and the operations of memory – relationships that have been seen to dominate many of the textual enquiries of his contemporaries, such as Mary Sidney and John Donne: 'He that feares death, or mournes it, in the just, | Shewes of the resurrection little trust' (viii.37: 1–2). A similar sentiment had been expressed by Shakespeare's Feste in *Twelfth Night* when he insists to Olivia, 'The more fool, madonna, to mourn for your brother's soul, being in heaven' (I.v.67–8). However, in Jonson's 'To Heaven' the penitent voice prays less obliquely to a 'Great God': 'My judge, my witnesse, and my aduocate' (viii.122: 12). In this instance, the identity of the penitent self is constituted solely in terms of the irrepressible memory of sin and the urgent desire for divine grace: 'How can I doubt to finde thee euer, here? | I know my state, both full of shame, and scorne' (viii.122: 16–17). At such moments, the reader discovers once again Jonson's poetic voices meditating human aspiration by staging scenes of personal and collective retrospection. In 'On My First Daughter', Jonson commemorates the loss of an infant by carefully piecing together two narratives of recollection: as the speaker revisits the familiar stoical idea that 'all heauens gifts [are] heauens due', we are reminded that this loan has now been redeemed at the behest of the heavens; and the daughter Mary also secures the echo of an identification with 'heauens Queene' (viii.33: 3, 7).[34] Interestingly, the rather plaintive wit being exercised in this instance would be displayed much more extravagantly later in 'An Epigram to the Queen, then lying in. 1630'. Robert C. Evans argues that 'Although Jonson was a master of literary tropes and classical conventions, his use of them often suggests a recognition of their tactical value as much as a purely "literary" interest in generic experimentation'.[35] In this particular lyric of 1630, Jonson does indeed draw upon the linguistic memories of Catholic prayers *tactically*, and conflates a celebration of Henrietta Maria in her confinement unexpectedly with a rather different annunciation: 'Haile *Mary*, full of honours, to my Queene, | The Mother of our Prince?' (viii.238: 5–6). Yet in his more elegiac writing such as 'On My First Daughter' and 'On My First Son', Jonson is not only pondering the nature of earthly transience, he endeavours to compensate for the evanescence of human life with textual plenitude – lending magnitude to the expression of grief and consolation through recourse to the resources of religious litany and classical diction. 'On My First Son' recalls the solemn strains of both the burial service and Martial's elegies; and these familiar discursive frames give shape and substance to this carefully modulated lament.

More generally, the narrative emphases at work here and elsewhere throughout Jonson's *œuvre* upon forbearance, fortitude, emotional restraint and a painfully achieved *contemptus mundi* indicate the broad influence of stoical philosophy, which was enjoying a renewal of interest across Europe in the sixteenth century and which appears to have been largely nourished by the study of such widely available works as Cicero's *De Officiis*, *De Senectute* and the *Tusculan Disputations*, along with Seneca's dialogues, closet dramas and letters. The intellectual interest in stoicism was significantly fuelled in this period by the work of the Flemish humanist Justus Lipsius with such contributions as his essay *On Constancy* (1584), which was translated by Sir John Stradling as *Two Books of Constancy* in 1594. The endeavours of Lipsius to reconcile some aspects of Christian belief with the broader thrust of classical stoicism had an enormous influence upon scholarship and political thinking at the close of the sixteenth century and the early decades of the seventeenth in England. Certainly, evidence of such philosophical speculations can be witnessed in a number of widely differing textual examples from Jonson's works and those of his contemporaries, ranging from Shakespeare's *Julius Caesar*, *Hamlet*, Montaigne's and Bacon's essays, to Chapman's tragedies and Milton's epic verse.

A SUFFICIENT MEMORY

In the case of his lyric tributes to his friend Sir John Roe (who, he declared in his conversations with Drummond, 'died in his armes of the pest', i. 137: 185–6), Jonson returns repeatedly to the question of how to discriminate between competing modes of commemoration (affective and poetic) – indeed, how to remember adequately. In 'Ile not offend thee with a vaine teare more', the encounter with 'Glad-mention'd ROE' furnishes the poet with a strategic opportunity to reflect upon the memorial obligations of the living. In another epigram, on this occasion to William Roe, Jonson had conjured up the vision of 'good ÆNEAS [who] past through fire, | Through seas, stormes, tempests: and imbarqu'd for hell' ('To William Roe' (viii.81: 12–14)). Through the heroic life of this idealised son of merchant stock, the reader is encouraged to bear witness to the fulfilment of exceptional human achievement. Both imaginatively and temporally, William Roe is shown to realise the aspirations of empire-builders, pursuers of fortune in his role as a latter-day Aeneas. However, in the case of the elegy 'Ile not offend … ' addressed to John Roe, the obligations of memory extend not only to honouring the dead but also to equally pressing concerns relating to the nature of mortality itself.

> … thou art but gone before,
> Whither the world must follow. And I, now,
> Breathe to expect my when, and make my how.
> Which if most gracious heauen grant like thine,
> Who wets my grave, can be no friend of mine.
> (viii.37: 2–6)

Interestingly, if Jonson himself underlined that '*There* is a greater Reverence had of things remote, or strange to us, then of much better, if they bee neerer, and fall under our sense. Men, and almost all sort of creatures, have their reputation by distance' (viii.609: 1489–92), in his own elegiac writing he repeatedly endowed his poetic enquiries with a sense of *gravitas* by stressing the reverence owed to the ethical inheritance bequeathed by the deceased. The humanist emphasis upon the constant rescrutinising of the past (thus generating ever more refined interpretations of it) is deeply related to Jonson's enquiries into human perfectibility.

One of the dominant ways in which he encouraged reader investigation into the classical past was through the exploitation of the cult of friendship inherited from the ancients. Famously, in *The Nichomachean Ethics*, Aristotle had insisted that 'The perfect form of friendship is that between the good, and those who resemble each other in virtue'.[36] Later, in Cicero's *De Amicitia* (which was widely taught in Tudor schools and, indeed, across early modern Europe), Laelius affirms that

> such is my enjoyment in the recollection of our friendship that I feel as if my life has been happy because it was spent with Scipio … I am not so much delighted by reputation for wisdom … as I am by the hope that the memory of our friendship will always endure … If my recollection and memory of these things had died with him, I could not now by any means endure the loss of a man so very near and dear to me. But those experiences with him are not dead; rather they are nourished and made more vivid by my reflection and memory.[37]

This Ciceronian narrative enjoyed wide currency throughout the early modern period: Sidney's Musidorus, for example, affirms 'but till I haue [Pyrocles] againe … I am in deed nothing: and therefore my storie is of nothing'.[38] The most notable example of Jonson committing himself poetically to this classical tradition is his elegy 'To the Immortal Memory, and Friendship of that Noble Pair, Sir Lucius Cary, and Sir H. Morison'. Here, the organisation of encomium into Pindaric choric strophes engenders a poetic narrative in which friendship is articulated in terms of a range of expectations derived from antiquity. We move from the recesses of mythology, as the brave Infant of Saguntum returns to the womb in the prospect of Hannibal's sack of the town, to the contrasting 'stand', unveiling 'one [who has] outliv'd his Peeres, | And told forth fourescore yeares': 'What did this Stirrer, but die late?' This ageing nonentity is developed as a foil to the fallen Morison, 'A perfect Patriot, and a noble friend, | But most, a vertuous Sonne' (viii.243–4: 25–6, 30, 46–7). We are asked to remain ever mindful that 'in short measures, life may perfect be' (viii.245: 75). Cary is then drawn into this poetic vision, which has been carefully stage-managed by the artful poet, as the adoring friend. In this way the poet and his subjects are all imaginatively found to invest in a narrative of cultural idealism bequeathed to future generations.

> The Counter-Turn.
>
> Call, noble *Lucius*, then for Wine,
> And let thy lookes with gladnesse shine:
> Accept this garland, plant it on thy Head,
> And thinke, nay know, thy *Morison*'s not dead.
> Hee leap'd the present age,
> Possest with holy rage,
> To see that bright eternall Day:
> Of which we *Priests*, and *Poëts* say
> Such truths, as we expect for happy men,
> And there he lives with memorie; and Ben.
>
> The Stand.
>
> Ionson, who sung this of him, ere he went
> Himselfe to rest …
> (viii.245–6: 76–87)

Straddling the worlds of the 'Counter-Turn' and the 'Stand', those of the quick and the dead, Jonson finally celebrates the men as 'Two Names of Friendship, but one Starre' (viii.246: 98). By inscribing Cary, Morison and himself within a centuries-old tradition of male devotion, Jonson gives a voice to an apparently timeless reality – a reality to which his verse must be seen to belong. He redeems Morison's death from mortal defeat by allowing us to forge an undying textual relationship with him. In claiming the right of the heroic past to coexist with a heroic present, Jonson avoids disconcerting Cary with the realisation that he has been drafted into a glorious world inhabited by those beyond the grave – and thus, the Jonsonian act of sober recollection re-establishes our close proximity to the virtuous life, rather than our lamentable distance from the deceased.[39]

It is thus everywhere apparent in his verse that as a poet endlessly fascinated with the business of commemoration and ethical surveillance, Jonson frequently observed his chosen subjects through the lenses of classical precedent (both formal and historical). Richard Dutton has persuasively analysed the influence of the classical precept of *laudando praecipere* (to lead or instruct by praising) as a driving, if not defining, force in Jonson's poetic undertaking.[40] This principle was particularly associated by the age with Pliny's *Letters* (III.18.1–3) and is addressed explicitly by Francis Bacon in his essay 'Of Praise': 'when by telling me what they are, they represent to them what they should be'.[41] And the past could not fail to nourish such enquiries pursued by the living. A hundred years earlier, Machiavelli had argued in *The Discourses* that 'If the present be compared with the remote past, it is easily seen that in all cities and in all peoples there are the same desires and the same passions as there always were'.[42] Indeed, amid Jonson's own circle of acquaintance such sentiments clearly had some currency. The diplomat Henry Wotton proposed that

In reading of history, a soldier should draw the platform of battles he meets with, plant the squadrons and order the whole frame as he finds it written, so he shall print it firmly in his mind and apt his mind for actions. A politique should find the characters of personages and apply them to some of the court he lives in, which will likewise confirm his memory and give scope and matter for conjecture and invention.[43]

One of Jonson's most arresting meditations on the past occurs in 'An Elegy on the Lady Jane Pawlet, Marchioness of Winton'. Here, the competing desires to praise and to grieve excite the poetic environment as Pawlet's ghost is discovered beckoning the speaker forward. Determined not simply to recite a litany of facts and titles ('Shee was the Lady *Jane*, and *Marchionisse* | Of *Winchester*; the Heralds can tell this', viii.269: 19–20), the speaker once again insists that the prime motive for honouring the distinguished lives of others is to establish an enduring narrative of human exemplarity for succeeding generations: 'And, in her last act, taught the Standers-by, | With admiration, and applause to die!' (viii. 270: 61–2). This determination 'to shew the right way to those that come after' (as expressed in *Timber, or Discoveries*, viii.617: 1758–9) means that the model of Pawlet's life is made to extend beyond the field of temporal experience and to resolve crises of faith for those who remain.

> And, but for that Contention, and brave strife,
> The Christian hath t'enjoy the future life,
> Hee were the wretched'st of the race of men:
> But as he soares at that, he bruiseth then
> The Serpents head: Gets above Death, and Sinne,
> And, sure of Heaven, rides triumphing in.
> (viii.271–2: 95–100)

In such a poem, Jonson ponders in a variety of ways how loss may be culturally digested. Indeed, he explores how death may unexpectedly constitute an opportunity to rescript the cultural narrative of memory and to resist the appalling spectacle of human decline.

MEMORY AND EXEMPLARITY

Stephen Orgel has argued convincingly that whereas 'Jonsonian drama presents no image of heroic virtue ... the poetry of the *Epigrams*, *The Forest*, and *The Underwood* celebrates numerous figures who have, like Hercules, made the exemplary choice and stand as models to mankind'.[44] In 'To the Ghost of Martial', Jonson reveals (like Surrey in his own poetic tribute to the Latin poet) a deep-seated fascination with the ways in which relations with the past may be beneficially forged and renegotiated textually. Elsewhere, we are asked to bear witness to the achievement of like-minded contemporaries who wish to share his commitment to renew, through cultural and textual acts of *translatio*, the writings of classical authors for present consumption. Clement Edmonds, for example, the translator of Caesar's *Commentaries*, is hailed as one who surpasses his rivals, for none 'can so speak CÆSAR, as thy labours doe' (viii.71: 12). Of equal significance in this poetic tribute to Edwards is Jonson's strategic placement of himself as *primo inter pares*, adjudicating upon the performance of others from an exalted position of erudition and poetic privilege. We may identify evidence of similar strategies elsewhere in his poetry, most famously in the dedicatory lyric to Shakespeare's 1623 First Folio. In 'To the Memory of My Beloved Master William Shakespeare, and What He Hath Left Us', if the fellow poet is primarily the subject of a textual monumentalisation, Jonson's reader is very quickly made aware that one of the principal ways in which we are to take the measure of the fallen bard is to place him against the speaker himself:

> To draw no enuy (*Shakespeare*) on thy name,
> Am I thus ample to thy Booke, and Fame:

> While I confesse thy writings to be such,
> As neither *Man*, nor *Muse*, can praise too much.
> 'Tis true, and all men's suffrage.
>
> (viii.390: 1–5)

When Jonson turns his attentions to another fellow poet and dramatist, George Chapman, he finds a 'worthy and honoured friend' who reaffirms his own great merit through the translation of Hesiod 'who hadst before wrought in rich *Homers* mine'.

> If all the vulgar Tongues, that speake this day,
> Were askt of thy Discoueries; They must say,
> To the Greeke coast thine onely knew the way.
>
> (viii.388: 3, 7–9)

From this perspective, the parochial and unambitious minds of those, like the 'Mere English Censurer', who fail to engage with the inestimable legacy of Roman and Greek writing, also fail to appreciate the close relationship between memory and self-knowledge. However, equally interestingly, Jonson makes the point at a number of junctures in *Timber, or Discoveries* that the past must not be seen to represent a terminus of human enquiry or to exhaust the possibilities of human achievement: 'I cannot thinke *Nature* is so spent, and decay'd, that she can bring forth nothing worth her former yeares. She is always the same, like her selfe: And when she collects her strength, is abler still. Men are decay'd, and studies: Shee is not' (viii.567: 124–8).[45] This sentiment had been expressed by earlier generations of scholars such as Juan Luis Vives ('It is far more profitable to learning to form a critical judgement on the writings of the great authors, than to merely acquiesce in their authority'[46]) and is equally apparent in the writings of his contemporary Francis Bacon, who railed in *The Advancement of Learning*, 'why should a few received authors stand up like Hercules' columns, beyond which there should be no sailing or discovering'.[47] Nonetheless, when Jonson wished to give a full account of a Shakespeare or an actor like Edward Alleyn, it seems his celebrated subject could only be fully realised through recourse to classical analogy:

> As skilfull ROSCIVS, and grave ÆSOPE
> …
> ALLEN, I should pause to publish thee?
> Who both their graces in thy selfe hast more
> Out-stript, then they did all that went before.
>
> (viii.56–7: 3, 8–10)

REMEMBERING JONSON

Jonson's unwavering engagement with the heritage of the past may be one of the reasons why Stanley Fish has insisted that his 'habit of beginning awkwardly is not simply a mannerism but is intimately related to the project of his poetry, and indeed represents a questioning of that project, since the issue always seems to be whether or not the poem can do what it sets out to do'.[48] Part of the poetic difficulty to which Fish has convincingly drawn attention is that Jonson never sought to divorce artistic creativity from an increasingly ambitious investment in *imitatio*. Clearly relying heavily upon arguments propounded in Seneca's 'Letter to Lucilius' (84) and Horace's *Ars Poetica* concerning what the true aims of the translator should be, he affirmed in *Timber, or Discoveries* that

> The third requisite in our *Poet*, or Maker, is *Imitation*, to bee able to convert the substance, or Riches of an other Poet, to his owne use. To make choise of one man above the rest, and so to follow him, till he grow very Hee: or, so like him, as the Copie may be mistaken for the Principall. Not, as a Creature, that swallowes, what it takes in, crude, raw, or indigested; but, that feedes with an Appetite, and hath a Stomacke to concoct, devide, and turne all into nourishment. Not, to imitate servilely, as *Horace* saith, and catch at vices, for vertue: but, to draw forth out of the best, and choisest flowers, with the Bee, and turne all into Honey, worke it into one relish, and savour: make our *Imitation* sweet: observe, how the best writers have imitated, and follow them.[49]

Jonson's painstaking interrogation of our commitments to the past was being mirrored widely in this period in the field of historiography, often stimulated in England by the growing appreciation of European humanist scholarship. It has been estimated that there were over two hundred editions of seventy-nine different chronicles between the establishment of the printing presses and the end of the seventeenth century in England. As is well known, Shakespeare was clearly familiar with a number of these productions, such as those composed by Hall, Holinshed and Stow, and exploited them for dramatic purposes. As part of this consuming cultural interest in textual/historical recuperation, we might also look to the proliferation of classical translations, to the religious narrativisation of Protestantism by Bale and Foxe, to other, quite different works such as the composite narratives of chorography that moved between geographical and economic description to historical exploits, legendry and folklore. Camden's *Britannia*, for example, drew sustenance from a burgeoning antiquarian movement that harked back to the achievements and ambitions of John Leland during the reign of Henry VIII. As was discussed in the Introduction, the endeavours of the itinerant Leland to present his sovereign with a survey of 'your whole world and empire of England' proved to be seminal for subsequent generations of scholars determined to reclaim the native histories of the British Isles through the careful scrutiny of their archaeology, topography and political development, for example. If Leland's ambitious undertaking remained (perhaps inevitably) incomplete at his death (which was itself preceded by the collapse of his sanity), it would be taken up later in a more focused fashion during Elizabeth's reign by figures such as William Lambarde with his *Perambulation of Kent* (1576), John Stow with his *Survey of London* (1598) and Richard Carew with his *Survey of Cornwall* (1602).

In the company of antiquaries, translators, historians and philologists, Jonson wished to affirm a pattern of intellectual resemblance and community, and to identify a common desire to return to precious cultural legacies that required strenuous interpretative labour. It mattered little whether he turned his attention to linguistic decorum, theatrical representations of classical heroism, the physical monument of Penshurst or the textual remains of Shakespeare, Jonson was eager to establish the indissoluble links between present experience and past narrative. Whatever their material forms, as Peter Sherlock has persuasively argued, 'Monuments told posterity what should be known about the past ... Early modern memorials should be analysed as sites that strove to change the memory of their subjects, as well as objects that created continuity'. However, whereas Sherlock considers the ways in which funerary monuments may 'do the work of memory independently ... [discharging] the society that produced or inherits them from the obligation to remember', Jonson's textual encomia constitute reaffirmations of that very obligation.[50] The recoverable past offered the opportunity to extend and perhaps to complete heroic aspiration: it offered a measure of intellectual achievement and a paradigm for human creativity, textual, cultural and (on rarer occasions, in his *œuvre*) spiritual. Jonson worked from the premiss that a knowledge of the past might hold in check the evolution of a hostile or unremarkable present, stressing in the dedication to the Folio edition of *Every Man in His Humor* that 'It is a fraile memorie, that remembers but present things'.[51] In many ways one of Jonson's most arresting poetic meditations upon the life solely spent among 'present things' is his 'Execration upon Vulcan'. Here, he lamented the domestic fire that apparently laid waste to his work in progress – 'And why to me this, thou lame Lord of Fire'. In general, this mock-heroic apostrophe keenly communicates the vulnerability and disorientation experienced by those robbed of the physical remains of the past: 'Thou mightst … have kept me dying a whole age, | Not ravish'd all hence in a minutes rage' (viii.202, 205: 1, 55–6). The speaker grieves among other things for the loss of a history of Henry V, a grammar, a chronicle of his journey to Scotland in 1618. He then compares Vulcan's conquest of his library to that of the Globe in 1613, which burnt down as a consequence of cannons fired during a performance of Shakespeare and Fletcher's *All is True, or Henry VIII*. In both cases, the limping god emerges as a lord of urban misrule.

Underlying the whole of Jonson's poetic writing is the central humanist belief that the progress of learning is linked to the goal of human perfectibility, that a recoverable past presents the possibility of recoverable virtue. In his poetry the need to recuperate and to preserve always competes with the need to create. Shortly after his death in 1637 a volume entitled *Jonsonus Virbius* was published to signal his passing. Jonson had himself provided the lead for his own commemoration when he hailed the achievements of fellow writers (both living and dead) such as Shakespeare, Donne and Bacon. If his enthusiastic and long-term commitment to elegiac writing had clearly mapped out how he wished his own death to be received, he had already built a significant part of his monument by overseeing the publication of his *Works* during his own lifetime in 1616. The First Folio constituted his most substantial bid to be preserved (as Shakespeare would be in the later 1623 Folio), to have 'a Moniment, without a tombe' (viii.391: 23).

Generally, in reviewing the commendatory lyrics dedicated to Jonson throughout his life, it becomes increasingly apparent that his sympathetic readers responded acutely to anxieties that had haunted him as a writer throughout his career. In his poetic tribute to the unpopular *Catiline*, for example, Francis Beaumont urged the poet to draw consolation from posterity:

> If thou had'st itch'd after the wild applause
> Of common people, and had'st made thy Lawes
> In writing, such, as catch'd at present voyce,
> I should commend the thing, but not thy choyce.
> But thou has squar'd thy rules, by what is good;
> And art three ages yet, from understood:
> And (I dare say) in it, there lies much wit
> Lost, till thy readers can grow up to it.
> Which they can nere outgrow, to find it ill,
> But must fall backe againe, or like it still.[52]

In a similarly effusive display, John Fletcher also pronounced that the 'labours' of *Catiline* 'shall outlive thee; and, like gold | Stampt for continuance, shall be current, where | There is a Sunne, a People, or a Yeare' (xi.325–7). Whereas Jonson reasoned with his 'learned Critic' that 'a sprigge of bayes, giuen by thee, | Shall out-liue gyrlands, stolne from the chast tree' (viii.32: 5–6), in more recent times Paul Ricoeur has probed the question of elegiac writing and textual survival in a more sombre fashion:

Elegies on the human condition, ranging in their modulations from lamentation to resignation, have never ceased to sing of the contrast between the time that remains and we who are merely passing. It is only the 'they' that never dies? If we hold time to be infinite, is this only because we are concealing our own finitude from ourselves? And if we say that time flies, is this simply because we are fleeing the idea of our Being-towards-the-end?[53]

If Jonson's poetry constantly prompts us to remember, to return to the originary sites of cultural and literary tradition in the West, it also forcefully impresses upon us how strategic the faculty of memory remains for moral and cultural (self-)scrutiny. Like many of his contemporaries, he showed himself unable to divorce thought itself from the business of remembering. However, in the next and final chapter, it will become clear that memory would not always dominate early modern understandings of the act of cognition and the formulation of subjectivity. Yet, if in the postmodern age the past may never be sufficiently lost, Jonson's poetry clearly challenges us to return to that very past in order to secure a fuller appreciation of what we may become.

Plato was not content with the Learning, that *Athens* could give him, but sail'd into *Italy* for *Pythagoras* knowledge: And yet not thinking himselfe sufficiently inform'd, went into *Egypt* to the Priests, and learned their mysteries. Hee labour'd, so must wee. Many things may be learn'd together, and perform'd in one point of time; as Musicians exercise their memory, their voice, their fingers, and sometime their head, and feet at once.[54]

CHAPTER 8

'This art of memory': Francis Bacon, memory and the discourses of power

> Truth stands open to all. It is not as yet taken possession of. Much of truth has been left for future generations to discover.
> Juan Luis Vives, *On Education*[1]

After waiting interminably for political preferment during the reign of Elizabeth I, Francis Bacon (1561–1626) was knighted by the newly instituted James I of England in 1603 and as his star rose he went on to become King's Counsel in 1604, Solicitor-General in 1607, Attorney-General in 1613, a Privy Counsellor in 1616, Lord Keeper in 1617 and Lord Chancellor in 1618. At the height of his career in public affairs, he was created Baron Verulam in 1618, and Viscount St Albans in the following year. However, his distinctive work as a thinker and a writer[2] was often necessarily performed during fallow periods in his career when he was not fully occupied in public affairs, yet his aspiration 'to stretch the deplorably narrow limits of man's dominion over the universe to their promised bounds' did not go unrecognised by those around him.[3] If, in his *Essaies Politicke, and Morall* (1608), one of Bacon's contemporaries and fellow essayists, Daniel Tuvill '(Gent.)', stressed in general terms that 'There is no better marke of a true generous disposition, then to attempt those things, which are hard to be achiued', by 1615 Nicholas Breton had dedicated his collection *Characters vpon essaies morall, and diuine* to 'The Honorable, and my much worthy honored, truly learned, and Iudicious Knight, Sr Francis Bacon, his Majesties Attourney Generall', proposing that his own essays, or 'Trauells of my Spirit', were but 'Imitators of your breaking the ice'.[4] Indeed, from the early seventeenth century, Bacon was repeatedly associated with innovation – on occasions, perplexing innovation. James VI/I reputedly observed that the scientific thinking of this most eminent lawyer was 'like the peace of God, which passeth understanding'.[5]

MEMORY AND MODERNITY

And now, my son, I do not conceal from you that we must find a way of clearing sham philosophers out of our path. Your philosophers are more fabulous than poets. They debauch our minds. They substitute a false coinage for the true. And worse still are the satellites and parasites of the great ones, the whole mob of professorial teachers ... generally speaking science is to be sought from the light of nature, not from the darkness of antiquity. It matters not what has been done; our business is to see what can be done. If a kingdom won in victorious fighting were offered to you, would you refuse it unless you had followed up the clues of ancient genealogies to prove that your ancestors had held it before? So much for the remote fastnesses of antiquity.[6]

Given that many of his most celebrated writings express a consuming interest in the 'progress or proficience'[7] of scientific thought (such as may be witnessed here in the *Temporis Partus Masculus* [1602–3]), Bacon might be imagined to have precious little to do with early modern discourses of *memoria*. He was, and is, widely associated with a commitment to inauguration: the reform of intellectual taxonomies, the complete revision of analytical practice, the re-evaluation of technological possibility – in short, with *the new*. His energetic engagement with the political life of early seventeenth-century England would appear to leave little room in the minds of many of his critics and readers for the picture of a man immersed in the business of recollection. Nonetheless, it might not be wholly counter-intuitive to reposition memory more centrally in Bacon's intellectual undertaking.

As David Colclough has underlined, for many later generations Bacon 'seems always to be standing on the threshold between premodernity and modernity ... [making] him the archetypal "early modern" writer'.[8] And, indeed, before scrutinising the natural philosopher's textual negotiations with memorial thinking, it might be helpful to reflect upon the ways in which he has been characterised (and notably characterised himself) as the High Priest presiding at the dawn of a new age of intellectual discovery. This kind of cultural production certainly prevails in the *Temporis Partus Masculus*. Here, we are summoned into an audience with a Platonic mentor instructing a duly appreciative tutee. The medieval insistence upon a *contemptus mundi*, the desirability of severing bonds of affection with this mortal existence, continued to have a powerful hold over the meditative life of very many in the early modern period – Bacon's fellow essayist, Robert Johnson, for example, speculated in his own *Essaies* (1601), 'how can they bee carried to embrace worthy deedes, who so highly prize this interim of life ... how can they be liberal, whose mindes confined to the world, think of liuing continually?'⁹ However, if in *Temporis Partus Masculus* time and space are invested in an urgent appeal to bleach or cleanse the mind, Bacon is not in this instance concerned with matters spiritual, as Donne had been. He is concentrating upon expelling the mental detritus accumulated from the textual remains of centuries given over to sterile ruminations of philosophers. As he acknowledged in *The Advancement of Learning*, the demands of the modern age meant that precedence must now be accorded to a *vita activa* devoted entirely to innovative, rational, methodical scientific enquiry – and 'men must know, that in this theatre of man's life it is reserved only for God and angels to be lookers on'.[10]

Bacon's unfailing promotion of the material environment as the proper object of human investigation placed him not only in opposition to medieval traditions of spiritual dedication but also in a number of ways to many of the dominant epistemological discourses inherited from the classical period. The Platonic (and Aristotelian) emphases that the laws governing temporality were radically different from those operating in realms elsewhere in the universe would come under vigorous interrogation in his treatises. Plato had associated the terrestrial with the mutable, and had deemed it incapable of yielding eternal truths. However, Bacon continued to resist such doctrines fiercely as they challenged the very core of his intellectual project of empiricism: 'For neither is heaven indued with that eternity which they suppose nor, the earth with that mutability.'[11] Whereas Plato had insisted that all *true* (read, apodictic) knowledge, to which the human mind had access, derived from experiences with a prenatal existence and was retrieved with the assistance of memory, Bacon's scientific undertaking vigorously promoted the systematic commemoration, not of inherited knowledge, but of knowledge gained solely *a posteriori* – as may be witnessed in the prefatory discussion to *The Great Instauration*:

> Not that I would be understood to mean that nothing whatever has been done in so many ages by so great labours. We have no reason to be ashamed of the discoveries which have been made, and no doubt the ancients proved themselves in everything that turns on wit and abstract meditation, wonderful men. But as in former ages when men sailed only by observation of the stars, they could indeed coast along the shores of the old continent or cross a few small and mediterranean seas ... but before we can reach the remoter and more hidden parts of nature, it is necessary that a more perfect use and application of the human mind and intellect be introduced.[12]

The university system of learning that Bacon and his contemporaries had undergone frequently depended upon intellectual enquiry guided by (sometimes confined to) explication of Aristotelian propositions. In terms of knowledge acquisition and retention, despite the fact that Aristotle's writings were more clearly shaped than those of Plato by cognitive and medical theories that affirmed the strategic role of the senses (most particularly relating to visual images) and deliberative acts of recollection (relating to the material universe and expressed through the sequential organisation of ideas), Bacon reserved a profoundly humanist scepticism for the manner in which such texts from antiquity had been mediated to later generations. He remained convinced that the interpreters of Aristotle had established a learning environment in which the scholar was given every encouragement to turn away from the cultural imperative of intellectual discovery: when invoking the authority of Aristotle, for example, Aquinas had simply recorded in his own writings 'Philosophus dixit'.

In the *Valerius Terminus: Of the Interpretation of Nature* (c.1603?) Bacon argued that all too often the educationalist 'desireth rather present satisfaction than expectant search'. And, as a consequence of centuries thus spent in aimless mental perambulations, society's energies had become wholly exercised by philosophical ephemera and theological aporia – in short, an age of intellectual mediocrity had come into being: 'Then begin men to aspire to the second prizes' (iii. 226). Under such a regime, human enquiry was driven by dialectical procedures of conceptual interrogation, rather than any acquaintance with what might now be termed the critical apparatus of observation, experimentation, data analysis and storage, or empirically based hypothesis.[13] In this context, it is worthwhile underlining that Bacon in general was more deeply preoccupied with questions of perception than those of logic, and this fact may offer valuable insights into his recurring interest in the role that memory might play in the progress of learning:

> a lack I find in the exercises used in the universities, which do make too great a divorce between invention and memory. For their speeches are either premeditate, in *verbis conceptis*, where nothing is left to invention; or merely *ex-temporal*, where little is left to memory. Whereas in life and action there is least use of either of these, but rather of intermixtures of premeditation and invention, notes and memory.[14]

Unlike the Sceptics (and most particularly the Pyrrhonian Sceptics), who 'affirm only that nothing can be known', Bacon insisted rather that 'we claim that not many things in nature can be known by the method now in use' (Aphorism XXXVII (iv. 53)). As a consequence, he regularly expressed his horror at the ways in which the intellectual legacies from the past had warped the progress of knowledge in his own age, as becomes abundantly clear in the following example from the 'Aphorisms concerning the Interpretation of Nature and the Kingdom of Man' from the *Novum Organum* (published 1620):

> if a man turn from the workshop to the library, and wonder at the immense variety of books he sees there, let him but examine and diligently inspect their matter and contents, and his wonder will assuredly be turned the other way; for after observing their endless repetitions, and how men are ever saying and doing what has been said and done before, he will pass from admiration of the variety to astonishment at the poverty and scantiness of the subjects which till now have occupied and possessed the minds of men.[15]

In this way, if an engagement with the experience of the past was no longer perceived as spiritually restorative, as it had been for Plato, or as an indispensable operation in many cognitive procedures, as it had been for Aristotle, for Bacon such an encounter remained valuable for its epiphanic potential, for presenting a *terminus a quo*. Nonetheless, while he was at pains to stress the sterile nature of so many encounters with the textual remains of the past, we should be mindful that for many of his contemporaries this fund of speculation, rumination and irresolvable enquiry remained all too tempting. A generation later, Sir Thomas Browne might still be heard confessing excitedly that he was 'naturally inclined to that which misguided zeal terms superstition'.[16] Refusing to luxuriate thus in aporetic conundrums or to disengage (in the manner of some Sceptics) from the *vita activa* in an attitude of estranged resignation, Bacon offered inductive thinking as a necessary escape, nay deliverance, from the intellectual labyrinth in which humanity presently found itself: 'human knowledge, as we have it, is a mere medley and undigested mass, made up of much credulity and much accident, and also of the childish notions which we at first imbibed' (Aphorism XCVII (iv. 93)). In the *Cogitata et Visa* ('Thoughts and Conclusions, or The Interpretation of Nature, or A Science Productive of Works', 1607, published 1653) this innovative *modus operandi* is unveiled as a master weapon with which to challenge the present pedagogic edifice: 'The syllogism being disposed of, what have we left? Induction. This is the one last refuge and support. On it are centred all hopes. This is the method which by slow and faithful toil gathers information from things and brings it to the understanding.'[17] And what was this intellectual redemption in the shape of the inductive method? Bacon answered in 'The Plan of the Work' to *The Great Instauration*, that

> my plan is to proceed regularly and gradually from one axiom to another, so that the most general are not reached till the last: but then when you do come to them you find them to be not empty notions, but well defined, and such as

nature would really recognise as better known to her, and such as lie at the heart and marrow of things.[18]

There has been a good measure of heated debate down the centuries regarding the exact nature and potential of Bacon's inductive, or hypothetico-inductive, or theoretico-inductive method;[19] yet, despite critical disagreement regarding Bacon's paradigms for knowledge-acquisition, it remains striking that he acknowledged on a number of occasions that his undertaking would necessarily involve a treatment of the faculty of memory that had so exercised the minds of his forebears in philosophical enquiry: 'The great help to the memory is *writing*; and it must be taken as a rule that memory without this aid is unequal to matters of much length and accuracy; and that its unwritten evidence ought by no means to be allowed' (iv. 435).[20] If only a limited power is accorded to memory in this instance, it might be added that Bacon's commitment to intellectual innovation did not prevent him at any time in his career from availing himself of hitherto authoritative constructs of the faculty (such as the Platonic theory of *anamnesis*) – when it served his own ends. This may be witnessed in the encomium addressed to James VI/I at the beginning of *The Advancement of Learning* (1605):

I have often thought that of all the persons living that I have known, your Majesty were the best instance to make a man of Plato's opinion, that all knowledge is but remembrance, and that the mind of man by nature knoweth all things, and hath but her own native and original notions (which by the strangeness and darkness of this tabernacle of the body are sequestered) again revived and restored.[21]

And, as we have seen, it is possible to discover Bacon exploiting the medieval discourse of spiritual cleansing and mental catharsis with a secular analogue in mind. In many of his writings, the purging of the benighted consciousness is counselled in order to make room for an unimpeded engagement with an intelligible material environment, and with the new methodologies that such investigations warranted – all leading in good time to the parthenogenesis of a new intellectual community, 'with minds washed clean from opinions ... becoming again as little children' (v. 132, 133).[22] The familiarity of such grandiloquent rhetoric heralding the birth of new political, or in this case, epistemological epochs in more recent times should not lead us to underestimate the radical nature of such a creed in a society where a great many invested deeply in the received wisdom of the past. In his own *Essayes*, published at the beginning of the seventeenth century, Sir William Cornwallis had no hesitation in affirming that 'We are beholding to times past, they haue shewed vs the ends of all Courses'.[23] Interestingly, it might also be added in this context that, with regard to his 'essays', Bacon asked his readers to exercise *their* own memories. As was discussed in Chapter 7, Jonson remonstrated with his 'Mere English Censurer' for the parochial nature of his poetic sensibilities,[24] and Bacon responded in a similar manner when introducing this 'new' form of writing, the 'essay': he argued that 'The word is late, but the thing is auncient'. Even if this apparently 'new' genre suggested etymologically the commitment to 'try' or 'experiment', he insisted that we should look back beyond recent productions by Michel de Montaigne to the examples of Seneca's epistles to Lucilius, which 'if one mark them well, [they] are *Essays*, that is, dispersed meditations, though conveyed in the form of epistles'.[25]

MEMORY AND PROFICIENCE

If at such moments Bacon can be discovered, like many of his contemporaries, seeking cultural validation for his textual endeavours by acknowledging his debts to the literatures of antiquity, and by reassuring his readership of his active participation in the humanist project of *aemulatio*, such considerations were often only preliminary to a broader concern with the salvific prospect of a new scientific age. The very title of the *Temporis Partus Masculus* hailed the advent of a new age of 'operative' knowledge involving, it seems, the 'masculine' or 'vigorous birth of time'. In the *Cogitationes de Natura Rerum* (Thoughts on the Nature of Things (1604)), Bacon argued that 'One whose object is to achieve an active natural philosophy must concern himself principally with the investigation of motion. To investigate, or exercise one's imagination, about the inactive principles of things is fit only for one whose purpose is *to* provide matter for talk and disputation'.[26] However, within the broader context of this study, it is surely significant that the journeying into this newly minted historical moment is mapped in Bacon's writing along a *via negativa*: the emergent order is frequently defined (at least initially) through its antitheses, which is to say the prevailing schemes of knowledge acquisition.

The *Temporis Partus Masculus* has been interpreted critically as one of Bacon's most passionate attacks upon the ills of received thinking. Nonetheless, more generally throughout his scientific writing there remained a recurrent stress upon the urgent need for a radical discontinuity in intellectual practices, and this could be articulated with a highly metaphorical language of innovation, birthing and maturation.

In the 'Aphorisms Concerning the Interpretation of Nature', readers are informed that 'It is idle to expect great advancement in science from the superinducing and engrafting of new things upon old. We must begin anew from the very foundations unless we would revolve for ever in a circle with mean and contemptible progress' (Aphorism XXXI (iv. 52)). Elsewhere, in the *Cogitata et Visa*, a more impatient Bacon is unmasked:

> Men's anticipations of the new are fashioned on the model of the old. The old governs their imagination. Yet this is a completely fallacious pattern of thought. There is no universal law that discoveries fetched up from the source and fount of things must flow down to us along familiar channels.[27]

Indeed, despite his sometimes extended appraisals of the intellectual legacies of antiquity in *Temporis Partus Masculus*, he clearly looked forward to a watershed moment of cultural parturition in order to confound once and for all the hold that Error and Superstition maintained upon the human mind: 'on waxen tablets you cannot write anything new until you rub out the old. With the mind it is not so there you cannot rub out the old until you have written in the new.'[28] Significantly, it was in this very work that Bacon styled himself as a latter-day 'Columbus': 'And therefore it is fit that I publish and set forth those conjectures of mine which make hope in this matter reasonable, just as Columbus did, before that wonderful voyage of his across the Atlantic' (iv. 91). Yet, if the carefully orchestrated staging of the intellectual as pioneering colonialist is not uncommon in Bacon's writing, Denise Albanese remains persuasive in her contention that in his utopian fiction *The New Atlantis* (published 1627), 'it is the phenomenal world of nature, rather than the natural world of savages, that stands as the object of conquest'.[29]

The Advancement of Learning proved to be Bacon's only philosophical text in English to be published in his lifetime. His other publications in this field more ambitiously targeted an international audience and thus, given the intellectual context of the age, engaged with what was at once the *lingua franca* of learned debate across early modern Europe and a strategic affirmation of cultural memory, namely Latin. In the Latin preface to the *Novum Organum*, Bacon argued that 'my object [is] to open a new way for the understanding, a way … untried and unknown'. If the old world were to be sundered from the new (that is, a 'course for the recovery of a sound and healthy condition'), then 'the entire work of the understanding [must] be commenced afresh' (iv. 40–1). This was so much the case that, by the time of the writing of the *Novum Organum*, Bacon was willing to cast himself as a redemptive figure for an age teetering on the edge of profound epistemological change, an inspired evangelist for an erring flock:

> But if any man there be who, not content to rest in and use the knowledge which has already been discovered, aspires to penetrate further; to overcome, not an adversary in argument, but nature in action; to seek, not pretty and probable conjectures, but certain and demonstrable knowledge; I invite all such to join themselves, as true sons of knowledge, with me, that passing by the outer courts of nature, which numbers have trodden, we may find a way at length into her inner chambers.[30]

This stands as one of many examples of Bacon's gendered discourse of knowledge acquisition in which the future holds the promise of a fecund and yielding Nature submitting to the penetrative enquiries of the inquisitive patriarch.[31] Indeed, such highly figurative language is clearly influenced by magical and alchemical traditions of writing in which the studious interpreter determines to harness Nature and bring about change with systematic experiment – albeit, Bacon often contended, such practices were wrapped in secrecy and prone to charlatanism. However, the 'novum organum' or 'new tool' of knowledge remains in *The New Atlantis* under the control of highly respected, but rather mysterious, brethren. Furthermore, in the *Temporis Partus Masculus*, if Bacon's readers can look forward to a time when 'the tradition of science may mature and spread like some lively vigorous vine', we are also assured that this 'science must be such as to select her followers, who must be worthy to be adopted into her family'.[32] We are invited to behold the birth of a new breed of intellectuals who are, it seems, unshaken in faith and uncontaminated by prejudices inherited from the past: 'We have as yet no natural philosophy that is pure; all is tainted and corrupted; in Aristotle's school by logic; in Plato's by natural theology; in the second school of Platonists, such as Proclus and others, by mathematics … From a natural philosophy pure and unmixed, better things are to be expected' (Aphorism XCVI (iv. 93)).[33] Nonetheless, if Bacon's *new* generations of intellectuals may be preparing a *new* age of discovery, they often resemble uncannily the alchemists and magi whom they were supposed to be supplanting.[34]

MEMORY AND EPISTEMOLOGY: A VEXED ENQUIRY

So much for the visionary. On further examination, this justly celebrated commitment to a new era of cognitive achievement on Bacon's part may be found to be tempered increasingly by an awareness of the seemingly inevitable meanderings of the human intellect: 'For the mind of man is far from the nature of a clear and equal glass, wherein the beams of things should reflect according to their true incidence; nay, it is rather like an enchanted glass, full of superstition and imposture, if it be not delivered and reduced' (iii. 394–5). Ultimately, Bacon's rhetoric of discovery, questing and, indeed, of *instauration* – his very concept of legitimate intellectual activity – discloses an evolving dialogue with the past and a complex meditation upon the very function of memory, despite his many and various protestations to the contrary. The pedagogue argues in the *Temporis Partus Masculus* that 'it would not be a proper thing for me, who am preparing things useful for the future of the human race, to bury myself in the study of ancient literature'.[35] Yet we frequently encounter in Bacon's writing an irrepressible desire to survey the intellectual legacies from the past before mounting a refutation of them:

> The sciences which we possess come for the most part from the Greeks. For what has been added by Roman, Arabic, or later writers is not much nor of much importance; and whatever it is, it is built on the foundation of Greek discoveries. Now the wisdom of the Greeks was professorial and much given to disputations; a kind of wisdom most adverse to the inquisition of truth.[36]

There are any number of examples throughout Bacon's writing of this denigration of Europe's intellectual inheritance: most famously, we learn in 'Preface' to *The Great Instauration* that 'Time is like a river, which has brought down to us things light and puffed up, while those which are weighty and solid have sunk' (iv .15).[37] However, as we delve further into his enquiries, it is not only early modern intellectual society in general which is in the grip of flawed philosophies, Bacon himself cannot refrain, it seems, from exercising his cultural memory, from risking further contamination with intellectual ephemera, and from returning to prior scenes of enquiry in search of possible truths that might *just possibly* be uncovered within their midst. He remains mindful in *The Advancement of Learning*, for example, of Martin Luther, who was 'enforced to awake all antiquity, and to call former times to his succours to make a party against the present time: so that the ancient authors, both in divinity and in humanity, which had long time slept in libraries, began generally to be read and revolved' (iii. 283).[38] Yet memory alone, it seemed, could not support his momentous undertaking; the project he proposed in the 'Aphorisms' had to be driven by systematic investigation:

> when, though the memory of things be decayed and almost lost, yet acute and industrious persons, by a certain persevering and scrupulous diligence, contrive out of genealogies, annals, titles … as well public as private, fragments

of histories … contrive, I say, from all these things or some of them, to recover somewhat from the deluge of time: a work laborious indeed, but agreeable to men and joined with a kind of reverence.[39]

It has already been indicated how the symbolic architecture of Titian's painting *An Allegory of Prudence* (Figure 1) may be seen to constitute one of the many early modern responses to the Ciceronian identification and moralisation of *memoria* in *De Inventione*. In the *Temporis Partus Masculus* Bacon would develop his own secular figuration of this schema, asserting that 'it is important to understand how the present is like a seer with two faces, one looking towards the future, the other towards the past'.[40] If Bacon frequently expressed a violent distaste for the pedagogic regime of the kind he and his contemporaries had met with at the universities, he also came to recognise, on occasions, that those who shaped it may not have been wholly devoid of intellectual curiosity or insight: 'if those schoolmen to their great thirst of truth and unwearied travail of wit had joined variety and universality of reading and contemplation, they had proved excellent lights, to the great advancement of all learning and knowledge' (*The Advancement of Learning* (see iii. 287)). Bacon's writings indicate a growing realisation that there can be no autonomy from the philosophical past without first acknowledging its intellectual commitments and, most importantly, its untapped potential: thus, the resolve to establish a radical discontinuity between past and future epistemologies (the desire to discriminate between authentic and inauthentic intellectual enquiry) may not only involve in due course the *Othering* the past, but also initially picking over its remains: 'my book of Advancement of Learning … exhibits a mixture of new conceits and old; whereas the Instauration gives the new unmixed, otherwise than with some little aspersion of the old for taste's sake' (vii. 13). Indeed, the very undertaking of his *Sapientia Veterum* (The Wisdom of the Ancients) was to analyse fables bequeathed to us from the earliest human communities, and to unlock their didactic potential as 'sacred relics and light airs breathing out of better times' (vi. 698). Elsewhere, the textual and intellectual journey undertaken in *The New Atlantis* represents a complex engagement with the past that looks back to cultural structures established by the Greeks, Romans, Egyptians, in addition to the Early Church, in order to demonstrate what guise a seventeenth-century future might assume:

You shall understand (that which perhaps you will scarce think credible) that about three thousand years ago or somewhat more, the navigation of the world, (specially for remote voyages,) was greater than at this day. Do not think with yourselves that I know not how much it is increased with you within these six score years; I know it well: and yet I say greater then than now.⁴¹

In such fictive worlds, the Jacobean present may be characterised by failing powers of memory or, equally plausibly, by the imperfect exertion of the faculty, and Bacon was determined to highlight what he saw as the fault-lines of the cultural mindset that the past had bequeathed to his society and to expose the challenges that might hinder epistemological change. Most famously, he delineated what he considered to be the spectres that continued to haunt or rather obstruct the pathway to human progress, styling them as idols.⁴² The 'idola tribus' (or idols of the tribe) represented the distorting power of human nature itself to measure the material world in terms of its own needs, appetites and desires, thus creating an extension of its own selfhood (see Aphorisms XL–XLIV (iv. 54–5)). The 'idola specus' (or idols of the cave) communicated the particular limitations of a human mind owing to circumstances of psychological and material development, whereas the 'idola fori' (or idols of the marketplace) referred to the errors generated within human society where the flawed use of language and patterns of received thinking leads to futile polemic. Finally, the 'idola theatri' (or idols of the theatre) were expressed as fallacious philosophies and intellectual procedures inherited from the past, which, in turn, bred further falsehoods.⁴³

But do you suppose, when all the approaches and entrances to men's minds are beset and blocked by the most obscure idols – idols deeply implanted and, as it were, burned in – that any clean and polished surface remains in the mirror of the mind on which the genuine natural light of things can fall? A new method must be found for quiet entry into minds so choked and overgrown.⁴⁴

Yet, as time elapsed, Bacon himself became increasingly aware of his intellectual investment in the faculty of memory, of the sustained nature of his negotiations with the past. He wrote to Isaac Casaubon in 1609 that 'I seem to have my conversation among the ancients more than among these with whom I live' (xi. 146–7). If, as we witnessed in Chapter 1, Petrarch had confided that 'I am happier with the dead than the living', such an intellectual sensibility only served to render the dispirited Bacon with a growing sense of melancholy.⁴⁵

MEMORY AND HISTORY

Bacon's early patron, Robert Devereux, second Earl of Essex, had written to the Earl of Rutland in 1595, 'Above all other books be conversant in the

Histories, for they will best instruct you in matter, moral, military, and politic, by which, in which, you must ripen and settle your judgement',[46] and it was inevitable that the Age's consuming interest in the ancient discipline would find a voice in Bacon's own meditations upon the functions of memory (most particularly, narratives of collective cultural memory) in later life. After his political defeat in 1621, one of the projects upon which he immediately embarked was *The History of the Reign of King Henry the Seventh* – and this narrative remained for many the authoritative account of the subject until the nineteenth century. Bacon had been particularly eager in the 'Description of the Intellectual Globe' (1612) to see the development of historical writing anchored, like so many of Jonson's lyrics, in the depiction of extraordinary specimens of humanity: 'History is properly concerned with individuals … For the images of individuals are received by the sense and fixed in the memory. They pass into the memory whole, just as they present themselves. Then the mind recalls and reviews them' (v. 503). And, in direct comparison with the textual strategies adopted by Donne in his sermons, Bacon appeared to believe that the very specificity of such narratives would fix the attention of readers and most readily stimulate reflection and enquiry.

As was appreciated in Chapter 7, the enormous interest in history and historiography more generally in the sixteenth century, nourished by humanist endeavours across Europe, had led in England to a marked growth in classical translations, civic chronologies, county portraits, political mythologies, accounts of native history (given further impetus by the establishment of the Society of Antiquaries in the 1580s), martyrologies, as well as dozens of editions of chronicles as the century unfolded. And Bacon himself remained in no doubt concerning the venerable ambitions of such an academic undertaking:

For to carry the mind in writing back into the past, and bring it into sympathy with antiquity; diligently to examine, freely and faithfully to report, and by the light of words to place as it were before the eyes, the revolutions of times, the characters of persons, the fluctuations of counsels, the courses and currents of actions, the bottoms of pretences, and the secrets of governments; is a task of great labour and judgment.[47]

When he turned to a detailed consideration of the discipline of History itself, Bacon sought to define its properties, as Philip Sidney had done during the reign of Elizabeth in *An Apology for Poetry* (published 1595) in opposition to those of Poetry and Philosophy. In the *De Augmentis*, the categories of history, poetry and philosophy were aligned with the subdivisions of the rational soul, namely memory, imagination, and reason (iv. 292). History was then divided further into 'natural' and 'civil' history, and then again into 'memorials' (or bald accounts of past events), 'antiquities' (relating to recovered objects and records) and 'perfect' history (including more developed and focused material such as chronicle, biography and narrative of particular experiences) (iv. 303). Bacon's contemporary, Walter Ralegh, offered Jacobean readers in 1614 a compendious *History of the World* (which in the event only extended to approximately 130 BC). However, rather than being interested in History as a sequential narrative, which stressed the workings of Providence and the moral instruction to be gleaned from flawed human experience *pace* Ralegh, Bacon, like many humanist historians, looked eagerly to the processes of causation in his accounts of human vicissitudes. Indeed, he went further in *The Advancement of Learning* to stress the demanding nature of the interpretative labour that such endeavours required for all parties concerned: 'It is the true office of history to present the events themselves, together with the counsels; and to leave the observations and conclusions thereupon to the liberty and faculty of every man's judgment' (iii. 339).

Bacon shared the belief of many of his contemporaries that the past remained in intimate dialogue with the present, and that its study thus became an invaluable, and inevitable, procedure for appreciating the nature of the most pressing affairs that confronted later ages. He theorised that historical narrativisation was not designed primarily as an opportunity for the reader or writer to involve themselves in extensions of sympathy or imaginative recognition, but for the provision of a more deliberative, exploitable knowledge.[48] Moreover, if the reading of History and the keeping of written records of all kinds remained central to Bacon's vision of cognitive development for humanity, in the *Novum Organum* he reflected more generally upon how writing assisted and, indeed, might establish the parameters of memorial powers:

> But even after such a store of natural history and experience as is required for the work of the understanding or of philosophy, shall be ready at hand, still the understanding is by no means competent to deal with it offhand and by memory alone; no more than if a man should hope by force of memory to retain and make himself master of the computation of an ephemeris ... no course of invention can be satisfactory unless it be carried on in writing.[49]

Here, Bacon is addressing in a rather oblique manner the age-old Platonic arguments that writing might act as a corrosive force upon memory, gnawing away at its achievements. However, it is evident that both Platonic and Baconian arguments concur in affirming that the act of writing itself would signal the extent of human memorial prowess. Reinforcing the primacy of spiritual apprehension, in Socrates's tale in the *Phaedrus* the God Theuth informs the Egyptian king Ammon that writing 'will introduce forgetfulness into the soul of those who learn it … you provide your students with the appearance of wisdom, not with its reality'.[50] However, for Bacon, both History and Natural Philosophy were cognate in that they required the accurate transcription of evidence and carefully recorded deliberation so that human knowledge might continue to progress and remain open to scrutiny. Whereas he acknowledged that 'The custody or retaining of knowledge is either in Writing or Memory', it remained an unassailable truth for him that 'The great help to the memory is writing' (iii. 397; iv. 435). If his intellectual programme often voiced vigorous opposition to the kinds of assertions propounded in the *Phaedrus*, elsewhere Bacon's recurring investigations into the manifold properties of memory (textual, historiographical, rhetorical, pedagogic) may indeed link more closely to Platonic premises. Plato had pondered the cyclical nature of Time's passage in the shape of the Great Year when the universe returned to its original configuration (e.g., *Timaeus* 39d–e) and later formulations of the *circuitus temporum* continued to enjoy widespread interest throughout the early modern period. Among Latin literatures, exposure to this thinking might be variously gained by the early modern reader from a reading of Cicero's *De Re Publica*, *De Divinatione* and the letters to Atticus, for example, or Seneca's *De Brevitate Vitae*. In more recent times, humanist scholars had stressed the critical importance of historical studies, most especially if credence were given to this enduring notion of the cyclical development of Time – thus rendering the recollection and the analysis of the past all the more imperative. In *The Discourses*, Machiavelli had drawn upon this fund of ideas, stressing 'E questo è il cerchio nel quale girando tutte le republiche si sono governate et si governano' ['This, then, is the cycle through which all commonwealths pass, whether they govern themselves or are governed'].[51] Rather than mapping Time along linear axes, in his essay 'Of Vicissitude of Things' Bacon speaks of the 'turning wheels of vicissitude', and in an address to the Commons in 1607 he insisted that 'the time past is a pattern of the time to come' (vi. 517 and x. 311). He later offered a more refined strain of this belief in *De Augmentis*, arguing that the study of the 'latest' history yields the most certain results: 'For why should not that which has been lately done without any subsequent inconvenience be done again?' (Aphorism XXIII (v. 92)). If Ralegh, one of his most notable contemporaries participating in the debate surrounding historiography, submitted dolefully that 'wee may gather out of History … the comparison and application of other mens fore-passed miseries, with our owne like errours and ill deseruings', Bacon refused to construct futurity in such abject terms.[52] Rather than relying upon the guidance of 'fore-passed miseries', Bacon argued that memory could never operate as an intellectual *terminus ad quem* in the new scientific age of the seventeenth century. However, as we shall see, the discrepancy between the Baconian creed and its implementation can become increasingly evident under more sustained examination. With reference to the history of Henry VII, John Kenyon is timely in his emphasis that 'its sources were restricted, much more so than Bacon pretended – almost all his quotations are invented. It is really little more than an impressionistic sketch'.[53]

THE DISCIPLINE OF MEMORY: STATEMENT AND COUNTERSTATEMENT

Drawing deeply upon Senecan theories of translation, Bacon is perhaps most persuasive in his vision in 'The Refutation of Philosophies' of the discriminating intellectual drawing sustenance from a host of different sources:

> Now, sons, all are agreed that the arts and sciences fall under one of two categories, the empirical and the rational. What we have not been allowed to see till now is the proper mingling of the two. The Empirics, like ants, gather and consume. The Rationalists, like spiders, spin webs out of themselves. The Bee adopts the middle course, drawing her material from the flowers of the garden or the field, but transforming it by a faculty peculiar to herself. Such should be the activity of a genuine philosophy. It should draw its material from natural history and mechanical experience, but not take it unaltered into the memory, but digest and assimilate it for storing in the understanding.[54]

This kind of epistemological syncretism, forging strong links between systematic rational enquiry and the acquisition of pragmatic knowledge, clearly involves a high degree of creative expertise, whether it is in Seneca's ideal practice of translation or Bacon's hallowed quest for materialist knowledge. If John Kenyon reproaches Bacon for an overindulgence in Thucydidean creativity when approaching his subject of Henry VII, there are other, perplexing examples in Bacon's *œuvre* where the match between objectives and praxis remains uneasy. His *Historia Ventorum* (History of the Winds, published in 1622 in the *Historia Naturalis*) is a case in point. As can be seen in Figure 4, Bacon was at pains throughout his discussion

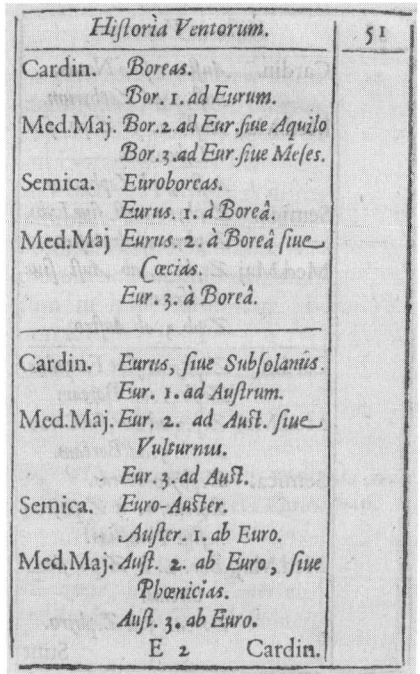
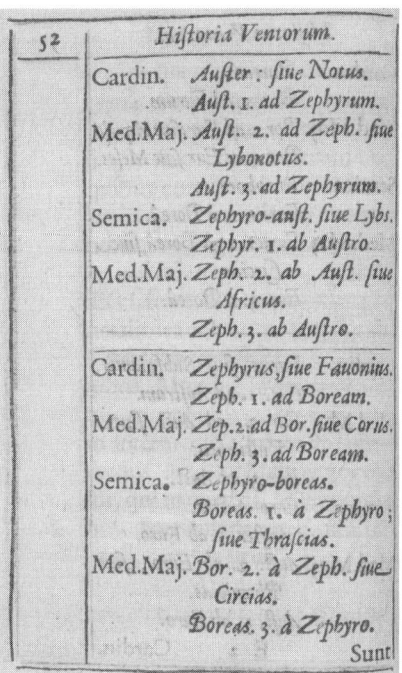

Figure 4. Francis Bacon, *Historia Ventorum* in *Historia Natvralis et Experimentalis ad Condendam Philosphiam siue, Phænomena Vniversi: Quæ est Instaurationis Magnæ Pars Tertia* (1622), pp. 51–2. Reproduced by permission of The Huntington Library, San Marino, California.

to identify, categorise, record and to store contentions and 'findings' in a coherent and systematic manner for the archive of the future. The reader is informed that 'For the sake of clearness and to assist the memory, we give a new set of names to the winds according to their order and degrees, instead of using the old proper names', and we are promptly furnished with an analytic listing to assist with this purpose (v. 145). Typographical formats, such as those offered in the *Historia Ventorum*, are thus deployed as spatial or organisational devices for knowledge acquisition: 'It does the mind a power of good to see how finite and comprehensible is the nature of things in tangible bodies. For the table gets to grips with nature as if in a wrestling match. Let no one therefore go astray or go in for fictions or dreams.'[35] Tables, diagrams and listings might also assist the investigator's memory in delimiting the field of enquiry prior to the formulation of the requisite axioms: 'hitherto more has been done in matter of invention by thinking than by writing ... little is to be hoped ... unless all the particulars which pertain to the subject of inquiry shall, by means of Tables of Discovery, apt, well arranged and, as it were, animate, be drawn up and marshalled; and the mind be set to work upon the helps duly prepared and digested which these tables supply' (iv. 96). Memory, with its grand store of sense impressions and cognitive associations, must thus give place to meticulous written records, enabling the careful processing of all results with the arrangement of data into tables. Nonetheless, the manner in which knowledge might be organised for future retrieval clearly continued to preoccupy a number of minds in the early modern period. In *The Holy State* (1642), for example, Thomas Fuller cautioned, '*Adventure not all thy learning in one bottom, but divide it betwixt thy Memory and thy Note-books.*'[56]

The whole discussion of the *Historia Ventorum* is punctuated with a host of *aperçus* on the chosen subject, reporting, for example, that 'The west winds are more violent than the east, and do more bend and wrench trees', and that 'Wet weather with an east wind continues longer than with a west, and generally lasts a whole day' (v. 157). Despite his declared quarry of 'certain' knowledge, in the *Historia Ventorum* Bacon produced a narrative that clearly demonstrated that his Age could not count on having the necessary (technological) knowledge or resources to perform adequate scrutiny and appraisal of such a subject. Confronted with this impassable gulf, this absolute dearth of materials and instruments with which to acquire the requisite data, Bacon tendered a carefully crafted amalgam of assertions, mostly lifted from the literatures of antiquity. The result is a discussion in which even observable fact is compelled to yield to all manner of accounts from folklore, mythology and speculation:

Pliny observes that in large pastures shepherds should take care to drive their flocks to the north side, that they may feed opposite to the south. For if they feed opposite the north, they get foot-rot, scouring, and blear eyes. The north wind likewise impairs their generative powers, so that if they look against the north wind as they copulate, they mostly produce ewe-lambs.[57]

Elsewhere, following an analogous *modus operandi* in the *Historia Densi et Rari* (History of Dense and Rare; or of the Coition and Expansion of Matter in Space (1623)), the reader is duly informed that 'Received opinion has it that at full moon the humours and juices not just in animals but also in plants swell and fill up the hollows more ... Butterflies moreover, which drop down dead in winter, get life and motion back again when they are put by the fire or in the Sun's rays'.[58] And in the *Sylva Sylvarum or A Natural History in Ten Centuries*, the speaker argues that 'it is true that the water of Nilus is sweeter than other waters in taste; and it is excellent good for the stone, and hypochondriacal melancholy' (ii. 587).

Bacon has deservedly won admiration down the centuries for seeking to establish an epoch-making intellectual programme for future enquiry: the momentous nature of such an undertaking is generously signalled at the very beginning, or 'Prooemium', to *The Great Instauration* that 'Francis of Verulam reasoned thus with himself, and judged it to be for the interest of the present and future generations that they should be made acquainted with his thoughts' (iv. 7).[59] However, Bacon may also demonstrate on occasions a prodigious reliance upon the very thing he repeatedly vilified – a memorial fund of apodictic knowledge. At such moments, we may witness not only the collapse of his declared aims but also the exhaustion of his Age's prevailing intellectual regime. Graham Rees concludes crisply that 'All in all, the *Historia ventorum* accomplishes the very considerable feat of making the weather boring' and laments that 'It contains little or nothing in the way of prodigies or weather marvels' and 'precious little jocundity'.[60] Yet, given the pursuit of his ambitious and particular goals at the turn of the seventeenth century, it remains unsurprising that even Bacon can find himself stymied in such enquiries when often the most that he can share with his readers is received thinking, lacunae and aporia (epistmological, perceptual, memorial or otherwise): 'The knowledge of the local origins of the winds is a difficult inquiry; for whence the wind cometh and whither it goeth is regarded even in Scripture as a mystery' (v. 159).

BACON AND THE *ARS MEMORATIVA*

In *De Augmentis*, Bacon lavishes a good measure of praise upon the practice of commonplacing, while remaining fully cognisant of the contrary (Platonic) arguments against the textualisation of memorial knowledge, and of the dismal failings of the commonplacing 'methods' in operation in his own times:

> there can hardly be anything more useful even for the old and popular sciences, than a sound help for the memory; that is a good and learned Digest of Common Places. I am aware indeed that the transferring of the things we read and learn into common-place books is thought by some to be detrimental to learning, as retarding the course of the reader and inviting the memory to take holiday. Nevertheless … I hold diligence and labour in the entry of common places to be a matter of great use and support in studying; as that which supplies matter to invention, and contracts the sight of the judgment to a point. But yet it is true

that of the methods and frameworks of common places which I have hitherto seen, there is none of any worth; all of them carrying in their titles merely the face of a school and not of a world; and using vulgar and pedantical divisions, not such as pierce to the pith and heart of things.[61]

Such discussions not only offer strategic insights into Bacon's appreciation that rational enquiry and meditation might involve recollection in order to function properly ('he who remembers or recollects, thinks' (see iv. 325)), they also shed light upon the ways in which the philosopher's intellectual ambitions were repeatedly thwarted by what he perceived as the blight of inane scholarly conventions and practices which had endured into the Jacobean present.

In her own wide-ranging and illuminating critical discussion, Victoria E. Burke has explored at length some of the broader anxieties surrounding 'memorial books' and commonplacing in seventeenth-century England, highlighting that, despite the intellectual ambitiousness of lawyers' commonplace books,

typically the rhetoric surrounding these compilations portrays an anxiety about a perceived slipping away from the original purpose of this form. Ideally, the form represented a record of a deep knowledge of the classics, an engagement with ancient culture, leading to one's own writing and speaking in an ethically informed manner. But if commonplace books aid the frailty of memory by amassing what other people think, then there is no guarantee that the compiler will exert the discipline of internalizing the knowledge for ethical behaviour.[62]

The growing emphasis in the early modern period upon the professionalisation of scholarly pursuits and public service inevitably had an impact upon the ways in which the faculty of memory was perceived, most particularly relating to the conditions of its mediation. As we have seen, as far back as antiquity there had been notable concerns voiced focusing upon the potentially attritional relationship between memory and textuality. Committed to the written record for the 'proficience' and preservation of human knowledge, Bacon nevertheless acknowledged that recollection might have an ethical as well as epistemological function, and that the human memory itself would benefit from a rigorous training regime. In this scheme of things, however, the subject's memorial improvement would not rely upon the *ars memorativa* but upon the *axiom-isation* of learning. In his *Apophthegms New and Old* (published 1624) he meditated upon the sustained benefits to a well-furnished mind of such a practice: apophthegms 'serve to be interlaced in continued speech. They serve to be recited upon occasion of themselves. They serve if you take out the kernel of them and make them your own' (vii. 123). Elsewhere, in a letter

(1596–1604?) to Sir Henry Savile, he underlined that the faculty might be significantly improved ('Artificial memory greatly holpen by exercise' (vii. 101)) if carefully subjected to incremental demands: 'the experience is manifest enough that the motions and faculties of the wit and memory may be not only governed and guided, but also confirmed and enlarged, by custom and exercise duly applied: as if a man exercise shooting, he shall not only shoot nearer the mark but also draw a stronger bow' (vii. 97). Thus, in this context, it must come as no surprise that in *De Augmentis* Bacon's readers are asked to assume an attitude of unrestrained awe when summoned into the presence of the memory expert:

> What a wonderful thing, for example, is that which is told of Caesar that he could dictate to five secretaries at once ... A thing inferior in use, but as a matter of display and ability perhaps still greater, is that which Cicero relates of his master Archias – that he could speak extempore a great number of excellent verses about anything that happened to be going on at the time. That Cyrus or Scipio could call so many thousands of men by name was a great feat of memory.[63]

Bacon's responses to the question of memorial training remained nuanced and supple in nature. He was no more implacable in his antagonism towards such crafts than he was towards the practices of alchemy – as we have seen, regarding experimentation and methodology, he could acknowledge on occasions that the enquiries of earlier centuries might still warrant considered attention. In his letter to Savile cited above, Bacon advised that the (wayward) memory might be held in check by demanding academic pursuits – 'if want of memory grow through lightness of wit and want of stayed attention, then the mathematics or the law helpeth; because they are things wherein if the mind once roam it cannot recover' (vii. 102). Equally strikingly, the philosopher also considered that dramatic representation might be beneficial in stimulating the power of recall and in assisting the socialisation of the [male] student: 'stage-playing ... strengthens the memory, regulates the tone and effect of the voice ... gives not a little assurance, and accustoms men to bear being looked at' (iv. 496). However, Bacon refrains from espousing or advocating the more formalised *ars memorativa*, nor is he any more sympathetic than the generation of Erasmus had been to the seemingly aimless practices of rote-learning, which continued to be witnessed in all manner of learning environments throughout the period. In his letter to Savile, he reiterated that he remained profoundly unpersuaded by the current 'exercises in the universities and schools', which compelled students 'either to speak by heart that which is set down *verbatim* or to speak *ex tempore*', instead of encouraging young minds 'to consider of heads; and then to form and fit the speech *ex tempore*. This would be done in two manners, both with writing and tables' (vii. 103). Indeed, in *De Augmentis*, he chose to follow in the footsteps of earlier generations of humanist scholars, arguing that

> for my own part (owing perhaps to the life of business I have led) I am ever disposed to make small account of things which make parade of art but are of no use. For the being able to repeat at once and in the same order a great number of names or words upon a single hearing, or to make a number of verses extempore on any subject … all such things I esteem no more than I do the tricks and antics of clowns and rope-dancers.[64]

When John Aubrey visited the Bacon family house at Gorhambury, he speculated whether Sir Nicholas Bacon (father to Francis) had not been mindful of the *ars memorativa* when he first conceived of certain aspects of the building's architecture: 'a stately gallery, whose glass windows are all painted; and every pane with several figures of beast, bird and flower: perhaps his lordship might use them as topics for local memory.'[65] Whatever the case, in *The Advancement of Learning*, Bacon himself focused specifically upon the *ars memorativa* that had so exercised some of the greatest intellects down the ages, pondering how the imaginative organisation of images (*imagines*) into architectural spaces (*loci*) might assist the performances of the rhetorician: 'This art of memory is but built upon two intentions; the one prenotion, the other emblem. Prenotion dischargeth the indefinite seeking of that we would remember, and directeth us to seek in a narrow compass, that is, somewhat that hath congruity with our place of memory.' Nonetheless, Bacon clearly believed that the satisfactory performance of rational enquiry (as opposed to that of memorial retention) required something more rigorous than the execution of mental gymnastics: 'Emblem reduceth conceits intellectual to images sensible, which strike the memory more; out of which axioms may be drawn much better practique than that in use; and besides which axioms, there are divers more touching help of memory, not inferior to them.' Desirous of promoting systematic investigation involving identification and painstaking categorisation in response to the laws of inductive thinking, Bacon unsurprisingly soon loses patience with the figurative nature of the diction and intellectual proceedings of the *ars memorativa*: 'But I did in the beginning distinguish, not to report those things deficient, which are but only ill managed' (iii. 398–9).[66] Similarly minded later in the century, Thomas Fuller would in turn offer his own vigorous treatment in *The Holy State* (1642) of the *ars memorativa*, claiming that

Artificiall memory is rather a trick then an art, and more for the gain of the teacher then profit of the learners. Like the tossing of a pike, which is no part of the postures and motions thereof, and is rather for ostentation then use, to shew the strength and nimblenesse of the arm, and is often used by wandring Souldiers as an introduction to beg. Understand it of the artificiall rules which at this day are delivered by Memory-mountebanks; for sure an art thereof may be made (wherein as yet the world is defective) and that no more destructive to naturall Memory then spectacles are to eyes, which girls in Holland wear from 12 years of age.[67]

In reviewing the multifariousness of Bacon's scholarly pursuits, Brian Vickers draws attention to an early 1594 notebook in which 'he seems to have set himself an exercise, writing out from memory all the quotations he could remember, a total of over 1,600 items, including 255 from Erasmus' *Adagia*, 110 from Virgil, 107 from the Bible, 46 from Ovid, a huge collection (443) of proverbs in Latin, French, Spanish, and Italian, together with a large number of metaphors, similes, and "mottoes", or brief phrases'.[68] Thus, even relatively early in his career, as he sought patrons among the elite of Elizabethan society, Bacon could clearly give ample testimony of his own formidable memorial expertise when called upon to do so.

In an early semi-dramatic piece, 'Of Tribute', he contended that 'A man is but what he knoweth' – but then there were always those troubling questions concerning how knowledge might be acquired and retained. Moreover, the very status of the *man who knoweth* did not go unquestioned in his own times. If there had been widespread evidence in the sixteenth century of the veneration for gifted scholars such as Erasmus, Philipp Melanchthon also submitted in one of his own learned orations to a university audience that, 'we scholars are not only despised, but also hated. Many believe that our labours are not something necessary for life, but slothful leisure. In fact, they even curse the theologians as "outcasts" and a plague of the state'.[69] In the next century, Bacon himself often poured scorn upon many of the superstitious practices of his contemporaries and forebears, but it is apparent that he was also keenly sensitive to the isolation that he experienced in Jacobean society. He remarked rather histrionically in 1608:

I have not even a person with whom I can converse on such subjects … why, I met not long ago a certain evil-eyed old fortune-telling woman, who … prophesied that my offspring should die in the desert.[70]

BACON REMEMBERING AND REMEMBERED

As his intellectual career progressed, Bacon was often drawn to conceive of the accumulation of knowledge (most particularly, 'the progress of the sciences') and the shape of the future in terms of conquest, acquisition and achievement (see viii. 123). In his essay 'Of Plantations' he argued that 'Plantations are amongst ancient, primitive, and heroical works', but then immediately conceded, 'when the world was young, it begat more children; but now it is old, it begets fewer' (vi. 457). His intellectual project was not, and indeed could not be, founded on apodictic pronouncements – he remained painfully aware that the present was not *inevitably* an improvement upon the past, and the future of humanity did not promise *inevitably* the advancement of learning: 'by far the greatest obstacle to the progress of the sciences and to the undertaking of new tasks and provinces therein, is found in this – that men despair and think things impossible' (iv. 90).

Given the often persuasive nature of Bacon's scientific evangelism and our subsequent knowledge of the development of the Scientific Revolution, we can lose sight of the very real opposition that such thinking encountered in early modern society. His fellow essayist Sir William Cornwallis, for example, would have been a notably reluctant member of Bacon's new, unfailingly inquisitive community of intellectuals: 'When I thinke of the abilities of man, I promise myselfe much out of my reading, but it prooues not so, Time goeth, and I turne leaues yet still finde my selfe in the state of ignorance … for I will choose rather to be an honest man then a good Logitian.'[71] The recurring thrust in Bacon's writing is that human potential can only be truly fulfilled by committing ourselves unceasingly to the expansion of materialist knowledge through carefully focused intellectual enquiry. Indeed, he honoured Julius Caesar precisely because 'in will and appetite he was one who never rested in what he had got, but ever pressed forward to timings beyond', and described his own ambition to his cousin Robert Cecil in July 1603 as one who hoped to 'be able to maintain memory and merit of the times succeeding' (vi. 341; x. 80).

Among his own contemporaries, Ben Jonson claimed Bacon as one of the most significant figures of the age in the 'Scriptorum Catalogus' of his own commonplace book, *Timber, or Discoveries*. In this distinguished roll of honour, Bacon was allowed to rub shoulders with Ralegh, Hooker and Sidney among others. Jonson hailed the *Novum Organum* as 'not penetrated, nor understood' by 'superficiall men', but proclaimed grandiloquently that 'it really openeth all defects of Learning whatsoever; and is a Booke'.[72] Later in the seventeenth century, a similarly minded Dryden would celebrate Bacon as one to whom the world 'does not only owe | Its present knowledge, but its future too'.[73] Indeed, there would have been no praise more eagerly anticipated by the natural philosopher who had, he declared in 'A New Abecedarium of Nature', 'little faith in the genius of our times' and thus devoted himself to 'posterity … knowing well enough the nature of the things that I impart, I deal out work for ages to come'.[74]

The critical reception of Bacon's natural philosophy continues to respond to the contrary motions so often discovered at the very heart of his intellectual meditations. Andrew Barnaby and Lisa J. Schnell, for example, have stressed that 'Bacon scholars have always been tempted to situate his writings at the beginning of something'.[75] However, equally convincingly, Charles Whitney argues that 'Bacon involves himself in a contradiction by judging, independently of the past, that the past must remain the basis for judgment'.[76] In fact, Bacon never really freed himself from the thrall of the past and on occasions he actively sought it out to dramatic effect, declaring, for example, to Buckingham in 1620 that, despite his fall from power, 'The King's state, if I should now die and were opened, would be found at my heart, as Queen Mary said of Calais' (xiv. 110). Ultimately, it may be most useful to view the natural philosopher as investing at regular intervals in what William E. Engel has termed 'monitory' memory (admonishing us to remember what may occur or what *is* to occur) and 'projective' memory (placing ourselves in the future and engaging with it in terms of our own prior mental narratives of fear and desire).[77] Both discourses demand that we make leaps of the imagination in time and in space.

At the base of Nicholas Hilliard's miniature (Figure 5) of the eighteen-year-old Bacon is marked 'Si tabula daretur digna, animum mallem' ['if one could but paint his mind'].[78] The course of this discussion has been governed by the desire to uncover some of the more neglected aspects to the cast of this mind. In defeat, at the end of his life, Bacon wrote a dedicatory address to Lancelot Andrewes, painting his own predicament in the 'examples of calamity in others'. In his determination to underline the precept from Ecclesiastes that 'no new thing is happened unto us', he alighted upon the examples of Demosthenes, Cicero and Seneca as worthy lenses through which to contemplate his own fall from power (see vii. 12). Indeed, he wrote to James VI/I in the aftermath of his disgrace in 1621 confessing

> I do now feed myself upon remembrance, how when your Majesty used to go a progress, what loving and confident charges you were wont to give me touching your business. For as Aristotle saith, young men may be happy by hope, so why should not old men, and sequestered men, by remembrance?[79]

Figure 5. Francis Bacon by Nicholas Hilliard © National Portrait Gallery, London.
Watercolour and bodycolour on vellum laid on card, 1578.

Thus, at the end of his life, he came to realise that there could in fact be no limit to his dealings with the past, and that he could not pass on a legacy (epistemological or political) to future generations that was not subject to dispute. In his own will, he submitted that 'for my name and memory, I leave it to men's charitable speeches, and to foreign nations, and the next ages' (xiv. 539). And it is clear that his memory has not always fared well. Whereas in 'Of Education' (1644) a Baconite Milton would argue that 'our hopeful youth' might journey to the outside world 'not to learn principles, but to enlarge experience and make wise observation', by the nineteenth century, voices of dissent regarding Bacon's *modus operandi* were more in evidence: George Henry Lewes, for example, gave him notably short shrift, remarking that the early modern philosopher 'may excite our admiration historically; [but] his method excites no admiration for its present intrinsic value'.[80] The conflicted memorialisation of Bacon's thinking has continued on into the modern age. Arthur B. Ferguson observes in his account of early modern historiography that 'Francis Bacon … demands our special attention, for no one of his generation reveals more clearly the developmental tendency in late Renaissance thought, or, more subtly, its limitations'; and, in turn, Julie Robin Solomon argues that 'Bacon's formulation of a discourse of scientific objectivity is a complex, dialectical, often contradictory, and ambiguous exercise'.[81]

However, if the pressures of memory understandably seem to have borne down increasingly upon the fallen Lord Chancellor in his final years, it should perhaps be remembered that the ungovernable faculty had been integrated firmly into the edifice of his intellectual project from the very beginning.

All those present pronounced the address worthy of the greatness of the human race and name, and deserving to be called candid rather than arrogant. They talked to one another saying that they were like men who had come suddenly out of thick shade into the open light and were for the moment dazzled, but carried with them a sure and happy augury of better sight to come.

Then the narrator asked me what I had to say to it. 'I am happy', I said, 'at what you had to tell.' 'Then', said he, 'if, as you say, you like it, will you, when you write on these matters, find room to include my report and not suffer the fruit of my travels to perish.' 'A fair request', said I, 'and I shall not forget.'[82]

Notes

INTRODUCTION: 'THE DARK BACKWARD AND ABYSM OF TIME'

1 William Shakespeare, *The Tempest*, ed. Frank Kermode (London: Methuen; New York: Arden, 1985).
2 Paul Ricoeur, *Time and Narrative*, vol. iii, trans. Kathleen Blamey and David Pellauer (University of Chicago Press, 1988), p. 227.
3 Paul Ricoeur, *Oneself as Another* (University of Chicago Press, 1992), pp. 140–1.
4 Andreas Huyssen, *Twilight Memories: Marking Time in a Culture of Amnesia* (New York and London: Routledge, 1995), p. 2.
5 Sir Philip Sidney, *The Countesse of Pembrokes Arcadia* (1593), Bk I, ch. 10, sig. 17^v–18^r.
6 See respectively, Pierre Nora, 'Entre mémoire et histoire' (pp. xvii–xlii), in Pierre Nora, *Les Lieux de mémoire*, vol. i (Paris: Editions Gallimard, 1984), p. xix; Mary Warnock, *Memory* (London: Faber and Faber, 1987), p. 6.
7 'To the Reader', in John Northbrooke, *Spiritus est vicarius Christi in terra* (1577), sig. A3^r.
8 'The Printer to the Reader', in John Rainolds, *Th'overthrow of stage-playes* (Oxford, 1599), sig. A2^r–A2^v.
9 (Attributed to) William Basse, *A Helpe to memory and discourse*, 2nd edn (1630; 1st pub. 1619), pp. 20–1.
10 Huyssen, *Twilight Memories*, p. 1.
11 Nora, 'Entre mémoire et histoire', *Les Lieux de mémoire*, vol. i, p. xvii.
12 William Rankins, *A Mirrour of Monsters* (1587), pp. 8–9.
13 He adds wistfully: 'At least, this has been true until very recent times.' See J. H. Plumb, *The Death of the Past* (Basingstoke: Macmillan, 1969), p. 41.
14 Mary J. Carruthers, *The Book of Memory: A Study of Memory in Medieval Culture* (Cambridge University Press, 1990), p. 1.
15 Frances A. Yates, *The Art of Memory* (London: Routledge and Kegan Paul, 1966); Paolo Rossi, *Logic and the Art of Memory: The Quest for a Universal Language*, trans. Stephen Clucas (London: Athlone, 2000); Janet Coleman, *Ancient and Medieval Memories: Studies in the Reconstruction of the Past* (Cambridge University Press, 1992); Lina Bolzoni, *The Gallery of Memory:*

Literary and Iconographic Models in the Age of the Printing Press, trans. Jeremy Parzen (University of Toronto Press, 2001).
16 See Carruthers, *The Book of Memory*, pp. 260 ff.
17 'Of the exercises of memorye and of the thre excellent continences of the tounge, wrathe, and the handes. Cap. x.', from *The education or bringinge vp of children, translated oute of Plutarche by syr Thomas Eliot knyght* (1532), sig. D4ᵛ–E1ʳ.
18 *The Castel of Memorie ... Made by Gulielmus Gratarolus ...* (1562), sig. B5ʳ.
19 *Meno* 81 c–d. Taken from G. M. A. Grube's translation in Plato, *Complete Works*, ed. John M. Cooper *et al.* (Indianapolis, IN and Cambridge: Hackett Publishing, 1997), p. 880.
20 *Phaedo* 75 e. See G. M. A. Grube's translation in Plato, *Complete Works*, p. 66.
21 *Theaetetus* 191 d–e. See M. J. Levett's translation (rev. Myles Burnyeat) in Plato, *Complete Works*, p. 212. In this context, see also 197 d–e and 198 d later in the same dialogue.
22 *Phaedo* 65 b, 65 c. See Plato, *Complete Works*, pp. 56–7.
23 Michel de Montaigne, *The Essayes*, 2nd edn (1613; 1st pub. 1603), Bk II, ch.12, p. 259.
24 Bk I, ch. 9: 'Of Lyers', in Montaigne, *The Essayes*, 2nd edn (1613), p. 15.
25 Francis Bacon, *The Works of Francis Bacon*, ed. J. Spedding, R. L. Ellis and D. D. Heath, 14 vols. (London: Longman *et al.*, 1857–74), iv. 325.
26 Thomas Hobbes, *Elements of Philosophy* (1656), Pt IV, xxv, 1, p. 290.
27 Book II, ch. 17: 'Of Presumption', in Montaigne, *The Essayes*, 2nd edn (1613), pp. 367–8.
28 Sigmund Freud, 'The Psychopathology of Everyday Life' (1901), in Sigmund Freud, *The Standard Edition of the Complete Psychological Works of Sigmund Freud* (London: Vintage, 2001), vi. 6, 7, 43.
29 Gratarolo, *The Castel of Memorie*, sig. B1ʳ.
30 Aristotle, *History of Animals*, i. 489b, trans. d'A. W. Thompson, in *The Complete Works of Aristotle: The Revised Oxford Translation*, ed. Jonathan Barnes (Bollingen Series LXXI-2), vol. i (Princeton University Press, 1984), 778.
31 Aristotle, *De Memoria et Reminiscentia*, 450a 20–30; 'On Memory', trans. J. I. Beare, *Complete Works*, i. 715.
32 Henri Bergson, *Matter and Memory*, trans. Nancy Margaret Paul and W. Scott Palmer (London: Swan Sonnenschein, 1991), p. 13.
33 'Cryptomnesia', in C. G. Jung, *The Collected Works of C. G. Jung: Psychiatric Studies*, trans. R. F. C. Hull, vol. i (London: Routledge & Kegan Paul, 1957), pp. 95–6, 98.
34 *On Memory*, 450a1 1. See Aristotle, *Complete Works*, p. 714.
35 *On Memory*, 453a1 5. See Aristotle, *Complete Works*, pp. 719–20.
36 *On Memory*, 450a1 12, 452 a1 13, 452 a1 17. See Aristotle, *Complete Works*, pp. 716, 718. In this context, see also the *Topics*, Bk VIII, 1 155b5, in Aristotle, *Complete Works*, p. 261.
37 See John Aubrey, *Aubrey's Brief Lives*, ed. Oliver Lawson Dick (London: Secker and Warburg, 1960), p. cv.

38 Cicero, *De Oratore*, II.ixxxvi.352–4, trans. E. W. Sutton and H. Rackham, Loeb Classical Library, 2 vols. (London: William Heinemann; Cambridge, MA: Harvard University Press, 1942), i. 465–7.
39 Elder Seneca, *Declamations*, trans. M. Winterbottom, Loeb Classical Library, 2 vols. (London: William Heinemann; Cambridge, MA: Harvard University Press, 1974), vol. i, *Controversiae*, Bk 1, Preface, 2, p. 5.
40 See [Elder] Pliny, *Natural History*, trans. H. Rackham, vol. ii (London: William Heinemann; Cambridge, MA: Harvard University Press, 1942), VII.xxiv–88, p. 563.
41 'The Induction', ll. 99–107, in John Marston, *The Malcontent*, ed. W. David Kay (London: A & C Black; New York: W. W. Norton, 2007), p. 14.
42 See the following section: 'Of an oracion deliberatiue': 'The narracion', in Leonard Cox, *The Art or Crafte of Rhetoryke* (1532), sig. D5^v.
43 John Brinsley, *Ludus literarius* (1612), p. 234.
44 The 1618 title is *Mnemonica, siue reminiscendi ars è puris artis naturaeque fontibus hausta, & in tres libros digesta*. In 1621, Willis published *The Art of Memory so far forth as it dependeth vpon places and idea's Written first in Latine*.
45 John Willis, *Mnemonica, or The Art of Memory drained out of the pure Fountains of Art & Nature digested into Three Books. Also a Physical Treatise of cherishing Natural Memory; diligently collected out of divers learned Mens Writings* (1661), pp. 140–1.
46 Warnock, *Memory*, p. 1.
47 *On Memory*, 453a1 15, 453b1 1. See Aristotle, *Complete Works*, p. 720.
48 Richard Edwards, *The excellent comedie of two the moste faithfullest freendes, Damon and Pithias* (1571), sig. C2^r.
49 Boncompagno da Signa, *Rhetorica novissima*, Bk 8. 'De Memoria', in Mary Carruthers and Jan M. Ziolkowski (eds.), *The Medieval Craft of Memory: An Anthology of Texts and Pictures* (Philadelphia: University of Pennsylvania Press, 2002), p. 108.
50 See Rossi, *Logic and the Art of Memory*, p. 25.
51 Gratarolo, *The Castel of Memorie*, sig. B3^v, C1^v, E1^v–E2^r.
52 See chap. 10, 'Of Memory', in Thomas Fuller, *The Holy State* (Cambridge, 1642), p. 176.
53 [Cicero], *Ad C. Herennium, De Ratione Dicendi* (*Rhetorica ad Herennium*), trans. Harry Caplan, Loeb Classical Library (London: William Heinemann; Cambridge, MA: Harvard University Press, 1954), III.xvi.28, p. 207.
54 *Ad C. Herennium*, II.xvi.28, pp. 264–5.
55 Quintilian, *The Institutio Oratoria of Quintilian*, trans. H. E. Butler (London: William Heinemann; Cambridge, MA: Harvard University Press, 1936), vol. iv: Bk XI.2.1, 18, 20–1, pp. 213, 221, 223.
56 We might also cite in this context of influential European tracts on the art of memory, Johann Romberch's *Congestorium artificiose memorie* (Venice, 1533), and Jacopo Publicio's *Oratoriae artis epitomata* (Venice, 1482).
57 'The prologue to this present boke', in Petrus Ravennas, *The Art of Memory, that otherwyse is called the Phenix* (c.1548), sig. A2^r.

58 Cited here from later edition: *The historie of graunde Amoure and la bell Pucel, called the Pastime of plesure co[n]teining the knowledge of the seue[n] sciences, [and] the course of mans life in this worlde* (1554), sig. F2ᵛ.
59 *The myrrour [and] dyscrypcyon of the worlde with many meruaylles [And] the vii. scyences as gramaye, rethorike wyth the arte of memorye, logyke, geometrye … and then arimetryke … and astronomy …* (1527), sig. D3ᵛ.
60 *De Oratore* II.xiv.62; trans. Sutton and Rackham, i. 243.
61 See respectively, Gratarolo, *The Castel of Memorie*, sig. A5ᵛ; John Foxe, *Pandectae locurum communium* (1572), sig. A3ᵛ.
62 See Walter J. Ong, *Ramus: Method, and the Decay of Dialogue* (Chicago and London: University of Chicago Press, 2004), esp. pp. 225 ff.; Rossi, *Logic and the Art of Memory*, pp. 97–102.
63 Abraham Fraunce, *The lawiers logike exemplifying the praecepts of logike by the practise of the common lawe* (1588), esp. fols. 1ᵛ, 4ʳ, 10ʳ⁻ᵛ, 34ᵛ, 80ᵛ, 88ʳ, 116ʳ.
64 Sir Philip Sidney, *A Defence of Poetry*, ed. Jan Van Dorsten (Oxford University Press, 1978), p. 51.
65 Sidney, *Arcadia*, Bk 1, ch. 1, sig. 1ᵛ. In this context, see also Bk 2, ch. 2, sig. 53ʳ.
66 Willis, *Mnemonica* (1661), pp. 52–3.
67 See *De Inventione* II.lii.158–liii, in Cicero, *De Inventione, De Optimo Genere Oratorum, Topica*, trans. H. M. Hubbell, Loeb Classical Library (London: William Heinemann; Cambridge, MA: Harvard University Press, 1949), p. 327.
68 Fernando Bouza, *Communication, Knowledge, and Memory in Early Modern Spain*, trans. Sonia López and Michael Agnew (Philadelphia: University of Pennsylvania Press, 1999), p. 3.
69 For an illuminating discussion of the artistic environments of the medieval and sixteenth centuries that also may have had a shaping influence upon this painting, see Simona Cohen, 'Titian's London Allegory and the Three Beasts of his *selva oscura*', *Renaissance Studies* 14:1 (March 2000), 46–69.
70 See, *On The Holy Trinity*, Bk x, ch. 11, in Philip Schaff (ed.), *A Select Library of the Nicene and Post-Nicene Fathers of the Christian Church*, vol. iii (Edinburgh: T & T Clark; Grand Rapids, MI: Eerdmans, 1993), p. 143.
71 Saint Augustine, *Confessions*, Bk x, viii (12), trans. Henry Chadwick, World's Classics (New York: Oxford University Press, 1991), p. 185.
72 Warnock, *Memory*, p. 16.
73 *Confessions*, Bk x, xiv (22), p. 192.
74 *Confessions*, Bk x, xii (19), xv (22), pp. 190, 192.
75 *Confessions*, Bk x, xvi (25), p. 193.
76 *Confessions*, Bk xi, xviii (23), xx (26), respectively, pp. 234, 235.
77 Albertus Magnus, *Liber de memoria & reminiscentia, Parva naturalia* [a commentary on Aristotle's *De Memoria et Reminiscentia*], trans. Jan M. Ziolkowski, in Carruthers and Ziolkowski, *The Medieval Craft of Memory*, p. 130.
78 See the translation of *De Bono*, in Carruthers, *The Book of Memory*, p. 268. For further discussion here, see Coleman, *Ancient and Medieval Memories*, pp. 62 ff.
79 See *De Bono*, in Carruthers, *The Book of Memory*, p. 269. For further discussion, see *The Book of Memory*, pp. 70 ff., 139 ff.

80 Aquinas, *In Aristotelis libros, De sensu et sensato, De memoria et reminscentia commentarium*, trans. John Burchill, in Carruthers and Ziolkowski, *The Medieval Craft of Memory*, p. 156.
81 Aquinas, *In Aristotelis libros*, in Carruthers and Ziolkowski, *The Medieval Craft of Memory*, p. 186.
82 See *Summa Theologiæ* 1a.84, 3 in Aquinas, *Summa Theologiæ*, vol. xii, ed. Paul T. Durbin (London: Eyre and Spottiswoode; New York: McGraw-Hill, 1968), p. 21.
83 Edmund of Abingdon, *The myrrour of the chyrche* (1521), sig. A3^v–A4^r.
84 Erasmus, *A booke called in latyn Enchiridion militis christiani, and in englysshe the manuell of the christen knyght* (1533), sig. Q7^v–Q8^r.
85 Quoted by Charles Fantazzi, in Juan Luis Vives, *The Education of a Christian Woman: A Sixteenth-Century Manual*, ed. and trans. Charles Fantazzi (Chicago and London: University of Chicago Press, 2000), p. 9.
86 Juan Luis Vives, *Vives: On Education: A Translation of 'De Tradendis Disciplinis' of Juan Luis Vives*, trans. Foster Watson (Cambridge University Press, 1913), p. 166. This sentiment is echoed a century later by John Brinsley in *The posing of the parts* (1615), sig. A2^v.
87 Vives, *Vives: On Education*, pp. 81, 95.
88 Vives, *Vives: On Education*, pp. 108–9.
89 *Parabolae* 72.1 (1534), in Erasmus, *The Collected Works of Erasmus*, vol. xxiii, ed. Craig R. Thompson, trans. R. A. B. Mynors (Toronto: University of Toronto Press, 1978), p. 212.
90 See *De ratione studii*, in Erasmus, *The Collected Works of Erasmus*, vol. xxiv, ed. Craig R. Thompson (University of Toronto Press, 1978), 671.
91 See, for example, Seneca, Letter LXXXIV, in Seneca, *Ad Lucilium Epistulae Morales*, trans. Richard M. Gummere, Loeb Classical Library, vol. ii (London: William Heinemann, 1930), pp. 277–81.
92 See John Nichols, *The Progresses and Public Processions of Queen Elizabeth*, 2 vols. (London: Nichols & Son, 1788), i. 10.
93 *Parabolae* (1534), in Erasmus, *The Collected Works*, xxiii. 244.
94 'To the most eminent scholar Martin Dorp, Theologian. Louvain' (1515). See More, *The Complete Works of St Thomas More*, vol. xv, ed. Daniel Kinney (New Haven, CT and London: Yale University Press, 1986), p. 47.
95 'The Argument', in George Gascoigne, *Glasse of gouernement: A tragicall comedie* (1575), sig. A3^r.
96 In this context, see Brinsley, *Ludus literarius*, p. 5, for example.
97 'The Author to the Reader', in William Camden, *Britain, or A chorographicall description of the most flourishing kingdomes, England, Scotland, and Ireland, and the ilands adioyning, our of the depth of antiquitie* (1610), sig. *5.
98 'Amyot to the readers', in Plutarch, *The lives of the noble Grecians and Romanes ... translated out of Greeke into French by Iames Amyot ... and out of French into Englishe, by Thomas North*, 2nd edn (1579), sig. *III^v.
99 Cited in Philip Schwyzer, *Literature, Nationalism, and Memory in Early Modern England and Wales* (Cambridge University Press, 2004), p. 61.

100 'TO THE HIGH AND MIGHTIE PRINCE *CHARLES Prince of Wales*', in Sir John Hayward, *The liues of the III. Normans, Kings of England William the first. William the second. Henrie the first* (1613), sig. A2ᵛ.
101 Bolzoni, *The Gallery of Memory*, see pp. 132–3.
102 Bolzoni, *The Gallery of Memory*, pp. 133–4.
103 Hélène Cixous, *Le Troisième Corps* (Paris: Grasset, 1970), p. 191.
104 Da Signa, *Rhetorica novissima*: Book 8 'De Memoria'. See Carruthers and Ziolkowski, *The Medieval Craft of Memory*, p. 106.
105 *The Castel of Memorie*, sig. B1ᵛ–B3ʳ.
106 Gilles Deleuze and Félix Guattari, *Anti-Oedipus: Capitalism and Schizophrenia*, trans. Robert Hurley et al. (London: Athlone Press, 1984), p. 42.
107 *Apius and Virginia* (1575), ed. Ronald B. McKerrow and W. W. Greg (London: Chiswick Press/Malone Reprints, 1911), sig. E3ʳ–E3ᵛ.
108 The cast for this scene details 'MEMORIE. ANAMNESTES. PHANTASTES. SENS. COM.' See Thomas Tomkis, *Lingua: or The combat of the tongue, and the fiue senses for superiority. A pleasant comoedie* (1607), sig. D3ᵛ. I am grateful to Dr Lina Perkins Wilder (Carleton College) for drawing my attention to this text.
109 Ricoeur, *Time and Narrative*, iii. 93.
110 Sidney, *Arcadia*, Bk I, ch.1, sig. A1ᵛ.
111 Mary Sidney Herbert, *The Collected Works of Mary Sidney Herbert, Countess of Pembroke*, ed. Margaret P. Hannay, Noel J. Kinnamen and Michael G. Brennan, 2 vols. (Oxford: Clarendon Press, 1998), vol. i, *Poems, Translations and Correspondence*, p. 295.
112 Richard Sennett, 'Disturbing Memories', in Patricia Fara and Karalyn Patterson (eds.), *Memory* (Cambridge University Press, 1998), p. 11.
113 Cited in Elizabeth Elliott, '"A memorie nouriched by images": Reforming the Art of Memory' in William Fowler's *Tarantula of Love*', *Journal of the Northern Renaissance*, 'Memory and the Northern Renaissance', 2:1 (Spring 2010).
114 Fulke Greville, *The Life of the renowned Sir Philip Sidney* (1652), ch. 1, p. 3.
115 Francis Bacon, *The Advancement of Learning and New Atlantis*, ed. Arthur Johnston (Oxford: Clarendon Press, 1980), iii.316.
116 Bouza, *Communication, Knowledge, and Memory in Early Modern Spain*, p. 2.
117 Giambattista Vico, *The New Science of Giambattista Vico*, trans. Thomas Goddard Bergin and Max Harold Fisch (Ithaca, NY and London: Cornell University Press, 1984). See respectively, Bk II: Poetic Wisdom, ch. 2 (699), pp. 264–5; Bk III: Discovery of the True Homer, ix (819), pp. 313–14.

1 'TO SEKE THE PLACE WHERE I MY SELF HADD LOST': ACTS OF MEMORY IN THE POETRY OF HENRY HOWARD, EARL OF SURREY

1 Puttenham, *The Arte of English Poesie* (1589), ed. Edward Arber (Westminster: A. Constable, 1895), p. 31: I.xix.

2 Juan Luis Vives, *On Education: A Translation of 'De Tradendis Disciplinis' of Juan Luis Vives*, trans. Foster Watson (Cambridge University Press, 1913), pp. 101–2.
3 The texts of Surrey's poems are taken from the following edition: Henry Howard, Earl of Surrey, *Poems*, ed. Emrys Jones (Oxford: Clarendon Press, 1964).
4 Greg Walker, *Writing Under Tyranny: English Literature and the Henrician Reformation* (Oxford University Press, 2005), p. 25.
5 Cited in Elizabeth Heale, *Wyatt, Surrey and Early Tudor Poetry* (London: Longman, 1998), p. 8.
6 Henry Howard, Earl of Surrey, *Selected Poems*, ed. Dennis Keene (Manchester: Carcanet, 1985), p. 14.
7 Alastair Fowler, *Conceitful Thought: The Interpretation of English Renaissance Poems* (Edinburgh University Press, 1975), p. 1.
8 Rory Rapple, *Martial Power and Elizabethan Political Culture: Military Men in England and Ireland, 1558–1594* (Cambridge University Press, 2009), p. 37.
9 C. W. Jentoft, 'Rhetoric and Structure in the Poetry of Henry Howard, Earl of Surrey', Ph.D. thesis, Ohio State University (1969), p. 2. Surrey's most recent biographer, Jessie Childs, appears equally cheerless: 'the Earl of Surrey is today an unfamiliar figure'. See Jessie Childs, *Henry VIII's Last Victim: The Life and Times of Henry Howard, Earl of Surrey* (London: Jonathan Cape, 2006), p. 3.
10 J. W. Lever, *The Elizabethan Love Sonnet* (London: Methuen, 1978), p. 38.
11 C. S. Lewis, *English Literature in the Sixteenth Century Excluding Drama* (Oxford: Clarendon Press, 1954), pp. 64, 234.
12 Heale, *Wyatt, Surrey and Early Tudor Poetry*, p. 3.
13 Sir Philip Sidney, *A Defence of Poetry*, ed. Jan Van Dorsten (Oxford University Press, 1978), p. 64.
14 See Agnes Heller, *Renaissance Man*, trans. Richard E. Allen (London: Routledge, 1978), p. 90. See also William A. Sessions, *Henry Howard, Earl of Surrey* (Boston, MA: Twayne, 1986), p. 23.
15 See respectively, Sir Thomas Elyot, *The Book named the gouernour* (1531), sig. F3^r: I.xii. 'Why gentilmen in this present tyme be nat equall in doctryne to the aunctient noble men'; Vives, *On Education*, p. 74.
16 *De Vita Solitaria*, Bk I, 1st Tractate, ch. 9. See Petrarch, *The Life of Solitude*, trans. Jacob Zeitlin (Urbana: University of Illinois Press, 1924), p. 151.
17 Jentoft, 'Rhetoric and Structure in the Poetry of Henry Howard', p. 44.
18 Sessions, *Henry Howard, Earl of Surrey*, p. 60.
19 Walker, *Writing Under Tyranny*, p. 432.
20 Sir Thomas Elyot, *The bankette of sapience* (1539), sig. B2^r.
21 Walter R. Davis, 'Contexts in Surrey's Poetry', *ELR* 4 (1974), p. 45. See also Sessions, *Henry Howard, Earl of Surrey*, p. 60.
22 John Willis, *Mnemonica; or, the Art of Memory* (London: Leonard Sowersby, 1661), p. 10.
23 Walker, *Writing Under Tyranny*, p. 404.
24 Elyot, *The Book named the gouernour*, sig. H1^v: Bk III.xxiv, 'Of Experience which haue preceded our tyme, with a defence of histories'.

25 *De Vita Solitaria*, Bk 1, 1st Tractate, ch. 4. See Petrarch, *The Life of Solitude*, trans. Zeitlin, pp. 135–6. In this context, see also Paul Oskar Kristeller, 'The Active and Contemplative Life in Renaissance Humanism', in Brian Vickers (ed.), *Arbeit, Musse, Meditation: Studies in the Vita activa and Vita contemplativa* (Zurich: Verlag des Fachvereine, 1991), pp. 139, 140.
26 Sonnet I, 1–2. For text and translation, see Garcilaso de la Vega, Sonnet I, in Edith Grossman (ed. and trans.), *The Golden Age: Poems of the Spanish Renaissance* (New York and London: W. W. Norton, 2007), pp. 42–3. (This mode is also taken up later in the century by Lope de Vega (1562–1635) – see *Rimas Sacras*, I.) In this context, see also Garcilaso de la Vega's sonnet x in which 'dulces prendas' (sweet mementoes) are accused of wishing 'verme morir entre memorias tristes' (to see me die of memories filled with grief) – sonnet x, 1, 14. See Grossman, *The Golden Age*, pp. 44–5.
27 Stephen Foley, 'The Honorable Style of Henry Howard, Earl of Surrey: A Critical Reading of Surrey's Poetry', unpub. Ph.D. thesis, Yale University (1979), p. 105.
28 *De Vita Solitaria*, Bk 1, 5th Tractate, ch. 4. See Petrarch, *The Life of Solitude*, trans. Zeitlin, p. 162.
29 See 'Introduction', in Vickers, *Arbeit, Musse, Meditation*, p. 2.
30 See respectively, C. S. Lewis, *Poetry and Prose in the Sixteenth Century* (Oxford: Clarendon Press, 1997), p. 231; Alicia Ostriker, 'Thomas Wyatt and Henry Surrey: Dissonance and Harmony in Lyric Form', *New Literary History* 1 (1970), p. 401.
31 See canzone 129 in Petrarch, *Canzoniere: Selected Poems*, trans. Anthony Mortimer (London: Penguin, 2002), pp. 62–3.
32 See canzone 272 in Petrarch, *Canzoniere: Selected Poems*, pp. 124–5.
33 H. A. Mason, *Humanism and Poetry in the Early Tudor Period* (London: Routledge, 1959), p. 239.
34 Peter M. Sacks, *The English Elegy: Studies in the Genre from Spenser to Yeats* (Baltimore, MD and London: Johns Hopkins University Press, 1985), p. 23.
35 Fowler, *Conceitful Thought*, p. 24.
36 Lewis, *English Literature in the Sixteenth Century Excluding Drama*, p. 231.
37 Cited in J. J. Scarisbrick, *Henry VIII* (London: Eyre Methuen, 1976), p. 621.
38 See Petrarch, *Canzoniere: Selected Poems*, pp. 88–9, 124–5. In this context, see sonnet 34 in Spenser's *Amoretti*: 'Lyke as a ship that through the Ocean wyde'.
39 Rather than Penelope, Sessions contends that in this poem, 'With the motifs of dreams and absence of the lover, the real subtext for this poem emerges: Vergil's Dido'. See *Henry Howard, Earl of Surrey*, p. 79.
40 See 'Le Narssis, pris d'Ovide, à François Charbonnier, Angevin', from Ronsard's collection *Le Bocage* (1554), in Pierre de Ronsard, *Œuvres complètes*, vol. vi, ed. Paul Laumonier (Paris: Hachette, 1930), pp. 75–6, ll. v.37–42. Translation from Pierre de Ronsard, *Selected Poems*, ed. and trans. Malcolm Quainton and Elizabeth Vinestock (London: Penguin, 2002), p. 118.
41 A. C. Spearing, *Mediaeval to Renaissance in English Poetry* (Cambridge University Press, 1985), p. 316.
42 Heale, *Wyatt, Surrey and Early Tudor Poetry*, p. 45.

43 Vives's text was first published in Latin in 1523 and its English translation was published in 1529. The text is anthologised in Kate Aughterson (ed.), *Renaissance Woman: Constructions of Femininity in England* (London: Routledge, 1995), p. 71.
44 Cited in Howard, Earl of Surrey, *Poems*, p. xxx.
45 Horace, *Satires, Epistles and Ars Poetica*, trans. H. Rushton Fairclough, Loeb Classical Library (London: William Heinemann; Cambridge, MA: Harvard University Press, 1991), ll. 128 ff., p. 461. See also Seneca, *Ad Lucilium Epistulae Morales*, trans. Richard M. Gummere, Loeb Classical Library, vol. ii (London: William Heinemann, 1930), pp. 279–80.
46 Pierre de Ronsard, *Œuvres complètes*, vol. ii, ed. Gustave Cohen (Paris: Gallimard/Pléiade, 1950), p. 1024.
47 Notwithstanding, in his *Ciceronianus* (1528) Erasmus insisted that in order to fulfil their creative potential later generations should distinguish their textual voices from those revered from the past. See *The Collected Works of Erasmus: Literary and Educational Writings*, vol. vi, ed. A. H. T. Levi (University of Toronto Press, 1986), p. 368.
48 For further discussion of early modern contexts for the *Aeneid* later in the century with reference to *Hamlet*, see Andrew Hiscock, *The Uses of this World: Thinking Space in Marlowe, Shakespeare, Cary and Jonson* (Cardiff: University of Wales Press, 2004), pp. 32–51.
49 Spearing, *Mediaeval to Renaissance in English Poetry*, p. 313.
50 Patricia Thomson, 'Wyatt and Surrey', in Christopher Ricks (ed.), *English Poetry and Prose, 1540–1674* (Harmondsworth: Penguin, 1993), p. 17.
51 Quoted in Jasper Ridley, *Henry VIII* (London: Constable, 1987), p. 345.
52 See Alistair Fox, *Politics and Literature in the Reigns of Henry VII and Henry VIII* (Oxford: Blackwell, 1989), p. 287.
53 See Susan Brigden, 'Henry Howard, Earl of Surrey and the "Conjured League"', *The Historical Journal* 37:3 (1994), 528.
54 See Howard, Earl of Surrey, *Poems*, p. xxiii.
55 See, for example, Roger Ascham, *The Scholemaster or plaine and perfite way of teachyng children* (1570), Book II: 'Imitatio', fol. 45 ff.
56 Puttenham, *The Arte of English Poesie*, p. 20.
57 Epigram LX, ll. 3, 5.
58 William Camden, *Britain, or A chorographicall description* (1610), pp. 8–9.
59 See Virgil, *Eclogues, Georgics, Aeneid I–VI*, trans. H. Rushton Fairclough, rev. G. P. Goold, Loeb Classical Library (Cambridge, MA and London: Harvard University Press, 1999), pp. 28–9. Unless indicated otherwise (as is the case above), the translations that follow in the notes are my own.
60 Heale, *Wyatt, Surrey and Early Tudor Poetry*, pp. 21–2.
61 See respectively, 'A Madame Marguerite, Soeur du Roy, Duchesse de Savoye' and 'Au Seigneur de Carnavalet', Ronsard, *Œuvres complètes*, i. 374, 379.
62 See canzone 74 in *Canzoniere*, pp. 38–9.
63 Canzone 129 in *Canzoniere*, pp. 66–7. See also canzone 126 and canzone 128.

64 See 'Epitaphe d'Anne, Duc de Montmorency, Pair est Connestable de France', Ronsard, *Œuvres complètes*, ii. 510.
65 See *Canzoniere*, pp. 56–7.
66 See *Canzoniere*, pp. 90–1.
67 In this context, see also Walker, *Writing Under Tyranny*, pp. 394, 396 and Colin Burrow, 'The Experience of Exclusion: Literature and Politics in the Reigns of Henry VII and Henry VIII', in David Wallace (ed.), *The Cambridge History of Medieval English Literature* (Cambridge University Press, 1999), p. 814.
68 C. W. Jentoft, 'Surrey's Five Elegies: Rhetoric, Structure, and the Poetry of Praise', *PMLA* 91 (1976), 23–4.
69 William A. Sessions, 'Surrey's Wyatt: Autumn 1542 and the New Poet', in Peter C. Herman (ed.), *Rethinking the Henrician Era: Essays on Early Tudor Texts and Contexts* (Urbana and Chicago: University of Illinois Press, 1994), p. 187.
70 Dennis Kay, *Melodious Tears: The English Funeral Elegy from Spenser to Milton* (Oxford: Clarendon Press, 1990), pp. 10–11.
71 Sessions, 'Surrey's Wyatt', p. 171.
72 See Thomas Whythorne, *Autobiography of Thomas Whythorne*, ed. James M. Osbourne (Oxford: Clarendon Press, 1961), p. 14.
73 Puttenham, *The Arte of English Poesie*, pp. 48–9: I.xxxi.
74 Cited in Sessions, 'Surrey's Wyatt', p. 176.
75 See respectively, 'A Preface, or rather a Briefe Apologie of Poetrie, and of the Author and Translator of this Poem', in Lodovico Ariosto, *Orlando Furioso in English. Heroical Verse by Iohn Harington* (1591), sig. ¶8ʳ; Thomas Nashe, *The Unfortunate Traveller* (1594); also *The Unfortunate Traveller*, in Paul Salzman (ed.), *An Anthology of Elizabethan Prose Fiction* (Oxford University Press, 1987), pp. 237, 239.

2 'REMEMBRE NOT (LORDE) MYNE OFFENCES': KATHERINE PARR AND THE POLITICS OF RECOLLECTION

1 All references (cited as *Prayers* in the text) are taken from Catharine [Katherine] Parr, *Prayers or medytacions* (1545). References to *The Lamentacion of a synner* are taken from Catharine [Katherine] Parr, *The Lamentacion of a synner* (London, 1547).
2 There also appeared an almost identical publication to the *Prayers or medytacions* from Berthelet's presses that is also dated June 1545, but which is attributed by Susan E. James to April 1545. This volume is entitled *Prayers stirring the mind unto heavenly meditations* and has the two concluding prayers of the first edition of *Prayers or medytacions*.
3 Initially, the collection was brought to a close with two prayers: 'A praier for the kynge' and 'A praier for men to saie enteryng into battayle'. Three more prayers were added for the November 1545 edition: 'A deuoute praier to be daiely saied' (extending material of the Lord's Prayer), 'An other praier', and 'A deuoute praier' (these latter two more clearly influenced by the conventions of the Psalms).

4 See Richard Younge, *The victory of patience and benefit of affliction* (1636), sig. A4ᵛ.
5 The previous year Elizabeth had sent Parr a copy of one of the latter's favourite works, Marguerite de Navarre's *Le Miroir de l'âme pécheresse*, with her own prose translation into English.
6 B. J. H. Biggs queries whether Whitford was indeed the translator of this edition. See B. J. H. Biggs (ed.), *The Imitation of Christ: The First English Translation of the 'Imitatio Christi'*, Early English Text Society (Oxford University Press, 1997), p. vii.
7 Greg Walker, *Writing Under Tyranny: English Literature and the Henrician Reformation* (Oxford University Press, 2005), p. 48.
8 For further discussion here, see Dakota L. Hamilton, 'The Household of Queen Katherine Parr', unpub. D.Phil. thesis, University of Oxford (1992), pp. 329–31. The sources for Hamilton's illuminating discussion are E. Charlton, 'Notes on Katherine Parr's Prayer Book Preserved at Sudeley Castle', *Notes and Queries* 2:44 (1850), 212, and Emma Dent, *Annals of Winchcombe and Sudeley* (London: John Murray, 1877), p. 182. See also James Kelsey McConica, *English Humanists and Reformation Politics under Henry VIII and Edward VI* (Oxford: Clarendon Press, 1965), pp. 204–5.
9 John Chrysostom, *A sermon of Saint Chrysostom ... translated into Englishe ... by Thomas Lupsette Londoner* (1542), sig. c8ᵛ.
10 The Latin anthology *Psalmi seu Precatores ex variis Scripturae locis collectae* (first published in Cologne in 1525 and attributed to John Fisher, Bishop of Rochester) had been published by Berthelet in April 1544.
11 William Atkinson, *A full deuoute and gostely treatyse* (1504), sig. A3ʳ.
12 Susan Wabuda, 'The Woman with the Rock: The Controversy on Women and Bible Reading', in Susan Wabuda and Caroline Litzenberger (eds.), *Belief and Practice in Reformation England* (Aldershot: Ashgate, 1998), p. 54.
13 McConica, *English Humanists and Reformation Politics*, p. 203.
14 Erasmus, *An exhortation to the diligent studye of scripture* (1529), no sig. 8th and 9th printed leaves in prefatory address to 'Christen Reader'.
15 See *De Conscribendi Epistolis*, in Erasmus, *The Collected Works of Erasmus*, vol. xxv, ed. J. K. Sowards (Toronto, Buffalo, NY and London: University of Toronto Press, 1985), pp. 32, 194.
16 Erasmus, *Preparation to deathe A booke as deuout as eloquent* (1538), sig. D4ᵛ.
17 See Henry Ellis (ed.), *Original Letters, Illustrative of English History*, 3 vols. (London: Harding, Triphook and Lepard, 1824), i. 239 ff.
18 David Scott Kastan, 'Print, Literary Culture and the Book Trade', in David Loewenstein and Janel Mueller, *Cambridge History of Early Modern English Literature* (Cambridge University Press, 2002), p. 90.
19 Thomas Lupset, *A compendious and a very frutefull treatyse* (1534), p. 37.
20 Susan E. James draws attention to the fact that Parr's mother wrote in 1524 to Lord Dacre with reference to Tunstall (then Bishop of London) that she valued 'the advice of my lord of London'. See Susan E. James, *Kateryn Parr* (Aldershot: Ashgate, 1999), p. 29.

21 See Cuthbert Tunstall, *Certaine godly and deuout prayers* (1558), sig B1ᵛ–B2ʳ.
22 See respectively, Erasmus, *Preparation to deathe* (1538), sig. D4ᵛ; John Hooper, *A Declaration of the ten holy co[m]maundments of allmygthye God* (1549), ch. 11, sig. CXCIII or O3ᵛ.
23 See 'To the moste vertuous Ladie Quene Katerine, late wife to the moste noble, and moste victorious king Henry the eigh of most famous memories, Nicolas Udal your moste humble seruaunt wisheth health, grace, and consolacion in our Lorde Jesus Christe euerlastyng', in Erasmus, *The first tome or volume* (1548), fol. XVIᵛ.
24 James, *Kateryn Parr*, p. 228.
25 In this, modern criticism is following Strype's lead who had submitted in his *Ecclesiastical Memorials* that he was 'apt to think Queen *Katherin* herself might do one at least, and perhaps that upon St *Matthew*'. See John Strype, *Ecclesiastical memorials* (1721), vol. ii, Bk 1, p. 30.
26 *In[j]unccions geuen by the moste excellent prince, Edward the sixt ... to al and singuler his louyng subiectes, as well of the clergie, as of the laietie* (1547), sig. C3ᵛ.
27 *In[j]unccions*, sig. A4ʳ.
28 Simon Fish, *A supplication of the poore commons Whereunto is added the supplication of beggers*, 2nd edn (1546), sig. 267 (A2ʳ), 297 (C1ʳ).
29 'W. T. vnto the Reader', in William Tyndale, *The Newe Testament* (Antwerp, 1534), sig. *6ʳ–*6ᵛ.
30 'An answere vnto the fyrst chapyter of Tyndales boke, why he translateth this wode chyrche in to thys worde congregacion', in Sir Thomas More, *The confutacyon of Tyndales answere* (1532–3), sig. XCV.
31 Walker, *Writing Under Tyranny*, p. 25.
32 Quoted in Walker, *Writing Under Tyranny*, p. 135.
33 See Thomas Lupset, *An exhortation to yonge men*, 2nd edn (1535), sig. 42ʳ.
34 Paul L. Hughes and James F. Larkin (eds.), *Tudor Royal Proclamations*, 3 vols. (New Haven, CT: Yale University Press, 1964–9), i. 296–8.
35 Cited in Kenneth Charlton and Margaret Spufford, 'Literacy, Society and Education', in Loewenstein and Mueller, *Cambridge History of Early Modern English Literature*, p. 30.
36 William Tyndale, *Prolog in to the seconde boke of Moses called Exodus. Second boke of Moses, called Exodus ...* [The Pentateuch] (1530), sig. A6ᵛ.
37 See also 'Tourne not thy face from me, deferre not thy visityng of me, ne withdraw not thy comfortes, leste happely my soule be made as drie earthe without the water of grace' (Tyndale, *Prolog in to the seconde boke of Moses called Exodus*, sig. D1ʳ).
38 Bernard of Clairvaux, *The meditat[i]ons of saint Bernard* (1496), sig. A3ʳ, A3ᵛ. This particular collection is reprinted in 1499 and 1525 in the early Tudor period, and accompanied by published translations of Bernard's 'Golden Epistle' and the 'Treatise of Good Living'.
39 Augustine, *Confessions*, trans. Henry Chadwick, World's Classics (Oxford University Press, 1998), Bk X, xiv (22), p. 192.

40 For further discussion here, see Janet Coleman, *Ancient and Medieval Memories: Studies in the Reconstruction of the Past* (Cambridge University Press, 1992), pp. 182 ff.
41 Erasmus, *A booke called in latyn Enchiridion militis christiani, and in englysshe the manuell of the christen knyght* (1533), sig. A6^v.
42 See, for example, John Donne, *The Sermons of John Donne, in Ten Volumes*, ed. George R. Potter and Evelyn M. Simpson (Berkeley and Los Angeles: University of California Press, 1953–62), ii. 11.236.
43 John N. King, *English Reformation Literature: The Tudor Origins of the Protestant Tradition* (Princeton University Press, 1982), p. 16.
44 See posthumous publication of Latimer's sermons: *27 sermons preached by … the ryght Reuerende father Maister Hugh Latimer*, 2nd edn (1562), sig. 56^v.
45 See William Baldwin, *A treatise of morall phylosophie* (1547), sig. K2^r.
46 Henry Brinkelow, *The lamentacyon of a Christe[n]*, 2nd edn (1548).
47 Brinkelow, *The lamentacyon of a Christe[n]*, sig. A2^r–A2^v, A3^r–A3^v.
48 Brinkelow, *The lamentacyon of a Christe[n]*, sig. D2^v, D3^r, D4^r.
49 Janel Mueller, 'A Tudor Queen Finds Voice: Katherine Parr's *Lamentation of a Sinner*', in Heather Dubrow and Richard Strier (eds.), *The Historical Renaissance: New Essays on Tudor and Stuart Literature and Culture* (University of Chicago Press, 1988), pp. 27–8.
50 *The Letters of Stephen Gardiner*, ed. James Arthur Muller (Cambridge University Press, 1933), p. 163.
51 *The Lamentacion of a synner*, sig. A4^r, F5^v.
52 John Foxe, *Acts and Monuments* (1570), Bk VIII, p. 1422.
53 For further discussion here, see Andrew Hiscock, '"A supernal liuely fayth": Katherine Parr and the Authoring of Devotion', *Women's Writing* 9:2 (2002), 177–97.
54 James, *Kateryn Parr*, p. 265.
55 Parr, *The Lamentacion of a synner*, sig. B4^r–B4^v.
56 This is taken from the later English translation. See Martin Luther, *A treatise, touching the libertie of a Christian* (1579), sig. D5^v.
57 'An homelie, or sermon, of good woorkes annexed vnto the faithe', in *Certayne sermons, or homelies appoynted by the kynges Maiestie* (1547), sig. H3^r.
58 Foxe, *Acts and Monuments* (1570 edn), Bk VIII, p. 1424.
59 A. G. Dickens, *The English Reformation* (London: Fontana/Collins, 1978), p. 52.
60 See *The First and Second Prayer Books of Edward VI*, introduction by Revd E. C. S. Gibson (London: Dent, 1964), p. 3.
61 *Concerning the Ministry*, 1523. The Latin text is excerpted in B. J. Kidd (ed.), *Documents Illustrative of the Continental Reformation* (Oxford: Clarendon Press, 1911), p. 124.
62 Parr, *The Lamentacion of a synner*, sig. A5^v, D2^v–D3^r.
63 For Cecil's comments, see prefatory epistle to Parr, *The Lamentacion of a synner*, unnumbered.
64 Prefatory epistle to the Parr, *The Lamentacion of a synner*, unnumbered.
65 As has been appreciated above, the exception here would be Margaret Beaufort.
66 James, *Kateryn Parr*, p. 239.

67 Parr, *The Lamentacion of a synner*, sig. A1ʳ–A1ᵛ.
68 Parr, *The Lamentacion of a synner*, sig. A4ᵛ.
69 For further discussion here, see Mueller, 'A Tudor Queen Finds Voice', pp. 19, 24–5, 31–3; James, *Kateryn Parr*, p. 205; W. P. Haugaard, 'Katherine Parr: The Religious Convictions of a Renaissance Queen', *Renaissance Quarterly* 22:4 (1969), p. 349; Janel Mueller, 'Complications of Intertextuality: John Fisher, Katherine Parr, and "The Book of the Cruxifix"', in Claude J. Summers and Ted-Larry Pebworth (eds.), *Representing Women in Renaissance England* (Columbia: University of Missouri Press, 1997), pp. 29–30; Hamilton, 'The Household of Queen Katherine Parr', p. 365; McConica, *English Humanists*, pp. 204–5.
70 Mueller, 'Complications of Intertextuality', p. 29.
71 King, *English Reformation Literature*, p. 89.
72 Wabuda, 'The Woman with the Rock', p. 56.
73 See respectively, 26 Jan. 1547: Bullinger receives information from Richard Hilles who is in Strasbourg that Parr and Earl of Hertford are sympathetic to reformed religion (Henry VIII, *Letters and Papers, Foreign and Domestic, of the Reign of Henry VIII, 1509–1547*, ed. J. S. Brewer, J. Gairdner and R. H. Brodie, 22 vols. (London: 1862–1932), vol. xxi, ii.752); John Buxton, *Calendar of Letters, Despatches, and State Papers, Relating to the Negotiations Between England and Spain, 1485–1552* [*Calendar of State Papers, Spain*], vol. viii (1545–6), ed. Martin A. S. Hume (1904), 368 (Henry VIII, *Letters and Papers*, vol. xxi, ii. 756); 5 Dec. 1547: Imperial ambassador reports to Charles V that mass no longer celebrated in households cited above, *Calendar of State Papers, Spain*, vol. ix. 221. I am indebted to Dakota L. Hamilton's thesis for drawing my attention to these details in 'The Household of Queen Katherine Parr', pp. 325–7.
74 *Kateryn Parr*, p. 234.
75 See respectively, Carole Levin, 'Women in *The Book of Martyrs* as Models of Behaviour in Tudor England', *International Journal of Women's Studies* (Canada) 4:2 (1981), p. 205; Foxe, *Acts and Monuments* (1570), Bk viii, p. 1422.
76 Foxe, *Acts and Monuments* (1570), Bk viii, p. 1424.
77 See respectively, Roland H. Bainton, *Women of the Reformation in France and England* (Minneapolis, MN: Augsburg Publishing House, 1973), p. 159; David Loades, *The Tudor Queens of England* (London: Continuum, 2009), pp. 133, 135.
78 Mueller, 'Complications of Intertextuality', p. 26.
79 George Sandys, *Anglorum speculum, or, The worthies of England in church and state* (1684), p. 839.

3 'BETTER A FEW THINGS WELL PONDERED, THAN TO TROUBLE THE MEMORY WITH TOO MUCH': TROUBLING MEMORY AND MARTYR IN FOXE'S *ACTS AND MONUMENTS*

1 Foxe, *Acts and Monuments* (1583), p. 1718; all following London editions abbreviated in the text as *Acts*, followed by the date of publication. Biblical citations respectively, from John 19, 1 Cor. 15, 2 Tim. 3, John 15, Col. 2 and John 15.

2 Foxe drew his text from a work previously published by John Olde. See Nicholas Ridley and Hugh Latimer, *Certein godly, learned and comfortable conference between N. Rydeley bishoppe of London, and Hughe Latymer* (1556).

3 Indeed, as Patrick Collinson has observed, 'We now know that Foxe himself was responsible for almost none of the words of the most famous story of all, the martyrdom of Ridley and Latimer, or perhaps only for the lines beginning "Be of good comfort Master Ridley", which made their first appearance in 1570.' See Patrick Collinson, 'John Foxe and National Consciousness', in Christopher Highley and John N. King (eds.), *John Foxe and His World* (Aldershot: Ashgate, 2002), p. 13.

4 Helen C. White makes the important point that 'To us today the word "martyr" in its commonest use suggests "sufferer". But in the beginning of Christian history it meant "witness"'. See Helen C. White, *Tudor Books of Saints and Martyrs* (Madison: University of Wisconsin Press, 1963), p. 4.

5 For further discussion here, see Jane Facey, 'John Foxe and the Defence of the English Church', in Peter Lake and Maria Dowling (eds.), *Protestantism and the National Church in Sixteenth-Century England* (London: Croom Helm, 1987), pp. 174 ff.

6 Juan Luis Vives, *An introduction to wysedome* (1558), sig. C4^{r-v}.

7 See 'A. P. to the Reader', in Sir John Hayward, *The first part of the life and raigne of King Henrie the IV* (1599), sig. A3^{r}.

8 *Acts* [1583], p. 1395.

9 Foxe, *Pandectae locurum communium* (1572), sig. A3^{r}.

10 I am indebted for these calculations to the following studies: Warren W. Wooden, *John Foxe* (Boston, MA: Twayne, 1983), pp. 20, 50; Margaret Aston and Elizabeth Ingram, 'The Iconography of *The Acts and Monuments*', in David Loades (ed.), *John Foxe and the English Reformation* (Aldershot: Scolar Press, 1997), pp. 79–80.

11 John N. King, 'Religious Dissidence in Foxe's *Book of Martyrs*: Humanism or Heresy?', *Religion and Literature* 32:2 (2000), p. 141.

12 For further discussion here, see Patrick Collinson, 'John Foxe and National Consciousness', in Highley and King, *John Foxe and His World*, p. 26.

13 *A Booke of certaine Canons, concernyng some parte of the discipline of the Church of England* (1571), sig. A3^{r}. David Loades underlines that 'Many parishes followed of their own volition … It was never a popular book in the sense of widespread ownership, because it was far too bulky, and far too expensive, for the average literate Englishman to buy'. See 'Introduction: John Foxe and the Editors', in Loades, *John Foxe and the English Reformation*, p. 4.

14 William Harrison, 'A Description of England': Bk II, ch. 9 'Of Pallaces belonging to the prince, and court of Englande', in Raphael Holinshed, *The first volume of the chronicles of England, Scotlande, and Irelande* (1577), p. 84.

15 Foxe scholarship has also noted the importance of the works of Matthias Flacius of Illyria (such as the *Catalogus Testium Veritatis*) and the Magdeburg Centuries that he edited. Also of particular influence on Foxe is the religio-historical writing of John Bale. For further reading, see Wooden, *John Foxe*,

esp. pp. 26 ff.; V. Norskov Olsen, *John Foxe and the Elizabethan Church* (Los Angeles: University of California Press, 1973), esp. pp. 20 ff.
16 For a lively discussion here, see Deborah Anne Meister, 'The Burning Bush: Tudor Martyrs and the Construction of Subjectivity in the English Renaissance', Ph.D. thesis, University of California, Los Angeles (1999), p. 70.
17 For further discussion of critical and theoretical appreciations of Foxe's narrative experimentation, see Andrew Hiscock, '"writers to solemnise and celebrate … Actes and memory": Foxe and the Business of Textual Memory', in Andrew Hiscock (ed.), *The Yearbook of English Studies: Tudor Literature*, 38:1 & 38:2 (2008), 68–85.
18 See Sharon Achinstein, 'John Foxe and the Jews', *Renaissance Quarterly* 54 (Spring 2001), p. 87 and Richard Helgerson, *Forms of Nationhood: The Elizabethan Writing of England* (Chicago and London: University of Chicago Press, 1992), p. 253. See also, for example, Colin Burrow, 'The Sixteenth Century', in Arthur F. Kinney (ed.), *The Cambridge Companion to English Literature, 1500–1600* (Cambridge University Press, 2000), p. 18; Isabelle Fernandes, 'Les Représentations du martyr dans *The Acts and Monuments* de John Foxe, ou la tentation théâtrale', *Revue des Sciences Humaines* 269 (2003), 135–51; Patrick Collinson, 'Truth and Legend: The Veracity of John Foxe's Book of Martyrs', in A. C. Duke and C. A. Tomse (eds.), *Clio's Mirror: Historiography in Britain and the Netherlands* (Zutphen: De Walburg Pers., 1985), p. 31.
19 *Acts* [1583], pp. 1177–8.
20 *Acts* [1563], p. 1471.
21 *Acts* [1583], p. 1717.
22 R. Malcolm Smuts, *Culture and Power in England, 1585–1685* (London: Macmillan, 1999), p. 41.
23 For an interesting discussion of the humanist context for Foxe's approach to the writing of history, see Ruth Ann Jones, 'John Foxe and the Humanist Concept of History', Ph.D. thesis, University of Missouri-Columbia (1989), esp. pp. 156 ff.
24 *Acts* [1563], p. 137. In this context, see also *Acts and Monuments* (1570), p. 63.
25 *Acts* [1563], p. 675. For discussion of the importance of the secular narrative of Roman history in *The Acts and Monuments*, see Michael S. Pucci, 'Reforming Roman Emperors: John Foxe's Characterization of Constantine in the *Acts and Monuments*', in David Loades (ed.), *John Foxe: An Historical Perspective* (Aldershot: Ashgate, 1999), pp. 30–51; Tom Betteridge, 'From Prophetic to Apocalyptic: John Foxe and the Writing of History', in Loades, *John Foxe and the English Reformation*, esp. pp. 217–19.
26 John N. King, *English Reformation Literature: The Tudor Origins of the Protestant Tradition* (Princeton University Press, 1982), p. 437. Warren W. Wooden underlines that, 'despite an almost medieval controlling design and an embarrassingly frank bias in the work, many modern scholars have come to concede that Foxe's respect for documentation and habit of including primary sources in his text marks a significant advance in the development of English historiography' (Wooden, *John Foxe*, p. 21).

27 See David Daniell, 'Tyndale and Foxe', in Loades, *John Foxe: An Historical Perspective*, p. 19. For further discussion here, see John N. King, 'Fiction and Fact in Foxe's Book of Martyrs', in Loades, *John Foxe and the English Reformation*, pp. 14–15; D. R. Woolf, 'The Rhetoric of Martyrdom: Generic Contradiction and Narrative Strategy in John Foxe's *Acts and Monuments*', in Thomas F. Mayer and D. R. Woolf (eds.), *The Rhetorics of Life-Writing in Early Modern Europe: Forms of Biography from Cassandra Fedele to Louis XIV* (Ann Arbor: University of Michigan Press, 1995), pp. 269–70.
28 'To the Professed Friends and Followers of the Pope's Proceedings'.
29 Anthony Low, *The Reinvention of Love* (Cambridge University Press, 1993), p. 53.
30 See 'The Author to the Reader', in William Camden, *Britain, or A chorographicall description of the most flourishing kingdomes, England, Scotland, and Ireland, and the ilands adioyning, our of the depth of antiquitie* (1610), sig. *6.
31 For further discussion here, see F. J. Levy, *Tudor Historical Thought* (San Marino, CA: Huntington Library, 1967), p. 102.
32 For further discussion here, see Meister, 'The Burning Bush', p. 89.
33 See *A Sermon of Christ Crucified* (1570), sig. B2^v–B3^r.
34 Facey, 'John Foxe and the Defence of the English Church', in Lake and Dowling, *Protestantism and the National Church in Sixteenth-Century England*, p. 167. Frances Yates also made the broad point that 'Roughly speaking, for Foxe the church was pure when persecuted under the pagan emperors and when early Christian emperors guided its councils; impure when the bishops of Rome took the lead'. See *Astraea: The Imperial Theme in the Sixteenth Century* (London and Boston, MA: Routledge and Kegan Paul, 1975), p. 43.
35 Alec Ryrie, 'The Unsteady Beginnings of English Protestant Martyrology', in David Loades (ed.), *John Foxe: An Historical Perspective* (Aldershot: Ashgate, 1982), p. 437. See also Helgerson's contention that 'Fundamental to apocalyptic as a narrative form is the continuing struggle between mighty opposites: Christ and Antichrist, God and Satan, the true church and the church of this world' (*Forms of Nationhood*, p. 256).
36 *Acts* [1583], p. 1146.
37 *Acts* [1583], p. 1419.
38 *Acts* [1583], p. 1794.
39 For further discussion here, see Olsen, *John Foxe and the Elizabethan Church*, pp. 134 ff.
40 *Acts* [1563], sig. B6^r.
41 For further discussion here, see A. Forty, 'Introduction', in A. Forty and S. Küchler (eds.), *The Art of Forgetting* (Oxford: Berg, 1999) and C. N. Seremtakis, *The Senses Still: Perception and Memory as Material Culture in Modernity* (University of Chicago Press, 1994). In this context, Arthur B. Ferguson is particularly illuminating in his discussion of Reformist bibliolatry. See *Clio Unbound: Perception of the Social and Cultural Past in Renaissance England* (Durham, NC: Duke University Press, 1979), pp. 133 ff.

42 Helen C. White stresses that 'When the invention of printing came to make books cheaper and so more easily available to the reading public, the Legenda Aurea led even the Bible in number of imprints, one hundred and fifty-six as against one hundred and twenty-eight for the fifteenth century' (*Tudor Books of Saints and Martyrs*, p. 26). The last recorded publication of the *Golden Legend* was by Wynkyn de Worde in August 1527.
43 Translated from 1563 prefatory address 'As Doctum Lectorem', cited at Loades, *John Foxe and the English Reformation*, p. 210. Indeed, John N. King notes that 'Except for a brief interval under Henry VIII, the only vernacular form in which English laymen could approach the Bible prior to Edward VI's reign was Caxton's translation of Jacobus de Voragine's *The Golden Legend*. This collection of saints' lives occupied a place in late medieval lay devotion similar to that which the Bible had held in the early Christian period' (*English Reformation Literature*, p. 38). For further evidence of Foxean debunking of the *Legenda Aurea* in *The Acts and Monuments*, see Foxe's record of Edward VI's supposedly derisive response to the legend of St George (*Acts* [1583], p. 1395).
44 *Acts* [1583], p. 88.
45 *Acts* [1583], p. 2033. For further discussion here, see White, *Tudor Books of Saints and Martyrs*, p. 164.
46 In this context, see also *Acts and Monuments* (1583), p. 1717.
47 Daniell, 'Tyndale and Foxe', in Loades, *John Foxe: An Historical Perspective*, p. 24. For the critical debate concerning the generic affinities of *The Acts and Monuments*, see, for example, Wooden, *John Foxe*, pp. 42–3, and Woolf in 'The Rhetoric of Martyrdom', in Mayer and Woolf, *The Rhetorics of Life-Writing in Early Modern Europe*, pp. 243–82.
48 *Acts* [1583], pp. 1703–4. Nevertheless, perhaps one of the most arresting narratives of captivity for Foxe's reader is that which is devoted to John Bolton, who in 1554 was persecuted for his public repudiation of the Catholic mass. See *Acts and Monuments* (1563), p. 1017.
49 *Acts* [1583], p. 1819.
50 Catherine Cubitt, 'Memory and Narrative in the Cult of Early Anglo-Saxon Saints', in Yitzhak Hen and Matthew Innes (eds.), *The Uses of the Past in the Early Middle Ages* (Cambridge University Press, 2000), p. 30.
51 I. Ross Bartlett, 'John Foxe as Hagiographer: The Question Revisited', *Sixteenth Century Journal* 27:4 (1995), 773.
52 For further discussion here, see Helgerson, *Forms of Nationhood*, pp. 269 ff.; Fernandes, 'Les Représentations du martyr', pp. 135–51.
53 Interestingly, Foxe the Protestant is keen to underline in a postscript, 'Such was then (sayeth Eusebius) the blessed bonde of mariage among the Saintes of God', *Acts and Monuments* (1570), p. 55 (pagination not corrected).
54 *Acts* [1583], p. 1032.
55 *Acts* [1583], p. 1557.
56 William Haller, *Foxe's Book of Martyrs and the Elect Nation* (London: Jonathan Cape, 1963), p. 50.
57 Cubitt, 'Memory and Narrative', in Hen and Innes, *The Uses of the Past*, p. 34.

58 Ernest Renan, 'Qu'est-ce qu'une nation?' – 1882 lecture. For further discussion, see Martin Thorn's translation 'What is a Nation?', in Homi K. Bhabha (ed.), *Nation and Narration* (New York: Routledge, 1990), p. 11. See also discussion of Foxean formulations of the English nation in David Loades, 'Literature and National Identity', in David Loewenstein and Janel Mueller (eds.), *The Cambridge History of Early Modern English Literature* (Cambridge University Press, 2002), esp. pp. 227 ff.; Claire McEachern, *The Poetics of English Nationhood, 1590–1612* (Cambridge University Press, 1996), esp. pp. 30 ff.; Andrew Escobedo, *Nationalism and Historical Loss in Renaissance England: Foxe, Dee, Spenser and Milton* (Ithaca, NY and London: Cornell University Press, 2004), p. 4.
59 *Acts* [1583], p. 557. For further discussion here, see V. Norskov Olsen, *John Foxe and the Elizabethan Church*, p. 52.
60 Garrett Sullivan Jr, *Memory and Forgetting in English Renaissance Drama* (Cambridge University Press, 2005), p. 2.
61 Foxe, *A Sermon of Christ Crucified* (1570), sig. c4^v. Although preachers such as Hugh Latimer, for example, were equally willing to remind those in authority of their own obligations, he blasted during one of his Easter sermons to the court, 'And, you rulers and officers, be wise and circumspecte, loke to your charge & see you do your duties; and rather be gladde to amend your yll liuyng, then to be angrye when you are warned or tolde of your faulte.' See *A notable sermon of ye reuerende father Maister Hughe Latemar which he preached in ye Shrouds at paules churche in London, on the xviii. daye of Ianuary 1548* (1548), sig. B1^r.
62 Foxe, *A Sermon preached at the Christening of a certaine Iew* (1578), sig. M4^r–M4^v.
63 Foxe, *A Sermon of Christ Crucified* (1570), sig. D4^r–D4^v.
64 For further consideration of typological interpretation in *The Acts and Monuments*, see Wooden, *John Foxe*, esp. pp. 52 ff.
65 Sharon Achinstein, 'John Foxe and the Jews', p. 99.
66 *Acts* [1570], p. 139 (pagination not corrected).
67 Pucci, 'Reforming Roman Emperors: John Foxe's Characterization of Constantine in the *Acts and Monuments*', in Loades, *John Foxe: An Historical Perspective*, p. 33.
68 Patrick Collinson emphasises the disenchantment of many radical Elizabethan Protestants by the 1570s 'in a country still menaced from within and without by resurgent Catholicism, and by no means safe in the hands of a Queen whose own religious commitment appeared to be lukewarm'. See 'Literature and the Church', in Loewenstein and Mueller, *Cambridge History of Early Modern Literature*, p. 383.
69 Pagination not corrected.
70 Wooden, *John Foxe*, p. 24.
71 *Acts* [1570], p. 91 (pagination not corrected).
72 Pagination not corrected.

73 Claire McEachern, 'Introduction', in Claire McEachern and Debora Shuger (eds.), *Religion and Culture in Renaissance England* (Cambridge University Press, 1997), p. 4.
74 *Timber, or Discoveries*, in Ben Jonson, *Ben Jonson*, ed. C. H. Herford and Percy and Evelyn Simpson, 11 vols. (Oxford: Clarendon Press 1925–52), viii. 578.

4 TEXT, RECOLLECTION AND ELIZABETHAN FICTION: NASHE, DELONEY, GASCOIGNE

1 Thomas Nashe, *The vnfortunate traueller. Or, The life of Iacke Wilton* (1594), sig. L3^v. Hereafter, *The vnfortunate traueller*.
2 Thomas Wilson, *The Arte of Rhetorique for the vse of all suche as are studious of eloquence* (1553), fol. 112.
3 Mikhail Bakhtin, 'Epic and Novel: Toward a Methodology for the Study of the Novel', in M. M. Bakhtin, *The Dialogic Imagination: Four Essays*, ed. Michael Holquist, trans. Caryl Emerson and Michael Holquist (Austin: Texas University Press, 2000), p. 23.
4 *The vnfortunate traueller*, sig. L3^v.
5 Arthur Kinney, *Humanist Poetics: Thought, Rhetoric, and Fiction in Sixteenth-Century England* (Amherst: Massachusetts University Press, 1986), p. 336.
6 Richard Terdiman, *Present Past: Modernity and the Memory Crisis* (Ithaca, NY and London: Cornell University Press, 1993), p. 12.
7 In this context, see Patrick H. Hutton, *History as an Art of Memory* (Hanover, NH and London: University of Vermont/University Press of New England, 1993), p. 19: 'With the coming of print culture, memory was historicized in more concrete ways. Print culture textualized the past … The textualizing of collective memory deepened the readers' awareness of temporality, and this in turn led to the recasting of mnemonic schemes, previously conceived spatially, onto timelines on which historical events served as places of memory … The past could be neither repeated (as in oral culture) nor resurrected (as in manuscript culture) but only reconstructed.'
8 Miguel de Cervantes Saavedra, *Don Quixote*, pt. 1, ch. 15. See Cervantes, *The Adventures of Don Quixote*, trans. J. M. Cohen (Harmondsworth: Penguin, 1981), p. 116.
9 *Don Quixote*, pt. 1, ch. 25. See *Don Quixote*, trans. Cohen, p. 211.
10 *Don Quixote*, pt. 1, ch. 13. See *Don Quixote*, trans. Cohen, p. 97.
11 Bakhtin, 'Epic and Novel', p. 19. In this context, Kim L. Worthington is also helpful in her investigations into the ways in which memory and narrative may interact to offer the possibility of 'a more or less stable conceptual framework from which to begin to understand the present and anticipate the future'. See *Self as Narrative: Subjectivity and Community in Contemporary Fiction* (Oxford: Clarendon Press, 1996), pp. 15 ff.
12 Bakhtin, 'Epic and Novel', p. 19.
13 Nashe, *The vnfortunate traueller*, sig. L3^v–L4^v.
14 Walter C. Davis, *Idea and Act in Elizabethan Fiction* (Princeton University Press, 1969), p. 136.

15 Nashe, *The vnfortunate traueller*, sig. F3ᵛ.
16 Davis, *Idea and Act in Elizabethan Fiction*, p. 217.
17 See respectively, *The Defense of Poesy*, ll. 802–12, in *Sir Philip Sidney: A Critical Edition of the Major Works*, ed. Katherine Duncan-Jones (Oxford University Press, 1989), pp. 231–2; Ben Jonson, *Ben Jonson*, ed. C. H. Herford and Percy and Evelyn Simpson, 11 vols. (Oxford: Clarendon Press 1925–52), vii. 256 (ll. 214–16). See also *The Poetaster* in which Caesar blurs his own identity with that of his bard: 'Welcome to CAESAR, VIRGIL. CAESAR, and VIRGIL | Shall differ but in sound; to CAESAR, VIRGIL | (Of his expressed greatnesse) shall be made | A second sur-name, and to VIRGIL, CAESAR' (v.ii.2–5). See *Ben Jonson*, iv. 294.
18 See Petrarch, *Canzoniere: Selected Poems*, trans. Anthony Mortimer (London: Penguin, 2002), pp. 42–3.
19 William A. Sessions, 'Surrey's Wyatt: Autumn 1542 and the New Poet', in Peter C. Herman (ed.), *Rethinking the Henrician Era: Essays on Early Tudor Texts and Contexts* (Urbana and Chicago: University of Illinois Press, 1994), p. 171.
20 See respectively, Ann Rosalind Jones, 'Inside the Outsider: Nashe's *vnfortunate traueller* and Bakhtin's Polyphonic Novel', *ELH* 50 (1983), p. 78; *The vnfortunate traueller*, sig. A4ʳ–A4ᵛ.
21 Nashe, *The vnfortunate traueller*, sig. C4ᵛ.
22 Nashe, *The vnfortunate traueller*, sig. L2ᵛ–L3ʳ.
23 John Carey, 'Sixteenth- and Seventeenth-Century Prose', in Christopher Ricks (ed.), *English Poetry and Prose, 1540–1674* (Harmondsworth: Penguin, 1993), p. 361.
24 For wider discussion of Jack's social vision of the masquing realm of 'Dry dusty' in this text, see Andrew Hiscock, '"Blabbing leaves of betraying paper": Configuring the Past in Gascoigne's *Adventures of Master F. J.*, Nashe's *The Unfortunate Traveller* and Deloney's *Jack of Newbury*', *English* 52:202 (Spring 2003), pp. 4–5.
25 Thomas Deloney, *The pleasant historie of Iohn Winchcomb in his* [younger] *yeares called Iack of Newbury*, 10th repr. (1626), sig. M1ᵛ–M2ʳ. Hereafter, *Jack of Newbury*.
26 Garrett Sullivan Jr, *Memory and Forgetting in English Renaissance Drama* (Cambridge University Press, 2005), p. 40.
27 John Stow, *A Survey of the Cities of London and Westminster ... Written at first in the Year MDXCVIII. By John Stow ... Now Lastly Corrected, Improved, and very much Enlarged ... By John Strype*, 2 vols. (1720), ii. 333. For further details, see Eugene P. Wright, *Thomas Deloney* (Boston, MA: Twayne, 1981), pp. 54 ff.; Jane M. Kinney, 'Rewriting History: Thomas Deloney's *Jack of Newbury*', *West Virginia University Philological Papers* 44 (1998–9), pp. 51–2.
28 'Popular-Festive Forms and Images in Rabelais', in Mikhail Bakhtin, *Rabelais and His World*, trans. Hélène Iswolsky (Bloomington: Indiana University Press, 1984), p. 255.
29 Kinney, 'Rewriting History: Thomas Deloney's *Jack of Newbury*', p. 50.

30 David Margolies, *Novel and Society in Elizabethan England* (London: Croom Helm, 1985), p. 144.
31 Judith Broome Mesa-Pelly, 'Fantasy and Social Change in Thomas Deloney's *Jack of Newbury* and *Thomas of Reading*', *Studies in the Humanities* 23:1 (1996), p. 87.
32 Laura Caroline Stevenson, *Praise and Paradox: Merchants and Craftsmen in Elizabethan Popular Literature* (Cambridge University Press, 1984), p. 2.
33 Norman Jones, *The English Reformation: Religion and Cultural Adaptation* (Oxford: Blackwell, 2002), p. 115. In this context, Christopher Burlinson in his study of Spenserian poetics has drawn attention to changing cultural responses to the statements made by the construction of the gallery during the sixteenth century: 'The gallery is a place where expectations and systems of power can be upended and overturned.' See *Allegory, Space and the Material World in the Writings of Edmund Spenser* (Cambridge: D.S. Brewer, 2006), p. 69.
34 Bakhtin, 'Epic and Novel', p. 18. Concerning the degree to which Gascoigne was aspiring to 'gentlemanly' status with the publication of *A Hundreth Sundrie Flowres*, see Gillian Austen, *George Gascoigne* (Cambridge: D. S. Brewer, 2008), pp. 69 ff.
35 Sir Philip Sidney, *The Countesse of Pembrokes Arcadia* (1593), Bk 1, ch. 3, sig. 5^r.
36 Sidney, *Arcadia*, Bk 1, ch. 13, sig. 25^v.
37 Thomas Deloney, *Jack of Newbury*, sig. G4^r.
38 'To the reuerende Diuines, vnto whome these Posies shall happen to be presented ... ', in *The Posies of George Gascoigne Esquire. Corrected, perfected, and augmented by the Author* (1575), sig. ¶2^r.
39 For further discussion here, see Austen, *George Gascoigne*, pp. 75 ff.
40 Gascoigne, *The Posies*, sig. K3^r.
41 Moreover, in the 1575 version: the prefatory material involving A.B., H.W and G.T. is dispensed with; one Bartello is credited with authorship and the setting for the narrative is moved to Italy; the narrator G.T. is lost; some erotic scenes are toned down and some poems removed; the character of Frances dies without redemption; F.J. goes off to lament in Venice; and the Elinor character appears to prosper. For further discussion here, see: Josephine Bloomfield, 'Gascoigne's *Master F. J.* as a Renaissance Proto-Novel', *Essays in Literature* 19:2 (1992), 163–72; Charles W. Smith, 'Structural and Thematic Unity in Gascoigne's *The Adventures of Master F. J.*', *Papers on Language and Literature* 2 (1966), 99–108.
42 'A Pleasant discourse of the aduentures passed by Master F.J.', in George Gascoigne, *A hundreth sundrie flowres* ... (1573), p. 203. Hereafter, 'Pleasant discourse'.
43 William Webbe, *A discourse of English poetrie Together with the author's iudgment, touching the reformation of our English verse* (1586), sig. I3^r.
44 Gascoigne, 'Pleasant discourse', p. 247.
45 In this context, David W. Price is illuminating in a more generalised discussion of polyvocality in textualised representations of the past. See *History*

Made, History Imagined: Contemporary Literature, Poiesis and the Past (Urbana and Chicago: University of Illinois Press, 1999), esp. pp. 9 ff.
46 Gillian Austen, 'Gascoigne's *Master F. J.* and its Revision, or, "You ain't heard nothin' yet!"', in Wolfgang Görtschacher and Holger Klein (eds.), *Narrative Strategies in Early English Fiction* (Lewiston, NY: Edwin Mellen, 1995), p. 77.
47 Gascoigne, 'Pleasant discourse', pp. 244–5.
48 See respectively, F. Schelling, *The Life and Writings of George Gascoigne* (Boston, MA: Ginn, 1893), pp. 18–19; R. S. White, *Shakespeare and the Romance Ending* (Newcastle upon Tyne: Tyneside Press, 1981), p. 12.
49 Michel Foucault, 'Film and Popular Memory', trans. Martin Jordin, in Michel Foucault, *Foucault Live (Interviews 1966–84)*, ed. Sylvère Lotringer (New York: Semiotext(e), 1989), p. 92.
50 Lynette McGrath, 'George Gascoigne's Moral Satire: The Didacticism of Convention in *The Adventures of Master F. J.*', *Journal of English and Germanic Philology* 11 (1971), 432–50.
51 Gascoigne, 'Pleasant discourse', p. 231.
52 Gascoigne, 'Pleasant discourse', p. 234.
53 Subsequently, after the secretary's return to the house, Gascoigne's reader is informed, 'it fell out that the *Secretary* hauing bin of long time absent, & thereby his quils & pennes not worn so neer as they were wont to be, did now prick such faire large notes, y^t his Mistres liked better to sing faburden vnder him, than to descant any longer vppon F. J.'s playne song' (p. 272).
54 'Epic and Novel', p. 7.
55 C. S. Lewis, *English Literature in the Sixteenth Century Excluding Drama* (Oxford: Clarendon Press, 1954), p. 418.
56 Carey, 'Sixteenth- and Seventeenth-Century Prose', p. 348.
57 See respectively, A. C. Hamilton, 'Elizabethan Romance: The Example of Prose Fiction', *ELH* 49:1 (1982), p. 287; Andrew Hadfield, 'Prose Fiction', in Michael Hattaway (ed.), *A Companion to English Renaissance Literature and Culture* (Oxford: Blackwell, 2000), p. 576.
58 R. Malcolm Smuts, *Culture and Power in England, 1585–1685* (London: Macmillan, 1999), p. 4.
59 Hadfield, 'Prose Fiction', p. 579.
60 Thomas Healy, *New Latitudes: Theory and English Renaissance Literature* (London: Edward Arnold, 1992), p. 4.
61 Elizabeth Tonkin, *Narrating our Pasts: The Social Construction of Oral History* (Cambridge University Press, 1992), p. 9.
62 Nashe, *The vnfortunate traueller*, sig. A2^r, O4^r.

5 THE DOLEFUL CLORINDA? MARY SIDNEY, COUNTESS OF PEMBROKE, AND THE VOCATION OF MEMORY

1 See Cicero, *Tusculun Disputations*, trans. J. E. King (London: William Heinemann; Cambridge MA: Harvard University Press, 1950), pp. 68–9.

2 Sir Edward Denny to Lady Mary Wroth. HMC, Salisbury (Cecil), XXII, 161. Quoted in Josephine A. Roberts (ed.), *The Poems of Lady Mary Wroth* (Baton Rouge: Lousiana State University Press, 1983), p. 239.
 3 Fulke Greville, *The Life of the renowned Sir Philip Sidney* (1652), p. 3.
 4 'To My Deare Lady and Sister, The Covntess of Pembroke', in Sir Philip Sidney, *The Countess of Pembrokes Arcadia. Written by Sir Philip Sidney Knight. Now since the first edition augmented and ended* (1593), sig. ¶3ᵛ.
 5 'To The Reader', in Sidney, *The Countess of Pembrokes Arcadia*, sig. ¶4ʳ.
 6 Sidney, *The Countesse of Pembrokes Arcadia*, Bk 1, ch. 1, sig. A1ʳ.
 7 Quoted in Kate Aughterson (ed.), *Renaissance Woman: Construction of Femininity in England* (London: Routledge, 1995), p. 27.
 8 Mary Ellen Lamb, 'The Countess of Pembroke's Patronage', *English Literary Renaissance* 12:2 (1982), 162.
 9 'To the Right Honourable and Most Vertuous Lady, the Countesse of Pembroke'. See Edmund Spenser, *The Faerie Queene*, ed. Thomas P. Roche Jr and C. Patrick O'Donnell Jr (Harmondsworth: Penguin, 1987), p. 32.
10 *Complaints Containing sundrie small poemes of the worlds vanitie* (1591), sig. A3ʳ, A3ᵛ.
11 For further discussion here, see H. R. Woudhuysen, *Sir Philip Sidney and the Circulation of Manuscripts, 1558–1640* (Oxford: Clarendon Press, 1996); Arthur F. Marotti and Michael D. Bristol (eds.), *Print, Manuscript & Performance: The Changing Relations of the Media in Early Modern England* (Columbus: Ohio State University Press, 2000); William H. Sherman, *John Dee: The Politics of Reading and Writing in the English Renaissance* (Amherst: University of Massachusetts Press, 1995); Peter Beal, *In Praise of Scribes: Manuscripts and their Makers in Seventeenth-Century England* (Oxford: Clarendon Press, 1998); Alexandra Shepard and Phil Withington (eds.), *Communities in Early Modern England: Networks, Place, Rhetoric* (Manchester University Press, 2000).
12 Elisabeth van Houts, *Memory and Gender in Medieval Europe, 900–1200* (London: Palgrave, 1999), p. 6.
13 'The epistle to the reader', in Richard Younge, *The victory of patience and benefit of affliction … together with a counterpoyson or antipoyson against all griefe* (1636), sig. A2ʳ.
14 Margaret P. Hannay, '"House-confinèd maids": the Presentation of Women's Role in the Psalmes of the Countess of Pembroke', *English Literary Renaissance* 24:1 (Winter 1994), 44–5.
15 Michel de Montaigne, *The Essayes*, 2nd edn (1613; 1st pub. 1603), Bk 1, ch. 9, p. 15.
16 'A Dedication to Sir Philip Sidney', ch. XIV. See *The Prose Works of Fulke Greville, Lord Brooke*, ed. John Gouws (Oxford: Clarendon Press, 1986), p. 93.
17 Paul Ricoeur, *Time and Narrative*, vol. I, trans. Kathleen McLaughlin and David Pellauer (University of Chicago Press, 1984), p. 3.
18 Paul Antze, 'Telling Stories, Making Selves: Memory and Identity in Multiple Personality Disorder', in Paul Antze and Michael Lambek (eds.), *Tense Past: Cultural Essays in Trauma and Memory* (New York: Routledge, 1996), p. 10.

19 *De Memoria et Reminiscentia* 450a25.
20 All citations of Pembroke's writing are taken from Mary Sidney Herbert, *The Collected Works of Mary Sidney Herbert, Countess of Pembroke*, ed. Margaret P. Hannay, Noel J. Kinnamon and Michael G. Brennan, 2 vols. (Oxford: Clarendon Press, 1998).
21 Suzanne Trill, 'Spectres and Sisters: Mary Sidney and the "Perennial Puzzle" of Renaissance Women's Writing', in Gordon McMullan (ed.), *Renaissance Configurations: Voices/Bodies/Spaces, 1580–1690* (London: Macmillan, 1998), p. 202.
22 Elizabeth Mary Tilyou, 'Fician Element in Selected Poems of Mary Sidney Herbert, Countess of Pembroke', in Dorothy L. Latz (ed.), *Neglected English Literature: Recusant Writings of the 16th–17th Centuries* (Salzburg: Institut für Anglistik und Amerikanistik, 1997), p. 50.
23 Richard Hooker, *A remedie against sorrow and feare, delivered in a funerall sermon* (1612), p. 8.
24 Michael Neill, *Issues of Death: Mortality and Identity in English Renaissance Tragedy* (Oxford: Clarendon Press, 1998), p. 2.
25 'To the Reader', in Anne Dowriche, *The French historie* (1589), sig. A3^v.
26 Mary Ellen Lamb, *Gender and Authorship in the Sidney Circle* (Madison: University of Wisconsin Press, 1990), p. 10.
27 Montaigne, *The Essayes*, 2nd edn (1613), sig. A2^r.
28 *Marcus Tullius Ciceroes thre bookes of duties* (1558), sig. C3^r. Quoted in Rivkah Zim, *English Metrical Psalms: Poetry as Praise and Prayer, 1535–1601* (Cambridge University Press, 1987), p. 12. In this context, see Kathleen M. Swaim, 'Contextualising Mary Sidney's Psalms', *Christianity and Literature* 48:3 (Spring 1999), 257.
29 'To the moste puissant prince, and our moste redoubted soueraigne Lord Edward the sixthe … [by] Nicolas Udal', in Erasmus, *The first tome or volume of the Paraphrase of Erasmus upon the Newe Testamente* (1548), sig. B3^v.
30 Robert Garnier, *Œuvres complètes*, vol. i, ed. Lucien Pinvert (Paris: Garnier Frères, 1923), p. 165.
31 'The Translator to the Reader earnestlye desyreth grace, mercy, and peace', in William Fulwood, *The Castel of Memorie … Made by Gulielmus Gratarolus* (1562), sig. A6^r–A6^v.
32 For further discussion here, see, for example, *The Collected Works of Mary Sidney Herbert, Countess of Pembroke*, i. 39 ff.
33 For further discussion here, see Andrew Hiscock, *The Uses of this World: Thinking Space in Marlowe, Shakespeare, Cary and Jonson* (Cardiff: University of Wales Press, 2004), pp. 83–113.
34 Karen Raber, *Dramatic Difference: Gender, Class and Genre in the Early Modern Closet Drama* (Newark: University of Delaware Press, 2001), p. 44.
35 Thomas Lupset, *A compendious and a very frutefull treatyse, teachynge the waye of dyenge well written to a frende* (1534), sig. D1^v–D2^r.
36 *A discourse of life and death. Written in French by Ph. Mornay. Antonius, a tragædie written also in French by Ro. Garnier. Both done in English by the Countesse of Pembroke* (1592), sig. A2^r.

37 For further discussion here, see Katherine Duncan-Jones and Jan Van Dorsten (eds.), *Miscellaneous Prose of Sir Philip Sidney* (Oxford: Clarendon Press, 1973), pp. 155 ff.
38 Victor Skretkowicz, 'Mary Sidney Herbert's Antonius, English Philhellenism and the Protestant Cause', *Women's Writing* 6:1 (1999), 8.
39 Chapter IV in Elizabeth Grymeston, *Miscelanea, Meditations, Memoratiues* (1604), sig. C3^r.
40 'Death's Duel', in *John Donne: Selected Prose*, ed. Helen Gardner and Timothy Healy (Oxford: Clarendon Press, 1967), p. 382.
41 *A discourse of life and death*, sig. A3^r, D3^r.
42 *A discourse of life and death*, sig. C3^r, D2^r.
43 Raphael Holinshed, *The Third volume of Chronicles* (1587), p. 1551.
44 Peter Sherlock, *Monuments and Memory in Early Modern England* (Aldershot: Ashgate, 2008), p. 126.
45 Gary Waller notes that Roger Ascham 'bewailed that Englishmen revered the Trionfi above Genesis'. See *Mary Sidney, Countess of Pembroke: A Critical Study of her Writings and Literary Milieu* (University of Salzburg, 1979), p. 144.
46 Lamb, *Gender and Authorship in the Sidney Circle*, p. 141. See also Trill, 'Spectres and Sisters', in McMullan, *Renaissance Configurations*, p. 197.
47 'Proposition', in Sidney, *A Defence of Poetry*, ed. Jan Van Dorsten, p. 25. For an invaluable discussion here, see Zim, *English Metrical Psalms*, pp. 1 ff.
48 *De Memoria et Reminiscentia* 449b30, in Richard Sorabji (ed.), *Aristotle on Memory* (London: Duckworth, 1972), p. 48.
49 Fulwood, *The Castel of Memorie*, sig. F6^r.
50 For an overview of this, see Sidney Herbert, *The Collected Works*, ed. Hannay et al., pp. 119 ff.; Waller, *Mary Sidney, Countess of Pembroke*; Margaret P. Hannay, *Philip's Phoenix*, p. 65.
51 Edmund Spenser, *Colin Clouts come home againe* (1595), sig. F4^v.
52 Peter M. Sacks, *The English Elegy: Studies in the Genre from Spenser to Yeats* (Baltimore, MD: Johns Hopkins University Press, 1985), p. 2.
53 Angelica Goodden, *The Backward Look: Memory and the Writing Self in France, 1580–1920* (Oxford: Legenda, 2000), p. 3.
54 Grymeston, *Miscelanea, Meditations Memoratiues*, sig. B3^r.
55 Sigmund Freud, 'Mourning and Melancholia', in Sigmund Freud, *The Standard Edition of the Complete Psychological Works of Sigmund Freud*, trans. James Strachey et al., vol. xiv (London: Hogarth, 1957), p. 244.
56 Dennis Kay, *Melodious Tears: The English Funeral Elegy from Spenser to Milton* (Oxford: Clarendon Press, 1990), pp. 2–3.
57 Paul Ricoeur, *Time and Narrative*, vol. iii, trans. Kathleen Blamey and David Pellauer (University of Chicago Press, 1988), p. 100.
58 Quoted in D. R. Woolf, 'Two Elizabeths? James I and the Late Queen's Famous Memory', *Canadian Journal of History/Annales Canadiennes d'Histoire* 20:2 (Aug. 1985), 189.
59 See *Aeneid* I: 203.
60 Kay, *Melodious Tears*, p. 7.

61 Thomas Wilson, *The Art of Rhetoric*, Bk I, 'Of Comforting' (1560). See Thomas Wilson, *The Art of Rhetoric*, ed. Peter E. Medine (University Park: Pennsylvania State University Press, 1993), p. 103. This volume was dedicated by Wilson in 1560 to John Dudley, Earl of Warwick.
62 In the context of modern theorising concerning melancholia and mourning, see, for example, Julia Kristeva, *Black Sun: Depression and Melancholia*, trans. Leon S. Roudiez (New York: Columbia University Press, 1989); Wendy Wheeler, 'In the Middle of Ordinary Things: Rites, Procedures and (Last) Orders', *New Formations* 34 (1988), 129–51; 'Melancholic Modernity and Contemporary Grief: The Novels of Graham Swift', *Literature and the Contemporary: Fictions and Theories of the Present*, ed. Roger Luckhurst and Peter Marks (New York: Longman, 1999), pp. 63–79.
63 Kate Chedgzoy, *Women's Writing in the British Atlantic World: Memory, Place and History, 1550–1700* (Cambridge University Press, 2007), p. 9.
64 See 'A Letter written by Sir Philip Sidney to Queen Elizabeth, touching her marriage with Monsieur', in Katherine Duncan-Jones and Jan Van Dorsten (eds.), *Miscellaneous Prose of Sir Philip Sidney* (Oxford: Clarendon Press, 1973), pp. 46–57.
65 In this context, see James Cleland, *Hero–paideia, or The institution of a young noble man* (London, 1607), p. 179.
66 Goodden, *The Backward Look*, p. 13.
67 Zim, *English Metrical Psalms*, p. 2.
68 In this context, see John N. King, *English Reformation Literature: The Tudor Origins of the Protestant Tradition* (Princeton University Press, 1982), pp. 232–3.
69 Wendy Wall, *The Imprint of Gender: Authorship and Publication in the English Renaissance* (Ithaca, NY: Cornell University Press, 1993), p. 312.
70 *Dialogus Ciceronianus* (1527). See Erasmus, *The Collected Works of Erasmus*, vol. xxviii, trans. Betty I. Knott (University of Toronto Press, 1986), p. 447.
71 Fernando Bouza, *Communication, Knowledge, and Memory in Early Modern Spain*, trans. Sonia López and Michael Agnew (Philadelphia: University of Pennsylvania Press, 1999), p. 3.
72 John Donne, *The Sermons of John Donne, in Ten Volumes*, ed. George R. Potter and Evelyn M. Simpson (Berkeley and Los Angeles: University of California Press, 1953–62), vol. viii, sermon 2, p. 86.
73 Hannibal Hamlin, *Psalm Culture and Early Modern English Literature* (Cambridge University Press, 2004), p. 131.
74 Jean Calvin, *The Psalmes of Dauid and others. With M. Iohn Caluins commentaries*, trans. Arthur Golding (1571), sig.*6ᵛ.
75 Sir Philip Sidney, *Defence of Poesie, Astrophil and Stella and Other Writings*, ed. Elizabeth Porges-Watson (London: Everyman/Dent, 1997), ll. 19–21, p. 87.
76 Clarke, *Isabella Whitney, Mary Sidney and Aemilia Lanyer*, p. xi.
77 For further discussion of the important dimensions of early manuscript culture, see, for example, Woudhuysen, *Sir Philip Sidney and the Circulation of Manuscripts*; Marotti and Bristol, *Print, Manuscript, Performance*; Eugene R. Kintgern, *Reading in Tudor England* (University of Pittsburgh Press, 1996);

Arthur F. Marotti, *Manuscript, Print, and the English Renaissance Lyric* (Ithaca, NY: Cornell University Press, 1995); W. Speed Hill (ed.), *New Ways of Looking at Old Texts: Papers of the Renaissance English Text Society, 1985–1997*, vol. cvii (Binghamton, NY: Medieval and Renaissance Texts and Studies, 1993).

78 'Upon the translation of the Psalms by Sir Philip Sidney, and the Countess of Pembroke his sister', ll. 46, 14, 21–2. See John Donne, *The Complete English Poems*, ed. A. J. Smith (Harmondsworth: Penguin, 1977), pp. 332–3.

79 See 'A Treatise on Playe. By Sir John Harrington. Never Printede', written during Elizabeth's reign, in Sir John Harrington, *Nugae Antiquae: Being a Miscellaneous Collection of Original Papers in Prose and Verse Written in the Reigns of Henry VIII, Edward VI, Elizabeth, James I, &c.*, 2 vols. (1769), ii. 6. See also Samuel Daniel, 'To the Right Honourable, the Lady *Marie*, Countesse of PEMBROOKE', in Daniel, *DELIA and ROSAMUND augmented CLEOPATRA*, sig. H6^v.

80 Gary F. Waller, '"This Matching of Contraries": Calvinism and Courtly Philosophy in the Sidney Psalms', *English Studies* 55 (1974), p. 23.

81 Nicholas Breton, *The pilgrimage to paradise, ioyned with the Countesse of Penbrookes loue* (1592, 1st pub. 1591), sig. ¶2.

82 Samuel Daniel, *The ciuile wars* (1609), sig. A2^r.

83 *The Advancement of Learning*, Book One, in Francis Bacon, *The Works of Francis Bacon*, ed. J. Spedding, R. L. Ellis and D. D. Heath, 14 vols. (London: Longman *et al.*, 1857–74), vi. 7, pp. 38–9.

84 Steven W. May, *The Elizabethan Courtier Poets* (Asheville: Pegasus Press/University of North Carolina Press, 1999), p. 177.

85 'Examination', in Sidney, *A Defence of Poetry*, ed. Jan Van Dorsten, ll. 22–4, p. 43.

86 Quoted in Margaret P. Hannay, 'The Countess of Pembroke's Agency in Print and Scribal Culture', in George L. Justice and Nathan Tinker (eds.), *Women's Writing and the Circulation of Ideas: Manuscript Publication in England, 1550–1880* (Cambridge University Press, 2002), p. 23.

87 William Browne, *Poems of William Browne of Tavistock*, ed. George Goodwin (n.d.), ii. 294. Quoted in Gary F. Waller, *The Triumph of Death and Other Unpublished and Uncollected Poems by Mary Sidney, Countess of Pembroke (1561–1621)* (Salzburg: Institute of English Language and Literature, 1977), p. 1.

88 Wall, *The Imprint of Gender*, p. 319.

89 Tina Krontiris, *Oppositional Voices: Women as Writers and Translators of Literature in the English Renaissance* (London: Routledge, 1992), p. 65.

90 Ricoeur, *Time and Narrative*, iii. 181.

91 Sigmund Freud, *The Interpretation of Dreams*, vol. iv, trans. James Strachey, ed. James Strachey *et al.*, Penguin Freud Library (Harmondsworth: Penguin, 1991; 1st pub. 1958), pp. 79, 656.

92 Sir Thomas Browne, *Hydriotaphia, Urn-Burial, or A Brief Discourse of the Sepulchral Urns lately found in Norfolk*, ch. IV. See Sir Thomas Browne,

Religio Medici, Hydriotaphia, and The Garden of Cyrus, ed. Robin Robbins (Oxford: Clarendon Press, 1982), pp. 128, 129–30.

6 'TELL ME, WHERE ALL PAST YEARES ARE': JOHN DONNE AND THE OBLIGATIONS OF MEMORY

1 Cited in Edmund Gosse, *The Life and Letters of John Donne*, 2 vols. (London: William Heinemann, 1899), i. 190–1.
2 The urgency of his situation is expressed in Donne's letters throughout this period, as may be testified in his 1607 letter 'To the Honourable Knight Sir Henry GOODYER, *one of the Gentlemen of his Majesty's Privy Chamber*'. See Gosse, *Life and Letters*, i. 156.
3 All textual references to Donne's published sermons are taken from *The Sermons of John Donne, in Ten Volumes*, ed. George R. Potter and Evelyn M. Simpson (Berkeley and Los Angeles: University of California Press, 1953–62). References are cited as: volume, sermon number, page number.
4 William Drummond of Hawthornden, 'Information by Ben Johnston to W.D. when came to Scotland upon foot 1619', in Ben Jonson, *Ben Jonson*, ed. C. H. Herford and Percy and Evelyn Simpson, 11 vols. (Oxford: Clarendon Press 1925–52), i. 135, 138.
5 See A. J. Smith (ed.), *John Donne: The Critical Heritage* (London: Routledge and Kegan Paul, 1975), p. 67.
6 Izaak Walton, *The Life of Dr. John Donne, late Dean of St Paul's Church London* (1670, 1st pub. 1640), in Izaak Walton, *The Lives of Dr. John Donne, Sir Henry Wootton, Mr. Richard Hooker, Mr. George Herbert 1670* (Menston: Scolar Press Facsimiles, 1969), p. 37.
7 See Walton, *The Life of Dr. John Donne*, pp. 43, 74.
8 See Smith, *John Donne: The Critical Heritage*, p. 126.
9 Cited in R. C. Bald, *John Donne: A Life* (Oxford: Clarendon Press, 1970), p. 342.
10 *Sermons*, ii.11.244. In this context, see also John Donne, *Devotions Upon Emergent Occasions*, ed. Anthony Raspa (Montreal: McGill-Queen's University Press, 1975), xiv Devotion: Prayer, p. 71. For differing critical discussions, see Gillian R. Evans, 'John Donne and the Augustinian Paradox of Sin', *Review of English Studies* 33:129 (Feb. 1982), 4–5; Roger Pooley, *English Prose of the Seventeenth Century, 1590–1700* (London: Longman, 1992), p. 111.
11 See William Drummond's account in *Ben Jonson*, i. 136.
12 *Sermons*, iii.3.110.
13 Thought by Gosse to date from 1603 or 1604. Cited in Gosse, *Life and Letters*, i. 122.
14 Chapter 24: 'Of Pedantisme'. See Montaigne, *Essayes* (1613), p. 62.
15 See Donne, *The Complete English Poems*, p. 176.
16 See Walton, *The Life of John Donne*, pp. 61–2.
17 *Sermons*, ii.2.73–4.
18 See Malcolm Mackenzie Ross, *Poetry and Dogma* (New York: Octagon Books, 1969), p. 59.

19 *Sermons*, ii.2.74.
20 See also Jeffrey Johnson, *The Theology of John Donne* (Cambridge: D. S. Brewer, 1999), p. 12.
21 For further discussion here, see Noralyn Masselink, 'Donne's Epistemology and the Appeal to Memory', *John Donne Journal* 8:1–2 (1989), 57, 62, 70; Terry G. Sherwood, *Fulfilling the Circle: A Study of John Donne's Thought* (University of Toronto Press, 1984), pp. 35 ff.
22 See also *Sermons*, iv.12.306.
23 All textual references to Donne's English poetry are taken from John Donne, *The Complete English Poems*, ed. A. J. Smith (Harmondsworth: Penguin, 1977).
24 For translation, see Horace, *The Complete Odes and Epodes*, trans. William Guy Shepherd (Harmondsworth: Penguin, 1983), p. 164.
25 See *Devotions Upon Emergent Occasions*, fourth Meditation: 'Meditation', p. 19.
26 See Gosse, *Life and Letters*, i. 234–5.
27 Indeed, in a christening sermon he takes up Saint Jerome's emphasis that 'A man may be an *adulterer* in his wives bosom; though he seek not strange women' (*Sermons*, v.5.120).
28 Interestingly, in this context, Cedric Brown identifies a recurrent anxiety in Donne's poetic tributes on the part of the writer in search of patronage that 'memory might fade and with it, the cumulative recognition of past gifts and services'. See Cedric C. Brown, 'Presence, Obligation and Memory in John Donne's Texts for the Countess of Bedford', *Renaissance Studies* 22:1 (2008), p. 71.
29 See Judith Scherer Herz, '"An excellent Exercise of Wit that Speaks so well of Ill": Donne and the Poetics of Concealment', in Claude J. Summers and Ted-Larry Pebworth (eds.), *The Eagle and the Dove: Reassessing John Donne* (Columbia: University of Missouri Press, 1986), p. 3.
30 See the tenth paradox in John Donne, *Paradoxes and Problems*, ed. Helen Peters (Oxford: Clarendon Press, 1980), p. 21.
31 See 'General Introduction' to John Donne, *The Elegies and The Songs and Sonnets*, ed. Helen Gardner (Oxford: Clarendon Press, 1965), p. xlvi.
32 See also *Sermons*, ii.1.64.
33 See Achsah Guibbory, *The Map of Time: Seventeenth-Century English Literature and Ideas of Pattern in History* (Urbana and Chicago: University of Illinois Press, 1986), p. 88 and Achsah Guibbory, 'John Donne and Memory as "the Art of Salvation"', *Huntington Library Quarterly* 43 (1980), 263.
34 See Noralyn Masselink, 'Memory in John Donne's Sermons: "Readie"? or Not?', *South Atlantic Review* 63:2 (1998), 99.
35 'The ninth Chapter. Of Lyers', in *Essayes* (1613), p. 15.
36 See Edith Grossman (ed. and trans.), *The Golden Age: Poems of the Spanish Renaissance* (New York and London: W. W. Norton, 2007), pp. 106–7.
37 F. C. Bartlett, *Remembering: A Study in Experimental and Social Psychology* (Cambridge University Press, 1932), p. 213.
38 The key discussion of this trinity of will, understanding and memory by Augustine is in *De Trinitate*: 'these three are one, one life, one mind, one

essence'. See *On The Holy Trinity*, Bk x, ch. 11, in Philip Schaff (ed.), *A Select Library of the Nicene and Post-Nicene Fathers of the Christian Church*, vol. iii (Edinburgh: T & T Clark; Grand Rapids, MI: Eerdmans, 1993), p. 143. This becomes a central tenet of Donne's preaching throughout his career; see, for example, *Sermons*, iii.5.154; vi.3.81.

39 *Sermons*, ix.2.84. This widespread Augustinian influence is also in evidence, for example, in the *Devotions Upon Emergent Occasions* – see the fifth Meditation. For further discussion here, see Walter R. Davis, 'Meditation, Typology, and the Structure of John Donne's Sermons', in Summers and Pebworth, *The Eagle and the Dove*, pp. 184–5 ff.

40 See 'John Donne and Memory as "the Art of Salvation"', pp. 261–2. In this context, see also Johnson, *The Theology of John Donne*, p. 13; Robert L. Hickey, 'Donne's Art of Memory', *Tennessee Studies in Literature* 3 (1958), 29–36.

41 In this context, see also *Sermons*, vi.5.116; vii.2.78; vii.12.314.

42 In this context, see Daniel W. Doerksen, 'Polemist or Pastor? Donne and Moderate Calvinist Conformity', in Mary Arshagouni Papazian (ed.), *John Donne and the Protestant Reformation: New Perspectives* (Detroit, MI: Wayne State University Press, 2003), pp. 15, 21.

43 Richard Greenham, *Propositions containing answers to certaine demaunds in divers spirituall matters* (1597), pp. 2–3.

44 See 'Donne's Epistemology', pp. 57–88.

45 In this context, see, for example, *Biathanatos* (New York: Facsimile Text Society, 1930), pt 3, dist. 1, sect. 1, p. 153.

46 *Sermons*, ii.11.237.

47 *Ancient and Medieval Memories*, p. 155.

48 *Ancient and Medieval Memories*, p. 181.

49 *Sermons*, v.16.318–19.

50 Mary Warnock, *Memory* (London: Faber and Faber, 1987), p. 1. For further discussion here with reference to Donne, see Sherwood, *Fulfilling the Circle*, pp. 67 ff.

51 See *De Memoria et Reminscentia* 453a14, in Richard Sorabji (ed.), *Aristotle on Memory* (London: Duckworth, 1972), p. 59.

52 For more detailed discussion here, see Frances A. Yates, *The Art of Memory* (London: Routledge and Kegan Paul, 1966), pp. 59–60, 69 ff.

53 In the context of Donne, see Gosse, *Life and Letters*, i. 175.

54 Ruth E. Harvey, *The Inward Wits: Psychological Theory in the Middle Ages and the Renaissance* (London: Warburg Institute/University of London, 1975), p. 46.

55 For further discussion here, see Harvey, *The Inward Wits*, pp. 10 ff.

56 *Essayes* (1603), p. 389.

57 Roger B. Rollin, '"Fantastique Ague": The Holy Sonnets and Religious Melancholy', in Summers and Pebworth, *The Eagle and the Dove*, p. 131.

58 Harvey, *The Inward Wits*, pp. 53 ff.

59 See also here Guibbory, *The Map of Time*, p. 96.

60 This is cited in Barbara Kiefer Lewalski, *Protestant Poetics and the Seventeenth-Century Religious Lyric* (Princeton University Press, 1979), p. 150.

61 For further discussion here of Donne's poem in the context of 'remembered wisdom', see Donald M. Friedman, 'Memory and the Art of Salvation in Donne's Good Friday Poem', *English Literary Renaissance* 3 (1973), 418–42.
62 See Dryden's prefatory letter to his *Eleonora: A Panegyrical Poem Dedicated to the Memory of the Late Countess of Abingdon* (1692), quoted in Smith, *John Donne: The Critical Heritage*, p. 150.
63 See respectively, David Lowenthal, *The Past is a Foreign Country* (Cambridge University Press, 1985), pp. 136–8; *The Works of Francis Bacon*, ed. J. Spedding, R. L. Ellis and D. D. Heath, 14 vols. (London: Longman *et al.*, 1857–74), iii. 291. See also Aphorism LXXXIV.
64 See Grossman, *The Golden Age*, pp. 172–3.
65 See Drummond, 'Information by Ben Johnston', in *Ben Jonson*, i. 133.
66 *Sermons*, vii.3.103.
67 *Paradoxes and Problems*, p. 24.
68 See Stanley Fish, 'Masculine Persuasive Force: Donne and Verbal Power', in Elizabeth D. Harvey and Katherine Eisaman Maus (eds.), *Soliciting Interpretation* (University of Chicago Press, 1990), p. 223.
69 *Essayes* (1603), p. 16.
70 'Unguided tour', in *The Susan Sontag Reader*, introduction by Elizabeth Hardwick (Harmondsworth: Penguin, 1982), p. 372.
71 Philipp Wolf, *Modernization and the Crisis of Memory: John Donne to Don DeLillo* (Amsterdam: Rodopi Press: 2002), pp. 31–2.
72 Walton, *The Life of Dr. John Donne*, p. 75.
73 See Smith, *John Donne: The Critical Heritage*, pp. 91, 93.
74 See Smith, *John Donne: The Critical Heritage*, pp. 308, 285.
75 See *Essays in Divinity*, Bk II, pt I, pp. 43–4.
76 See T. S. Eliot, 'Donne in our Time', in Theodore Spencer (ed.), *A Garland for John Donne, 1631–1931* (Gloucester, MA: Peter Smith, 1958), pp. 18, 19. With reference to Grierson, see *The Poems of John Donne*, ed. Herbert J. C. Grierson, 2 vols. (Oxford University Press, 1912).
77 See Smith, *John Donne: The Critical Heritage*, p. 137.
78 *Sermons*, ii.11.248.

7 'OF ALL THE POWERS OF THE MIND … THE MOST DELICATE AND FRAILE': THE POETRY OF BEN JONSON AND THE RENEWAL OF MEMORY

1 'To Leo X', 1 Feb. 1516, letter 384 in *The Collected Works of Erasmus: The Correspondence of Erasmus—letters 298 to 445 (1514–1516)*, vol. iii, trans. R. A. B. Mynors and D. F. S. Thomson, annot. James K. McConica (Toronto and Buffalo, NY: University of Toronto Press, 1976), pp. 221–2.
2 *Timber, or Discoveries*, in Ben Jonson, *Ben Jonson*, ed. C. H. Herford and Percy and Evelyn Simpson, 11 vols. (Oxford: Clarendon Press 1925–52), viii. 578–9 (ll. 479–94). Further textual references refer to this series of Jonson's works and are rendered in the following format: volume, page, line (e.g., viii.578–9: 479–94).

3 Sir Henry Wotton, *A parallel betweene Robert late Earle of Essex, and George late Duke of Buckingham* (1641), p. 1.
4 Maxime 89 in 1678 edition. See *La Rochefoucauld: Œuvres complètes*, ed. L. Martin-Chauffier *et al.* (Paris: Gallimard, 1964), p. 415. In this context, see Richard Dutton, *Ben Jonson: To the First Folio* (Cambridge University Press, 1983), p. 133.
5 George Parfitt, 'Ethical Thought and Ben Jonson's Poetry', *Studies in English Literature* 9 (1969), 133.
6 David Norbrook, *Poetry and Politics in the English Renaissance*, rev. edn (Oxford University Press, 2002), p. 155.
7 Fernando Bouza, *Communication, Knowledge, and Memory in Early Modern Spain*, trans. Sonia López and Michael Agnew (Philadelphia: University of Pennsylvania Press, 1999), p. 21.
8 Sir Robert Naunton, *Fragmenta Regalia or Observations on Queen Elizabeth, Her Times and Favourites*, ed. J. S. Cerovski (Washington, DC and London: Folger Shakespeare Library, 1985), p. 43.
9 Virgil, *Aeneid*, 4.335–6. For this translation, see Virgil, *Eclogues, Georgics, Aeneid I–VI*, trans. H. Rushton Fairclough, rev. G. P. Goold, Loeb Classical Library (Cambridge, MA and London: Harvard University Press, 1999), pp. 444–5.
10 Paul Ricoeur, *Time and Narrative*, vol. iii, trans. Kathleen Blamey and David Pellauer (University of Chicago Press, 1988), p. 227.
11 Francis Bacon, *The Advancement of Learning and New Atlantis*, ed. Arthur Johnston (Oxford: Clarendon Press, 1980): 'The Second Book', xvii.10, p. 137.
12 Brian Vickers underlines that 'The Renaissance was fundamentally a notebook culture, its greatest literary productions displaying what has been called a *stile a mosaico*'. See *Francis Bacon: The Major Works*, ed. Brian Vickers (Oxford University Press, 1996), p. xlii.
13 Sara van den Berg, 'True Relation: The Life and Career of Ben Jonson', in Richard Harp and Stanley Stewart (eds.), *The Cambridge Companion to Ben Jonson* (Cambridge University Press, 2000), p. 1.
14 From 'Of Lyers', in Michel de Montaigne, *The Essayes* (1603), p. 15.
15 Raymond Tallis, 'A Critique of Neuromythology', in R. Tallis and H. Robinson (eds.), *The Pursuit of Mind* (Manchester: Carcanet Press, 1991), p. 101. This position is discussed by Emmanuel Prower in his essay 'Memory as Sign', in Wojciech H. Kalaga and Tadeusz Rachwal (eds.), *Memory–Remembering–Forgetting* (Frankfurt: Peter Lang, 1999), pp. 18 ff.
16 Robin Sowerby, *The Classical Legacy in Renaissance Poetry* (London: Longman, 1994), p. 145.
17 Janet Coleman, *Ancient and Medieval Memories: Studies in the Reconstruction of the Past* (Cambridge University Press, 1992), p. 8.
18 Kate Chedgzoy, *Women's Writing in the British Atlantic World: Memory, Place and History, 1550–1700* (Cambridge University Press, 2007), p. 18.
19 'To the Great Example of Honor and Vertue, The Most Noble William Earle of Pembroke, L. Chamberlaine, &c.' See *Ben Jonson*, viii. 25–6: 4, 40–2.

20 'A Study of Ben Jonson', in Algernon Charles Swinburne, *The Complete Works of Algernon Charles Swinburne*, ed. Sir Edmund Gosse and Thomas James Wise, vol. xii, Bonchurch edition: *Prose Works*, vol. ii (London: William Heinemann; New York: Gabriel Wells, 1926), pp. 65–6.
21 Swinburne, 'A Study of Ben Jonson', p. 66.
22 Sir Philip Sidney, *The Countesse of Pembrokes Arcadia* (1593). See respectively, Bk i, ch. 2, sig. 4^r; Bk i, ch. 4, sig. 8^r.
23 'An exhortacion concerning good order and obedience, to rulers and Magistreates', in *Certayne sermons appoynted by the Quenes Maiestie* (1559), sig. R3^r.
24 'An exhortacion', in *Certayne sermons*, sig. R3^r.
25 See respectively, Raymond Williams, *The Country and the City* (Oxford University Press, 1973); Don E. Wayne, *Penshurst: The Semiotics of Place and the Poetics of History* (Madison: University of Wisconsin Press, 1984); Rhonda Lemke Sanford, *Maps and Memory in Early Modern England* (Basingstoke: Palgrave, 2002).
26 Heather Dubrow, *Shakespeare and Domestic Loss: Forms of Deprivation, Mourning and Recuperation* (Cambridge University Press, 1999), p. 56.
27 For further discussion here concerning the discourses of memory and futurity in this period, see Andrew Hiscock: '*To Provide for the Future, and Times Succeeding*: Walter Ralegh and the Progress of Time', in Andrea Brady and Emily Butterworth (eds.), *Renaissance Futures* (London: Routledge, 2009), pp. 90–109 and 'Ralegh and the Arts of Memory', *Literature Compass* 4 (July 2007), 1030–58.
28 William E. Engel, *Mapping Mortality: The Persistence of Memory and Melancholy in Early Modern England*, Massachusetts Studies in Early Modern Culture (Amherst: University of Massachusetts Press, 1995), pp. 66, 67, 68.
29 Sara van den Berg, *The Action of Ben Jonson's Poetry* (Newark: University of Delaware Press, 1987), p. 28.
30 In this context, it is interesting to note R. G. Collingwood's contention that 'A mind which knows its own change is by that very knowledge lifted above change. History, and the same is true of memory ... is the mind's triumph over time. In the ... process of thought, the past lives in the present, not as a mere "trace" or effect of itself on the physical organism, but as the object of the mind's historical knowledge of itself in an eternal present'. See R. G. Collingwood, *Speculum Mentis, or the Map of Knowledge* (Oxford: Clarendon Press, 1924).
31 *Ben Jonson*, vi.475. See also Lady Frampul's exclamation at iii.ii.241–2: 'How swift is time, and slily steales away | From them would hug it, value it, embrace it?' (*Ben Jonson*, vi.458).
32 *De Oratore* ii.ix.36. See Cicero, *De Oratore*, trans. E. W. Sutton and H. Rackham, Loeb edn, 2 vols. (London: William Heinemann; Cambridge, MA: Harvard University Press, 1942), i. 225; *Ben Jonson*, viii.176: 15–18.
33 'Oration on the life of Aristotle' (1537), in Philipp Melanchthon, *Orations on Philosophy and Education*, ed. Sachiko Kusukawa (Cambridge University Press, 1999), p. 205.

34 For an interesting discussion of Jonson's textual acts of mourning in the context of early modern traditions of rigorism, see G. W. Pigman III, 'Suppressed Grief in Jonson's Funeral Poetry', *ELR* 13:2 (Spring 1983), 203–20.
35 Robert C. Evans, *Ben Jonson and the Poetics of Patronage* (Lewisburg, PA, London and Toronto: Bucknell University Press/Associated University Presses, 1989), p. 153.
36 Aristotle, *The Nichomachean Ethics*, trans. H. Rackham, Loeb Classical Library (London: William Heinemann; Cambridge, MA: Harvard University Press, 1962), p. 461: VIII.iii.6.
37 Cicero, *De Senectute, De Amicitia, De Divinatione*, trans. William Armistead Falconer, Loeb Classical Library (London: William Heinemann; Cambridge, MA: Harvard University Press, 1946), pp. 125 (IV.15), 211 (XXVII.104).
38 Sidney, *Arcadia* (1593), Bk I, ch. 2, sig. 4^r.
39 In this context, see: Earl Miner, *The Cavalier Mode from Jonson to Cotton* (Princeton University Press, 1971), p. 44; Dutton, *Ben Jonson: To The First Folio*, p. 108.
40 Dutton, *Ben Jonson: To the First Folio*, p. 83.
41 Bacon, *Francis Bacon*, ed. Vickers, p. 443.
42 Niccolò Machiavelli, *The Discourses*, ed. Bernard Crick, trans. Leslie J. Walker and Brian Richardson (Harmondsworth: Penguin, 1978), Bk 1.39, pp. 207–8.
43 Logan Pearsall Smith (ed.), *Life and Letters of Henry Wotton*, vol. ii (Oxford University Press, 1907), p. 494.
44 Stephen Orgel, *The Jonsonian Masque* (Cambridge, MA: Harvard University Press, 1965), p. 190.
45 In this context of 'Jonsonian' authority, see Robert C. Evans, *Habits of Mind: Evidence and Effects of Ben Jonson's Reading* (Lewisburg, PA and London: Bucknell University Press/Associated University Presses, 1995), p. 34.
46 Vives, *On Education: A Translation of the* De tradendis disciplinis *of Juan Luis Vives*, ed. and trans. Foster Watson (Totowa, NJ: Rowman and Littlefield, 1977 [1913]), p. 101.
47 *The Advancement of Learning*, Book II, 'To the King'. See Bacon, *The Works of Francis Bacon*, ed. J. Spedding, R. L. Ellis and D. D. Heath, 14 vols. (London: Longman et al., 1857–74), iii. 321. See also Jonson's *Timber, or Discoveries*, in *Ben Jonson*, viii.627: 2095–8.
48 Stanley Fish, 'Authors-Readers: Jonson's Community of the Same', *Representations* 7 (Summer 1984), p. 28.
49 *Ben Jonson*, viii.638–9: 2466–80.
50 Peter Sherlock, *Monuments and Memory in Early Modern England* (Aldershot: Ashgate, 2008), pp. 3, 5.
51 See *Ben Jonson*, iii.301: 8–9.
52 *Ben Jonson*, xi.325.
53 Ricoeur, *Time and Narrative*, iii. 93.
54 *Timber, or Discoveries*, in *Ben Jonson*, viii.619: 1832–40.

8 'THIS ART OF MEMORY': FRANCIS BACON, MEMORY AND THE DISCOURSES OF POWER

1. Juan Luis Vives, *On Education: A Translation of the* De tradendis disciplinis *of Juan Luis Vives*, ed. and trans. Foster Watson (Totowa, NJ: Rowman and Littlefield, 1977 [1913]), p. 9.
2. Unless otherwise indicated, all textual references are to *The Works of Francis Bacon*, ed. J. Spedding, R. L. Ellis and D. D. Heath, 14 vols. (London: Longman *et al.*, 1857–74).
3. Translation from the *Temporis Partus Masculus* (1602–3), in Benjamin Farrington, *The Philosophy of Francis Bacon* (Liverpool University Press, 1964), p. 62. In this context, see also Aphorism CXIII, *The Works of Francis Bacon*, iv. 102.
4. See respectively, Daniel Tuvill (D. T.), *Essaies politicke, and morall* (London: Humphrey Lownes, 1608), sig. 17^r. 'Of Paines and Industrie'; Nicholas Breton, *Characters vpon essaies morall, and diuine* (London: Edw. Griffin, 1615), sig. A3^{r-v}.
5. Cited in Charles Whitney, *Francis Bacon and Modernity* (New Haven, CT: Yale University Press, 1986), p. 17.
6. Farrington, *The Philosophy of Francis Bacon*, pp. 63, 69.
7. *The Advancement of Learning*, *The Works of Francis Bacon*, iii. 268.
8. David Colclough, '"Non canimus surdis, respondent omnia sylvai": Francis Bacon and the Transmission of Knowledge', in Philippa Berry and Margaret Tudeau-Clayton (eds.), *Textures of Renaissance Knowledge* (Manchester University Press, 2003), p. 81.
9. Robert Johnson, *Essaies, or rather Imperfect offers* (London: John Windet, 1601), sig. B1^v. 'Of Greatness of Mind'.
10. *The Advancement of Learning*, Book Two, *The Works of Francis Bacon*, iii. 421.
11. Translation of *Cogitationes de Natura Rerum*. See *The Works of Francis Bacon*, v. 437.
12. Translation of the preface to *The Great Instauration*. See *The Works of Francis Bacon*, iv. 18. In this context, see also *The Works of Francis Bacon*, iv. 363.
13. On Bacon's rejection of the syllogism as an intellectual procedure, see Brian Vickers, 'Bacon Among the Literati: Science and Language', *Comparative Criticism* 13 (1991), 261.
14. *The Works of Francis Bacon*, iii. 326. For an analogous enquiry in the modern period, see Henri Bergson, *Matter and Memory*, trans. Nancy Margaret Paul and W. Scott Palmer (London: Swan Sonnenschein, 1991), p. 72.
15. Aphorism LXXXV, *The Works of Francis Bacon*, iv. 83–4.
16. *Religio Medici*, 'The First Part', sections 3, 10. See Sir Thomas Browne, *Religio Medici, Hydriotaphia and The Garden of Cyrus*, ed. Robin Robbins (Oxford: Clarendon Press, 1982), p. 4.
17. See the translation of *Cogitata et Visa* in Farrington, *The Philosophy of Francis Bacon*, p. 89. For further discussion here, see Perez Zagorin, *Francis Bacon* (Princeton University Press, 1998), p. 102; Lisa Jardine, 'Experientia

literata or Novum Organum? The Dilemma of Bacon's Scientific Method', in William A. Sessions (ed.), *Francis Bacon's Legacy of Texts* (New York: AMS Press, 1990), p. 52.
18 *The Works of Francis Bacon*, iv. 25.
19 For contemporary critical voices on this matter, see, for example, Zagorin, *Francis Bacon*, p. 103; Michel Malherbe, 'Bacon's Method of Science', in Markku Peltonen (ed.), *The Cambridge Companion to Bacon* (Cambridge University Press, 1996), p. 76; Ian Box, *The Social Thought of Francis Bacon* (Lampeter: Edwin Mellen Press, 1989), p. 94.
20 Some of the reservations that his critics have expressed with regard to this combination of theorising and induction are that Bacon failed: to take sufficient account of the role of mathematics in scientific investigation; to comprehend that a field of enquiry might involve non-finite and inaccessible specimens; to build sufficient room in his thinking for creative hypothesis; to account for the fact that experiment must be guided by a larger generalisation to be tested, yet his method is initiated by individual enquiries; to realise that a phenomenon might be caused by multiple factors and have a plurality of properties.
21 'To The King'; see *The Works of Francis Bacon*, iii. 261–2.
22 See also Lisa Jardine, 'Experientia literata or Novum Organum?', p. 54.
23 'Of Imitation'. See Sir William Cornwallis, *Essayes by Sir William Corne-Waleys the younger, Knight*, vol. i (London: S. Stafford, 1600), sig. M2^r–M2^v.
24 See Chapter 7, n. 19 and the discussion to which it refers.
25 'To the Most High and Excellent Prince, Henry, Prince of Wales, Duke of Cornwall, and Earl of Chester'. See 11.340. See also Cornwallis's 'Of Essayes & Bookes', in *Essayes*, vol. ii (London: R. Read, 1601), sig. Gg8^v. Michael Kiernan makes the point that Plutarch's *Moralia* (which Bacon knew) provided Bacon also with a source from antiquity for his 'essay' genre. See Francis Bacon, *The Essayes or Counsels, Civill and Morall*, ed. Michael Kiernan, The Oxford Francis Bacon, vol. xv (Oxford: Clarendon Press, 2000), p. xlvii.
26 See Farrington, *The Philosophy of Francis Bacon*, p. 40. With reference to this discussion of the need for pragmatic knowledge, see also *The Works of Francis Bacon*, iv. 47, 110, 119.
27 See Farrington, *The Philosophy of Francis Bacon*, p. 96.
28 See Farrington, *The Philosophy of Francis Bacon*, p. 71. In this context, see also John C. Briggs, *Francis Bacon and the Rhetoric of Nature* (Cambridge, MA: Harvard University Press, 1989), p. 132.
29 See Denise Albanese, *New Science, New World* (Durham, NC and London: Duke University Press, 1996), p. 103.
30 Preface to *Novum Organum*. See *The Works of Francis Bacon*, iv. 42. In this context, see also Francis Bacon, *Francis Bacon: Philosophical Studies c.1611–c.1619*, ed. Graham Rees, The Oxford Francis Bacon, vol. iv (Oxford: Clarendon Press, 2003), p. 3; Arthur B. Ferguson, *Clio Unbound: Perception of the Social and Cultural Past in Renaissance England* (Durham, NC: Duke University Press, 1979), p. 407.

31 In this context, see also: Charles Whitney, *Francis Bacon and Modernity*, p. 123; Jose Maria Rodriguez Garcia, 'Solitude and Procreation in Francis Bacon's Scientific Writings: The Spanish Connection', *Comparative Literature Studies* 35:3 (1998), p. 281; Catherine Gimelli Martin, 'The Feminine Birth of the Mind: Regendering the Empirical Subject Bacon and his Followers', in Julie Robin Solomon and Catherine Gimelli Martin (eds.), *Francis Bacon and the Refiguring of Early Modern Thought* (Aldershot: Ashgate, 2005), p. 70.
32 See Farrington, *The Philosophy of Francis Bacon*, p. 62. In this context, see also *The Works of Francis Bacon*, v. 133 and Elizabeth Hanson's *Discovering the Subject in Renaissance England* (Cambridge University Press, 1998), p. 126.
33 In this context, see also Walter Ralegh's *The History of World* (1614), 1.i.7, p. 8.
34 See *The Works of Francis Bacon*, iii. 331. See also the *Temporis Partus Masculus* in this context: Farrington, *The Philosophy of Francis Bacon*, pp. 67, 68.
35 See Farrington, *The Philosophy of Francis Bacon*, p. 67.
36 Aphorism LXXI, *The Works of Francis Bacon*, iv. 72–3.
37 In this context, see also Aphorism LXXVIII, *The Works of Francis Bacon*, iv. 77; Bacon, *Francis Bacon: Philosophical Studies c.1611–c.1619*, pp. 3–5.
38 He subsequently bemoans the fact that the renewal of interest in languages led to a fascination for *verba* rather than *res*.
39 *The Advancement of Learning*, *The Works of Francis Bacon*, iv. 303–4.
40 See Farrington, *The Philosophy of Francis Bacon*, p. 68.
41 *The Works of Francis Bacon*, iii. 140
42 This discourse is widely in evidence in Bacon's writing. See, for example, the Preface to *The Great Instauration*, *The Works of Francis Bacon*, iv. 14–15.
43 In this context, see Andrew Barnaby, '"Things Themselves": Francis Bacon's Epistemological Reform and the Maintenance of the State', *Renaissance and Reformation* 21:4 (1997), p. 63.
44 See the *Temporis Partus Masculus*, in Farrington, *The Philosophy of Francis Bacon*, p. 62.
45 Cited in Thomas M. Greene, *The Light in Troy: Imitation and Discovery in Renaissance Poetry* (New Haven, CT: Yale University Press, 1982), p. 8.
46 Walter Bourchier Devereux, *Lives and Letters of the Devereux, Earls of Essex in the Reigns of Elizabeth, James I and Charles I, 1540–1646* (London: John Murray, 1853), i. 329 – Letter XCIII. For wider discussion of the authorship of these letters, see Paul E. J. Hammer, 'Letters of Travel Advice from the Earl of Essex to the Earl of Rutland', *Philological Quarterly* 74:3 (Summer 1995), 317–25.
47 *The Works of Francis Bacon*, iv. 302.
48 This Ciceronian idea concerning the 'exploitable' exemplarity of history is taken up in a number of different places in Bacon's writing. See, for example, the third chapter of 'A Description of the Intellectual Globe' (Bacon, *Francis Bacon: Philosophical Studies c.1611–c.1619*, p. 105).
49 Aphorism CI, *The Works of Francis Bacon*, iv. 96.

50 *Phaedrus* 275a (trans. Alexander Nehamas and Paul Woodruff), in Plato, *Complete Works*, ed. John M. Cooper *et al.* (Indianapolis, IN and Cambridge: Hackett Publishing, 1997), pp. 551–2. For a sixteenth-century intervention in this debate, see Lodowick Lloyd, *The Pilgrimage of Princes* (1573). 'Of Memorie and Obliuion', p. 137.
51 See Niccolò Machiavelli, *The Discourses*, ed. Bernard Crick, trans. Leslie J. Walker and Brian Richardson (Harmondsworth: Penguin, 1978), i.ii, p. 109.
52 'The Preface' in Sir Walter Ralegh, *The History of the World* (1614).
53 John Kenyon, *The History Men: The Historical Profession in England since the Renaissance* (London: Weidenfeld and Nicolson, 1993), p. 13.
54 See translation of 'The Refutation of Philosophies', in Farrington, *The Philosophy of Francis Bacon*, p. 131. With reference to the bee metaphor, see Seneca's 84th letter to Lucilius.
55 Translation of *Historia Densi et Rari*, in Francis Bacon, *The Instauratio magna: Last Writings*, ed. Graham Rees, The Oxford Francis Bacon, vol. xiii (Oxford: Clarendon Press, 2000), p. 49.
56 See Chapter 10 'Of Memory', in Thomas Fuller, *The Holy State* (Cambridge, 1642), pp. 175–6.
57 *The Works of Francis Bacon*, v. 156.
58 See Bacon, *Francis Bacon: Philosophical Studies c.1611–c.1619*, p. 85.
59 A similar sentiment is expressed in 'A New Abecedarium of Nature'. See Bacon, *The Instauratio magna: Last Writings*, ed. Rees, p. 223.
60 Francis Bacon, *The Instauratio magna, Part III: Historia naturalis et experimentalis: Historia ventorum and Historia vitæ & mortis*, ed. Graham Rees with Maria Wakely, The Oxford Francis Bacon, vol. xii (Oxford: Clarendon Press, 2007), pp. xlv, xlvi.
61 *The Works of Francis Bacon*, iv. 435.
62 Victoria E. Burke, '"Memorial Books": Commonplaces, Gender, and Manuscript Compilation in Seventeenth-Century England', in Donald Beecher and Grant Williams (eds.), *Ars Reminiscendi: Mind and Memory in Renaissance Culture* (Toronto: Centre for Reformation and Renaissance, 2009), p. 122.
63 *The Works of Francis Bacon*, iv. 374.
64 *The Works of Francis Bacon*, iv. 436.
65 John Aubrey, *Brief Lives*, ed. Richard Barber (Suffolk: Boydell & Brewer, 1982), p. 31.
66 See also *The Works of Francis Bacon*, ii. 659, iii. 552–3, iv. 127, 163, 435–7, vii. 101. For further discussion here, see also James Stephens, *Francis Bacon and the Style of Science* (University of Chicago Press, 1975), pp. 69 ff.
67 See Chapter 10 'Of Memory', in Fuller, *The Holy State*, p. 174.
68 See *Francis Bacon: The Major Works*, ed. Brian Vickers (Oxford University Press, 1996), pp. xlii–xliii.
69 Melanchthon, 'Oration on the necessity of joining together the schools and ministry of the Gospel' (1543), in Philipp Melanchthon, *Orations on Philosophy and Education*, ed. Sachiko Kusukawa (Cambridge University Press, 1999), p. 9.

70 See translation of 'The Refutation of Philosophies', in Farrington, *The Philosophy of Francis Bacon*, p. 104.
71 Cornwallis, 'Of Essayes and Bookes', *Essayes*, vol. ii, sig. Hh1^{r-v}.
72 See *Timber, or Discoveries*, in Ben Jonson, *Ben Jonson*, ed. C. H. Herford and Percy and Evelyn Simpson, 11 vols. (Oxford: Clarendon Press, 1925–52), vii. 592.
73 'To my Honour'd Friend, Dr Charleton', ll. 23–4. Critical attention has also been drawn to the establishment of a Baconian college in Cowley's *Davideis*, ll. 663–934.
74 'A New Abecedarium of Nature', in *The Instauratio magna: Last Writings*, ed. Rees, p. 173. See also *The Works of Francis Bacon*, iv. 53.
75 Andrew Barnaby and Lisa J. Schnell, *Literate Experience: The Work of Knowing in Seventeenth-Century English Writing* (New York: Palgrave, 2002), p. 24.
76 Whitney, *Francis Bacon and Modernity*, p. 180.
77 William E. Engel, *Mapping Mortality: The Persistence of Memory and Melancholy in Early Modern England*, Massachusetts Studies in Early Modern Culture (Amherst: University of Massachusetts Press, 1995), pp. 54 ff.
78 See *The Works of Francis Bacon*, viii. 7.
79 *The Works of Francis Bacon*, xiv. 297.
80 See respectively, 'Of Education', in John Milton, *The Complete English Poems, Of Education, Areopagitica*, ed. Gordon Campbell (London: Dent/Everyman, 1993), p. 569; George Henry Lewes, *A Biographical History of Philosophy*, 4 vols. (London, 1852–3), iii. 33.
81 See respectively: Arthur B. Ferguson, *Clio Unbound*, p. 405; Julie Robin Solomon, *Objectivity in the Making: Francis Bacon and the Politics of Inquiry* (Baltimore, MD: Johns Hopkins University Press, 1998), p. xii.
82 'The Refutation of Philosophies', translation in Farrington, *The Philosophy of Francis Bacon*, p. 133.

Select Bibliography

Achinstein, Sharon. 'John Foxe and the Jews', *Renaissance Quarterly* 54 (Spring 2001), 86–120.
Albanese, Denise. *New Science, New World* (Durham, NC and London: Duke University Press, 1996).
Albertus Magnus. *Liber de memoria & reminiscentia, Parva naturalia* [a commentary on Aristotle's *De Memoria et Reminiscentia*], trans. Jan M. Ziolkowski, in Mary Carruthers and Jan M. Ziolkowski (eds.), *The Medieval Craft of Memory: An Anthology of Texts and Pictures* (Philadelphia: University of Pennsylvania Press, 2002).
Albott, Robert. *Wits theatre of the little world* (London, 1599).
Anderson, Fulton H. *Francis Bacon: His Career and his Thought* (Westport, CT: Greenwood Press, 1978).
Antze, Paul. 'Telling Stories, Making Selves: Memory and Identity in Multiple Personality Disorder', in Paul Antze and Michael Lambek (eds.), *Tense Past: Cultural Essays in Trauma and Memory* (New York: Routledge, 1996).
Aquinas, Thomas. *In Aristotelis libros, De sensu et sensato, De memoria et reminscentia commentarium*, trans. John Burchill, in Mary Carruthers and Jan M. Ziolkowski (eds.), *The Medieval Craft of Memory: An Anthology of Texts and Pictures* (Philadelphia: University of Pennsylvania Press, 2002).
  Summa Theologiæ, vol. xii, ed. Paul T. Durbin (London: Eyre and Spottiswoode; New York: McGraw-Hill, 1968).
Ariosto, Lodovico. *Orlando Furioso in English. Heroical Verse by Iohn Harington* (London, 1591).
Aristotle. *Aristotle on Memory*, ed. Richard Sorabji (London: Duckworth, 1972).
  Aristotles politiques, or Discourses of gouernment. Translated out of Greeke into French, with expositions taken out of the best authours, specially out of Aristotle himselfe, and out of Plato ... By Loys Le Roy, called Regius. Translated out of French into English (London, 1598).
  The Complete Works of Aristotle: The Revised Oxford Translation, ed. Jonathan Barnes (Bollingen Series LXXI-2), vol. i (Princeton University Press, 1984).
  The Nichomachean Ethics, trans. H. Rackham, Loeb Classical Library (London: William Heinemann; Cambridge, MA: Harvard University Press, 1962).
Ascham, Roger. *The Scholemaster or plaine and perfite way of teachyng children* (London, 1570).

Aston, Margaret and Elizabeth Ingram. 'The Iconography of *The Acts and Monuments*', in David Loades (ed.), *John Foxe and the English Reformation* (Aldershot: Scolar Press, 1997).

Atkinson, William. *A ful deuout and gostely treatyse of the imitacyon and folowynge the blessed lyfe of our moste mercyful sauyour cryste* (London, 1504).

Aubrey, John. *Aubrey's Brief Lives*, ed. Oliver Lawson Dick (London: Secker and Warburg, 1960).

Brief Lives, ed. Richard Barber (Suffolk: Boydell & Brewer, 1982).

Aughterson, Kate (ed.). *Renaissance Woman: Constructions of Femininity in England* (London: Routledge, 1995).

Augustine, Saint (Bishop of Hippo). *Confessions*, trans. Henry Chadwick, World's Classics (New York: Oxford University Press, 1991).

Austen, Gillian. 'Gascoigne's *Master F. J.* and its Revision, or, "You ain't heard nothin' yet!"', in Wolfgang Görtschacher and Holger Klein (eds.), *Narrative Strategies in Early English Fiction* (Lewiston, NY: Edwin Mellen, 1995).

George Gascoigne (Cambridge: D. S. Brewer, 2008).

Bacon, Francis. *The Advancement of Learning and New Atlantis*, ed. Arthur Johnston (Oxford: Clarendon Press, 1980).

The Essayes or Counsels, Civill and Morall, ed. Michael Kiernan, The Oxford Francis Bacon, vol. xv (Oxford: Clarendon Press, 2000).

Francis Bacon: The Major Works, ed. Brian Vickers (Oxford University Press, 1996).

Francis Bacon: Philosophical Studies c.1611–c.1619, ed. Graham Rees, The Oxford Francis Bacon, vol. iv (Oxford: Clarendon Press, 2003).

The historie of the raigne of King Henry the Seuenth (London, 1622).

The Instauratio magna, Part III: Historia naturalis et experimentalis: Historia ventorum and Historia vitæ & mortis, ed. Graham Rees with Maria Wakely, The Oxford Francis Bacon, vol. xii (Oxford: Clarendon Press, 2007).

The Instauratio magna: Last Writings, ed. Graham Rees, The Oxford Francis Bacon, vol. xiii (Oxford: Clarendon Press, 2000).

The Works of Francis Bacon, ed. J. Spedding, R. L. Ellis and D. D. Heath, 14 vols. (London: Longman et al., 1857–74).

Bainton, Roland H. *Women of the Reformation in France and England* (Minneapolis, MN: Augsburg Publishing House, 1973).

Baker-Smith, Dominic. 'Uses of Plato by Erasmus and More', in Anna Baldwin and Sarah Hutton (eds.), *Platonism and the English Imagination* (Cambridge University Press, 1994).

Bakhtin, Mikhail. 'Epic and Novel: Toward a Methodology for the Study of the Novel', in M. M. Bakhtin, *The Dialogic Imagination: Four Essays*, ed. Michael Holquist, trans. Caryl Emerson and Michael Holquist (Austin: Texas University Press, 2000).

'Popular-Festive Forms and Images in Rabelais', in Mikhail Bakhtin, *Rabelais and His World*, trans. Helene Iswolsky (Bloomington: Indiana University Press, 1984).

Bald, R. C. *John Donne: A Life* (Oxford: Clarendon Press, 1970).

Baldo, Jonathan. 'Wars of Memory in *Henry V*', *Shakespeare Quarterly* 47 (1996), 132–59.

Baldwin, William. *A treatise of morall phylosophie contaynyng the sayinges of the wyse. Gathered and Englyshed by Wyl[lia]m Baldwyn. The seconde boke intytled, of preceptes and counsayles; Of Deathe, not to be feared. Cap. v. The summe of all* (London, 1547).

Barnaby, Andrew. '"Things Themselves": Francis Bacon's Epistemological Reform and the Maintenance of the State', *Renaissance and Reformation* 21:4 (1997), 57–80.

Barnaby, Andrew and Lisa J. Schnell, *Literate Experience: The Work of Knowing in Seventeenth-Century English Writing* (New York: Palgrave, 2002).

Bartlett, F. C. *Remembering: A Study in Experimental and Social Psychology* (Cambridge University Press, 1932).

Bartlett, I. Ross. 'John Foxe as Hagiographer: The Question Revisited', *Sixteenth Century Journal* 27:4 (1995), 771–89.

Basse, William (attrib.). *A Helpe to memory and discourse*, 2nd edn (London, 1630; 1st pub. 1619).

Baxter, Nathaniel. *Sir Philip Sidney's Ourania* (London, 1606).

Beal, Peter. *In Praise of Scribes: Manuscripts and their Makers in Seventeenth-Century England* (Oxford: Clarendon Press, 1998).

Beilin, Elaine. *Redeeming Eve: Women Writers of the English Renaissance* (Princeton University Press, 1987).

Bergson, Henri. *Matter and Memory*, trans. Nancy Margaret Paul and W. Scott Palmer (London: Swan Sonnenschein, 1991).

Bernard of Clairvaux. *The meditat[i]ons of saint Bernard* (London, 1496).

Betteridge, Tom. 'From Prophetic to Apocalyptic: John Foxe and the Writing of History', in David Loades (ed.), *John Foxe and the English Reformation* (Aldershot: Scolar Press, 1997).

Biggs, B. J. H. (ed.), *The Imitation of Christ: The First English Translation of the 'Imitatio Christi'*, Early English Text Society (Oxford University Press, 1997).

Bloomfield, Josephine. 'Gascoigne's *Master F. J.* as a Renaissance Proto-Novel', *Essays in Literature* 19:2 (1992), 163–72.

Blundeville, Thomas. *The arte of logick Plainely taught in the English tongue, according to the best approued authors …* (1617).

Bolzoni, Lina. *The Gallery of Memory: Literary and Iconographic Models in the Age of the Printing Press*, trans. Jeremy Parzen (University of Toronto Press, 2001).

Bouza, Fernando. *Communication, Knowledge, and Memory in Early Modern Spain*, trans. Sonia López and Michael Agnew (Philadelphia: University of Pennsylvania Press, 1999).

Box, Ian. *The Social Thought of Francis Bacon* (Lampeter: Edwin Mellen Press, 1989).

Breton, Nicholas. *Characters vpon essaies morall, and diuine written for those good spirits, that will take them in good part, and make vse of them to good purpose* (London: Edw. Griffin, 1615).

Melancholike humours, in verses of diuerse natures (1600).
The pilgrimage to paradise, ioyned with the Countesse of Penbrookes loue, compiled in verse by Nicholas Breton Gentleman (London, 1592; 1st pub. 1591).
Brigden, Susan. 'Henry Howard, Earl of Surrey and the "Conjured League"', *The Historical Journal* 37:3 (1994).
Briggs, John C. *Francis Bacon and the Rhetoric of Nature* (Cambridge MA: Harvard University Press, 1989).
Brinkelow, Henry. *The lamentacyon of a Christe[n] agai[n]st the citye of London for some certaine greate vyces vsed theri[n]*, 2nd edn (London, 1548).
Brinsley, John. *Ludus literarius* (London, 1612).
The posing of the parts (London, 1615).
Brooks-Davies, Douglas (ed.). *Silver Poets of the Sixteenth Century* (London: Everyman, 1992).
Brown, Cedric C. 'Presence, Obligation and Memory in John Donne's Texts for the Countess of Bedford', *Renaissance Studies* 22:1 (2008), 63–85.
Browne, Sir Thomas. *Hydriotaphia, urne-buriall, or, a discourse of the sepulchrall urnes lately found in Norfolk. Together with the garden of Cyrus …* (London, 1658).
Religio Medici, Hydriotaphia, and The Garden of Cyrus, ed. Robin Robbins (Oxford: Clarendon Press, 1982).
Browne, William. *Poems of William Browne of Tavistock*, ed. George Goodwin (n.d.).
Burke, Peter. 'History as Social Memory', in Thomas Butler (ed.), *Memory: History, Culture and the Mind* (Oxford: Basil Blackwell, 1989), pp. 97–113.
The Renaissance Sense of the Past (London: Edward Arnold, 1969).
Burke, Victoria E. '"Memorial Books": Commonplaces, Gender, and Manuscript Compilation in Seventeenth-Century England', in Donald Beecher and Grant Williams (eds.), *Ars Reminiscendi: Mind and Memory in Renaissance Culture* (Toronto: Centre for Reformation and Renaissance, 2009), pp. 121–38.
Burlinson, Christopher. *Allegory, Space and the Material World in the Writings of Edmund Spenser* (Cambridge: D. S. Brewer, 2006).
Burrow, Colin. 'The Experience of Exclusion: Literature and Politics in the Reigns of Henry VII and Henry VIII', in David Wallace (ed.), *The Cambridge History of Medieval English Literature* (Cambridge University Press, 1999).
'The Sixteenth Century', in Arthur F. Kinney (ed.), *The Cambridge Companion to English Literature, 1500–1600* (Cambridge University Press, 2000).
Burton, Robert. *The Anatomy of Melancholy*, ed. Nicolas K. Kiessling *et al.* (Oxford: Clarendon Press, 1990), vol. ii.
Buxton, John. *Calendar of Letters, Despatches, and State Papers, Relating to the Negotiations Between England and Spain, 1485–1552* [*Calendar of State Papers, Spain*], vol. viii (London, 1545–6), ed. Martin A. S. Hume (1904).
Calendar of Letters, Despatches, and State Papers, Relating to the Negotiations Between England and Spain, 1485–1552 [*Calendar of State Papers, Spain*], vol. ix (London, 1547–49), ed. Martin A. S. Hume and Royall Tyler (1912).

A Tradition of Poetry (New York: St Martin's Press, 1967).
Calvin, Jean. *The Psalmes of Dauid and others. With M. Iohn Caluins commentaries*, trans. Arthur Golding (London, 1571).
Camden, William. *Britain, or A chorographicall description of the most flourishing kingdomes, England, Scotland, and Ireland, and the ilands adioyning, out of the depth of antiquitie* (London, 1610).
  Remaines of a Greater Worke Concerning Britaine (London, 1605).
Carey, John. *John Donne: Life, Mind and Art* (London: Faber and Faber, 1981).
  'Sixteenth- and Seventeenth-Century Prose', in Christopher Ricks (ed.), *English Poetry and Prose, 1540–1674* (Harmondsworth: Penguin, 1993).
Carruthers, Mary J. *The Book of Memory: A Study of Memory in Medieval Culture* (Cambridge University Press, 1990).
Carruthers, Mary J. and Jan M. Ziolkowski (eds.), *The Medieval Craft of Memory: An Anthology of Texts and Pictures* (Philadelphia: University of Pennsylvania Press, 2002).
Caxton, William. *The myrrour [and] dyscrypcyon of the worlde with many meruaylles [And] the vii. scyences as gramaye, rethorike wyth the arte of memorye, logyke, geometrye ... and then arimetryke ... and astronomy ...* (London, 1527).
Cervantes Saavedra, Miguel de. *The Adventures of Don Quixote*, trans. J. M. Cohen (Harmondsworth: Penguin, 1981; 1st pub. 1950).
Charlton, E. 'Notes on Katherine Parr's Prayer Book Preserved at Sudeley Castle', *Notes and Queries* 2:44 (1850), 212.
Charlton, Kenneth and Margaret Spufford. 'Literacy, Society and Education', in David Loewenstein and Janel Mueller (eds.), *Cambridge History of Early Modern English Literature* (Cambridge University Press, 2002).
Chedgzoy, Kate. *Women's Writing in the British Atlantic World: Memory, Place and History, 1550–1700* (Cambridge University Press, 2007).
Cheney, Donald. 'Narrative, Romance, and Epic', in Arthur F. Kinney (ed.), *The Cambridge Companion to English Literature, 1500–1600* (Cambridge University Press, 2000).
Childs, Jessie. *Henry VIII's Last Victim: The Life and Times of Henry Howard, Earl of Surrey* (London: Jonathan Cape, 2006).
Chrysostom, John. *A sermon of Saint Chrysostom ... translated into Englishe ... by Thomas Lupsette Londoner* (London, 1542).
Cicero. *De Inventione, De Optimo Genere Oratorum, Topica*, trans. H. M. Hubbell, Loeb Classical Library (London: William Heinemann; Cambridge, MA: Harvard University Press, 1949).
  De Oratore, trans. E. W. Sutton and H. Rackham, Loeb Classical Library, 2 vols. (London: William Heinemann; Cambridge, MA: Harvard University Press, 1942).
  De Senectute, De Amicitia, De Divinatione, trans. William Armistead Falconer, Loeb Classical Library (London: William Heinemann; Cambridge, MA: Harvard University Press, 1946).
  Tusculun Disputations, trans. J. E. King (London: William Heinemann; Cambridge MA: Harvard University Press, 1950).

[Pseudo-]Cicero. *Ad C. Herennium, De Ratione Dicendi* (*Rhetorica Ad Herennium*), trans. Harry Caplan, Loeb Classical Library (London: William Heinemann; Cambridge, MA: Harvard University Press, 1954) (tract wrongly attributed to Cicero in the early modern period).
Cixous, Hélène. *Le Troisième Corps* (Paris: Grasset, 1970).
Clarke, Danielle (ed.). *Isabella Whitney, Mary Sidney and Aemilia Lanyer: Renaissance Women Poets* (Harmondsworth: Penguin, 2000).
  '"Lover's Songs Shall Turne to Holy Psalmes": Mary Sidney and the Transformation of Petrarch', *Modern Language Review* 92:2 (Apr. 1997), 282–94.
Cleland, James. *Hero-paideia, or The institution of a young noble man* (London, 1607).
Cohen, Simona. 'Titian's London Allegory and the Three Beasts of his *selva oscura*', *Renaissance Studies* 14:1 (Mar. 2000), 46–69.
Colclough, David. '"Non canimus surdis, respondent omnia sylvai": Francis Bacon and the Transmission of Knowledge', in Philippa Berry and Margaret Tudeau-Clayton (eds.), *Textures of Renaissance Knowledge* (Manchester University Press, 2003).
Coleman, Janet. *Ancient and Medieval Memories: Studies in the Reconstruction of the Past* (Cambridge University Press, 1992).
Collingwood, R. G. *Speculum Mentis, or the Map of Knowledge* (Oxford: Clarendon Press, 1924).
Collinson, Patrick. 'John Foxe and National Consciousness', in Christopher Highley and John N. King (eds.), *John Foxe and His World* (Aldershot: Ashgate, 2002).
  'Truth and Legend: The Veracity of John Foxe's Book of Martyrs', in A. C. Duke and C. A. Tomse (eds.), *Clio's Mirror: Historiography in Britain and the Netherlands* (Zutphen: De Walburg Pers., 1985).
Conti, Natale. *Mythologiae sive explicationis fabularum libri decem* (Venice, 1551); French trans. *Mythologie* (Rouen, 1611).
Cope, Sir Anthony. *A godly meditacion upon xx. select psalmes of David* (London, 1548).
Cornwallis, Sir William. *Essayes by Sir William Corne-Waleys the younger, Knight*, 2 vols. (London: S. Stafford/R. Read, 1600–1).
Cox, Leonard. *The Art or Crafte of Rhetoryke* (London, 1532).
Cranmer, Thomas. 'A Prologue or Preface made by the most reuerende father in God, Thomas Archbishop of Cantuebury Metropolytan and Prymate of Englande', in *The Byble in Englyshe* (London, 1540).
Cranmer, Thomas, and Church of England. *Certayne sermons appoynted by the Quenes Maiestie, to be declared and read, by all persones, vycars, and curates, euery Sondaye and holy daye in theyr churches: and by her Graces aduyse perused & ouer sene, for the better vnderstandyng of the simple people: newly imprinted in partes accordynge as is mencioned in the booke of commune prayers* (London, 1559).
  Certayne sermons, or homelies appoynted by the kynges Maiestie (London, 1547).

Crawford, Anne (ed.). *Letters of the Queens of England, 1100–1547* (Stroud: Sutton, 1994).
Cressy, David and Lori Anne Ferrell (eds.). *Religion and Society in Early Modern England* (London: Routledge, 1996).
Cross, Claire. *Church and People, 1450–1660* (Glasgow: Fontana, 1976).
Cubitt, Catherine. 'Memory and Narrative in the Cult of Early Anglo-Saxon Saints', in Yitzhak Hen and Matthew Innes (eds.), *The Uses of the Past in the Early Middle Ages* (Cambridge University Press, 2000).
da Signa, Boncompagno. *Rhetorica novissima* ['De Memoria', trans. Sean Gallagher, pp. 105–17], in Mary Carruthers and Jan M. Ziolkowski (eds.), *The Medieval Craft of Memory: An Anthology of Texts and Pictures* (Philadelphia: University of Pennsylvania Press, 2002).
Daniel, Samuel. *The ciuile wars betweene the howses of Lancaster and Yorke corrected and continued by Samuel Daniel one of the groomes of hir Maiesties most honorable Priuie Chamber* (London, 1609).
  DELIA and ROSAMUND augmented CLEOPATRA (London, 1594).
Daniell, David. 'Tyndale and Foxe', in David Loades (ed.), *John Foxe: An Historical Perspective* (Aldershot: Ashgate, 1999).
Dauvois, Nathalie. *Mnémosyne: Ronsard, une poétique de la mémoire* (Paris: Honoré Champion, 1992).
Davis, Walter C. *Idea and Act in Elizabethan Fiction* (Princeton University Press, 1969).
Davis, Walter R. 'Contexts in Surrey's Poetry', *ELR* 4 (1974), 40–55.
  'Meditation, Typology, and the Structure of John Donne's Sermons', in Claude J. Summers and Ted-Larry Pebworth (eds.), *The Eagle and the Dove: Reassessing John Donne* (Columbia: University of Missouri Press, 1986).
de Certeau, Michel. *The Writing of History*, trans. Tom Conley (New York: Columbia University Press, 1988).
Deleuze, Gilles and Félix Guattari. *Anti-Oedipus: Capitalism and Schizophrenia*, trans. Robert Hurley *et al.*, introduction by Michel Foucault (London: Athlone Press, 1984).
Deloney, Thomas. *The pleasant historie of Iohn Winchcomb in his [younger] yeares called Iack of Newbury, the famous and worthy clothier of England; declaring his life and loue, together with his charitable deeds and great hospitalitie. And how hee set continually fiue hundred poore people at worke, to the great benefit of the common-wealth*, 10th repr. (London, 1626).
Dent, Emma. *Annals of Winchcombe and Sudeley* (London: John Murray, 1877).
Devereux, Walter Bourchier. *Lives and Letters of the Devereux, Earls of Essex in the Reigns of Elizabeth, James I and Charles I, 1540–1646* (London: John Murray, 1853), vol. i.
Dickens, A. G. *The English Reformation* (London: Fontana/Collins, 1978).
Distiller, Natasha. '"Philip's Phoenix"?: Mary Sidney Herbert and the Identity of Author', in Michael Pincombe (ed.), *The Anatomy of Tudor Literature* (Aldershot: Ashgate, 2001).

Doerksen, Daniel W. 'Polemist or Pastor? Donne and Moderate Calvinist Conformity', in Mary Arshagouni Papazian (ed.), *John Donne and the Protestant Reformation: New Perspectives* (Detroit, MI: Wayne State University Press, 2003).

Donne, John. *Biathanatos* (New York: Facsimile Text Society, 1930).
   The Complete English Poems, ed. A. J. Smith (Harmondsworth: Penguin, 1977).
   Devotions Upon Emergent Occasions, ed. Anthony Raspa (Montreal: McGill-Queen's University Press, 1975).
   The Elegies and The Songs and Sonnets, ed. Helen Gardner (Oxford: Clarendon Press, 1965).
   John Donne: Selected Prose, ed. Helen Gardner and Timothy Healy (Oxford: Clarendon Press, 1967).
   Paradoxes and Problems, ed. Helen Peters (Oxford: Clarendon Press, 1980).
   The Poems of John Donne, ed. Herbert J. C. Grierson, 2 vols. (Oxford University Press, 1912).
   Pseudo-Martyr, introduction by Francis Jacques Sypher (Delmar, NY: Scholars' Facsimiles and Reprints, 1974).
   The Sermons of John Donne, in Ten Volumes, ed. George R. Potter and Evelyn M. Simpson (Berkeley and Los Angeles: University of California Press, 1953–62).

Dowling, Maria. 'The Gospel and the Court: Reformation under Henry VIII', in Peter Lake and Maria Dowling (eds.), *Protestantism and the National Church in Sixteenth-Century England* (London: Croom Helm, 1987).

Dowriche, Anne. *The French historie* (London, 1589).

du Laurens, André. *A Discourse of the Preservation of Sight; of Melancholike Diseases; of Rheumes, and of Old Age* (London, 1594).

Dubrow, Heather. *Shakespeare and Domestic Loss: Forms of Deprivation, Mourning and Recuperation* (Cambridge University Press, 1999).

Duncan-Jones, Katherine and Jan Van Dorsten (eds.), *Miscellaneous Prose of Sir Philip Sidney* (Oxford: Clarendon Press, 1973).

Dutton, Richard. *Ben Jonson: To the First Folio* (Cambridge University Press, 1983).

Edmund of Abingdon, *The myrrour of the chyrche herefoloweth a deuout treatyse co[n]teyny[n]ge, necessary & confortable to the edyfycacion of the soule & body to the loue & grace of god* (London, 1521).

Edward VI. *The First and Second Prayer Books of Edward VI*, introduction by Revd E. C. S. Gibson (London: Dent, 1964).
   In[j]unccions geuen by the moste excellent prince, Edward the sixt ... to al and singuler his louyng subiectes, as well of the clergie, as of the laietie (London, 1547).

Edwards, Richard. *The excellent comedie of two the moste faithfullest freendes, Damon and Pithias Newly imprinted, as the same was shewed before the Queenes Maiestie, by the Children of her Graces Chappell ...* (London, 1571).

Eliot, T. S. 'Donne in our Time', in Theodore Spencer (ed.), *A Garland for John Donne, 1631–1931* (Gloucester, MA: Peter Smith, 1958).

Elliott, Elizabeth. '"A memorie nouriched by images": Reforming the Art of Memory in William Fowler's *Tarantula of Love*', *Journal of the Northern Renaissance*, 'Memory and the Northern Renaissance', 2:1 (Spring 2010): www.northern-renaissance.org/articles/A-memorie-nouriched-by-images-Reforming-the-Art-of-Memory-in-William-Fowlers-iTarantula-of-LoveibrElizabeth-Elliott/21.

Ellis, Henry (ed.). *Original Letters, Illustrative of English History*, 3 vols. (London: Harding, Triphook and Lepard, 1824), vol. i.

Elyot, Sir Thomas. *The bankette of sapience* (London, 1539).

The Book named the gouernour (London, 1531).

The Book Named the Governour (London: Everyman, 1962).

The education or bringinge vp of children, translated oute of Plutarche by syr Thomas Eliot knyght (London, 1532).

Engel, William E. *Mapping Mortality: The Persistence of Memory and Melancholy in Early Modern England*, Massachusetts Studies in Early Modern Culture (Amherst: University of Massachusetts Press, 1995).

'Montaigne's *Essais*: The Literary and Literal Digesting of a Life', in Thomas F. Mayer and D. R. Woolf (eds.), *The Rhetorics of Life-Writing in Early Modern Europe: Forms of Biography from Cassandra Fedele to Louis XIV* (Ann Arbor: University of Michigan Press, 1995).

England, Church of. *A Booke of certaine Canons, concernyng some parte of the discipline of the Church of England* (London, 1571).

Erasmus, Desiderius. *Apophthegmes ... First gathered and compiled in Latine by the ryght famous clerke Maister Erasmus of Roterdame. And now translated into Englyshe by Nicolas Vdall* (London, 1542).

A booke called in latyn Enchiridion militis christiani, and in englysshe the manuell of the christen knyght replenysshed with moste holsome preceptes, made by the famous clerke Erasmus of Roterdame, to the whiche is added a newe and meruaylous profytable preface (London, 1533).

The Collected Works of Erasmus, vol. xxiii, ed. Craig R. Thompson, trans. R. A. B. Mynors (University of Toronto Press, 1978).

The Collected Works of Erasmus, vol. xxiv, ed. Craig R. Thompson (University of Toronto Press, 1978).

The Collected Works of Erasmus, vol. xxv, ed. J. K. Sowards (Toronto, Buffalo, NY and London: University of Toronto Press, 1985).

The Collected Works of Erasmus, vol. xxviii, trans. Betty I. Knott (University of Toronto Press, 1986).

The Collected Works of Erasmus, vol. xl, ed. Craig R. Thompson (University of Toronto Press, 1997).

The Collected Works of Erasmus: The Correspondence of Erasmus—letters 298 to 445 (1514–1516), vol. iii, trans. R. A. B. Mynors and D. F. S. Thomson, annot. James K. McConica (Toronto and Buffalo, NY: University of Toronto Press, 1976).

The Collected Works of Erasmus: Literary and Educational Writings, vol. vi, ed. A. H. T. Levi (University of Toronto Press, 1986).

An exhortation to the diligent studye of scripture (London, 1529).

The first tome or volume of the Paraphrase of Erasmus upon the Newe Testamente (London, 1548).
Preparation to deathe A booke as deuout as eloquent (London, 1538).
Escobedo, Andrew. *Nationalism and Historical Loss in Renaissance England: Foxe, Dee, Spenser and Milton* (Ithaca, NY and London: Cornell University Press, 2004).
Evans, Gillian R. 'John Donne and the Augustinian Paradox of Sin', *Review of English Studies* 33:129 (Feb. 1982), 1–22.
Evans, Robert C. *Ben Jonson and the Poetics of Patronage* (Lewisburg, PA, London and Toronto: Bucknell University Press/Associated University Presses, 1989).
  Habits of Mind: Evidence and Effects of Ben Jonson's Reading (Lewisburg, PA and London: Bucknell University Press/Associated University Presses, 1995).
Facey, Jane. 'John Foxe and the Defence of the English Church', in Peter Lake and Maria Dowling (eds.), *Protestantism and the National Church in Sixteenth-Century England* (London: Croom Helm, 1987).
Farrington, Benjamin. *The Philosophy of Francis Bacon* (Liverpool University Press, 1964).
Felt, Shirley Ann Rader. 'John Donne's Sermons and the *Ars Moriendi*', Ph.D. thesis, University of California Riverside (1975).
Fenner, Dudley. *The artes of logike and rethorike …* (London, 1584).
Ferguson, Arthur B. *Clio Unbound: Perception of the Social and Cultural Past in Renaissance England* (Durham, NC: Duke University Press, 1979).
Fernandes, Isabelle. 'Les Représentations du martyr dans *The Acts and Monuments* de John Foxe, ou la tentation théâtrale', *Revue des Sciences Humaines* 269 (2003), 135–51.
Ferrand, Jacques. *Erotomania or A treatise discoursing of the essence, causes, symptomes, prognosticks, and cure of love, or erotique melancholy* (London, 1640).
Fish, Simon. *A supplication of the poore commons Whereunto is added the supplication of beggers*, 2nd edn (London, 1546).
Fish, Stanley. 'Authors-Readers: Jonson's Community of the Same', *Representations* 7 (Summer 1984), 26–58.
  'Masculine Persuasive Force: Donne and Verbal Power', in Elizabeth D. Harvey and Katherine Eisaman Maus (eds.), *Soliciting Interpretation* (University of Chicago Press, 1990).
[Fisher, John]. *Psalmi seu Precatores ex variis Scripturae locis collectae* (London, 1544; 1st pub. Cologne, 1525).
Fisken, Beth Wynne. '"The Art of Sacred Parody" in Mary Sidney's *Psalmes*', *Tulsa Studies in Women's Literature* 8:2 (1989), 223–39.
Fletcher, Phineas. *The purple island, or, The isle of man together with Piscatorie eclogs and other poeticall miscellanies* (London, 1633).
Foley, Stephen. 'The Honorable Style of Henry Howard, Earl of Surrey: A Critical Reading of Surrey's Poetry', unpub. Ph.D. thesis, Yale University (1979).
Forty, A. and S. Küchler (eds.). *The Art of Forgetting* (Oxford: Berg, 1999).

Foucault, Michel. 'Film and Popular Memory', trans. Martin Jordin, in Michel Foucault, *Foucault Live (Interviews 1966–84)*, ed. Sylvère Lotringer (New York: Semiotext(e), 1989), pp. 89–96.
Fowler, Alastair. *Conceitful Thought: The Interpretation of English Renaissance Poems* (Edinburgh University Press, 1975).
Fox, Alistair. *Politics and Literature in the Reigns of Henry VII and Henry VIII* (Oxford: Blackwell, 1989).
Foxe, John. *Acts and Monuments* (London, 1563).
  Acts and Monuments (London, 1570).
  Acts and Monuments (London, 1583).
  Pandectae locurum communium (London, 1572).
  A Sermon of Christ Crucified (London, 1570).
  A Sermon preached at the Christening of a certaine Iew (London, 1578).
Fraunce, Abraham. *The lawiers logike exemplifying the praecepts of logike by the practise of the common lawe* (London, 1588).
Freeman, Mark. *Rewriting the Self: History, Memory, Narrative* (London: Routledge, 1993).
Freud, Sigmund. *The Interpretation of Dreams*, vol. iv, trans. James Strachey, ed. James Strachey *et al.*, Penguin Freud Library (Harmondsworth: Penguin, 1991; 1st pub. 1958).
  'Mourning and Melancholia', in Sigmund Freud, *The Standard Edition of the Complete Psychological Works of Sigmund Freud*, trans. James Strachey *et al.*, vol. xiv (London: Hogarth, 1957).
  'The Psychopathology of Everyday Life' (1901), in Sigmund Freud, *The Standard Edition of the Complete Psychological Works of Sigmund Freud*, vol. vi (London: Vintage, 2001).
Friedman, Donald M. 'Memory and the Art of Salvation in Donne's Good Friday Poem', *English Literary Renaissance* 3 (1973), 418–42.
Frith, John. *A disputacion of Purgatorye* (London, 1533).
Fuller, Thomas. *The Holy State* (Cambridge, 1642).
Fulwood, William. *The Castel of Memorie: wherein is conteyned the restoring, augmenting and conseruing of a memorye and remembraunce ... Made by Gulielmus Gratarolus ...* (London, 1562).
Gardiner, Stephen. *The Letters of Stephen Gardiner*, ed. James Arthur Muller (Cambridge University Press, 1933).
Gardner, Helen. 'General Introduction', in John Donne, *The Elegies and The Songs and Sonnets*, ed. with introduction by Helen Gardner (Oxford: Clarendon Press, 1965).
Garnier, Robert. *Œuvres complètes*, vol. i, ed. Lucien Pinvert (Paris: Garnier Frères, 1923).
Gascoigne, George. *The droomme of Doomes day Wherin the frailties and miseries of mans lyfe, are lyuely portrayed, and learnedly set forth. Deuided, as appeareth in the page next following. Translated and collected by George Gascoigne Esquyer* (London, 1576).
  Glasse of gouernement: A tragicall comedie (London, 1575).

A hundreth sundrie flowres bounde vp in one small poesie Gathered partely (by translation) in the fyne outlandish gardins of Euripides, Ouid, Petrarke, Ariosto, and others: and partle by inuention, out of our owne fruitefull orchardes in Englande: yelding sundrie sweete sauours of tragical, comical, and morall discourses … (London, 1573).

The Posies of George Gascoigne Esquire. Corrected, perfected, and augmented by the Author (London, 1575).

Goodden, Angelica. *The Backward Look: Memory and the Writing Self in France, 1580–1920* (Oxford: Legenda, 2000).

Gosse, Edmund. *The Life and Letters of John Donne*, 2 vols. (London: William Heinemann, 1899).

Gosson, Stephen. *The School of Abuse & Playes Confuted in Five Actions* (London, 1582).

Gratarolo, Gulielmo. *The Castel of Memorie … Made by Gulielmus Gratarolus …* (London, 1562).

Greene, Thomas M. *The Light in Troy: Imitation and Discovery in Renaissance Poetry* (New Haven, CT: Yale University Press, 1982).

Greenham, Richard. *Propositions containing answers to certaine demaunds in divers spirituall matters specially concerning the conscience oppressed with the griefe of sinne. With an epistle against hardnes of heart, made by that woorthie Preacher of the Gospell of Christ, M. R. Greenham Pastor of Drayton* (London, 1597).

Greville, Fulke. *The Life of the renowned Sir Philip Sidney* (London, 1652).

The Prose Works of Fulke Greville, Lord Brooke, ed. John Gouws (Oxford: Clarendon Press, 1986).

Grimald, Nicholas. *Marcus Tullius Ciceroes thre bookes of duties, to Marcus his sonne, turned out of latine into english, by Nicolas Grimalde. Wherunto the latine is adjoyned* (London, 1558).

Grossman, Edith (ed. and trans.). *The Golden Age: Poems of the Spanish Renaissance* (New York and London: W. W. Norton, 2007).

Grymeston, Elizabeth *Miscelanea, Meditations, Memoratiues* (London, 1604).

Guibbory, Achsah. 'John Donne and Memory as "the Art of Salvation"', *Huntington Library Quarterly* 43 (1980), 261–74.

The Map of Time: Seventeenth-Century English Literature and Ideas of Pattern in History (Urbana and Chicago: University of Illinois Press, 1986).

Hadfield, Andrew. *Literature, Politics and National Identity: Reformation to Renaissance* (Cambridge University Press, 1994).

'Prose Fiction', in Michael Hattaway (ed.), *A Companion to English Renaissance Literature and Culture* (Oxford: Blackwell, 2000), pp. 576–88.

Halbwachs, Maurice, *On Collective Memory*, trans. Lewis A. Coser (University of Chicago Press, 1992).

Hall, Basil. 'The Early Rise and Gradual Decline of Lutheranism in England (1520–1600)', in Derek Baker (ed.), *Reform and Reformation: England and the Continent c.1500–c.1750* (Oxford: Blackwell, 1979).

Haller, William. *Foxe's Book of Martyrs and the Elect Nation* (London: Jonathan Cape, 1963).

Hamilton, A. C. 'Elizabethan Romance: The Example of Prose Fiction', *ELH* 49:1 (1982), 287–99.

Hamilton, Dakota L. 'The Household of Queen Katherine Parr', unpub. D.Phil. thesis, University of Oxford (1992).

Hamlin, Hannibal. *Psalm Culture and Early Modern English Literature* (Cambridge University Press, 2004).

Hammer, Paul E. J. 'Letters of Travel Advice from the Earl of Essex to the Earl of Rutland', *Philological Quarterly* 74:3 (Summer 1995), 317–25.

The Polarisation of Elizabethan Politics: The Political Career of Robert Devereux, 2nd Earl of Essex, 1585–1597 (Cambridge University Press, 1999).

Hannay, Margaret P. 'The Countess of Pembroke's Agency in Print and Scribal Culture', in George L. Justice and Nathan Tinker (eds.), *Women's Writing and the Circulation of Ideas: Manuscript Publication in England, 1550–1880* (Cambridge University Press, 2002).

'"House-confinèd maids": The Presentation of Women's Role in the Psalmes of the Countess of Pembroke', *English Literary Renaissance* 24:1 (Winter 1994), 44–71.

Philip's Phoenix: Mary Sidney, Countess of Pembroke (Oxford University Press, 1990).

Hanson, Elizabeth. *Discovering the Subject in Renaissance England* (Cambridge University Press, 1998).

Hardy, Barbara. 'Shakespeare's Narrative Acts of Memory', *Essays in Criticism* 39:2 (Apr. 1989), 93–115.

Shakespeare's Storytellers: Dramatic Narration (London and Chester Springs, PA: Peter Owen, 1997).

Harington, Sir John. *Nugae Antiquae: Being a Miscellaneous Collection of Original Papers in Prose and Verse Written in the Reigns of Henry VIII, Edward VI, Elizabeth, James I, &c.*, 2 vols. (London, 1769), vol. ii.

Harrison, William. *The Description of England*, ed. Georges Edelen (Washington, DC and New York: Dover Publications, 1994; 1st pub. Ithaca, NY: Cornell University Press for Folger Shakespeare Library; 1968).

Harvey, Gabriel. *Ode Natalitia* (London, 1575).

Harvey, John. *An astrologicall addition, or supplement to be annexed to the late discourse vpon the great coniunction of Saturne …* (London, 1583).

Harvey Richard. *Ephemeron, sive paean, in gratiam perpurgatae reformataeque dialecticae* (London, 1583).

Philadelphus or A Defence of Brutes, and the Brutans History (London, 1593).

Harvey, Ruth E. *The Inward Wits: Psychological Theory in the Middle Ages and the Renaissance* (London: Warburg Institute/University of London, 1975).

Haugaard, W. P. 'Katherine Parr: The Religious Convictions of a Renaissance Queen', *Renaissance Quarterly* 22:4 (1969), 346–59.

Hawes, Stephen. *The historie of graunde Amoure and la bell Pucel, called the Pastime of plesure co[n]teining the knowledge of the seue[n] sciences, [and] the course of mans life in this worlde* (London, 1554; 1st pub. 1509).

Hayward, Sir John. *The first part of the life and raigne of King Henrie the IV* (London, 1599).
'TO THE HIGH AND MIGHTIE PRINCE *CHARLES Prince of Wales*', in Sir John Hayward, *The liues of the III. Normans, Kings of England William the first. William the second. Henrie the first* (London, 1613).
Heale, Elizabeth. *Wyatt, Surrey and Early Tudor Poetry* (London: Longman, 1998).
Healy, Thomas. *New Latitudes: Theory and English Renaissance Literature* (London: Edward Arnold, 1992).
Helgerson, Richard. *Forms of Nationhood: The Elizabethan Writing of England* (Chicago and London: University of Chicago Press, 1992).
Heller, Agnes. *Renaissance Man*, trans. Richard E. Allen (London: Routledge, 1978; 1st pub. 1967).
Henry VIII. *Letters and Papers, Foreign and Domestic, of the Reign of Henry VIII, 1509–1547*, ed. J. S. Brewer, J. Gairdner and R. H. Brodie, 22 vols. (London: 1862–1932).
Herbert, Mary Sidney. *The Collected Works of Mary Sidney Herbert, Countess of Pembroke*, ed. Margaret P. Hannay, Noel J. Kinnamon and Michael G. Brennan, 2 vols. (Oxford: Clarendon Press, 1998).
Herodotus. *The Histories*, trans. Aubrey de Selincourt (Harmondsworth: Penguin, 1954).
Herz, Judith Scherer. '"An excellent Exercise of Wit that Speaks so well of Ill": Donne and the Poetics of Concealment', in Claude J. Summers and Ted-Larry Pebworth (eds.), *The Eagle and the Dove: Reassessing John Donne* (Columbia: University of Missouri Press, 1986).
Hickey, Robert L. 'Donne's Art of Memory', *Tennessee Studies in Literature* 3 (1958), 29–36.
Hiscock, Andrew. '"Blabbing leaves of betraying paper": Configuring the Past in Gascoigne's *Adventures of Master F. J.*, Nashe's *The Unfortunate Traveller* and Deloney's *Jack of Newbury*', *English* 52:202 (Spring 2003), 1–20.
'Ralegh and the Arts of Memory', *Literature Compass* 4 (July 2007), 1030–58.
'"A supernal liuely fayth": Katherine Parr and the Authoring of Devotion', *Women's Writing* 9:2 (2002), 177–97.
'*To Provide for the Future, and Times Succeeding*: Walter Ralegh and the Progress of Time', in Andrea Brady and Emily Butterworth (eds.), *Uses of the Future in Early Modern Europe* (London: Routledge, 2009), pp. 90–109.
The Uses of this World: Thinking Space in Marlowe, Shakespeare, Cary and Jonson (Cardiff: University of Wales Press, 2004).
'"writers to solemnise and celebrate ... Actes and memory": Foxe and the Business of Textual Memory', in Andrew Hiscock (ed.), *The Yearbook of English Studies: Tudor Literature*, 38:1 & 38:2 (2008), 68–85.
Hobbes, Thomas. *Elements of Philosophy* (London, 1656).
Holinshed, Raphael. *The first volume of the chronicles of England, Scotlande, and Irelande* (London, 1577).

The Third volume of Chronicles, beginning at duke William the Norman, commonlie called the Conqueror; and descending by degrees of yeeres to all the kings and queenes of England in their orderlie successions ... (London, 1587).

Hooker, Richard. *A remedie against sorrow and feare, delivered in a funerall sermon* (London, 1612).

Hooper, John. *A Declaration of the ten holy co[m]maundments of allmygthye God* (London, 1549).

Horace. *The Complete Odes and Epodes*, trans. William Guy Shepherd (Harmondsworth: Penguin, 1983).

  Satires, Epistles and Ars Poetica, trans. H. Rushton Fairclough, Loeb Classical Library (London: William Heinemann; Cambridge, MA: Harvard University Press, 1991).

Howard, Henry, Earl of Surrey. *Selected Poems*, ed. Dennis Keene (Manchester: Carcanet, 1985).

  Poems, ed. Emrys Jones (Oxford: Clarendon Press, 1964).

  The Poems of Henry Howard Earl of Surrey, ed. F. M. Padelford (New York: Haskell House, 1966).

Huarte, Juan. *Examen de ingenios. The examination of mens wits ... Translated out of the Spanish tongue by M. Camillo Camili. Englished out of his Italian, by R[ichard] C[arew]* (London, 1594).

Hughes, Paul L. and James F. Larkin (eds.), *Tudor Royal Proclamations*, 3 vols. (New Haven, CT: Yale University Press, 1964–9), vol. i.

Hull, Suzanne W. *English Books for Women, 1475–1640* (San Marino, CA: Huntington Library, 1982).

Hutton, Patrick H. *History as an Art of Memory* (Hanover, NH and London: University of Vermont/University Press of New England, 1993).

Huyssen, Andreas. *Twilight Memories: Marking Time in a Culture of Amnesia* (New York and London: Routledge, 1995).

James, Susan E. *Kateryn Parr* (Aldershot: Ashgate, 1999).

Jardine, Lisa. 'Experientia literata or Novum Organum? The Dilemma of Bacon's Scientific Method', in William A. Sessions (ed.), *Francis Bacon's Legacy of Texts* (New York: AMS Press, 1990).

Jentoft, C. W. 'Rhetoric and Structure in the Poetry of Henry Howard, Earl of Surrey', Ph.D. thesis, Ohio State University (1969).

  'Surrey's Five Elegies: Rhetoric, Structure, and the Poetry of Praise', *PMLA* 91 (1976), 23–4.

  'Surrey's Four "Orations" and the Influence of Rhetoric on Dramatic Effect', *Papers on Language and Literature* 9 (1973), 250–1.

Johnson, Jeffrey. *The Theology of John Donne* (Cambridge: D. S. Brewer, 1999).

Johnson, Robert. *Essaies, or rather Imperfect offers* (London: John Windet, 1601).

Jones, Ann Rosalind. 'Inside the Outsider: Nashe's *vnfortunate traueller* and Bakhtin's Polyphonic Novel', *ELH* 50 (1983), 61–81.

Jones, Norman. *The English Reformation: Religion and Cultural Adaptation* (Oxford: Blackwell, 2002).

Jones, Ruth Ann. 'John Foxe and the Humanist Concept of History', Ph.D. thesis, University of Missouri-Columbia (1989).
Jonson, Ben. *Ben Jonson*, ed. C. H. Herford and Percy and Evelyn Simpson, 11 vols. (Oxford: Clarendon Press, 1925–52).
Jung, C. G. 'Cryptomnesia', in *The Collected Works of C. G. Jung: Psychiatric Studies*, trans. R. F. C. Hull, vol. i (London: Routledge and Kegan Paul, 1957).
Kastan, David Scott. 'Print, Literary Culture and the Book Trade', in David Loewenstein and Janel Mueller (eds.), *Cambridge History of Early Modern English Literature* (Cambridge University Press, 2002).
Kay, Dennis. *Melodious Tears: The English Funeral Elegy from Spenser to Milton* (Oxford: Clarendon Press, 1990).
Kenyon, John. *The History Men: The Historical Profession in England since the Renaissance* (London: Weidenfeld and Nicolson, 1993).
Kidd, B. J. (ed.). *Documents Illustrative of the Continental Reformation* (Oxford: Clarendon Press, 1911; repr. 1967).
King, John N. *English Reformation Literature: The Tudor Origins of the Protestant Tradition* (Princeton University Press, 1982).
  'Fiction and Fact in Foxe's *Book of Martyrs*', in David Loades, *John Foxe and the English Reformation* (Aldershot: Scolar Press, 1997).
  'Patronage and Piety', in Margaret P. Hannay, *Silent But for the Word: Tudor Women as Poets, Translators and Writers of Religious Works* (Kent, OH: Kent State University Press, 1992).
  'Religious Dissidence in Foxe's *Book of Martyrs*: Humanism or Heresy?', *Religion and Literature* 32:2 (2000), 141–56.
Kinney, Arthur. *Humanist Poetics: Thought, Rhetoric, and Fiction in Sixteenth-Century England* (Amherst: Massachusetts University Press, 1986).
Kinney, Jane M. 'Rewriting History: Thomas Deloney's *Jack of Newbury*', *West Virginia University Philological Papers* 44 (1998–9), 50–7.
Kintgern, Eugene R. *Reading in Tudor England* (University of Pittsburgh Press, 1996).
Kraye, Jill (ed.). *Cambridge Translations of Renaissance Philosophical Texts*, vol. i, *Moral Philosophy* (Cambridge University Press, 1997).
Kristeller, Paul Oskar. 'The Active and Contemplative Life in Renaissance Humanism', in Brian Vickers (ed.), *Arbeit, Musse, Meditation: Studies in the Vita activa and Vita contemplativa* (Zurich: Verlag des Fachvereine, 1991).
Kristeva, Julia. *Black Sun: Depression and Melancholia*, trans. Leon S. Roudiez (New York: Columbia University Press, 1989).
Krontiris, Tina. *Oppositional Voices: Women as Writers and Translators of Literature in the English Renaissance* (London: Routledge, 1992).
Küchler, Susanne and Walter Melion. 'Introduction', in Susanne Küchler and Walter Melion (eds.), *Images of Memory: On Remembering and Representation* (Washington, DC: Smithsonian Institute Press, 1991).
La Rochefoucauld, François de. *La Rochefoucauld: Œuvres complètes*, ed. L. Martin-Chauffier *et al.* (Paris: Gallimard, 1964).

Lake, Peter and Maria Dowling (eds.), *Protestantism and the National Church in Sixteenth-Century England* (London: Croom Helm, 1987).
Lamb, Mary Ellen. 'The Countess of Pembroke's Patronage', *English Literary Renaissance* 12:2 (1982), 162–79.
  Gender and Authorship in the Sidney Circle (Madison: University of Wisconsin Press, 1990).
  'The Myth of the Countess of Pembroke', *Yearbook of English Studies* 11 (1981), 194–202.
Lambek, Michael. 'The Past Imperfect: Remembering as Moral Practice', in Paul Antze and Michael Lambek (eds.), *Tense Past: Cultural Essays in Trauma and Memory* (New York: Routledge, 1996).
Latimer, Hugh. *A notable sermon of ye reuerende father Maister Hughe Latemar which he preached in ye Shrouds at paules churche in London, on the xviii. daye of Ianuary 1548* (London, 1548).
  27 sermons preached by the ryght Reuerende father in God and constant matir [sic] of Iesus Christe, Maister Hugh Latimer, as well such as in tymes past haue bene printed, as certayne other commyng to our handes of late, whych were yet neuer set forth in print. Faithfully perused [and] allowed accordying to the order appoynted in the Quenes Maiesties iniunctions, 2nd edn (London, 1562).
Le Goff, Jacques. *History and Memory*, trans. Steven Rendall and Elizabeth Claman (New York: Columbia University Press, 1992).
Lemnius, Levinus. *The touchstone of complexions … now Englished by Thomas Newton* (London, 1576).
Leroi-Gourhan, André. *Le Geste et la parole*, vol. ii, *La Mémoire et les rythmes* (Paris: Editions Albin Michel, 1965).
Lever, J. W. *The Elizabethan Love Sonnet* (London: Methuen, 1978; 1st pub. 1956).
Levin, Carole. 'Women in *The Book of Martyrs* as Models of Behaviour in Tudor England', *International Journal of Women's Studies* (Canada) 4:2 (1981), 196–207.
Levy, Allison. 'Augustine's Concessions and Other Failures: Mourning and Masculinity in Fifteenth-Century Tuscany', in Jennifer C. Vaught *et al.* (eds.), *Grief and Gender: 700–1700* (Basingstoke: Palgrave, 2003).
Levy, F. J. *Tudor Historical Thought* (San Marino, CA: Huntington Library, 1967).
Lewalski, Barbara Kiefer. *Protestant Poetics and the Seventeenth-Century Religious Lyric* (Princeton University Press, 1979).
Lewes, George Henry. *A Biographical History of Philosophy*, 4 vols. (London, 1852–3).
Lewis, C. S. *English Literature in the Sixteenth Century Excluding Drama* (Oxford: Clarendon Press, 1954; repr. 1959).
  Poetry and Prose in the Sixteenth Century (Oxford: Clarendon Press, 1997).
Lloyd, Lodowick. *The Pilgrimage of Princes, penned out of sundry Greeke and Latine authours* (London, 1573).
Loades, David (ed.). *John Foxe and the English Reformation* (Aldershot: Scolar Press, 1997).

'Literature and National Identity', in David Loewenstein and Janel Mueller (eds.), *The Cambridge History of Early Modern English Literature* (Cambridge University Press, 2002).
The Tudor Queens of England (London: Continuum, 2009).
Low, Anthony. *The Reinvention of Love* (Cambridge University Press, 1993).
Lowenthal, David. *The Past is a Foreign Country* (Cambridge University Press, 1985).
Lupset, Thomas. *A compendious and a very fruteful treatyse, teachynge the waye of dyenge well written to a frende, by the flowre of lerned men of his tyme, Thomas Lupsete Londoner, late deceassed, on whose soule Iesu haue mercy* (London, 1534).
An exhortation to yonge men perswading them to walke in the pathe way that leadeth to honeste and goodnes: writen to a frend of his by Thomas Lupsete Londoner, 2nd edn (London, 1535).
Luther, Martin. *A treatise, touching the libertie of a Christian. Written in Latin by Doctor Martine Luther, and translated into English by James Bell* (London, 1579).
McConica, James Kelsey. *English Humanists and Reformation Politics under Henry VIII and Edward VI* (Oxford: Clarendon Press, 1965).
McEachern, Claire. 'Introduction', in Claire McEachern and Debora Shuger (eds.), *Religion and Culture in Renaissance England* (Cambridge University Press, 1997).
The Poetics of English Nationhood, 1590–1612 (Cambridge University Press, 1996).
McGrath, Lynette. 'George Gascoigne's Moral Satire: The Didacticism of Convention in *The Adventures of Master F. J.*', *Journal of English and Germanic Philology* 11 (1971), 432–50.
Machiavelli, Niccolò. *The Discourses*, ed. Bernard Crick, trans. Leslie J. Walker and Brian Richardson (Harmondsworth: Penguin, 1978).
Mackie, J. D. *The Earlier Tudors, 1485–1558* (Oxford: Clarendon Press, 1966).
Makin, Bathsua. *An essay to revive the antient education of gentlewomen in religion, manners, arts & tongues* (London, 1673).
Malherbe, Michel. 'Bacon's Method of Science', in Markku Peltonen (ed.), *The Cambridge Companion to Bacon* (Cambridge University Press, 1996).
Margolies, David. *Novel and Society in Elizabethan England* (London: Croom Helm, 1985).
Marotti, Arthur F. *Manuscript, Print, and the English Renaissance Lyric* (Ithaca, NY and London: Cornell University Press, 1995).
Marotti, Arthur F. and Michael D. Bristol (eds.). *Print, Manuscript & Performance: The Changing Relations of the Media in Early Modern England* (Columbus: Ohio State University Press, 2000).
Marsham, Robert. 'On a Manuscript Book of Prayers … said to have been given by Queen Anne Boleyn to a Lady of the Wyatt Family', *Archaeologia* (Society of Antiquaries, London) 44:2 (1873), 259–72.
Marston, John. *The Malcontent*, ed. W. David Kay (London: A & C Black; New York: W. W. Norton, 2007).

Martin, Catherine Gimelli. 'The Feminine Birth of the Mind: Regendering the Empirical Subject in Bacon and his Followers', in Julie Robin Solomon and Catherine Gimelli Martin (eds.), *Francis Bacon and the Refiguring of Early Modern Thought* (Aldershot: Ashgate, 2005).

Martz, Louis. *The Poetry of Meditation: Study in English Religious Literature of the Seventeenth Century* (New Haven, CT: Yale University Press, 1954).

Mason, H. A. *Humanism and Poetry in the Early Tudor Period* (London: Routledge, 1959).

Masselink, Noralyn. 'Donne's Epistemology and the Appeal to Memory', *John Donne Journal* 8:1–2 (1989), 57–88.

  'Memory in John Donne's Sermons: "Readie"? or Not?', *South Atlantic Review* 63:2 (1998), 99–107.

May, Steven W. *The Elizabethan Courtier Poets* (Asheville: Pegasus Press/ University of North Carolina Press, 1999).

Meister, Deborah Anne. 'The Burning Bush: Tudor Martyrs and the Construction of Subjectivity in the English Renaissance', Ph.D. thesis, University of California, Los Angeles (1999).

Melanchthon, Philip. *Orations on Philosophy and Education*, ed. Sachiko Kusukawa (Cambridge University Press, 1999).

Mesa-Pelly, Judith Broome. 'Fantasy and Social Change in Thomas Deloney's *Jack of Newbury* and *Thomas of Reading*', *Studies in the Humanities* 23:1 (1996), 84–98.

Miller, Shannon. 'Mary Sidney and Gendered Strategies for the Writing of Poetry', in Barbara Smith *et al.* (eds.), *Write or Be Written: Early Modern Women Poets and Cultural Constraints* (Aldershot: Ashgate, 2001).

Milton, John. *The Complete English Poems, Of Education, Areopagitica*, ed. Gordon Campbell (London: Dent/Everyman, 1993).

Miner, Earl. *The Cavalier Mode from Jonson to Cotton* (Princeton University Press, 1971).

Misztal, Barbara A. *Theories of Social Remembering* (Maidenhead and Philadelphia: Open University Press, 2003).

Montaigne, Michel de. *The Essayes or Morall, Politike and Millitarie Discourses of Lo: Michaell de Montaigne … First written in French And now done in English by Iohn Florio* (London, 1603).

  The Essayes or Morall, Politike and Millitarie Discourses of Lo: Michaell de Montaigne … First written in French And now done in English by Iohn Florio, 2nd edn (London, 1613).

More, Sir Thomas. 'An answere vnto the fyrst chapyter of Tyndales boke, why he translateth this worde chyrche in to this worde congregacion', in Sir Thomas More, *The confutacyon of Tyndales answere* (London, 1532–3).

  The Complete Works of St Thomas More, vol. xv, ed. Daniel Kinney (New Haven, CT and London: Yale University Press, 1986).

Mornay, Philippe de. *A discourse of life and death. Written in French by Ph. Mornay. Antonius, a tragædie written also in French by Ro. Garnier. Both done in English by the Countesse of Pembroke* (London, 1592).

Mueller, Janel. 'Complications of Intertextuality: John Fisher, Katherine Parr, and "The Book of the Cruxifix"', in Claude J. Summers and Ted-Larry Pebworth (eds.), *Representing Women in Renaissance England* (Columbia: University of Missouri Press, 1997).
  'Devotion as Difference: Intertextuality in Queen Katherine Parr's *Prayers or Meditations* (1545)', *Huntington Library Quarterly* 53:3 (1990), 171–97.
  'A Tudor Queen Finds Voice: Katherine Parr's *Lamentation of a Sinner*', in Heather Dubrow and Richard Strier (eds.), *The Historical Renaissance: New Essays on Tudor and Stuart Literature and Culture* (University of Chicago Press, 1988).
Munday, Anthony. *A Second and Third Blast of Retrait from Plaies and Theaters* (London, 1580).
Nashe, Thomas. *The Unfortunate Traveller* (1594), in Paul Salzman (ed.), *An Anthology of Elizabethan Prose Fiction* (Oxford University Press, 1987).
  The vnfortunate traueller. Or, The life of Iacke Wilton (London, 1594).
Naunton, Sir Robert. *Fragmenta Regalia or Observations on Queen Elizabeth, Her Times and Favourites*, ed. J. S. Cerovski (Washington, DC and London: Folger Shakespeare Library, 1985).
Neill, Michael. *Issues of Death: Mortality and Identity in English Renaissance Tragedy* (Oxford: Clarendon Press, 1998).
Nichols, John. *The Progresses and Public Processions of Queen Elizabeth*, 2 vols. (London: Nichols & Son, 1788), vol. i.
Nietzsche, Friedrich. *The Complete Works of Friedrich Nietzsche*, ed. Oscar Levy, vol. ii, pt. ii (Edinburgh and London: T. N. Foulis, 1909).
Nora, Pierre. 'Entre mémoire et histoire' (pp. xvii–xlii), in Pierre Nora, *Les Lieux de mémoire*, vol. i (Paris: Editions Gallimard, 1984).
Norbrook, David. *Poetry and Politics in the English Renaissance*, rev. edn (Oxford University Press, 2002).
Norskov Olsen, V. *John Foxe and the Elizabethan Church* (Los Angeles: University of California Press, 1973).
Northbrooke, John. *Spiritus est vicarius Christi in terra* (London, 1577).
Norton, Thomas (and Thomas Sackville). *The tragedie of Gorboduc* (London, 1565).
Ong, Walter J. *Ramus: Method, and the Decay of Dialogue* (Chicago and London: University of Chicago Press, 2004).
Orgel, Stephen. *The Jonsonian Masque* (Cambridge, MA: Harvard University Press, 1965).
Ostriker, Alicia. 'Thomas Wyatt and Henry Surrey: Dissonance and Harmony in Lyric Form', *New Literary History* 1 (1970), 387–405.
Parfitt, George. 'Ethical Thought and Ben Jonson's Poetry', *Studies in English Literature* 9 (1969), 123–35.
Park, Katherine. 'The Organic Soul', in C. B. Schmitt *et al.* (eds.), *The Cambridge History of Renaissance Philosophy* (Cambridge University Press, 1992).
Parker, Michael P. 'Diamond's Dust: Carew, King and the Legacy of Donne', in Claude J. Summers and Ted-Larry Pebworth (eds.), *The Eagle and the Dove: Reassessing John Donne* (Columbia: University of Missouri Press, 1986).

Parr, Catharine [Katherine]. *The lamentacion of a sinner, made by y most vertuous Ladie, Quene Caterin, bewayling the ignoraunce of her blind life; set furth and put in print at the instaunt delite of the righte gracious ladie Caterin Duchesse of Suffolke, & the earnest requeste of the right honourable Lord, William Parre, Marquesse of Northampton* (London: Edward Whitchurch, Nov. 1547).

Prayers or medytacions, whereine the mynd is stirred, paciently to suffer all afflictions here, to set at nought the vayne prosperitee of this worlde, and alwaie to longe for the euerlastynge felicitee: Collected out of holy woorkes by the most virtuous and graciouse Princesse Katherine queen of Englande, Fraunce, and Irelande (London: Thomas Berthelet, Nov. 1545).

Prayers stirring the mind unto heavenly meditations collected out of holy works by the most virtuous and gracious princess Katherine queen of England, France, and Ireland and has the two concluding prayers of the first edition of *Prayers or medytacions* (London, 1545).

Parry, Graham. 'Literary Patronage', in David Loewenstein and Janel Mueller (eds.), *The Cambridge History of Early Modern English Literature* (Cambridge University Press, 2002).

Petrarch. *Canzoniere: Selected Poems*, trans. Anthony Mortimer (London: Penguin, 2002).

The Life of Solitude, trans. Jacob Zeitlin (Urbana: University of Illinois Press, 1924).

Pigman, G. W., III. 'Suppressed Grief in Jonson's Funeral Poetry', *ELR* 13:2 (Spring 1983), 203–20.

Plato. *Complete Works*, ed. John M. Cooper *et al.* (Indianapolis, IN and Cambridge: Hackett Publishing, 1997).

Pliny [Elder]. *Natural History*, trans. H. Rackham, vol. ii (London: William Heinemann; Cambridge, MA: Harvard University Press, 1942).

Plumb, J. H. *The Death of the Past* (Basingstoke: Macmillan, 1969).

Plutarch. *The lives of the noble Grecians and Romanes ... translated out of Greeke into French by Iames Amyot ... and out of French into Englishe, by Thomas North*, 2nd edn (London, 1579).

Pooley, Roger. *English Prose of the Seventeenth Century, 1590–1700* (London: Longman, 1992).

Praz, Mario. *Mnemosyne: The Parallel Between Literature and the Visual Arts* (Bollingen Series xxxv-16) (Princeton University Press, 1970).

Price, David W. *History Made, History Imagined: Contemporary Literature, Poiesis and the Past* (Urbana and Chicago: University of Illinois Press, 1999).

Prower, Emmanuel. 'Memory as Sign', in Wojciech H. Kalaga and Tadeusz Rachwal (eds.), *Memory–Remembering–Forgetting* (Frankfurt: Peter Lang, 1999).

Publicio, Jacopo. *Oratoriae artis epitomata* (Venice, 1482).

Pucci, Michael S. 'Reforming Roman Emperors: John Foxe's Characterization of Constantine in the *Acts and Monuments*', in David Loades (ed.), *John Foxe: An Historical Perspective* (Aldershot: Ashgate, 1999), pp. 30–51.

Puttenham, George. *The Arte of English Poesie* (1589), ed. Edward Arber (Westminster: A. Constable, 1895).

Quintilian. *The Institutio Oratoria of Quintilian*, trans. H. E. Butler (London: William Heinemann; Cambridge, MA: Harvard University Press, 1936), vol. iv.
R. B. [Richard Blower]. *Apius and Virginia* (1575), ed. Ronald B. McKerrow and W. W. Greg (London: Chiswick Press/Malone Reprints, 1911).
Raber, Karen. *Dramatic Difference: Gender, Class and Genre in the Early Modern Closet Drama* (Newark: University of Delaware Press, 2001).
Rainolds, John. *Th'overthrow of stage-playes* (Oxford, 1599).
Ralegh, Sir Walter. *The History of the World* (London, 1614).
Ramus, Petrus. *The art of arithmeticke ... translated into English by William Kempe* (London, 1592).
  Elementes of geometrie ... faithfully translated by Tho. Hood (London, 1590).
  The Latine grammar of P. Ramus translated into English (London, 1585).
  The logike of the most excellent philosopher P. Ramus ... (London, 1574).
Rankins, William. *A Mirrour of Monsters ...* (London, 1587).
Rapple, Rory. *Martial Power and Elizabethan Political Culture: Military Men in England and Ireland, 1558–1594* (Cambridge University Press, 2009).
Ravennas, Petrus [Pietro da Ravenna]. *The Art of Memory, that otherwyse is called the Phenix. A boke very behouefull and profytable to all professours of scyences. Grammaryens, rethoryciens dialectyke, legystes, phylosophres [and] theologiens* (c. 1548).
  Phoenix sive artificiosa memoria (Venice, 1491).
Renan, Ernest. 'What is a Nation?', trans. Martin Thorn, in Homi K. Bhabha (ed.), *Nation and Narration* (New York: Routledge, 1990), pp. 8–22.
Revard, Stella P. 'Donne and Propertius: Love and Death in London and Rome', in Claude J. Summers and Ted-Larry Pebworth (eds.), *The Eagle and the Dove: Reassessing John Donne* (Columbia: University of Missouri Press, 1986).
Ricoeur, Paul. *Oneself as Another* (University of Chicago Press, 1992).
  The Reality of the Historical Past (Milwaukee, WI: Marquette University Press, 1984).
  Time and Narrative, vol. i, trans. Kathleen McLaughlin and David Pellauer (University of Chicago Press, 1984).
  Time and Narrative, vol. iii, trans. Kathleen Blamey and David Pellauer (University of Chicago Press, 1988).
Ridley, Jasper. *Henry VIII* (London: Constable, 1987).
Ridley, Nicholas and Hugh Latimer. *Certein godly, learned and comfortable conference between N. Rydeley bishoppe of London, and Hughe Latymer* (London, 1556).
Roberts, Josephine A. (ed.). *The Poems of Lady Mary Wroth* (Baton Rouge: Lousiana State University Press, 1983).
Rodriguez Garcia, Jose Maria. 'Solitude and Procreation in Francis Bacon's Scientific Writings: The Spanish Connection', *Comparative Literature Studies* 35:3 (1998), 278–300.
Rollin, Roger B. '"Fantastique Ague": The Holy Sonnets and Religious Melancholy', in Claude J. Summers and Ted-Larry Pebworth (eds.), *The*

Eagle and the Dove: Reassessing John Donne (Columbia: University of Missouri Press, 1986).
Rollins, Hyder Edward (ed.). *Tottel's Miscellany (1557–1587)* (Cambridge, MA: Harvard University Press, 1965), vol. ii.
Romberch, Johann. *Congestorium artificiose memorie* (Venice, 1533).
Ronsard, Pierre de. *Œuvres complètes*, vol. vi, ed. Paul Laumonier (Paris: Hachette, 1930).
  Œuvres complètes, vol. ii, ed. Gustave Cohen (Paris: Gallimard/Pléiade, 1950).
  Selected Poems, ed. and trans. Malcolm Quainton and Elizabeth Vinestock (London: Penguin, 2002).
Ross, Malcolm Mackenzie. *Poetry and Dogma* (New York: Octagon Books, 1969).
Rossi, Paolo. *Logic and the Art of Memory: The Quest for a Universal Language*, trans. Stephen Clucas (London: Athlone, 2000).
Ryrie, Alec. 'The Unsteady Beginnings of English Protestant Martyrology', in David Loades (ed.), *John Foxe: An Historical Perspective* (Aldershot: Ashgate, 1982).
Sacks, Peter M. *The English Elegy: Studies in the Genre from Spenser to Yeats* (Baltimore, MD and London: Johns Hopkins University Press, 1985).
Salzman, Paul (ed.). *An Anthology of Elizabethan Prose Fiction* (Oxford University Press, 1987).
Sandys, George. *Anglorum speculum, or, The worthies of England in church and state* (London, 1684).
Sanford, Rhonda Lemke. *Maps and Memory in Early Modern England* (Basingstoke: Palgrave, 2002).
Scarisbrick, J. J. *Henry VIII* (London: Eyre Methuen, 1976).
Schaff, Philip (ed.). *A Select Library of the Nicene and Post-Nicene Fathers of the Christian Chu.ch*, vol. iii (Edinburgh: T & T Clark; Grand Rapids, MI: Eerdmans, 1993).
Schelling, F. *The Life and Writings of George Gascoigne* (Boston, MA: Ginn, 1893).
Schwyzer, Philip. *Literature, Nationalism, and Memory in Early Modern England and Wales* (Cambridge University Press, 2004).
Seneca [Elder]. *Declamations*, trans. M. Winterbottom, Loeb Classical Library, 2 vols. (London: William Heinemann; Cambridge, MA: Harvard University Press, 1974), vol. i.
Seneca, *Ad Lucilium Epistulae Morales*, trans. Richard M. Gummere, Loeb Classical Library, vol. i (London: William Heinemann, 1925).
  Ad Lucilium Epistulae Morales, trans. Richard M. Gummere, Loeb Classical Library, vol. ii (London: William Heinemann, 1930).
Sennett, Richard. 'Disturbing Memories', in Patricia Fara and Karalyn Patterson (eds.), *Memory* (Cambridge University Press, 1998), pp. 10–26.
Seremtakis, C. N. *The Senses Still: Perception and Memory as Material Culture in Modernity* (University of Chicago Press, 1994).
Sessions, William A. *Henry Howard, Earl of Surrey* (Boston, MA: Twayne, 1986).

'Surrey's Wyatt: Autumn 1542 and the New Poet', in Peter C. Herman (ed.), *Rethinking the Henrician Era: Essays on Early Tudor Texts and Contexts* (Urbana and Chicago: University of Illinois Press, 1994).

Shakespeare, William. *The Tempest*, ed. Frank Kermode (London: Methuen; New York: Arden, 1985).

Shepard, Alexandra and Phil Withington (eds.). *Communities in Early Modern England: Networks, Place, Rhetoric* (Manchester University Press, 2000).

Sherlock, Peter. *Monuments and Memory in Early Modern England* (Aldershot: Ashgate, 2008).

Sherman, William H. *John Dee: The Politics of Reading and Writing in the English Renaissance* (Amherst: University of Massachusetts Press, 1995).

Sherwood, Terry G. *Fulfilling the Circle: A Study of John Donne's Thought* (University of Toronto Press, 1984).

Sidney Herbert, Mary, Countess of Pembroke. *The Collected Works of Mary Sidney Herbert, Countess of Pembroke*, ed. Margaret P. Hannay, Noel J. Kinnamon and Michael G. Brennan, 2 vols. (Oxford: Clarendon Press, 1998).

Sidney, Sir Philip. *The Countess of Pembrokes Arcadia. Written by Sir Philip Sidney Knight. Now since the first edition augmented and ended* (London, 1593).

Defence of Poesie, Astrophil and Stella and Other Writings, ed. Elizabeth Porges-Watson (London: Everyman/Dent, 1997).

A Defence of Poetry, ed. Jan Van Dorsten (Oxford University Press, 1978).

'A Letter written by Sir Philip Sidney to Queen Elizabeth, touching her marriage with Monsieur', in Katherine Duncan-Jones and Jan Van Dorsten (eds.), *Miscellaneous Prose of Sir Philip Sidney* (Oxford: Clarendon Press, 1973), pp. 46–57.

Sir Philip Sidney: A Critical Edition of the Major Works, ed. Katherine Duncan-Jones (Oxford University Press, 1989).

Skretkowicz, Victor. 'Mary Sidney Herbert's Antonius, English Philhellenism and the Protestant Cause', *Women's Writing* 6:1 (1999), 7–25.

Smith, A. J. (ed.). *John Donne: The Critical Heritage* (London: Routledge and Kegan Paul, 1975).

Smith, Charles W. 'Structural and Thematic Unity in Gascoigne's *The Adventures of Master F. J.*', *Papers on Language and Literature* 2 (1966), 99–108.

Smith, Logan Pearsall (ed.). *Life and Letters of Henry Wotton*, vol. ii (Oxford University Press, 1907).

Smuts, R. Malcolm. *Culture and Power in England, 1585–1685* (London: Macmillan, 1999).

Solomon, Julie Robin. *Objectivity in the Making: Francis Bacon and the Politics of Inquiry* (Baltimore, MD: Johns Hopkins University Press, 1998).

Sontag, Susan. *The Susan Sontag Reader*, introduction by Elizabeth Hardwick (Harmondsworth: Penguin, 1982).

Sowerby, Robin. *The Classical Legacy in Renaissance Poetry* (London: Longman, 1994).

Spearing, A. C. *Mediaeval to Renaissance in English Poetry* (Cambridge University Press, 1985).

Speed, John. *The history of Great Britaine under the conquests of ye Romans, Saxons, Danes and Normans* (London, 1611).
Speed Hill, W. (ed.). *New Ways of Looking at Old Texts: Papers of the Renaissance English Text Society, 1985–1997*, vol. cvii (Binghamton, NY: Medieval and Renaissance Texts and Studies, 1993).
Spenser, Edmund. *Amoretti* (London, 1595).
  Colin Clouts come home againe (London, 1595).
  Complaints Containing sundrie small poemes of the worlds vanitie. Whereof the next page maketh mention (London, 1591).
  The Faerie Queene, ed. Thomas P. Roche Jr and C. Patrick O'Donnell Jr (Harmondsworth: Penguin, 1987).
  The Works of Edmund Spenser: A Variorum Edition, vol. x, *The Prose Works*, ed. Rudolf Gottfried (Baltimore, MD: Johns Hopkins University Press, 1949).
Stephens, James. *Francis Bacon and the Style of Science* (University of Chicago Press, 1975).
Stevenson, Laura Caroline *Praise and Paradox: Merchants and Craftsmen in Elizabethan Popular Literature* (Cambridge University Press, 1984).
Stow, John. *A Survey of the Cities of London and Westminster ... Written at first in the Year MDXCVIII. By John Stow ... Now Lastly Corrected, Improved, and very much Enlarged ... By John Strype*, 2 vols. (London, 1720), vol. ii.
Strype, John. *Ecclesiastical memorials; relating chiefly to religion, and the reformation of it, and the emergencies of the Church of England* (London, 1721).
Sullivan, Garrett, Jr. *Memory and Forgetting in English Renaissance Drama* (Cambridge University Press, 2005).
Summit, Jennifer. *Memory's Library: Medieval Books in Early Modern England* (Chicago and London: University of Chicago Press, 2008).
Swaim, Kathleen M. 'Contextualising Mary Sidney's Psalms', *Christianity and Literature* 48:3 (Spring 1999), 253–73.
Swinburne, Algernon Charles. *The Complete Works of Algernon Charles Swinburne*, ed. Sir Edmund Gosse and Thomas James Wise, vol. xii, Bonchurch edition: *Prose Works*, vol. ii (London: William Heinemann; New York: Gabriel Wells, 1926).
Tallis, Raymond. 'A Critique of Neuromythology', in R. Tallis and H. Robinson (eds.), *The Pursuit of Mind* (Manchester: Carcanet Press, 1991).
Tasso. *Godfrey of Bulloigne: or The recovery of Jerusalem. Done into English heroical verse, by Edward Fairfax, Gent.* (London, 1686).
Terdiman, Richard. *Present Past: Modernity and the Memory Crisis* (Ithaca, NY and London: Cornell University Press, 1993).
Thomson, Patricia. 'Wyatt and Surrey', in Christopher Ricks (ed.), *English Poetry and Prose, 1540–1674* (Harmondsworth: Penguin, 1993).
Tilyou, Elizabeth M. 'Fician Element in Selected Poems of Mary Sidney Herbert, Countess of Pembroke', in Dorothy L. Latz (ed.), *Neglected English Literature: Recusant Writings of the 16th–17th Centuries* (Salzburg: Institut für Anglistik und Amerikanistik, 1997).

Tomkis, Thomas. *Lingua: or The combat of the tongue, and the fiue senses for superiority. A pleasant comoedie* (London, 1607).
Tonkin, Elizabeth. *Narrating our Pasts: The Social Construction of Oral History* (Cambridge University Press, 1992).
Trill, Suzanne. 'Spectres and Sisters: Mary Sidney and the "Perennial Puzzle" of Renaissance Women's Writing', in Gordon McMullan (ed.), *Renaissance Configurations: Voices/Bodies/Spaces, 1580–1690* (London: Macmillan, 1998).
Tunstall, Cuthbert. *Certaine godly and deuout prayers. Made in latin by the Reuerend father in God, Cuthbert Tunstall, Bishop of Durham, and translated into Englishe by Thomas Paynell, clerke* (London, 1558).
Tuvill, Daniel (D.T.). *Essaies politicke, and morall* (London: Humphrey Lownes, 1608).
Tyndale, William. *The Newe Testament* (Antwerp, 1534).
  Prolog in to the seconde boke of Moses called Exodus. Second boke of Moses, called Exodus ... [The Pentateuch] (London, 1530).
Udall, Nicholas. 'To the moste vertuous Ladie Quene Katerine, late wife to the moste noble, and moste victorious king Henry the eigh[th] of most famous memories, Nicolas Udal your moste humble seruaunt wisheth health, grace, and consolacion in our Lorde Jesus Christe euerlastyng', in Desiderius Erasmus, *The first tome or volume* (London, 1548).
van den Berg, Sara. *The Action of Ben Jonson's Poetry* (Newark: University of Delaware Press, 1987).
  'True Relation: The Life and Career of Ben Jonson', in Richard Harp and Stanley Stewart (eds.), *The Cambridge Companion to Ben Jonson* (Cambridge University Press, 2000).
van Houts, Elisabeth. *Memory and Gender in Medieval Europe, 900–1200* (London: Palgrave, 1999).
Vickers, Brian. 'Bacon among the Literati: Science and Language', *Comparative Criticism* 13 (1991), 249–71.
Vico, Giambattista. *The New Science of Giambattista Vico*, trans. Thomas Goddard Bergin and Max Harold Fisch (Ithaca, NY and London: Cornell University Press, 1984).
Virgil. *Eclogues, Georgics, Aeneid I–VI*, trans. H. Rushton Fairclough, rev. G. P. Goold, Loeb Classical Library (Cambridge, MA and London: Harvard University Press, 1999).
Vives, Juan Luis. *The Education of a Christian Woman: A Sixteenth-Century Manual*, ed. and trans. Charles Fantazzi (Chicago and London: University of Chicago Press, 2000).
  An introduction to wysedome ... Translated into Englyshe, by Richard Moryson (London, 1558).
  On Education: A Translation of the De tradendis disciplinis *of Juan Luis Vives*, ed. and trans. Foster Watson (Totowa, NJ: Rowman and Littlefield, 1977 [1913]).
  On Education: A Translation of 'De Tradendis Disciplinis' of Juan Luis Vives, trans. Foster Watson (Cambridge University Press, 1913).

Wabuda, Susan. 'The Woman with the Rock: The Controversy on Women and Bible Reading', in Susan Wabuda and Caroline Litzenberger (eds.), *Belief and Practice in Reformation England* (Aldershot: Ashgate, 1998).

Waddington, Raymond B. '*Paradise Lost*: Memories are Made of This', in Donald Beecher and Grant Williams (eds.), *Ars Reminiscendi: Mind and Memory in Renaissance Culture* (Toronto: Centre for Reformation and Renaissance, 2009), pp. 213–27.

Walker, Greg. *Writing Under Tyranny: English Literature and the Henrician Reformation* (Oxford University Press, 2005).

Wall, Wendy. *The Imprint of Gender: Authorship and Publication in the English Renaissance* (Ithaca, NY: Cornell University Press, 1993).

Waller, Gary F. *Mary Sidney, Countess of Pembroke: A Critical Study of her Writings and Literary Milieu* (University of Salzburg, 1979).

'"This Matching of Contraries": Calvinism and Courtly Philosophy in the Sidney Psalms', *English Studies* 55 (1974), 22–31.

The Triumph of Death and Other Unpublished and Uncollected Poems by Mary Sidney, Countess of Pembroke (1561–1621) (Salzburg: Institute of English Language and Literature, 1977).

Walton, Izaak. *The Life of John Donne* (London, 1658; 1st pub. 1640).

The Lives of Dr. John Donne, Sir Henry Wootton, Mr. Richard Hooker, Mr. George Herbert 1670 (Menston: Scolar Press Facsimiles, 1969).

Warnock, Mary. *Memory* (London: Faber and Faber, 1987).

Watson, Thomas. *Compendium memoriae localis* (London, 1585).

The Hekatompathia : or, Passionate centurie of love (London, 1582).

Wayne, Don E. *Penshurst: The Semiotics of Place and the Poetics of History* (Madison: University of Wisconsin Press, 1984).

Webbe, William. *A discourse of English poetrie Together with the author's iudgment, touching the reformation of our English verse* (London, 1586).

Wheeler, Wendy. 'In the Middle of Ordinary Things: Rites, Procedures and (Last) Orders', *New Formations* 34 (1988), 129–51.

'Melancholic Modernity and Contemporary Grief: The Novels of Graham Swift', *Literature and the Contemporary: Fictions and Theories of the Present*, ed. Roger Luckhurst and Peter Marks (New York: Longman, 1999), pp. 63–79.

White, Helen C. *Tudor Books of Saints and Martyrs* (Madison: University of Wisconsin Press, 1963).

White, R. S. *Shakespeare and the Romance Ending* (Newcastle upon Tyne: Tyneside Press, 1981).

Whitney, Charles. *Francis Bacon and Modernity* (New Haven, CT: Yale University Press, 1986).

Whythorne, Thomas. *Autobiography of Thomas Whythorne*, ed. James M. Osbourne (Oxford: Clarendon Press, 1961).

Wilcox, Donald J. *The Measure of Times Past: Pre-Newtonian Chronologies and the Rhetoric of Relative Time* (University of Chicago Press, 1987).

Williams, Raymond. *The Country and the City* (Oxford University Press, 1973).

Willis, John. *The Art of Memory so far forth as it dependeth vpon places and idea's Written first in Latine, by Iohn Willis Bachelour in Diuinitie: and now published in English by the said author, with such alternations thereof as seemed needful* (London, 1621).
  Mnemonica, or The Art of Memory drained out of the pure Fountains of Art & Nature digested into Three Books. Also a Physical Treatise of cherishing Natural Memory; diligently collected out of divers learned Mens Writings (London: Leonard Sowersby, 1661).
  Mnemonica, siue reminiscendi ars è puris artis naturaeque fontibus hausta, & in tres libros digesta (London, 1618).
Wilson, Thomas. *The Art of Rhetoric*, ed. Peter E. Medine (University Park: Pennsylvania State University Press, 1993).
  The Arte of Rhetorique for the vse of all suche as are studious of eloquence (London, 1553).
Witherspoon, Alexander M. *The Influence of Robert Garnier on Elizabethan Drama* (New Haven, CT: Yale University Press, 1924).
Wolf, Philipp. *Modernization and the Crisis of Memory: John Donne to Don DeLillo* (Amsterdam: Rodopi Press: 2002).
Wooden, Warren W. *John Foxe* (Boston, MA: Twayne, 1983).
Woolf, D. R. 'The Rhetoric of Martyrdom: Generic Contradiction and Narrative Strategy in John Foxe's *Acts and Monuments*', in Thomas F. Mayer and D. R. Woolf (eds.), *The Rhetorics of Life-Writing in Early Modern Europe: Forms of Biography from Cassandra Fedele to Louis XIV* (Ann Arbor: University of Michigan Press, 1995).
  'Two Elizabeths? James I and the Late Queen's Famous Memory', *Canadian Journal of History/Annales Canadiennes d'Histoire* 20:2 (Aug. 1985), 167–91.
Worthington, Kim L. *Self as Narrative: Subjectivity and Community in Contemporary Fiction* (Oxford: Clarendon Press, 1996).
Wotton, Sir Henry. *A parallel betweene Robert late Earle of Essex, and George late Duke of Buckingham* (London, 1641).
Woudhuysen, H. R. *Sir Philip Sidney and the Circulation of Manuscripts, 1558–1640* (Oxford: Clarendon Press, 1996).
Wright, Eugene P. *Thomas Deloney* (Boston, MA: Twayne, 1981).
Wright, Thomas. *The passions of the minde* (London, 1601).
Yates, Frances A. *The Art of Memory* (London: Routledge and Kegan Paul, 1966).
  Astraea: The Imperial Theme in the Sixteenth Century (London and Boston, MA: Routledge and Kegan Paul, 1975).
Younge, Richard. *The victory of patience and benefit of affliction ... together with a counterpoyson or antipoyson against all griefe* (London, 1636).
Zagorin, Perez. *Francis Bacon* (Princeton University Press, 1998).
Zim, Rivkah. *English Metrical Psalms: Poetry as Praise and Prayer, 1535–1601* (Cambridge University Press, 1987).

Index

Achinstein, Sharon, 94, 110
Agrippa, Cornelius, 68, 120, 136
Albanese, Denise, 226
Albertus Magnus, 21, 180, 183
   De Bono, 21–2
Alleyn, Edward, 214
Andrewes, Lancelot, 190, 243
Anne of Cleves, 85, 88
Antze, Paul, 143
Apius and Virginia, 31
Aquinas, Thomas, 21, 22, 171, 180, 181, 183, 185, 222
   Summa Theologiæ, 22
Ariosto, 198
Aristotle, 11, 13, 31, 49, 143, 152, 171, 177, 179, 180, 182, 193, 210, 221, 222, 223, 227, 243
   De Anima, 11
   De Memoria et Reminiscentia, 10, 11, 12, 14, 20
   The History of Animals, 10
Ascham, Roger, 54
Askew, Anne, 80, 82, 104
Aubrey, John, 12, 240
Augustine, 20, 91, 101, 150, 166, 169, 170, 171, 172, 178, 179, 181, 185, 200, 275
   Confessions, 20, 21, 77, 78
   De Trinitate, 20
Aurelius, Marcus, 190
Austen, Gillian, 131
Averroes, 15
Avicenna, 15, 28, 29, 183

Bacon, Sir Francis, 8, 35–6, 187, 195, 217, 245, 282
   Advancement of Learning, 162, 214, 221, 224, 226, 228, 229, 232, 240
   Bacon remembered, 245
   Cogitata et Visa, 223, 226
   Cogitationes, 225
   Essays, 209, 212, 219, 225, 233, 242
   Henry VII, 28, 231, 234
   Historia Densi et Rari, 235, 236
   Historia Ventorum, 234, 235, 236, 237
   Letters, 230, 238, 239
   New Atlantis, 226, 227, 229
   Novum Organum, 222, 223, 226, 227, 228, 230, 232, 233, 242
   Sapientia Veterum, 229
   Temporis, 220, 225, 226, 227, 228, 229, 230
   Valerius Terminus, 222
Bacon, Sir Nicholas, 240
Bainton, Roland H., 88
Baker, Sir Richard, 167
Bakhtin, Mikhail, 114, 115, 116, 119, 124, 127, 135
Bald, R. C., 189
Baldwin, William, 27, 79
Bale, John, 27, 215
Barlow, John, Dean of Westbury, 38
Barnaby, Andrew, 243, 283
Bartlett, F. C., 178
Bartlett, I. Ross, 106
Baxter, Nathaniel, 162
Beaufort, Lady Margaret, 67
Beaumont, Francis, 200, 217
Becket, Thomas, 109
Becon, Thomas, 74, 140
Bentley, Thomas
   The monument of matrones, 81
Berg, Sara van den, 196, 203
Bergson, Henri, 247, 281
Bernard of Clairvaux, 66, 77–8, 181–2, 257
Berthelet, Thomas, 66
Biggs, B. J. H., 256
Boleyn, Anne, 67, 75
Bolton, John, 263
Bolzoni, Lina, 6, 28
Borough, Sir Thomas, 75
Boughton, Joan, 104
Bouza, Fernando, 19, 159, 194
Breton, Nicholas, 140, 161, 219
Brigden, Susan, 55
Brinkelow, Henry, 79, 80

Brinsley, John, 13
Brown, Cedric, 275
Browne, Sir Thomas, 164, 223
Browne, William, 163, 164
Buckingham, Duke of. *See* Villiers, George
Bullinger, Heinrich, 87
Burke, Victoria E., 238
Burlinson, Christopher, 267
Burrow, Colin, 255

Caesar, Julius, 239, 242
Caesar, Sir Julius, 33
Calvin, Jean, 159, 161, 180
Camden, William, 28, 199
  Britannia, 26, 27, 57, 99, 215
Carew, Richard
  Survey of Cornwall, 27, 216
Carew, Thomas, 190
Carey, John, 121, 135, 189
Carrara, Giammichele Alberto da, 14
Carruthers, Mary, 6
Cary, Sir Lucius, 211
Casaubon, Isaac, 230
Castel of Memorie, The (Gratarolo, Fulwood translation), 7, 10, 15, 17, 29, 147, 152
Castiglione, 161
Catullus, 197
Caxton, William, 55, 66, 263
  The myrrour, 17
Cecil, Robert, 1st Earl of Salisbury, 242
Cecil, William, Lord Burghley, 84
Cervantes, 115
Chapman, George, 209, 214
Charles I, 179
Chaucer, Geoffrey, 52, 129
Chedgzoy, Kate, 156, 198
Cheke, Sir John, 63
Childs, Jessie, 252
Cicero, 18, 21, 26, 35, 138, 146, 155, 180, 181, 193, 207, 209, 239, 243, 283
  De Amicitia, 210
  De Divinatione, 233
  De Inventione, 18, 180
  De Oratore, 12, 15, 17
  De Re Publica, 233
  Letters, 233
Cixous, Hélène, 29
Clapham, David, 68
Clarke, Danielle, 160
Clere, Sir Thomas, 58, 59
Cohen, Simona, 249
Colclough, David, 220
Coleman, Janet, 6, 16, 181, 182, 197
Colet, John, 51, 70
Collinson, Patrick, 260, 264

Cornwallis, Sir William, 224, 242
Coverdale, Miles, 74, 87
Cox, Leonard, 13
Cranmer, Thomas, 86, 94, 95
Cromwell, Thomas, 55, 75, 94
Cubitt, Catherine, 106, 108

Damon and Pithias, 14
Daniel, Samuel, 140, 151, 162
  The first fowre bookes, 28
Daniell, David, 98, 104
Dante, 100
Davis, Walter R., 117
Deleuze, Gilles, 30
Deloney, Thomas
  Elizabethan fiction remembered, 135–268
  Jack of Newbury, 33, 115, 121–8, 134
  Thomas of Reading, 126
Demosthenes, 243
Denny, Sir Edward, 138, 151, 164
Devereux, Robert, 2nd Earl of Essex, 18, 230
Dickens, A. G., 82
Digby, Sir Kenelm, 197
Dionysius Carthusianus, 67
Donne, John, 34, 39, 77, 78, 150, 161, 165–91, 197, 199, 200, 202, 208, 217, 221, 231
  Anniversaries, 186–8
  Biathanatos, 167
  Devotional verse, 178, 184–6
  Devotions Upon Emergent Occasions, 174, 274
  Donne remembered, 165–7, 188–91
  Essays in Divinity, 190
  Paradoxes and Problems, 177, 188
  Secular verse, 168, 172–4, 175–6, 177–8, 186
  Sermons, 159, 165, 167–72, 174, 177, 179–82, 183, 184, 185, 186, 188
Dorp, Martin, 25
Douglas, Gavin, 55
Dowriche, Anne, 145
Drayton, Michael, 195
Drummond, William, of Hawthornden, 166, 193, 195
Dryden, John, 242
Dubrow, Heather, 202
Dudley, John, Duke of Northumberland, 87
Dudley, Robert, Earl of Leicester, 140
Dutton, Richard, 212

Edmonds, Clement, 213
Edmund of Abingdon, 23
Edward Seymour, Duke of Somerset, 87
Edward the Confessor, 55
Edward VI, 32, 63, 86, 92, 94, 111, 140, 146, 263
  Injunctions, 72

Eliot, T. S., 39, 190, 196
Elizabeth I, 25, 56, 66, 81, 92, 99, 140, 142, 152, 156, 157, 163, 219, 231, 256
Elyot, Sir Thomas, 6, 40, 41, 42, 66, 73
Engel, William E., 203, 243
Erasmus, 17, 23, 24, 25, 40, 67, 68–70, 71–2, 74, 86, 95, 136, 146, 192, 239, 241, 254
  De Conscribendi Epistolis, 69
  De ratione studii, 24
  Dialogus Ciceronianus, 158
  Enchiridion militis Christiani, 23, 69, 78
  Parabolae, 25
  Paraclesis, 68
Eusebius of Caesarea, 93, 106
Evans, Robert C., 208, 280

Facey, Jane, 100
Ferguson, Arthur B., 245
Fetty, John, 105
Ficino, Marsilio
  Neoplatonism, 51, 144
Fish, Simon, 72, 73
Fish, Stanley, 188, 215
Fisher, John, Bishop of Rochester, 86, 256
Fitzroy, Henry, Duke of Richmond, 58, 59–60
Fletcher, John, 218
  Henry VIII, 217
Florio, John, 146
Foley, Stephen, 46
Foucault, Michel, 131
Fowler, Alastair, 38, 50
Fowler, William, 34
Foxe, John, 27, 32–3, 89, 90–112, 114, 119, 169, 170, 215
  Acts and Monuments, 27, 80, 81–2, 88, 90–1, 92–6, 97–109, 110–12, 143
  Foxe remembered, 111–12
  Pandectae locorum communium, 17, 92
  Sermon, Christening of a certaine Iew, 110
  Sermon of Christ Crucified, 100, 109, 110
  Sources, 260
Fraunce, Abraham, 18, 140, 162
Freud, Sigmund, 9, 154, 164
Frith, John, 72, 107
Fuller, Thomas, 12, 15, 236, 240

Galen, 15, 28, 182, 183
Gardiner, Stephen, Bishop of Winchester, 80, 81, 89, 102
Gardner, Helen, 177
Garnier, Robert, 34, 65, 140, 145–8, 152, 158
Gascoigne, George
  Elizabethan fiction remembered, 135–268
  Glasse of gouernement, 26
  Master F. J., 33, 115–16, 128–35
Gerson, Jean, 67
Golding, Arthur, 159
Goodden, Angelica, 153, 157
Goodwin, Christopher, 68
Gosynhill, Edward, 68
Gower, John, 42
Grafton, Richard, 27
Greenham, Richard, 180
Greville, Fulke, 139, 143, 155
  Life of Sidney, 35
Grey, Lady Jane, 101, 158
Grierson, Herbert J. C., 39, 190
Grimald, Nicholas, 146
Grymeston, Elizabeth, 150, 154
Guattari, Félix, 30
Guibbory, Achsah, 178, 179
Guicciardini, Francesco, 28

Hackett, Sir John, 73
Hadfield, Andrew, 135, 136
Hall, Edward, 27, 215
Haller, William, 108
Hamilton, A. C., 135
Hamilton, Dakota L., 87
Hamlin, Hannibal, 159
Hannay, Margaret P., 143
Harington, Sir John, 63, 161, 163
Harrison, William, 93
Harvey, Gabriel, 18
Harvey, Richard, 18
Harvey, Ruth E., 183
Hawes, Stephen
  Pastime of Pleasure, 17
Hayward, Sir John, 91
  Lives of Three Normans, 28
Hazlitt, William, 190
Heale, Elizabeth, 39, 52, 58
Healy, Thomas, 136
Heidegger, Martin, 32
Helgerson, Richard, 94, 262
Heller, Agnes, 40
Helpe to memory and discourse, A (attributed to William Basse), 5
Henrietta Maria, 208
Henry V, 109, 217
Henry VIII, 32, 38, 39, 41, 51, 67, 68, 72, 75, 79, 80, 81, 82, 85, 87, 114, 116, 120, 121, 123, 124, 126, 128, 136, 156, 216
Herbert, George, 159
Herz, Judith Scherer, 176
Hesiod, 214
Heywood, John, 63
Hilliard, Nicholas, 243
Hilton, Walter, 66

Index

Hiscock, Andrew, 254, 261, 266, 279
Hobbes, Thomas, 9
Holinshed, Raphael, 215
  Chronicles, 27, 143, 151
Hooker, Richard, 94, 145, 242
Hooper, John, 71
Horace, 54, 173, 194, 197, 215
Hotman, François, 145
Houts, Elizabeth van, 142
Howard, Catherine, 88
Howard, Henry, Earl of Surrey, 32, 37–64, 68, 97, 117–19, 120, 136, 146, 155, 156, 170, 213
  Aeneid, 53–8
  Elegies, 58–62
  Surrey remembered, 62–4
Hutton, Patrick H., 265
Huyssen, Andreas, 3, 5

James IV of Scotland, 124
James VI/I, 34, 165, 202, 219, 224, 243
James, Susan, 72, 80, 85, 88, 255, 256
Jentoft, C. W., 38, 41, 61
John of the Cross, St, 182
Johnson, Robert, 220
Jones, Ann Rosalind, 119
Jones, Emrys, 56
Jones, Norman, 126
Jonson, Ben, 34–5, 166, 167, 187, 189, 190, 192–218, 225, 231
  The Case is Altered, 193
  Catiline, 217, 218
  Every Man in His Humor, 216
  Haddington Masque, 118
  Jonson remembered, 215–18
  The New Inn, 207
  Timber, or Discoveries, 112, 192, 195, 212, 214, 215, 218, 242
  Volpone, 197
Julian of Norwich, 67
Jung, C. J., 11
Juvenal, 197

Kastan, David Scott, 70
Katherine of Aragon, 23, 67, 72, 123, 124
Kay, Dennis, 62, 154, 155
Keene, Dennis, 38
Kempe, Margery, 67
Kempis, Thomas à, 66, 75, 77
Kenyon, John, 234
Ker, Sir Robert, 167
Key, Thomas, 72
Kiernan, Michael, 282
King, Henry, 190
King, John N., 78, 87, 98, 263
Kinney, Arthur, 114

Kinney, Jane M., 125
Kristeva, Julia, 272
Krontiris, Tina, 164

La Rochefoucauld, François de, 193
Lamb, Mary Ellen, 140, 146, 152
Lambarde, William
  Perambulation of Kent, 27, 216
Lanyer, Aemilia, 142, 151
Latimer, Hugh, 78, 86, 90, 91, 104, 105, 264
Legenda Aurea, 103, 263
Leland, John, 27, 28, 62, 215
León, Fray Luis de, 178
Lever, J. W., 39
Levin, Carole, 88
Lewes, George Henry, 245
Lewis, C. S., 39, 48, 50, 135
Lichfield, John, 4
Linacre, William, 67
Lipsius, Justus, 209
Livy, 26, 202
Loades, David, 88, 260
Lok, Anne Vaughan, 158
Low, Anthony, 99
Lowenthal, David, 187
Lupset, Thomas, 66, 70, 74, 149
Luther, Martin, 70, 81, 83, 85, 120, 136, 150, 228
Lydgate, John, 42

McConica, James Kelsey, 67
McEachern, Claire, 112
McGrath, Lynette, 132
Machiavelli, Niccolò, 28
  Discourses, 212, 233
Maecenas, 203
Mann, F. O., 136
Margolies, David, 125
Marlowe, Christopher
  Dr Faustus, 207
Marston, John
  The Malcontent, 13
Martial, 41, 44, 58, 197, 209, 213
Marvell, Andrew, 207
Mary I, 71, 88, 92, 93, 101, 140, 243
Mason, H. A., 50
Masselink, Noralyn, 178, 180, 185
May, Steven W., 163
Melanchthon, Philipp, 25, 207, 241
Memory
  and Augustinian ideas, 20–3, 70–1, 77–8, 91, 113, 150, 166, 168, 169, 170, 178, 179, 185, 200
  and historiography, 27–8, 207, 215–17, 230–4, 283
  and Latin writers, 15–16, 155, 173, 192–3, 207, 208, 209, 213, 214, 237–41, 283

Memory (cont.)
  and mourning, 50, 139–40, 143, 145, 151, 153–61, 272
  and nation, 108–9
  and pedagogy, 26–7, 147, 224, 230, 234–7
  and religion, 102, 106, 108, 169–70
  and rhetoric, 15–16, 76, 92–3, 113, 173, 192–3, 237–41
  and the body, 13–15, 28–31, 77–8, 150, 179–88, 205–6
  and the humanists, 23–5, 39–48
  Aristotle, 10–12, 31, 102, 143, 152, 171, 177, 182, 193, 222, 223
  Moral, 13, 20
  Mythology, 6
  Plato, 7–8, 31, 143, 169, 170, 171, 178, 183, 197, 223, 224, 237
  Ramist influence, 17–18
Mesa-Pelly, Judith Broome, 125
Milton, John, 198, 209, 244
Mirror for Magistrates, A, 27
Montaigne, Michel de (Florio translation), 8, 9, 143, 168, 178, 184, 188, 196, 209, 225
More, Sir Thomas, 25, 67, 70, 73, 107, 120, 130, 136
Morison, Sir Henry, 211
Mornay, Philippe de, 65, 140, 149–51, 152
Mueller, Janel, 80, 86, 89

Nashe, Thomas
  Elizabethan fiction remembered, 135–268
  The Unfortunate Traveller, 33, 63, 113–15, 116–21, 134
Naunton, Sir Robert, 194
Navarre, Marguerite de, 256
Neill, Michael, 145
Neoplatonism. See Ficino, Marsilio
Neville, John, Lord Latimer, 75
Nora, Pierre, 4, 5
Norbrook, David, 194
Norden, John
  Middlesex, 27
North, Sir Thomas
  translation of Amyot's *Preface to Plutarch*, 26
Northbrooke, John, 4

Ong, Walter, 17
Orgel, Stephen, 213
Ostriker, Alicia, 48
Ovid, 241

Paget, Sir William, 80
Parfitt, George, 193
Parr, Katherine, 32, 65–89, 109, 170
  Lamentacion, 79–81, 83–7

Paraphrases, 71–2, 146
Parr remembered, 81
Prayers or medytacions, 65–7, 68, 75–9, 83, 84, 85, 86, 89, 255
Passe, Simon de, 140
Pembroke, Countess of, Mary Sidney.
  See Sidney, Mary
Petrarch, 34, 40, 43, 44, 47, 48, 49, 51, 53, 60, 61, 100, 117, 118, 132, 133, 140, 151–3, 155, 158, 173, 177, 230
Philips, Katherine, 138
Philpot, John, 107
Philpot, John, Archdeacon of Winchester, 105
Pigman III, G. W., 280
Plato, 11, 31, 169, 171, 178, 179, 183, 185, 197, 218, 221, 222, 223, 224, 227, 237
  Meno, 7
  Phaedo, 7, 8
  Phaedrus, 233
  Theaetetus, 7
  Timaeus, 233
Pliny the Elder, 236
  Naturalis Historia, 12
Pliny the Younger
  Letters, 212
Plumb, J. H., 6, 246
Plutarch, 6
Price, David W., 267
Publico, Jacopo, 248
Pucci, Michael S., 111
Puttenham, George, 37, 56, 63

Quevedo, Francisco de, 187
Quintilian, 193
  Institutio oratoria, 15, 16

Raber, Karen, 148
Rainolds, John, 4
Ralegh, Sir Walter, 188, 195, 242
  The History of the World, 28, 207, 232, 233
Ramus, 17
Rankins, William, 5
Rapple, Rory, 38
Ravenna, Pietro da
  Phoenix sive artificiosa memoria, 16
  The Art of Memory (Copland translation), 16
Razes (Abu Bakr Al-Razi), 183
Rees, Graham, 237
Renan, Ernest, 108
Rhetorica ad Herennium, 15, 16
Richard II, 97
Ricoeur, Paul, 2, 32, 143, 155, 164, 194, 218
Ridley, Nicholas, Bishop of London, 90, 91, 95, 101, 104
Roe, Sir John, 199, 209, 210

Roe, Sir Thomas, 200
Roe, William, 209
Rollin, Roger B., 184
Romberch, Johann, 248
Ronsard, Pierre de, 52, 58, 60
   La Franciade, 54
Ross, Malcolm Mackenzie, 170
Rossi, Paolo, 6, 14, 17
Rough, John, 104
Ryrie, Alec, 100

Sacks, Peter M., 50, 153
Sallust, 26
Samuel, Robert, 105
Sandys, George
   Anglorum speculum, 89
Sanford, Rhonda Lemke, 201
Savile, Sir Henry, 239
Schelling, Felix E., 131
Schnell, Lisa J., 243
Scott, Sir Walter, 198
Scrots, William, 45
Seneca the Elder, 168, 192
   Controversiae, 12
Seneca the Younger, 209, 234, 243
   De Brevitate Vitae, 233
   Letters, 215, 225
Sennett, Richard, 33
Serres, Jean de, 145
Sessions, W. A., 40, 41, 61, 62, 118, 253
Seymour, Edward, Duke of Somerset, 84
Seymour, Jane, 88
Seymour, Thomas, 79, 87, 88, 89
Shakespeare, 33, 200, 213, 215, 216
   Antony and Cleopatra, 148
   Hamlet, 3, 143, 209
   Henry VIII, 217
   Julius Caesar, 209
   Love's Labour's Lost, 30, 207
   Richard II, 143, 207
   Sonnets, 133
   The Tempest, 1–6
   Twelfth Night, 208
Sherlock, Peter, 151, 216
Sidney, Elizabeth, Countess of Rutland, 203
Sidney, Frances (née Walsingham), 140
Sidney, Lady Barbara (née Gamage), 202
Sidney, Lady Mary (née Dudley, 1530/5?–1586), 151
Sidney, Mary, Countess of Pembroke, 33–4, 56, 65, 138, 168, 208
   Dolefull Lay of Clorinda, 153–6
   Garnier, 140, 145–8, 152, 158
   Mary Sidney remembered, 161
   Mornay, 140, 149–51, 152

Pastoral Dialogue, 163
Petrarch, 140, 151–3, 158
Psalms, 34, 140, 142–5, 156–61
Sidney, Sir Philip, 35, 125, 129, 138, 139–42, 144, 145, 149, 151, 153, 154, 157, 163, 203, 204, 242
   Apology for Poetry, 18, 39, 118, 152, 159, 231
   Arcadia, 3, 18, 33, 127, 139, 200
   Astrophil and Stella, 34, 83
   Lady of May, 162
   Psalms, 34, 142, 158
Sidney, Sir Robert, 200, 202
Signa, Boncompagno da, 14, 29, 183
Simonides of Ceos, 12
Skretkowicz, Victor, 149
Smuts, R. Malcolm, 96, 136
Solomon, Julie Robin, 245
Southey, Robert, 190
Sowerby, Robin, 197
Spearing, A. C., 52, 54
Speed, John
   The Theatre of the Empire of Great Britaine, 28
Spenser, Edmund, 33, 82, 151, 194, 195
   Dolefull Lay of Clorinda, 153–6
   The Faerie Queene, 7, 30–1, 131, 141, 183
   The Ruins of Time, 141
Stevenson, Laura, 126
Stoicism, 209
Stow, John, 123, 215
   Summary of English Chronicles, 27
   Survey of London, 216
Stradling, Sir John, 209
Strype, John, 123
   Ecclesiastical memorials, 257
Sullivan Jr, Garrett, 109, 123
Suso, Henry (Amandus), 66
Swinburne, Algernon Charles, 198, 199
Symson, Cut[h]bert, 103, 104

Tacitus, 26, 202
Tallis, Raymond, 196
Tasso, 162
Taylor, Dr Rowland, 102
Temple, William, 18
Terdiman, Richard, 114
Thomson, Patricia, 54
Thucydides, 234
Tilyou, Elizabeth Mary, 144
Titian, 19, 180, 229
Tomkis, Thomas
   Lingua, 31
Tonkin, Elizabeth, 137
Tottel's Miscellany, 62
Trill, Suzanne, 144
Tunstall, Cuthbert, 67, 70–1, 74, 256

Tuvill, Daniel, 219
Tyndale, William, 73, 74, 76, 86, 98, 185

Udall, Nicholas, 71, 72, 146

Vaughan, Robert, 68
Vega, Garcilaso de la, 45, 253
Vega, Lope de, 253
Vere, Sir Horace, 194
Vickers, Brian, 48, 241, 278, 281
Vico, Giambattista, 36
Villiers, George, Duke of Buckingham, 243
Virgil, 55, 58, 117, 155, 202, 241
  Aeneid, 54, 58, 194
  Eclogues, 58
Vives, Juan Luis, 23, 53, 67, 91, 214, 219
  De Tradendis Disciplinis, 24, 37, 40

Wabuda, Susan, 67, 87
Walker, Greg, 37, 41, 42, 66, 73, 255
Wall, Wendy, 158, 163
Waller, Gary, 161
Walton, Izaak, 166, 168, 189
Warham, William, 70
Warnock, Mary, 4, 6, 14, 20, 182
Warton, Thomas, 53
Watson, Thomas, 18
Wayne, Don, 201
Webbe, John, 101
Webbe, William, 129

Webster, John
  The Duchess of Malfi, 525
Wheeler, Wendy, 272
White, Helen C., 260, 263
White, R. S., 131
White, Rawlins, 108
Whitford, Richard, 66, 77, 256
Whitney, Charles, 243
Whythorne, Thomas, 63
Williams, Raymond, 201
Willis, John, 13, 18, 42
Wilson, Thomas, 113, 155
Wolf, Philipp, 189
Wolsey, Thomas, Cardinal, 70
Wooden, Warren W., 111, 261
Worde, Wynken de, 66
Worthington, Kim L., 265
Wotton, Sir Henry, 192, 212
Wriothesley, Henry, Earl of Southampton, 116, 136
Wroth, Lady Mary
  Urania, 138–9
Wyatt, Sir Thomas, 39, 43, 48, 57, 58, 60–2, 63

Yates, Frances, 6, 16, 262
Younge, Richard, 66, 142

Zim, Rivkah, 158
Zwingli, Ulrich, 79

PR428.M44 H57 2011

Hiscock, Andrew, 1962-
JAN 3 0 2012
Reading memory in early
modern literature